RETURN ENGAGEMENTS

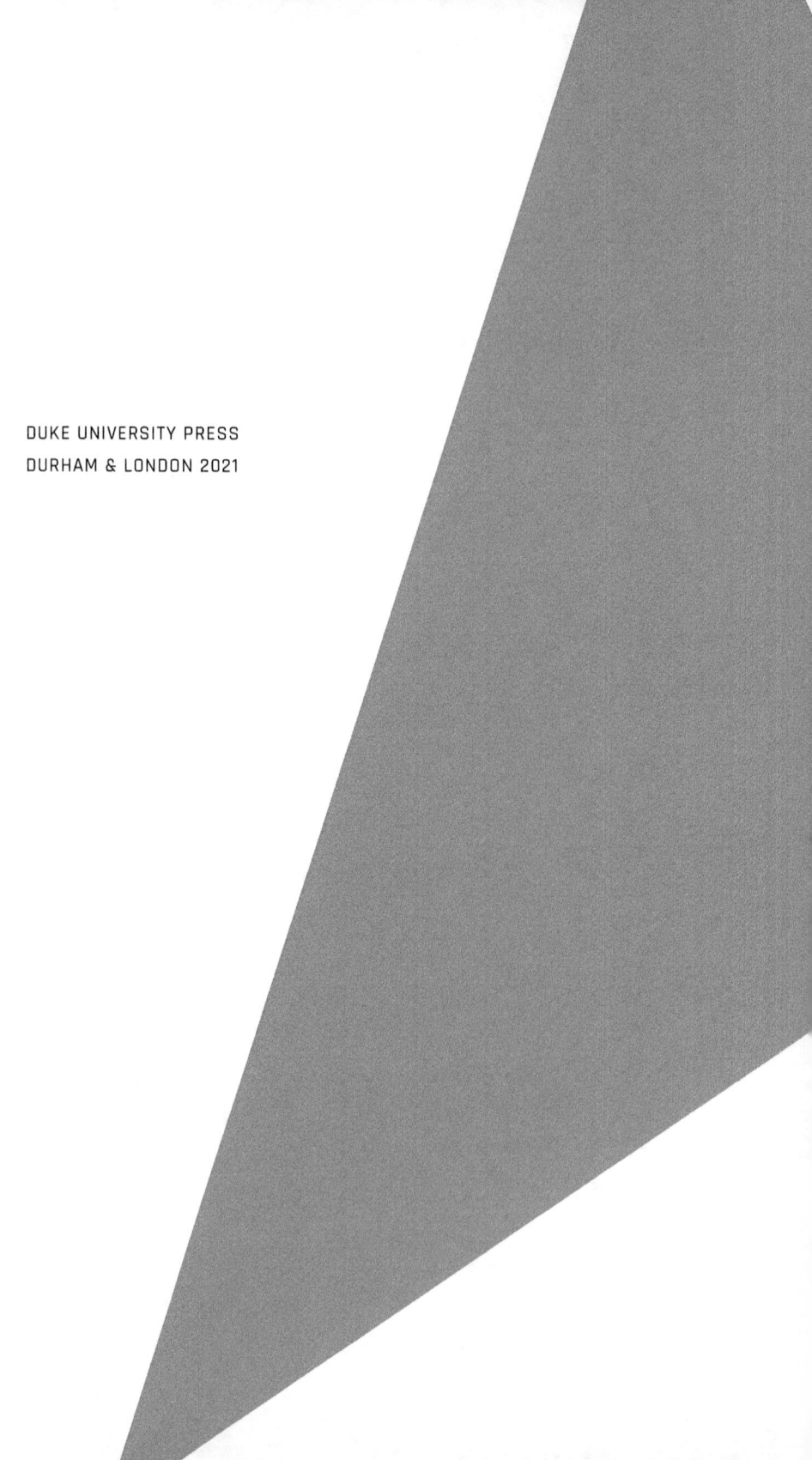

DUKE UNIVERSITY PRESS
DURHAM & LONDON 2021

CONTEMPORARY ART'S TRAUMAS
OF MODERNITY AND HISTORY IN
SÀI GÒN AND PHNOM PENH

VIỆT LÊ

return
ENGAGEMENTS

Designed by Aimee C. Harrison
Typeset in Minion Pro by Westchester Publishing Services

Library of Congress Cataloging-in-Publication Data
Names: Lê, Việt, author.
Title: Return engagements: contemporary art's traumas of modernity and history in
    Sài Gòn and Phnom Penh / Việt Lê.
Description: Durham: Duke University Press, 2021. | Includes bibliographical references
    and index.
Identifiers: LCCN 2020027530 (print) | LCCN 2020027531 (ebook)
ISBN 9781478010388 (hardcover)
ISBN 9781478010791 (paperback)
ISBN 9781478012931 (ebook)
Subjects: LCSH: Art, Vietnamese—21st century. | Arts, Cambodian—21st century. | Art,
    Modern—21st century. | Popular culture in art. | Psychic trauma in art. | Arts and
    society—Vietnam—Ho Chi Minh City. | Arts and society—Cambodia—Phnom Penh. |
    Vietnam War, 1961–1975—Art and the war. | Vietnam War, 1961–1975—Influence.
Classification: LCC N7314. L48 2021 (print) | LCC N7314 (ebook) | DDC 700.959709/05—dc23
LC record available at https://lccn.loc.gov/2020027530
LC ebook record available at https://lccn.loc.gov/2020027531

Duke University Press gratefully acknowledges the Visual Studies program and the
Visual & Critical Studies graduate program at California College of the Arts, which
provided funds toward the publication of this book.

Cover art: Việt Lê, "construct," 2016–20, digital C-print, 152.4 x 228.6 cm
(60 x 90 inches), ed. 3 + 1 AP, from the *lovebang!* series.

Thần giữ gia đình | For my family

contents

illustrations

Trauma returns most unexpectedly. Whenever I swam in a pool during my twenties, I'd stop halfway through the first lap, clinging to the lane divider, disoriented and gasping for breath. I felt as if I were about to drown. My midnight raft escape from Saì Gòn with my mom at age three had come back to me. When the panic receded, I swam on. I kept coming back to the pool and facing my panic attacks, determined to overcome my terror. By the time I was thirty I could swim with joy, and in my forties I swim for about an hour three times a week.

The body has its own logic, its own memory. The afterlife of trauma leaves invisible traces. My dangerous ocean escape and the laps I swim draw invisible lines. They have shaped who I am. I cannot capture how it feels to almost drown as you leave a country where your mother takes you into the water because she fears you will die on land. My passages since then have been physical and psychological. All I can offer to explain them is a tracing of these experiences. Language and logos fail us. There are inherent gaps in the act of tracing such experience, as well as the possibilities of traces, translations, and returns.

To return, as my trauma did to me, implies leaving at an earlier moment, whether a few moments or a lifetime of exile. To return is to take a risk, to be vulnerable. Lot's wife looks back and turns into a pillar of salt, stricken with grief. The cautionary tale warns us to not revisit the painful past. Otherwise we turn into a monument of tears.

If we glance back, we are doomed to be eternal melancholics, fixated on the unhealing wound. Truly returning, however, demands bifurcated vision. In returning one edges the past and confronts the jarring present. This bifurcated vision opens up future directions. To return is to look back and to look ahead. A hauntology, Avery Gordon and Jacques Derrida note, conjures at once revenant and arrivant. A return trip is both departure and arrival.

In examining cultural "structures" and state strictures I look at institutional and cultural practices from the ground up rather than the top down. Doing work on the ground and in the field as both insider and outsider is a position I share with many of the "diasporic" artists in the book. These artists have had access to education and opportunities "local" ones may not. I interrogate their position, addressing the void on scholarship on art and politics in the region and its diasporas.

Phnom Penh, Sài Gòn, and Little Saigon, Orange County, have all been home to me. When I return to them, whether the absence has been days or years, they look familiar yet not the same. The mental image of a particular place and time butts up against its current reality. Friends have new hairstyles, new relationships. Some have new additions to their families or different jobs. They may have moved somewhere else. New edifices replace familiar landmarks. Their newness makes them seem haughty, as if they are clearly superior to what preceded them. Everything and everyone has subtly or dramatically shifted. It takes time to readjust.

My mother feels it, too. Returning to Việt Nam for the first time in thirty years, my mother says, "Everything looks different." For human beings, the word *look* is key because it is the visual realm—and through visual culture—that first signals change. This book examines visual representation dealing with return. Upon return, we must reconcile the past and the present. We are confronted with the now. Upon return, the past, present, and future meld.

The first time I went back to Việt Nam, my uncle Cậu Út gave me the address of the home in Sài Gòn where I was born. He had stayed behind when my mother and I fled the country, ultimately barely surviving brutal concentration camps Hồ Chí Minh's government called "reeducation camps" for former dissidents. As I was growing up in the United States, my mother had wistfully described our house in Việt Nam as being airy with marble floors, a refuge amid turmoil. Having left at three, I had no conscious memories of the house. Late one damp night during a three-month visit to Sài Gòn I took a taxi with a friend to find the house. The taxi driver drove a mere fifteen minutes through the outskirts of the city center. I wanted to see it for my mother, who had not seen it since she fled Việt Nam more than three decades earlier.

My mother's quiet rage and sadness, my misapprehensions and adolescent volatility, our gulfs—this was all a blur to me: blurry black-and-white family photographs. I hoped that seeing our home would be like putting on my glasses: things would suddenly make sense, become crystalline. I cannot discern what happened before, after, in-between history and memory. I wanted to see what she conjured in her mind's eye, day after day, decade after decade.

Our first and last home in Việt Nam is now a narrow, storefront bridal shop; the upper floors were used as a residence, as many family-owned businesses were. The front was closed up for the night. It was nothing like I had imagined, nondescript. I felt no connection. I was about to knock, to ask to look around and ask about the current residents, out of curiosity, but realized that it was a rather odd request from a stranger. My friend sat watching in the taxi. After quickly strolling around the block, I returned to the taxi waiting to drive us back through the rain-slicked streets.

Some say retrospective vision is perfect, but I am left with blind traces. This "return" did not feel like a reckoning, a respite, a homecoming. The gulfs in memory and history remain. In an uncanny essay, Salman Rushdie writes of visiting his childhood home in Bombay, haunted by an old black-and-white photograph, after an absence of three decades. He also stands in front of his former home, his presence unknown to its current inhabitants. Memory, desire, and loss merge. Rushdie notes, "we will not be capable of reclaiming precisely the thing that was lost. . . . [W]e will in short, create fictions, not actual cities or villages, but invisible ones, imaginary homelands."[1] Our "real" and imaginary homelands are mere fictions, implausible creations—artifice and art.

Although I was disappointed by this reunion with my childhood home, I felt somewhat more at home in Sài Gòn than in Hà Nội, perhaps because Sài Gòn is a more urban space, more cosmopolitan. Several other Việt Kiều artists, overseas Vietnamese, stated they felt more comfortable living there than in Hà Nội, which was deemed too small; there were also fewer opportunities to find employment. Others defended Hà Nội's charm, scenery, and vibrant cultural scene. The intersections of the personal and political may account for these preferences.[2]

Networks

The sociologist Pierre Bourdieu has written extensively about the interwoven, interdependent networks that produce and reproduce the "economy of cultural goods": artists, art institutions, academics, critics, collectors, and so on.[3] I am inextricably bound to these networks—both the objective and object is art. Politics, privilege, and aesthetics are part of the mix. As a researcher at a North American university, independent international curator, boat refugee, conceptual artist, and queer male, I realize that my history, personal politics, and privilege (education, cultural capital, research funding, American citizenship, gender) puts me in an unequal standing with most of the subjects I write about, both local and diasporic artists and organizers. As a curator/researcher/artist in Việt Nam, I had preconceived notions of what "conceptual" art looks like, forged by my indoctrination into a very particular hegemonic art world: the one of international biennials, which privileges conceptual rigor over formal aesthetics, modeled on a teleological Western art history. I realize my complicity in this project and my problematic preference for certain aesthetic/conceptual discourses over others.

"Showing/telling" one part of the world about another has largely been my career. It will take a lifetime to scratch the surface. It is an act of translation. I interpret, filter, judge "local" activities for an international audience. I critique others like myself. Hypocrisy. Stuck in-between. I am called to represent "Vietnamese" artists to the rest of the world; I am called to represent the rest of the world to Vietnamese artists. What constitutes "Vietnamese" anyhow?

Artists function within art scenes that look different based on the point of view of the looker. I use a range of methodologies to understand how artists and cultural organizers self-identify and are identified by critics, gallerists, and arts organizations in Cambodia, Việt Nam, and its diasporas. As art history demonstrates, a work of art and artists do not exist in a vacuum. To grasp the complexity of an artwork, I rely on close readings of the work combined with studio visits and interviews whenever possible—what the art historian Margo Machida calls an "oral hermeneutics." I also consider critics' and viewers' reactions to the art piece or film. Through participant observation and oral interviews I gained insight about each artist's unique process. Within anthropology, a self-reflexive understanding of my position as a researcher and how it informs my relationships with my subjects is critical. For almost a decade I have built my professional and personal archives and relationships with the artists and communities I write about in this book.

I have attended countless screenings, openings, talks, and art-related events in Cambodia, Việt Nam, and the United States, among other countries. In turn, I have also given talks and participated in or organized exhibitions. I expect these professional and personal relationships will nurture and sustain me—emotionally and intellectually—for the rest of my life. These are the faces and places I will return to again and again.

As a returning Việt Kiều more than twenty years ago, I was haunted—doubled over with grief, confusion, rage at inequities. Double standards on both sides. I wondered, Who would I have been if my mother and father had stayed? I saw uncanny glimpses of myself on the street: office worker, street vendor, businessman, manual laborer, money boy. I would not have had the money to attend college, since my parents worked for the old regime. Several of my uncles spent years in the communist government's brutal reeducation camps, unable to provide for their families, returning as shrunken husks of men. Most of my cousins who stayed have a twelfth-grade education. Some toil in fields; others are well off, business-savvy. Who knows? One thing is certain: I would not be as overeducated and privileged as I am today. Although there are thriving queer communities in Việt Nam, perhaps I could not be as openly "out" in my professional life. Yet the boundaries between local and diasporic increasingly blur. My cousins' children have no memories of war, of poverty. As Việt Nam modernizes and adopts molecular identities, disparities fade, bygones are bygones. At least, that is what official rhetoric states. There is a new saying, "Việt Kiều không có cửa"—Việt Kiều are no longer on top (lit., Việt Kiều don't have a door). Locals have equaled, even surpassed, them in prestige and wealth. The divides have interchanged. Now we are peers, doubles. We are becoming each other. Việt Kiều and Vietnamese subjectivity is transforming in the new global economy. Dualities are gone. Or are they?

The City and the Country

If I doze off during the six-hour Mekong Express bus ride from Phnom Penh to Sài Gòn, I cannot tell when I wake up whether I am in the Cambodian or Vietnamese countryside. The expanses of green meld. Similar figures drive their motorbikes or cars through the dust, over gray paved roads. Occasionally on the air-conditioned bus a sun-scorched *barang* (Khmer for French; now used to refer to foreigners) tourist (or three) sports the ubiquitous shirt sold in both countries emblazoned with the cringe-inducing truism, "same same but different."

In Phnom Penh some of the neighborhoods remind me of Sài Gòn: the same stainless steel metalwork, the same pastel multi-story architecture. And in my neighborhood near Wat Mohamontrey and Tuol Sleng prison I hear the same Vietnamese voices echoing through the side alleys. I am delighted and slightly incredulous when any given street vendor thinks I am a Khmer "local." Despite a long history of ethnic tension, Vietnamese are the second-largest ethnic group in Cambodia, followed by Chinese; I am both Vietnamese and Chinese. Still I stubbornly try to pass as a "local" in both Việt Nam and Cambodia, with varying degrees of success. The similarities and differences between the two developing neighboring countries dumbfound me daily. Same same but different.

Lost Loves

Trauma returns unexpectedly. On August 20, 2011, I attended a fundraising screening in Phnom Penh for a feature film entitled *Lost Loves* (2010), by Chhay Bora, Cambodia's first independent film producer. The film concerns the life story of the filmmaker's mother in-law, who survived Pol Pot's nightmarish regime. It shows the protagonist, Nun Sila (played by Kauv Southeary), leaving Phnom Penh on foot in 1975 with her father, three daughters, son, and brother, joining a mass exodus abandoning what had been Cambodia's biggest city. They take one suitcase, which they eventually abandon. Paper money litters the streets like confetti—currency no longer has value. Along with other "new people" from the city, family members find work in Khmer Rouge–controlled countryside communes with "old people"—rural villagers. During the course of the movie, the protagonist loses most of her family one by one. Her infant daughter dies of illness. Her father is executed for being an intellectual. Her brother is bludgeoned to death for taking extra food. Her other daughter dies of malnutrition. In 1979 she returns by foot to what remains of Phnom Penh after the fall of the Khmer Rouge with her remaining two children.

Lost Loves echoed a striking image by the Berlin-based conceptual artist and philosopher Adrian Piper. In the picture, a young bright-eyed Caucasian man gazes into a mirror. Hennaed backward on his forehead and reflected in the mirror is the phrase "Everything will be taken away." For this open-call project, the artist invited strangers to live with this crimson text on their faces until the dye faded and write their reactions in a journal.[4] Henna is the color of dried blood. It is a meditation on suffering and impermanence.

While watching *Lost Loves* I kept thinking, "Everything will be taken away." When you have nothing, what is left? The tragedy is unrelenting. A visiting gallerist, Keng from Singapore, praised the tear-jerker's high production value but criticized it for being too melodramatic. Tevy, a Khmer painter, told me that her family, too, had to leave Phnom Penh by foot and eventually ended up in Battambang because of the forced evacuation. She confided that an uncle had died because he was educated. It was too difficult to watch, she said. I agreed. We half-joked that we would have been killed because we both wore glasses. During a scene of starvation, she told me that older family members recounted the insufferable years of labor and cruelty. Unhygienic conditions caused rashes; worms crawled out of their skin. I am reminded of my uncle's stories of his time in a Vietnamese concentration camp and his skeletal friends who died one by one—from starvation, from illness, from overwork.

I left Phnom Penh for Orange County, California, in November 2012, not to return until December 2016, then regularly thereafter to this day. Return is both departure and arrival. I left Phnom Penh then with a heavy heart for many reasons. Among them were witnessing the survivors of a traumatic past.

In another time and place, I scan the faces of survivors, the real-life counterparts of *Lost Loves* sitting in the Extraordinary Chambers in the Courts of Cambodia (ECCC), also referred to as the Khmer Rouge tribunal, far from the center of Phnom Penh. They are witnesses for the prosecution. One can read years of lack on their faces. One woman's dry lips are the color of dried blood. These witnesses come from both the city and the country-side seeking justice. The humid circulated summer air feels like a suffocating shroud. Outside the courtroom, construction cranes lift their silver necks skyward.

Friday, November 16, 2018, was the last day of the United Nations–sponsored Khmer Rouge tribunal. The ECCC, composed of Khmer and foreign prosecutors, found Nuon Chea, ninety-two, Pol Pot's right-hand man—known as "Brother Number Two"—guilty of genocide against ethnic Vietnamese, Cham Muslims, and past officials in the former Khmer Republic government. Khieu Samphan, eighty-seven, who was head of state, was convicted of genocide against the Vietnamese. Both men, tried together as Case 002/2, were sentenced to life in prison "for genocide and crimes against humanity carried out between 1977 and 1979."[5] This is the first and possibly the last time the tribunal "handed down the notoriously elusive verdict of genocide," writes the *Phnom Penh Post*.[6] Chea and Samphan can still appeal their case to the Supreme Court. Khieu Samphan appealed the verdict on November 20, 2018.[7] Previously, the duo had received the same life sentence in 2014 for the forced evacuation of Phnom Penh.

After Chea's and Samphan's 2018 genocide conviction, Deputy Prime Minister and Interior Minister Sar Kheng said that "there are no more defendants" and that "the process has ended." Underscoring this announcement, Sar Kheng, a former cadre, stated the following day, "I want to confirm that, because there are brothers and sisters who used to participate in activities with those leaders. . . . [D]o not be worried that investigations in this trial will continue—there are no more [Khmer Rouge leaders left]."[8] Yet the international side of the tribunal has argued that prosecutions should not be limited and should be processed as evidence arises. "This tension is at the heart of criticism by some trial analysts that the government of Prime Minister Hun Sen exerts undue influence in limiting prosecutions," reports the *New York Times*. The Cambodian historian David Chandler observes that Hun Sen "set the parameters [of the court] in the beginning and he never changed them."[9] A 2016 report by human rights lawyers cautioned against "ongoing government interference," which threatens the court's "legacy and legitimacy."[10] Four frustrated international judges have resigned. Chandler suggests that the first and only genocide verdict may be meant by the court as "sort of a farewell."[11]

Soy Sen, sixty, a trial witness and former Kriang Tachan prisoner, stated that victims are not compensated, and they are not happy with the verdict: "We cannot accept this. We want to see the court bring all the top Khmer Rouge leaders to justice. . . . [T]he leaders of the Khmer Rouge were not just four or five people but many."[12] In the decade since the tribunal was established, only three have been convicted.

The Khmer Rouge tribunal began on February 17, 2009. Case 001 was Kaing Guek Eav (also known as Duch), former chairman for the Khmer Rouge S-21 Tuol Sleng Detention Center. He was initially sentenced by the ECCC to thirty-five years for "crimes against humanity" and "brave breaches of the Geneva Convention of 1949"; the Supreme Court extended Duch's sentence to life imprisonment.[13]

On June 26, 2011, I attended the first day of the public hearings for Case 002, in which the four top leaders of the Khmer Rouge were put on trial. The ailing, elderly defendants included Pol Pot's second in command, Nuon Chea, then eighty-four; the past head of state, Khieu Samphan, seventy-nine; former Minister of Social Affairs Ieng Thirith, seventy-nine; and her husband, Ieng Sary, eighty-five, who was the foreign minister. All maintained their innocence. The latter two defendants died before receiving verdicts by the ECCC. Ieng Thirith was subsequently judged unfit to face trial and passed away in 2015. "Brother Number Three," Ieng Sary, ostensibly third in command, was eventually convicted of genocide but died in 2013.

On the first day of the 2011 trial of Case 002, the Dutch defense lawyer Michiel Pestman, speaking on behalf of Nuon Chea, said that the investigation had been "unfair" and called for the "terminat[ion]" of the proceedings.

In an argument I found unexpectedly convincing, Pestman questioned the very framework of the trials and the efficacy of the research teams. "Why were American bombings not investigated? And the dubious role of the Vietnamese?" he demanded. "Is the court trying to bury history?" Pestman argued that the trial was not taking in the whole picture of what happened, including the circumstances of the Khmer Rouge's rise to power and its aftermath. He accused the tribunal of wearing selective blinders. He called on its members to hold the United States accountable and to have a balanced perspective.

Wartime legacies linger in Southeast Asia and America. The effects of empire differ for refugees, Khmerican (Khmer American) deportees, and Vietnamese and Khmer nationals. Crater ponds—the result of U.S. bombs—dot the Khmer countryside. The Việt Nam War, Vietnamese invasion of Cambodia, and subsequent Vietnamese government intervention all have an ongoing impact. Cambodia does not exist in a geopolitical vacuum. I found myself agreeing with Pestman's critique that Cambodia under Pol Pot, and more recently, exists in a world in which the United States and Việt Nam have considerable influence. Ordinary transactions in Cambodia use U.S. dollars more often than the official riel. Vietnamese businesses crowd the streets of Phnom Penh. However, the trial will not, and should not, be terminated. There has to be a semblance of justice, however limited and blind. Cambodians are variably uninterested, disillusioned, and anxious about the return verdict—a distant horizon.

During a lunch break at the trial, I saw cameramen and journalists swarming around the painter Vann Nath, one of the few survivors of the torture prison Tuol Sleng; he is now deceased. I immediately recognized his shock of white hair and handsome, calm visage from documentaries and news articles. Everything had been taken away from him, too—his wife, his children, the world as he knew it. Day after day, victims and perpetrators arrived and departed. Day after day, the prosecution and the defense offered elaborate rational legal arguments. But this is not adequate for those among us who have lost everything. Nothing suffices. Why come back again and again? Let's return to the heart of the matter.

Acknowledgments

This book bears the traces of myriad returns to people, ideas, and places that have indelibly shifted my life. Instead of "turning away," bell hooks urges instead for a "return to love." These revisitations and revisions have been a return to—and a labor of—love. Revisiting a key figure and text in her memoir *Bone Black* (1996)[1] and again in her book *All About Love: New Visions* (2000), bell hooks recalls her girlhood: "Rilke gives meaning to the wilderness of spirit I am living in. His book is a world I enter and find myself. He tells me that everything terrible is really something helpless that wants help from us. I read *Letters to a Young Poet* over and over. I am drowning and it is the raft that takes me safely to the shore."[2] These journeys are tender and terrifying. In a world that feels at times like drowning, your words and embodied wisdoms are our raft. May we all regain our shores.

The shores, sleepy beaches, and low-slung cities of Southern California shaped my graduate horizons. From my time in the master of fine arts program in studio art at the University of California, Irvine, to the American studies and ethnicity doctoral program at the University of Southern California, and beyond, I witnessed engaged critical and creative rigor embodied by Allan de Souza, Macarena Gómez-Barris, Jack Halberstam, Janet Hoskins, Dorinne Kondo, Akira Lippit, Catherine Lord, Daniel J. Martinez, Richard Meyer, Glen Mimura, Panivong Norindr, David Román, Connie Samaras, and Karen Tongsen. I recall Linda Võ's kind urging to continue to pursue academia and her challenge to traverse disciplines of comfort. Similarly, Douglas Crimp modeled uneasy, unassailable politics and poetry. I miss him.

Between programs, the Fine Arts Work Center gave me space to bridge the worlds of art, creative writing, and academia: Gina Apostol, Carlos Jackson, Hunter O'Hanian, Jason Schneiderman, and Shimon Tanaka. Yong Soon Min as a mentor, friend, and collaborator dazzles with her generosity, humility, and magpie steel-sharp brilliance. Việt Nguyễn best exemplifies writerly passion and scholarly depth, as well as public intellectual and communal engagement. I look forward to sharing more transcontinental art adventures with the pioneering Bruce Yonemoto. I fondly recall the friendships forged in these graduate days: Beth Bird, Jih-Feh Cheng, Susan Choi, Cirilo Domine, Laura Fujikawa, Chris Hearle, Betti-Sue Hertz, Imani Kai, Dredge Kang, Nisha Kunte, Tala Mateo, Mytoan Nguyen-Akbar, Nguyễn Tấn Hoàng, Carrie Patterson, Seph Rodney, Anton Smith, John Won, and Mario Ybarra. I'm grateful to Wendy Cheng, Michelle Dizon, Eng-Beng Lim, and Hentyle Yapp for showing me by example how to negotiate the personal and the political.

Living in Phnom Penh for the first time as a doctoral researcher, I am indebted to Lyno Vuth, Erin Gleeson, Lim Sokchanlina, Khvay Samnang, Khong Vollack, Chum Chanveasna, Anida Yoeu Ali, Amy Sanford, Dana Langlois, Sokuntevy Oeur, Billy Lor, SA SA Projects, and Java Arts for their kindness, support, and friendship. In Hà Nội and Sài Gòn, Trần Lương, Nguyễn Quốc Thanh, Jamie Maxtone-Graham, Nguyễn Trinh Thi, Hanoi DocLab, Nguyễn Phương Linh, Gabby Miller, Tuan Mami, Quỳnh-Anh Trần, Jenny Trang Lê, Quỳnh Phạm, Nguyễn Như Huy, Uudam Nguyễn, Tuan Andrew Nguyễn, Zoe Butt, Sàn Art, and Ngoc Phan, among others, constellate another home. Within and outside Southeast Asia—and troubling these coordinates—Ute Meta Bauer, Brian Curtin, Kathleen Ditzig, Merv Espina, Patrick Flores, Roger Nelson, Manuel Ocampo, Sidd Perez, Russell Storer, John Tain, Henry Tan, Lynda Tay, June Yapp, and Green Papaya Projects have enlightened me on the urgent arts of curating, community building, and compassion.

Bridging these countries, and transgressing the local and the diasporic, I am indebted to the artists I write about in this book: Rithy Panh, Tiffany Chung, Vann Nath, Leang Seckon, Sandrine Llouquet, Phan Quang, Spencer Nakasako, Binh Danh, Mike Siv, and Đinh Q. Lê. Special thanks to Quỳnh Phạm and Tyler Rollins for championing your artists over the years.

During my postdoctorate at Academia Sinica in Taipei I was buoyed by my colleagues' intellectual camaraderie: Te-Hsing Shan, Chin-Tao Wu, Chi-

Ming Andy Wang, and Julia Chan. Again traversing disciplinary and geopolitical borders, my mentors and interlocutors in critical refugee studies, Southeast Asian studies, and cultural studies provide yet another refuge: Yến Lê Espiritu, Nguyễn-võ Thu-hương, Mariam Beevi Lam, Long Bui, Christine Balance, Thùy Võ Đặng, Lucy Burns, Caroline Kieu-Linh Valverde, Tram Lê, Cẩm Nhung Vũ, Christina Schwenkel, Joan Kee, Cathy Schlund-Vials, Marita Sturken, Jenna Grant, and Khathyra Um, among many others. The art historians Pamela Corey, Margo Machida, Moira Roth, and Nora Taylor have nurtured me through their incisively graceful work.

My California College of the Arts colleagues demonstrate daily that scholarship and artistic communities truly matter: Nilgun Bayraktar, Steven Beal, Tammy Rae Carland, Jackie Francis, Thomas Haakenson, Glen Helfand, Patricia G. Lange, Tirza Latimer, Maxwell Leung, Mia Liu, Beth Mangini, Ranu Mukherjee, Kim Nguyễn, Amy Phan, Jeanette Roan, Tina Takemoto, James Voorhies, and Kathy Zarur. My friends with ties to the Golden State inspire: Michele Carlson, Patty Chang, Abbey Chen, Dawn Nakaya Delk, Brian Doan, Shona Findlay, Ken Foster, Mark Johnson, David Kelley, Christine Kim, Bonnie Kwong, Lian Ladia, Andrew Lam, Ringo Lê, Rudy Lemke, Sonia Mak, Dominic Mangila, Marie Martraire, Marc Meyer, Trinh T. Minh-ha, Chuck Mobley, Genevieve Erin O' Brien, Mario Ontiveros, Myron Schulz, Shervin Shahbazi, Nayan Shaw, Valerie Soe, Priya Srinivasan, Tam Van Tran, Kristina Wong, and Paul Zaloom, among many more. Several fellowships, grants, and research and art residencies made this book possible: Art Matters; Camargo Foundation; Center for Khmer Studies (CKS); Civitella Ranieri Foundation; Fulbright-Hays; International Institute for Asian Studies (IIAS) Affiliated Senior Research Fellowship, Leiden University; Nanyang Technological University Centre for Contemporary Art Singapore; National Endowment for the Humanities Summer Institute at New York University; Southeast Asian Studies Summer Institute; Vietnamese Advanced Summer Institute; and Visual Communications. I am invigorated by Philippe Peycam's familial leadership at CKS and IIAS and his jouissance. I fine-tuned my research via several institutional invitations: Global Asia Exchange; Inter-Asian Connections IV: Instanbul, Koç University; Shanghai Biennale, Smithsonian National Portrait Gallery; and Waseda University. I'm honored by the kind invitations by Takashi Aso, Liu Jie, Sarah Newman, Henry Tsang, and Leslie Ureña, among others. Earlier, shorter versions of chapters of this book appear in *American Quarterly Journal*, *Visual Anthropology Journal*, and *Modern and Contemporary Southeast Asian Art: An Anthology*, edited by Nora Taylor and Boreth Ly.

Daily I am in touch with—and heartened by—Alexandra Chang, Laura Kina, and Alice Ming-Wai Jim, my comrades in arms at the *Asian Diasporic Visual Cultures in America* journal. I have learned so much from Mary Yu Danico about being a dedicated ally. I appreciate my collaborators in art, academia, and activism: Matt Austin, Anh Bui, Yiu Fai Chow, Jereon deKloet, Lan Duong, Ciara Ennis, Trangđài Glassey-Trầnguyễn, Laurie Lazer, Ysa Lê, Leta Ming, Ina Adele Ray, Kate Hers Rhee, Elyna Shukyri, Vivian Sming, Heather Snider, Jen Vanderpool, Faith Wilding, and countless others.

Boundless gratitude to Ken Wissoker for his steady support over the years. Also at Duke University Press, Josh Trannen, Susan Albury, Maria Volpe, and Elizabeth Ault tremendously helped steer smooth sails. I also appreciate Susan Deeks's gracious, thorough copyedits, as well as Aimee Harrison's thoughtful book design. I thank the anonymous readers for their keenly balanced insights. Kate Epstein worked her editorial magic with humor. Chương-Đài Võ—bạn thân and laser-minded editor—is part of the whole journey: San Diego, Sài Gòn, back, and beyond.

Likewise, my family joins me in spirit—near and away—always: Lê Lợi, Hồng Hoá, Catherine, Wai. For you, and with you, I venture to the farthest shores.

Acknowledgments

introduction

RISKY RETURNS, RESTAGINGS, AND REVOLUTIONS

Through the multivalent frame of "return engagements," this book examines modernity, popular visual culture, and trauma in contemporary
art in Southeast Asia and Asian America, with a focus on Việt Nam
and Cambodia—two countries linked historically and regionally with
each other and the United States. In this political-economic-cultural-
industrial critique I assert that artistic voices strategically emerge in
tandem with national, regional, and transnational socioeconomic
discourse. This project makes the hierarchies of art histories
and art markets—and the negotiations by artists, scholars, and
organizers—explicit. I highlight the frameworks of desirability
within the art market, scholarship, and institutions, as well as
efforts by artists and organizers to make themselves more desirable (and legible) to these external forces. I investigate the
desire of many contemporary experimental Cambodian and
Vietnamese local and diasporic artists to gain recognition
in the international art market and attain both symbolic
and real capital.

In its common usage, a *return engagement* is a public exhibition that is "performed, presented, or taking
place again."[1] It is the future promise of a past act; a
repeat performance on the stage. The restaging or
"reenactment," as it were, occurs in theater, but I
also extend it to other cultural arenas, including
theaters of war. I argue that the legacies and strategies of war, culture, and empire are intertwined,

recurring, reenacted. To revolt, we must grapple with the material, militarized, and metaphysical aspects of return. As Marita Sturken and Việt Thanh Nguyễn, among others, observe, wars are "staged" twice: once in combat, and then in memory, including in cultural productions (such as visual art and film, the focus of this book).

Art is an ideological and ontological battleground. One of Southeast Asia's most visible returning annual regional exhibitions is tellingly entitled Art Stage Singapore. Its name suggests the interplay—and tensions—between local and international arenas; artists are actors on this high-stakes (art) world "stage." Critics of international art biennales bemoan that the same jet-set circuit of well-known artists return again and again, in different climes at differing times—the future promise of a past act. At Art Stage Singapore, "emerging" and "established" artists are presented—the changing faces of the future of Southeast Asian art, whose works often grapple with the traumas of the past (wars) and present (modernity).

Beyond regional and international showcases, *stage* can also refer to the stages or cycles of life and death. In this sense, the word *return* also suggests cyclical motion, as in "revolve," as well as "revolution." The Spanish verb *volver* roughly translates as "to return" or "to become," and the French *revolutare* means "to roll or revolve."[2] To come back is to become (and to become undone), to transform—to evolve, personally and politically. The segments that follow outline my framing of return and its connection to revolt and revolution as cyclical engagements.

I recenter the importance of return in political and personal—critical and creative—change. Although now seen as linear, revolution is circular. "The development of two words, revolt and revolution, from the sense of a circular movement to the sense of a political rising, can hardly be simple coincidence," notes the cultural theorist Raymond Williams.[3] The word *revolution* is connected with "sudden and violent change."[4] In contemporary use, it is associated with both political and technological turns (e.g., Hong Kong's Umbrella Revolution of 2014; the digital revolution). The industrial revolution involved both democratic reform and technical inventions (steam engine, iron, steel).

To revolt, to revolve—return, turn again—and to engage in revolution are intrinsically linked. Tracing the etymology of *revolution*, Williams notes that the term encompasses power's cyclical nature. In its earliest English usage in the fourteenth century, the word indicated a "revolving movement in space or time." *Revolution*'s association with circular movement predated its political usage, but the two are tied. Shifting from "circular movment to a rising," Williams notes that *revolt* and *revolution* had two underlying connections. First, socioeconomic order is upended, the "low" putting themselves over the "high." The second connection is the image of the wheel of fortune: "men were revolved" around fortune's wheel, "topsy-turvy . . . first up, then down."[5] Through rebellion, the normalized top of society is upended by its lowest rungs.[6]

In both connections of *revolt* and *revolution*, top and bottom positions are reversed, repeatedly. "History from the bottom up"—scholarship focused on common struggles (embodied by C. L. R. James's *Black Jacobins* and Howard Zinn's *People's History of the United States*, among others)—marks a departure from elitist, "top-down" perspectives. The cultural critic and artist Nguyễn Tân Hoàng advocates for a queer "bottom" politics that unmoors top-bottom and black-white hierarchal binaries of racialized, sexualized representation—in politics, pornography, and mass and social media. While powerful interventions, these frameworks still reinscribe hegemonic frameworks, if only to invert them.[7] Instead of arborescent (hierarchical, tree-like, binary) or the rhizomatic (nomadic) knowledge championed by Gilles Deleuze and Félix Guattari, I am asserting a framework that is cyclical, circular, focused on engaged return. What we consider an overturning (revolution) is really a returning.

To return is to recognize repeating rhetoric (across continents, histories, disciplines) and long-term repercussions. The queer theorist Sara Ahmed observes, "The violence of revolting 'repeats' the violence which is its cause. . . . [R]evolutionaries expose violence, but the violence they expose is not recognized as violence: structural violence is veiled."[8] How, then, to recognize structural violence embedded in our institutions, embodied in ourselves?[9] As Frantz Fanon observes in *Black Skin, White Masks*, postcolonial subjects often reinstate neocolonial strictures and structures with more fervency than their colonial forebears.[10] With this in mind, the move toward a decolonial aesthetics merely masks a neocolonial ethics in which the glut of biennials and triennials within the "periphery" may not radically destabilize (art world) hierarchies. Ahmed writes, "To revolt is to be undone—it is to not produce an inheritance. And yet, a revolution does not empty the world of significance; it does not create blank pages. The writing might be on the wall, even when the walls come down."[11] As mentioned earlier, *volver* means both to return and to become. To revolt and to return (*volver*) is to be at once undone and to become—a potentiality. I link this to Deleuze and Guattari's concept of "becoming"—a process of exchange and transformation—that I elaborate on in chapter 2.

Revolt, revolve, return. In this framework, revolution does not obliterate "the writing on the wall." Yet this revolt, this return is queer in that it does not (re)produce an inheritance (heteronormative or homonormative). It does not replicate or repeat its root violence. To delink the veiled violence of empire and its cultural hegemony does not mean to shut it down (one cannot entirely erase its traces) or to let it shut one down.

There are affective components of revolution. To revolt is also the "willingness to be stressed, let the present get under your skin. To revolt is an "'out-of-skin' experience," as Ahmed notes.[12] To revolt, return (*volver, revolutar*) is to engage the senses, both corporeal and political. Finding something revolting or senseless gets "under your skin"—it may jolt you out of your body and into the political body—from apathy to engagement.

Affective Engagements

An engagement is a promise, an arrangement, an agreement—even a dispute. My concept encompasses both acceptance and refusal but most important, ambivalence. *Engagement* is defined as (1) a promise to wed; (2) a plan to meet someone or do something at a particular time; (3) the start of a military fight; and (4) involvement. In all instances, the term points at contingency, liminality: engagement is a process, a reckoning with your skins. By returning to the site of multiple engagements—military, social, business, and romantic—we recognize that rupture and desire are not separate affairs; they often inform one another.

Late capitalism encourages endless consumer desire: the promise of rapture without disruption. The term *disrupt* has been adopted within commodity's lexicon (for example, "She/he is disrupting the industry"). The Marxist philosopher Herbert Marcuse argues that capitalism anticipates and absorbs revolutionary sentiments. Yet this counterrevolution is largely preventative—it can be ruptured. Cultural production can be a tool of both domination and liberation.

Aesthetic engagement has long been used for political ends, with varying means. In the chapter entitled "Art and Revolution," Marcuse notes the varying strategies of art to reflect and change sociopolitical reality. The core dialectical tension is between "reality" and symbolic meaning: "political 'engagement' becomes a problem of 'technique,' and instead of translating art into reality it is translated to a new aesthetic form."[13] Regardless of formal or conceptual "technique," Marcuse supports art's subversive potential and its wide berth of (revolutionary) tactics.[14] These strategies can range from pop art appropriation to its opposite, an avant-gardist aesthetics of "total alienation," championed by Theodor Adorno.[15] For example, the composer John

4

Cage's aesthetics of alienation prioritizes silence and repetition—radical formal and conceptual gestures. Yet revolution is not erasure; Marcuse notes, "The most extreme political content does not repel traditional forms."[16] Again, revolution is not a "blank slate," erase the writing on a demolished wall.[17] Revolution is not amnesia but a re-membering, re-making, re-turning.

Dealing with damage requires an ethics of return that is not reactive but sustained, a gradual shifting of oneself and one's sphere. In *The Long Revolution*, Williams states, "We respond to disturbance not only by remaking ourselves, but if we can, by remaking the environment. . . . [T]his is not only how the artist lives and works, but how men live and work, in a long process, ending and beginning again."[18] By ending and beginning again and again, the world is remade, reenvisioned. Elaine Scarry also observes that after traumatic events in which the world is "undone," artists "remake," reconstitute the world again.[19] The ritual of return is both physical and metaphysical. As artists, we come back again and again to our studios, computers, desks—our paintings, pixels, and papers—our musings and our muses.

The remaking and reconnecting of ourselves and our environs—nature and humanity—is a steady process. Marcuse proposes that nature is key to bridging the personal and the political. Through Cartesian duality (mind/body split) we have become disconnected from both nature and our own nature. We have disassociated our individual bodies from the body politic. Citing the psychologist C. G. Jung, Williams outlines a dialectic between artists and their output, between individual and collective expression. Creativity is a process of return: "The general creative activity is a human process, of which the artist is, in his art, the impersonal embodiment, taking us back to the level of experience at which man lives, not the individual."[20] The creative process may not take us back to a primordial site (Charles Darwin) or a primal scene (Sigmund Freud)—it returns our humanity. Living, then, becomes quest and question ("how the artist works and lives," "the level of experience at which man lives"). The menace of death remains—physical death and social death.

After disturbance, what drives us to remake the world? In *Eros and Civilization*, Marcuse reframes Freud's "return of the repressed" and society's two main drives, eros and thanatos (sex and death), from the negative to the life-affirming. Nature (and human nature) is not seen as threatening. There is no need to subsume and subdue the natural through scientific rationality and disciplinary regimes. Instead of a force that needs to be dominated and sublimated, Marcuse argues for a liberatory politics that embraces eros (embodied knowledge/desire) alongside logos (rational knowledge/reason).[21] The word *desire* comes from the Latin phrase *de sidere*, meaning "from the stars." This suggests that our deepest desires entail reconsidering our earthbound orientations, returning to our true north, our guiding star. Postcolonial, queer, and feminist scholars also advocate for theories of subjectivity to supplant continental philosophy's overreliance on abstract objectivity.

Apart from the separation of mind and body, the core question is how we deal with eternal separation. Nietzsche's optimistic eternal return predated Freud's pessimistic return of the repressed. Some scholars have argued that the former influenced the latter.[22] Nietzsche's philosophical question obviates the psychosomatic quandary of inhibited instincts. Marcuse and Nietzsche (and Jacques Derrida later on) wrestled with the question of living knowing that we—and our loved ones—will die. In short, unless one's relationship to death is reconciled, individual liberation is impossible. The eternal return, or eternal recurrence, proposes that all energy recurs endlessly: we experience our lives and relationships infinitely. From the infinite to the infinitesimal, every interaction has profound significance: our fleeting interactions, our kindness (or lack thereof) to strangers. Hence, Nietzsche's concept of *amor fati* (love of fate) plays a crucial role: we must embrace the now, this ephemeral yet eternal conundrum. If we must return ad infinitum (literally or metaphorically), then we must affirm life again and again.[23] To live is to accept traumas and disappointment over and over again.[24] Nietzsche claims that only the *Übermensch*—idealized man—can appreciate this new, affirmative concept of life. Marcuse disagrees with this elitist vision and seeks egalitarian liberation for all humanity.

Buddhist philosophy is likewise concerned with liberation and return. Within a Buddhist cosmology, energy is also eternally recurring. Liberation is a question of choice. We choose to embrace this moment, our fate (*amor fati*). Boddhisattvas—those close to reaching enlightenment—choose to return again and again to help all suffering sentient beings find liberation. The Sōtō priest Kōtō Uchiyama writes, "For us as bodhisattvas, all aspects of life, including the fate of humanity itself, live within us."[25] There is no distinction between the inner and outer worlds. Liberation is creative act, deliberate action, not subject to fate (or "karma"). Williams notes that is the artist "taking us back" to the "experience at which [humankind] lives, and not the individual."[26] The Dalai Lama clarifies, "Literally, karma means 'action' and refers to the intentional acts of sentient beings. . . . Intentions results in acts. . . . The chain reaction of interlocking causes and effects operates not only in individuals but also for groups and societies, not just in one lifetime but across many lifetimes."[27] In a sense, this cycle of passions—wars and loves—recurs without end, as human history attests.

Bridging spiritual and scientific perspectives, the Dalai Lama engaged leading thinkers on infinite return and interconnectedness. He writes, "In physics, the deeply interdependent nature of reality has been brought into sharp focus by the EPR paradox—named after its creators [Albert Einstein, Boris Podolsky, and Nathan Rosen]. . . . There seems, according to quantum mechanics, to be a startling and profound interconnectedness at the heart of physics."[28] Other theories of the universe (e.g., big bounce, related to big bang) envision cyclical expansions and contractions of endless (and beginning-less) cosmos, akin to Indian Mahayana conceptions of an "incalculable" multiverse.[29] Like the ethos of Nietzsche's eternal return, the Dalai Lama states, "What we do and think in our own lives becomes extremely important as it affects everything we're connected to."[30] From the micro to the macro level, all is interdependent.

A return engagement takes us "back" from potentially isolating personal experience to empowering, politically transformative encounters. Through this tracing, I assert that discourses on revolution, liberation, and creation hinges on cyclical return, repetition—eternal return, karma. A concept tethered to revolution and liberation, the visual image and imagination is likewise linked to ideas of repetition. This logic can be traced to the nineteenth-century poet-philosopher Samuel Taylor Coleridge's assertion that artistic perception is a creative act (and not a mimetic one, as Renaissance worldviews, inherited from Plato and Aristotle, would have it). Rather than divine imitation, imagination is reiteration, a reflection of higher consciousness: "Imagination . . . is the living power and prime agent of all human perception, and as a *repetition* in the finite mind."[31] Imagination, creativity is a ritual, a return to the sacred—an individual's process of getting in touch with the "finite mind" and the infinite.[32] Fleeting individual views become enduring cultural expression. This is part of Williams's emergent "structure of feeling": the ineffable expressions of a cultural moment, political momentum.

Coming back time and again to psychological and physical spaces, imagined and real, we open up new ways to think about the relationship between self and other: humanity lives within us. Images are enacted. Imagination can be both grounded and metaphysical. In contrast, Marcuse idealizes the role of the imagination: utopic visions. As in Buddhist intentionality (karma as thoughts driving action), I see imagination as purpose-driven—intractable parts of mind, body, and spirit. The term *imagination* opens up political possibilities. It also evokes wars over images and ideology, including culture wars and cold and hot wars, then and now.

Arjun Appadurai notes in *Modernity at Large: Cultural Dimensions of Globalization* that, through individual and collective imaginaries, communities are created across physical and psychic boundaries. The imagination is viewed as a "social practice," not a fixed process that allows for multifaceted negotiations of space, temporality, and agency.[33] His celebratory call for examining media, mass migration, and the imagination is a provocative stance. He does not, however, fully address the complexities of such intersections; nor does he address the inequities of such interactions. Building on Benedict Anderson's notion of "imagined communities,"[34] my work highlights the differential hierarchies of legibility, privilege, marketing, and meaning in transnational cultural consumption and cultural work within a more localized, less universally cosmopolitan sphere. Framing communities connected through imagination as celebratory examples of heterogeneity, hybridity, and multiplicity can be dangerous.

Imagination has corporeal consequences. Consider the poet Claudia Rankine's fragment from *Citizen*: "Because white men can't / police their imagination / black men are dying."[35] Imagination is also ideology, insidious, invasive—at times, inspired. How do we use our imaginations, and how are we the image of our nations? The racialized violence on US soil also comprises acts of imagination, as Rankine suggests. According to the *Washington Post's* real-time National Police Shootings Database, there were 963 incidents of fatal deaths in 2016; 984 in 2017; 992 in 2018; and, in 2019, an average two deaths a day. As of August 2020, 1,000 people in the US have been shot and killed by the police since the beginning of the year, in the midst of a global pandemic and in light of protests in support of the Black Lives Matter movement.[36] Historicity repeats itself: the US Asian Exclusion Act of 1924 banned Asians and Arabs and restricted immigration for southern and eastern Europeans. The Obama administration deported more than 2.7 million immigrants, then the highest of any presidential administration.[37] In December 2017, President Donald Trump proposed restricting the number of immigrants to forty-five thousand.[38] Threats continue: walls for Mexico and Muslim bans. Banner years: Brexit, Rohingya refugees of genocide, international anti-immigrant sentiment in an age in which displacement is at its apex. Imagination as fear wreaks ceaseless havoc. Imagination as empathy calls us back to be engaged with those in need of help, infinitely.

Evolution and revolution appear to be temporal opposites, yet they are aligned. *Evolution* connotes slow biological Darwinian processes, whereas *revolution* implies rapid leaps. Evolution, like revolution, is a cyclical process. Evolution's Latin root (*evolver*) means a rolling out (or unrolling a book). Shifting from the literal (and literary—a book) to the metaphorical, evolution refers to "both to the divine creation and to the working-out, the developing formation, of Ideas or Ideal Principles. It is clear from the root sense . . . what is implied is the 'unrolling' of something that already exists," Williams writes.[39] Again, the creative act is a reiterative act—not spontaneously arising but eternal. This unfurling of "something that already exists" recalls both Western and Eastern scientific and philosophical constructs (eternal return, quantum physics, karma) discussed earlier. The expansion of deep wisdom is a continual working out, working through.

Evolution and revolution can be a dialectic. As stated earlier, one of revolution's root words, the French *revolutare* means "to roll." To roll (revolution) is to bind—to become bound to others in political solidarity. To become unbound, unbidden from the group (evolution) follows the logic of singular advancement: survival of the fittest. Yet to unroll "something that already exists" can be a movement encompassing the individual, social (Ideal Principles) and the spiritual (the divine). To become (*volver* "return") and to become undone (revolt) is to simultaneously bind oneself with embodied experience (eros) and unsheathe scrolls of knowledge (*logos*). It is telos and demos.

For a revolution in ethics and aesthetics to occur, we must abandon dyadic, linear, and reactionary thinking. Williams's call for a "Long Revolution" combines both aspects of evolution and revolution: the development of heightened consciousness. This is the "working out, working through" of an emancipatory cultural politics over an extended time frame. Williams's Long Revolution is a cultural one, which, he suggests, develops alongside democratic and industrial revolutions. His "short" revolutions are political uprisings, insurgencies: "We need not identify revolution with violence or with a sudden capture of state power. Even where such events occur, the essential transformation is indeed a long revolution." His conception of the Long Revolution is a process that arguably spans centuries and countries. This Long Revolution, I suggest, dovetails with Lisa Lowe's conception of the "intimacies" of the four continents in which seemingly disparate disciplines (history, area studies, anthropology) and disparate violence (e.g., slave trade, indigenous genocide, and so on) across time and space are indeed connected by empire's machinations and needs. Instead of taking this roving telescopic view, my study zooms in to focus on the long shadows of the Việt Nam War while keeping this wider geopolitical perspective in mind.

Marcuse and Williams both wrote during the "Vietnamese revolution" (as Anthony Barnett calls it in the updated preface to Williams's book).[40] Barnett observes that we are now indeed living in revolutionary times. The digital revolution has also precipitated political ones (Arab Spring, Taksim Square, and so on). Writing in the early 1970s, Marcuse explicitly references Việt Nam as a beacon, a potential, a paradigm of Third World resistance. And yes, he also references it as a pity and "true horror story": the killing of students at Kent State, "wholesale massacres" of Indochinese and others deemed "in revolt against governments subservient to imperialist [Western] forces."[41] Then, as now, the threat has shifted, but the attack continues: then against communism; now against terrorism, both domestically and abroad. *Volver* "revolt, return"; *revolutare* "revolution": at once undone and "to become." Then and now, Việt Nam returns as political and racialized specter, as Sylvia Chong suggests—a hauntology on the edges of perception. Chong's "Oriental obscene" at once obfuscates, hides "off-scene," the mise-en-scène of eternal racial triangulation for black, yellow, and white bodies within the North American political and mass-media imaginary. At the same time, it is a spectacle of raced, sexed violence on the air, on-screen again and again. Asian American scholars such as Long Bui, Chong, and V. T. Nguyễn, among others, assert that these repetitions continue from the Cold War to today, largely unchanged. Bui calls these valences the "returns of war," in which Vietnamization—Nixon's 1969 policy of public US military withdrawal that was actually a secret escalation—founded other foreign policies that leave legacies of debt from the past to the future through the figure of the refugee.[42]

Suffering Southeast Asian, Syrian, and North African refugees embody the pornography of violence, as I call it. This can be seen as the return of the repressed. The "Vietnamese revolution" succeeded and failed. I argue for an alternative reading in which haunting is not pathology. The recurring ghosts of empire are not symptoms of domination but, rather, spirits of liberation.

I argue that return is a strategic and revolutionary act. To return is to revolt, to be undone, to become. Williams proclaims, "I see revolution as the inevitable working through of a deep and tragic disorder, to which we can respond in varying ways."[43] Revolution can address traumatic wounds, redress a neoliberal world system in disorder, from short- to long-term strategies—the longue dureé.

Return marks a break, a reconsideration. In returning, something imperceptibly, irrevocably shifts. Revisiting psychic and physical spaces time and again, we open up new ways to think about the relationship between history and modernity, rupture and wholeness. In reengaging personal and public archives, artists and audiences alike participate in forming dialogues beyond dominant mass media and political narratives. These extended engagements, these return engagements, are vexed ones.

Return: YIELD PROFIT

A main focus of this book is the international art market's fetishization of trauma and transnational difference. For example, Southeast Asian artists are often rendered invisible unless they make work that plays into hypervisible discourses of trauma. For instance, Binh Danh—an Asian American artist born in 1977 to a Cambodian father and Vietnamese mother—has built a profitable career grappling with the aftermath of trauma. His best-known and most collected works are "chlorophyll prints" addressing the Việt Nam War. The prints are portraits of soldiers and civilians imprinted on leaves through a photosynthetic photographic process he developed. In 2011 he had a solo exhibition of chlorophyll prints and daguerreotypes at the North Carolina Museum of Art entitled *In the Eclipse of Angkor*. This body of work was the culmination of a trip to Angkor Wat, Cambodia's famous Khmer temple, in 2008, as well as to two sites associated with genocide in Cambodia: Tuol Sleng Genocide Museum and Choeung Ek.[44] Danh's daguerreotypes "Divinities of Angkor #1" (2008 [plate 1]) and "Ghost of Tuol Sleng Genocide Museum #2" (2008 [plate 2]) are, respectively, images of an អប្សរា (*apsara* "celestial female dancer/nymph") carving at Angkor Wat and a re-photograph of a young female victim of Tuol Sleng prison. It seems possible that these works refer to a phenomenon Phnom Penh–based curator Erin Gleeson has lamented: curators' and collectors' interest in art about Cambodia is often limited to depictions of "temples and trauma."[45] In this tourism through art, ancient ruins become aesthetic shorthand for the country. Psychic ruins become anesthetic.

The Asian American cultural studies scholar Cathy Schlund-Vials suggests that artists returning to Cambodia in body and in memory, such as Binh Danh, offer an "alternative memory" to US and Cambodian political amnesia. She notes that facets of the Khmer Rouge genocide are strategically recalled and forgotten by Khmer, Vietnamese, and American politicians— symptomatic of a "Cambodia Syndrome." I argue that cultural producers also engage with cultural institutions in a politics of strategic forgetting and remembering. The cultural industries in which artists such as Danh circulate fetishize such "alternative" visions and voices without the aim of a recuperative politics. Referencing the trauma studies scholar Jenny Edkins,

Schlund-Vials states that what is "at stake in such memory work is not what is represented but who is represented."[46]

US identity politics of the 1990s and its backlash has shown that a critical mass of critical voices (addressing race, class, gender, sexuality) do not radically change infrastructures. This redressing is window dressing. When the what and who get conflated—as in Danh's images of Khmer Rouge victims—the artist and his images of "trauma and temples" also collapse in a relational loop. One's subjectivity becomes objectified (as art objects). The question of "authentic" voices and images comes to the fore: who has the right—and institutional access—to represent such vexed stories, and in what manner?

Danh's predecessor is the Vietnamese American artist Đinh Q. Lê, who is based in Sài Gòn. Lê has built an even more impressive career out of the legacies of US military involvement in Cambodia, Việt Nam, and Laos. He was born 1968 in Hà Tiên, a Vietnamese town near the Cambodian border. In 2011, Lê's video installation *The Farmers and the Helicopter* (2006) was featured in a solo exhibition at the Museum of Modern Art in New York.[47] Lê has two series of work dealing with Cambodia—trauma and tourism—that arguably take a less didactic approach than Danh's work. The 1998 series *Splendor and Darkness* literally weaves together photographic images of Tuol Sleng victims and close-ups of Angkor Wat (both mainly black and white), forming an abstract tapestry of sorts, a dialectic of transcendence and terror. The solo show *The Hill of Poisonous Trees* a (translation of the Khmer words *Tuol Sleng*) at the PPOW gallery, New York City, in May 2008 revisits the infamous photographic archive of victims at the Tuol Sleng Genocide Museum. This series of "photo-weavings" superimposes the black-and-white images of victims with yellow-hued shots of the museum—its long halls, its small warren of prisons, and its torture chambers.

Both artists use formal innovations—Danh's "chlorophyll prints" and Lê's "photo-weavings"—to re-present temples and trauma. The formal innovations serve as an aesthetic filter and translation of otherwise gruesome and overused imagery. The formal quality of the work not only allows the viewer to engage in the subject matter but also contains it at a safe remove. All of those who have engaged in dark tourism (real or virtual) in Southeast Asia are familiar with the black-and-white photographic grids of Cambodian Khmer Rouge victims. Postcards and paintings of Angkor Wat traffic in clichés of bas-relief close-ups, sunrises, and sunsets—might artists refresh tourists' or gallery-goers' jaded outlook, providing a new angle? I do not explore the breadth of Danh's and Lê's works in this book because much has already been written on that subject. I do write about their work related to Cambodia here because I want to underscore the fact that visibility for artists from the "periphery" is still contingent on playing to the "center," as evidenced by their focus on temples and trauma. These are strategic uses of the periphery—or "strategic cartographies," a concept on which I elaborate.

Strategic Cartographies

Examining the oeuvre of artists with ties to Phnom Penh and Sài Gòn, such as Đinh Q. Lê and Binh Danh, I argue for a reconsideration of "diasporic" and "local." Overseas artists living in Southeast Asia may be marketed—and identify—as "local," whereas their "local" counterparts have "diasporic" outlooks. For these artists, "translations" of local issues are (self-)exploitative gestures. In a competitive international art market, I assert, these artists strategically position themselves as both insiders and outsiders.

I critically interrogate but do not abandon national and regional framings but, instead, ambivalently embrace and interrogate the categories and cartographies that determine "Southeast Asia" as a field. In doing so, I deliberately invoke this framing while, at the same time, I aim to decenter it. Artists must continually position themselves within a global art market, placing themselves within strategic cartographies to be legible. The "global turn" in contemporary art, sparked by the spectacular proliferation of art biennales (echoing imperialist World's Fairs of yesteryear) from Jakarta to Johannesburg, satiates the demands of "diversity" and dividends. Building on the postcolonial theorist Gayatri Spivak's "strategic essentialism," this book attempts to forge strategic cartographies, an affective unmapping and retracing of critical and creative connections within and outside Southeast Asia. Spivak writes about the ways in which multivalent identitarian groups (nationalities, minorities, ethnicities) deliberately present themselves outwardly as a unified entity toward common goals or interests, despite differences. This is "a strategic use of positivist essentialism in a scrupulously visible political interest."[48] In this frame, subalterns use normally stigmatizing stereotypes as empowering strategies to thwart domination. I move beyond subordinate-dominant binaries to think through how powerful narratives are at once construed and destabilized. What are the aesthetic and ethical ramifications—beyond identitarian politics and politicking—of producing and exhibiting (and critically examining) artwork now, at this "global turn"?[49]

Strategic cartographies deploy geographic and historical identities and (dis)identifications in a tactical manner.[50] This approach is a considered mapping of psychic and physical terrain, connections, disconnections, and affiliations. These subject positions based on national, regional, and transnational coordinates create uncertain terrain—it is both useful and fraught ground for creative and critical inquiries. I recognize epistemic and disciplinary violence, displacements: Enlightenment singular-perspective cartography, as well as area studies' colonial and Cold War antecedents. Strategic cartographies also evoke palimpsest (neo)colonial, neoliberal, transnational subjectivities as a way to acknowledge and thwart these framings.

Strategic cartographies also invoke the interventions of "critical cartography" and "critical art." The urban planner and theorist Annette Miae Kim proposes a "critical humanist cartography" as a means for geographers, artists, architects, and laypeople, among others, to "map the unmapped."[51] This aims to reconceive how political regimes' conventional maps and mapping of its subjects underscore power linked by policies, procedures, and cultural programming. Likewise, a critical art practice—and a practice of looking critically at art (institutions, producers, audiences)—foregrounds performative exchanges of influence. In dialogue with the postcolonial scholar Iain Chambers and the political theorist Chantal Mouffe, the art historian Anne Ring Petersen suggests that "critical art" "should be understood as a performative process of engagement and critical reflection which is undertaken by artists and audiences alike."[52] Artists and audiences critically align with, subvert, and create new geopolitical affiliations and affects.

As part of the uncertain terrain artists, audiences, and institutions are navigating, we are witnessing a shift in geopolitics: the faltering of the "American Century" (the United States' post–World War II socioeconomic dominance) and the hyped rise of the "Asian Century." Has the "Pacific Century" dawned? In the twenty-first century, which is also referred to as the "Asia-Pacific Century," the superpowers (China, India) and emerging Association of Southeast Asian Nations (ASEAN) "tiger economies" are reportedly displacing—and provincializing—Europe and the Atlantic. "The rest" beset the West.

Mimetic and Antimimetic Theories on Trauma and Art

To better understand Binh Danh's and Đinh Q. Lê's memorializing output—and, by extension, other diasporic artists who are part of the first and second generation of Vietnamese immigrants—I briefly discuss different approaches in trauma. The trauma theorist Ruth Leys examines the underlying assumptions of theoretical and clinical approaches on psychic trauma. Leys notes there are two basic currents in trauma theory, which have oscillated through time: (1) mimetic theory; and (2) antimimetic theory. Mimetic theory holds that "precisely because the victim cannot recall the original traumatogenic event, she is fated to act it out or in other ways imitate it."[53] Traumatized subjects cannot fully comprehend the original trauma or completely represent it; nor can they integrate it into their worldview. Antimimetic theories hold that the trauma is entirely external to the victim, and it is possible to recall and represent it.

Two historically contingent currents appear to overlap with psychoanalytic and Enlightenment approaches, with mimetic theory aligned with the former and antimimetic aligned with the latter. Mimetic theory is aligned with psychoanalytic approaches in that both are internally oriented; trauma is ingested, repressed. Within this framework, artists are melancholics who constantly revisit traumatic sites, incapable of resolution. Antimimetic theory may be aligned with Enlightenment approaches in that both are externally oriented. Trauma is an outside event that can be mastered, worked through more or less rationally. Within this view, artists gain mastery over trauma through mastery of its representations. However, Leys's Foucauldian genealogy points out that the mimetic and antimimetic paradigms do not resolve themselves. Rather there is a continuing and productive tension (often appearing within the body of work of a single theorist). This ambivalent tension is at the heart of Lê's practice. Lê refuses to offer a "complete" narrative of trauma. Instead, he offers the viewer disjointed fragments, quotations from mass media, and mental images.

Mimetic/antimimetic theories of trauma recall mimetic/antimimetic discourses in art. In Western aesthetic and philosophical traditions, the creative act was first seen as a mimetic act. Aristotle and Plato (and later, Renaissance thinkers influenced by them) asserted that artists only imitated God's creations. Aristotle claimed the importance of "the universal" (which was challenged then by Plato and is challenged now by postmoderns). In contrast to Plato, who saw art and fiction as mere copies of appearances, Aristotle maintained that art (and imitation) was the highest form of learning, getting beyond the specific singularities (of history). The "universal statements" found in art attested to divine ideas of permanence beyond earthly foibles.[54] We have inherited the distinction between the universal and the particular—empire and its "peripheries." Danh and Lê occupy "peripheral" subject positions as refugees and war survivors. Their narrative is not "universal," although displacement is one of the primary hallmarks of the

15

postmodern condition. Their particular histories (and art) do not address timeless grand themes, philosophical traditions.

In tracing the idea of the "creative," Williams states that the shift from art as mimesis to art as creative occurs as Western society transitions from a religious to a humanist framework.[55] Part of the shift to humanist conceptions includes the influence of psychoanalysis, particularly theories of the unconscious (Freud, Jung). Within this new paradigm, the subconscious psyche is the realm just beyond humankind's reach. (Previously that realm was the divine.) In getting in touch with his unconscious, the artist creates anew. Although artists are no longer inheritors of the divine, touched by genius, contemporary artists can be cultural ambassadors. Artists, then, are still conduits. Instead of being messiahs for heavenly realms, they are messengers of our earthly troubles.

In Eastern aesthetic traditions there is no such split between mimesis and abstraction. Representations of earthly realms (landscapes) are represented as voids—negative space is equally important as positive space. For instance, in traditional Chinese and Vietnamese landscape paintings the human subject is often dwarfed by vast mists, voids of cloud, sky. This is consistent with Confucian views of man and nature (man as a small part of nature and not apart from it). Likewise, there is no split among creative, philosophical, and critical inquiry. For centuries, philosopher-poet emperors and literati were seen as exemplary.

The (Western) model of art as mimetic (religious)/antimimetic (humanistic) appears to reverse theories of trauma outlined earlier. Again, in mimetic/psychoanalytic trauma systems, trauma is internal, to be repeated endlessly. In antimimetic/Enlightenment approaches to trauma, it is external, to be worked through. In all formulations, the dissonance between the sacred and the profane; mimicry and creation; unconscious and rational echoes an Apollonian-Dionysian ethos in which oppositional impulses cycle toward balance.

The trauma theorist Ann Kaplan notes that humanities research often does not account for "vicarious trauma"—that is, trauma that is not directly experienced but may manifest in various traumatic symptoms, such as generational trauma and the "empathetic" symptoms of professionals who work with trauma victims. Using the (Freudian) notion of transference, Dominick LaCapra describes similar symptoms as vicarious trauma resulting when "transference takes place in relations between people and . . . in one's relationship to the object of study itself."[56] Danh wrestles with this "vicarious trauma." As part of the so-called 1.5 generation—born to immigrant parents

16

and younger than sixteen before they immigrated—Danh experienced the effects of war and displacement firsthand but largely remembers it through secondhand accounts and media representation. His work does not offer a singular account of his personal traumatic experience but points to how generational trauma is transmitted: through snippets of images in movies and newspaper archives, through stories relatives tell, through the visage of passing strangers who bear the traces of painful pasts. The art of ambivalence, oscillation, and reframing alerts us to discrepant radical frames. Danh, Lê, and their artistic peers do not present authentic tales of woe but point at how constructed narratives of the past, present, and future collide. This is a form of adaptation, reinvention. Theirs is not a dyadic mimetic/antimimetic art in which traumas are endlessly reproduced or one in which there is complete healing. Return is grace.

The concept of "trauma" is often discussed within mainstream media without grounded specificity. Suffering is viewed as a basic human affliction. Tragic narratives are also hallmarks of "the universal," until they become too specific. As Judith Butler notes, certain lives are deemed more grievable than others.[57] Trauma does not transcend geopolitics. Trauma cannot be delinked from place and history, body and memory. The psychologist David Becker acknowledges the universalizing tendencies of the term *trauma* and trauma studies: "Trauma can only be understood with reference to the specific contexts in which it occurs."[58] Trauma is not an event unto itself but part of a social, cultural web: "In each different social context people should create their own definition within a framework, in which the basic focus is not so much on the symptoms of a person but on the sequential development of the traumatic situation."[59] The trauma theorists Jill Bennett and Rosanne Kennedy echo this critique, stating that psychoanalytic theory—and its largely US-centered research—while productive in analyzing Holocaust testimony and First World subjects and subjectivity, may not be appropriate for other contexts across the globe.[60] They call for a shift of the "monocultural discipline" into one "that can inform the study of memory within a global context."[61] They also suggest that postcolonial studies, while inherently engaged with trauma studies, should be more open to cultural studies frameworks that include artistic, aesthetic, and cinematic representations.[62]

While I appreciate the move for a more "diverse" trauma studies, the additive model (more global perspectives of suffering) does not shift pathologizing paradigms of revisiting past wounds. I assert that we must rethink how we conceive of "working on" and "working through" trauma, with all of its local and transnational implications.

Traumas and Modernities

Historic shocks and the trauma of modernization are not separate but are deeply intertwined. I examine the valences of trauma and modernity through visual cultural production. How do Southeast Asians, particularly Cambodians and Vietnamese, remember and represent the conflicts and postwar redevelopment in Southeast Asia? These changes are most apparent for humans in the realm of the visual for humans—changing cityscapes, marketing displays, government propaganda, and feature films.

I challenge the hypervisibility of trauma tropes in Western representations of Southeast Asia and the invisibility of other representational, sociopolitical, and historical narratives. Significant scholarship has addressed the Khmer Rouge and Cambodia's troubled past—distant and recent—and present and the connections inbetween. Similarly, in the United States Việt Nam has become a metonym for a defeated war. We see spectacles of suffering—a naked girl screaming in terror, center-framed; monks and gasoline; villages on fire; rooftop evacuations. My project highlights Cambodian and Vietnamese artistic responses beyond Western narratives of hysterical terror and historical tragedy.

What is the issue with ongoing representations and associations of Cambodia with genocide and Việt Nam with war? As Chong, Schlund-Vials, and V. T. Nguyễn assert, such rhetorical conflations serve as strategic reasons for continuing US violence abroad and at home. The dead justify more deaths. This book wrestles with the uneasy problematics of representation: logos, trauma, modernity. It deals with the politics of the art market, the marginalization of Southeast Asian art history within art history. Rather than fixed identities, I focus on process, displacement, repetition, and cycles. Dislocation, reiteration, and succession mark diaspora and the traumas of history and modernity.

Modernity is both nonlinear and traumatic. The project of modernity is also a historical one, not just a contemporary phenomenon. Different modernities are evident in the French colonial manses in Hà Nội, the Russian brutalist 1970s architecture of Hồ Chí Minh's mausoleum, and the angular modernist university buildings in Phnom Penh. Through visuality (and these buildings' stylistic markers) ideology is marked. Economic growth has created a dramatically shifting sociopolitical, economic, and cultural climate in both countries. Modern subjects in Vietnamese soap operas and Cambodian music videos are portrayed enjoying middle-class luxuries. Modernization, however, is also a traumatic process. Kaplan notes that "trauma is often

18

seen as inherently linked to modernity."[63] Although governments and mass media view them as positive growth, industrialization and globalization are inherently brutal. Modernity's assumed progress is lauded by the state, obscuring its violence. In the shadow of gleaming high-rises and glossy billboards lie deep inequities. Bright shopping malls erase the dark memory of displaced, impoverished populations once occupying the same territory.

Traumas such as military engagement and modernization return as thematic objects of desire and desired art objects on international art markets. I examine artists whose work revisits the traumas of genocide, war, or rapid development in their "homelands" in Southeast Asia. Their work both critiques and capitalizes on these shifts. On the international art market, devastating losses become transformed, translated into delectable art items. These art markets are sites of economic return for artists, gallerists, collectors, critics, and art institutions.

Return of the Real?

The art historian and critic Hal Foster stresses that within these models of trauma discourse, the artist-subject is "evacuated and elevated at once." Following this logic, artists such as Binh Danh and Đinh Q. Lê are voided of their individuality as they become representative voices within cultural institutions. They are at once insiders and outsiders, constrained by the limits of institutional knowledge. Foster contends that "trauma discourse magically resolves two contradictory imperatives in culture today: deconstructive analyses and identity."[64] Declared dead by poststructuralism, the author/artist experiences a "strange rebirth" to address multiculturalism's wants.[65] Foster views this "absentee authority" as a "significant turn" in cultural politics and contemporary art and criticism.[66]

To extend this example, Binh Danh's and Đinh Q. Lê's works do not overtly address their biographical histories. Their subject positions, however, lend authority to their works that both subverts and reinforces conceptions of Southeast Asia during and after US military involvement. Through works that deal with historical and contemporary traumas, singular universalizing discourses are deconstructed—yet the politics of identity are reaffirmed. Thus, Foster notes, "Here the return of the real converges with the return of the referential." "Referential" modes of art making and thinking of the 1970s and 1980s prioritize text and intertextuality—for artists and scholars, the traditional studio is replaced by the postmodern seminar room. The "return of the real" in art and theory heralded by the 1990s and beyond focuses again on identities and communities as embodied sites. In this turn, the multiplicity of artistic/authorial voices both "evacuates and elevates" the traumatized, minoritized subject. The Southeast Asian artist's placement within cultural institutions and canons is simultaneously a displacement.

Foster's book *Return of the Real* argues that the "return" or reappearance of late twentieth-century Western avant-garde artistic strategies (e.g., ready-made objects, pop-culture appropriation, monochrome painting) is not repetition or "belated" imitation of older models but, rather, productive reworkings of them. Lê's and Danh's appropriation of popular and vernacular cultures (film, photos) builds on Marcel Duchamp's and Andy Warhol's differing tactics while underscoring their blind spots.

Foster's conception of return differs from mine. He attempts to map a parallel genealogy of the Western avant-garde that simply enfolds "Others" within its art-history framework. Foster returns to Eurocentric modernist canons, whereas my notion of return highlights myriad modernities. Foster's art-history alternatives largely dismiss alterity, whereas subaltern strategies are core to my study. Excavating the "relation between turns in critical models and returns of historical practices," Foster asks, "how does a reconnection with a past practice support a disconnection from a present practice and/or a development of a new one?"[67] He traces the shift of medium-specific, New York–centric (minimalism, abstract expressionism) models to discourse-specific modalities, evidenced by the global turn in contemporary art. Echoing the art critic Douglas Crimp's rebuttal of Foster's book, I also argue against a revisionist art history and for a visual and cultural studies grounded in politics. Refusing Foster's assertion that art history is more "rigorous" than visual studies, Crimp declares, "What is at stake is not history per se, which is a fiction in any case, but what history, whose history, history to what purpose."[68] The next sections attempt to address questions of how art histories—and geopolitical histories—are mapped, and toward what ends.

Negative Return   MELANCHOLIA, LOSS, SELF

I advocate for a politics of "negative return"—an inversion. To return does not reinforce a binary between eternal melancholia and "proper" mourning à la Freud. Return does not mean a repetition compulsion. Within common usage, a negative return occurs when total losses outweigh the initial investment. Normally, we want nominally positive result—an outgrowth of our positivist system, which valorizes materiality, empirical evidence (facts, figures), and rationality over intuition and the metaphysical.

Instead, I reframe the "negative" as a desired outcome, against the background of teleological positivism. This "negative return" references Freud's theories on melancholia. Briefly, the melancholic subject forever mourns the lost object. Without successfully reconciling this grief, the melancholic subject is doomed to compulsively revisit this wound.

Postcolonial and feminist revisions—racial melancholia, melancholic migrants—address Freud and his adherents' blindness to the linked traumas of race, gender, class, and empire. David Eng argues in *Racial Castration* that psychoanalytic frames of melancholic return and loss pivot on "idealized images such as masculinity, heterosexuality and whiteness [and] also imply an obverse set of images such as femininity, homosexuality and racialization."[69] Hence, Foster's "return of the real" echoes ongoing rhetoric of the "return" of the dark primitive (racialized, sexualized threats)—against white virility, "high culture," abstraction—hallmarks of Western modernity. Thus, Jackson Pollock and his "action" paintings—the apex of modernist traditions—are obversely mirrored by minoritarian artists who get acted on by traumas such as imperial might or rampant modernization. They are bearers of an identity politics hinged on loss. In this frame, one is made through one's acts ("a man of action"); the other is unmade, undone. Sara Ahmed and Anne Cheng argue that, for racialized, minoritized subalterns, the wounds will never heal, as they are structurally omnipresent, intimately reenacted through micro- and macro-aggressions. Ahmed's "melancholic migrant" is eternally socioeconomically displaced, without recourse. Cheng's "melancholy of race" addresses the trauma of racialization that denies full subjectivity—second-class citizenship. These views of melancholia focus on the denial of personhood—a world shattering. Instead, I focus on negation as subject and world making and its opposite. Inaction is also political activity—passivity as resistance.

I also emphasize return's spatial dimensions. A melancholic requires a place to return to. A negative return is both action and site: it refuses a melancholic's frenzied repetitions. The site of slow, gradual, repeated return is the self. In his later works, Jung wrote about coming to terms with his shadow self as a process of self-actualization. Differing from Freud's unconscious, Jung's shadow concept evokes other archetypes: trickster, wolf, and so on. To become fully integrated, one has to embrace one's darkest aspects. We must choose to return to the troubling. In contrast to the Freudian view—patients assaulted by pathologies need to expel them—

a return to the Jungian shadow is a deliberate, sustained encounter, a return engagement. The shadow, the negative, must be continuously integrated over one's life. Instead of a possession (Freud's melancholic), darkness is assimilated.

Within indigenous American traditions, to become a leader the wounded healer has to undergo a traumatic process (e.g., serious physical or psychic illness). The shaman-to-be has to successfully heal herself or himself in order to heal others.[70] The dark period is a transformation. Similarly, in *Thus Spoke Zarathustra*, Nietzsche recognizes that man cannot ignore his pathos: "I must first go down . . . deeper into pain than ever I descended, down into its blackest flood. . . . Whence come the highest mountains? I once asked. Then I learned that they came out of the sea. The evidence is written in their rocks and in the walls of their peaks. It is out of the deepest depth that the highest must come to its height."[71] The dyad of "blackest" depth and height sees the need for both shadow and light.

The Enlightenment project (and science) is heralded for shedding light on the superstitions lurking within the medieval "Dark Ages"; for remedying the black plague. Likewise, imperial light ennobles the dark, savage continents. In *Atomic Light (Shadow Optics)*, however, Akira Lippit discusses the shadows of the twentieth century cast by modernity—new light-emitting, "avisual" technologies such as movies, X-ray, and atomic bombs—and their residual traces in postwar Japanese life and cinema.[72] In this context, the blinding radiance of an atomic blast reminds us that encountering light and shadow is also a matter of life and death.

Positivism's rhetoric is one of gain: capitalist accumulation, dominions and domination of peoples, places, and time. A negative return emphasizes loss—losing control, losing oneself. Referring to "shadow feminism" Jack Halberstam writes, "Loss enables another connection to other models of time, space, place and connection."[73] Shadow feminism, like Williams's Long Revolution, forgoes immediate political action and gratification for a longer time span. Other modalities of being (passivity, for instance, over activism) are sites of struggle. This struggle is sustained, repeated, engaged.

The negative return is returning to the void of unknowing—of not knowing precisely oneself (as active agent), of becoming undone in order to become again. Halberstam elaborates on negation's power: "This feminism, grounded in negation, refusal, passivity, absence and silence . . . [is] a shadow feminism which has nestled in more positivist accounts and unravels their logic within."[74] Like the wounded warrior, embracing the shadow is a negative return. There is both a self and a no-self—a disorientation and a reorientation—as one goes to the "deepest depth" and the highest heights. It is a topsy-turvy turning: one full revolution for one.

We all are entrenched within shadow and light—interpolated within empire, the machinations of capitalism. A shadow feminist response to empire's violence may be not overt action but vulnerability and grief as solidarity. In "Violence, Mourning, Politics," Butler observes, "To grieve, and to make grief itself into a resource for politics, is not to be resigned to inaction, but it may be understood as the slow process by which we develop a point of identification with suffering itself." How do we open ourselves up to be vulnerable, not as mere witnesses or bystanders, but to risk our grasp on our guarded identities and truly identify with the refugee, the displaced, the dispossessed? It is a mourning, letting go of the ego, the id, one's (global North) identities—a (dis)identification, if you will. Butler notes that the "disorientation of grief—'Who have I become,' or indeed, 'What is left of me?' 'What is it in the Other that I have lost?'—posits the 'I' in the mode of unknowingness."[75] Loss as a means for a different kind politics—an unraveling of self, an unknowingness—is a shadow process. It is a "dissolution of the persona."[76]

A politics of negative return is a position of ambivalence, uncertainty. I posit that being unable to place oneself, literally and metaphorically, is a pivot: it is a way of being, unnamed, unknown, unhinged from one's axis and *axis mundi*. One must lose personhood to form a new sense of self and the world. For artists and for art, a negative return is a risky proposal: it unbalances, unhinges. Yet this practice of separation and unity is crucial. The shaman has to journey, to leave in order to return with a message from the spirits to help others. Engaging the Jungian shadow is also a tenuous path of integration: "The ego and shadow are no longer divided but are brought together in an—admittedly precarious—unity."[77] For Marcuse, an art that contains its own contradictions is vital. He notes, "There is no work of art which does not break its own affirmative stance by 'the power of the negative,' which does not, in its very nature, evoke the words, the images of another reality, of another order repelled by the existing one yet alive in its memory and anticipation, alive in what happens to men and women and in their rebellion against it."[78] This sentiment echoes Halberstam's insistence that negation is a tactic to "unravel" capitalism's counterrevolution from within and from outside. Art can insist on negating itself and its conditions.

Binh Danh and Đinh Q. Lê both engage in negative returns: through strategic use of the periphery, they at once place and displace themselves and cultural institutions. They simultaneously reinforce and untether topologies of "temples and trauma." Their conceptual art can be seen as "passive," melancholic (versus "active" street protests or cheery pop art). Their conceptual interventions are a form of shadow politics. Marcuse maintains that the highest art must oscillate between jouissance and despair, being and nothing, action and inaction. He writes, "Where this tension between affirmation and negation, between pleasure and sorrow, higher and lower material culture no longer prevails, where the work no longer sustains the dialectical unity of what is and what can (and ought to) be, art has lost its truth, has lost itself."[79] Similar to Jung's and Nietzsche's claims, humanity (the questing artist) has to plumb the "blackest," deepest depths in order to alight. The internal "tensions" between negation and affirmation are also reflected in the mimesis/antimimesis theories on art and trauma outlined earlier in this introduction.

Danh and Lê's return engagements are not driven by manic neurosis (melancholia, repetition compulsion). Instead, their embrace of the shadow is intentional, measured. Their praxis centers the negative, void: multiplicity, unknowing—they are unplaceable and implacable.

Art Historicity THE GREAT DEBATE

Đinh Q. Lê and Binh Danh are among the most visible artists of Vietnamese descent on the international art scene. They are famous, but will they ever be included in the household-name, postage-stamp canon of Pollack and Warhol? Or will their ethnicity forever limit them? In her provocative essay "Why Have There Been No Great Vietnamese Artists?" Nora Taylor notes that "artists from peripheral loci of art production—that is, outside the Western art market centers in places such as Việt Nam—often 'exist' or are known only because Western galleries, art auction houses, or even art historians have situated them."

These institutional forces often reflect Eurocentric hierarchies. "Greatness" implies transcending the bonds of race and gender; to be "great," one has to create "timeless" works that speak to humanity. The title of Taylor's essay refers to the art historian Linda Nochlin's seminal feminist essay "Why Have There Been No Great Women Artists?" which highlights the gendered structural inequities within the art world. Gender, class, and race discrimination persists today both more distinctly and more imperceptibly. Multiculturalism's shadow obscures the lack of opportunities for marginalized artists through celebratory, tokenizing discourse. Global gendered economies of scale reveal a shifting world order that demands difference. Yet this quest for difference is homogenizing. Taylor observes that the identities of artists from the "periphery" are often lumped into a single ethnic or national frame.[80] Both Taylor and Nochlin critique the standards of greatness. Artists from peripheral sites are automatically constrained, geographically and ethnically. They cannot reach the upper pantheon of artists. Rhetorically, the parameters of greatness are indifferent to creed, color, and gender. In reality, however, artistic masters and their masterpieces reinscribe vast hierarchies.

The question of discovering a great Cambodian, Vietnamese, or any artist is a futile exercise. There is no point in raising the issue. "Why have there been no great Southeast Asian artists?" is a query that reveals the power structures and cultural biases by which "greatness" is evaluated and conferred. We must scrutinize the position of those asking and answering the inquiry, even if it is us. Yes, there have been great Khmer and Vietnamese artists, but they are heralded as masters within a national context and unknown elsewhere because of a lack of critical and commercial resources. Greatness is subjective. The sociologist Pierre Bourdieu has written about the "economy of cultural goods": the overlapping networks of art institutions, critics, artists, and academics.[81] Increasing numbers of dealers, collectors, curators, and critics are coming to Southeast Asia.

Within the past decade, the region's emerging art scenes have been trumpeted as the next hot thing. To use Việt Nam as a case study, an article published in the *New York Times* in 2017 proclaims "Vietnamese Art Has Never Been More Popular," noting that "some of Vietnam's greatest artists are enjoying a moment of increasing world attention," fetching record prices at Sotheby's and Christie's auctions.[82] In 2007, the same newspaper quoted the Southeast Asian art specialist Mok Kim Chuan (of Sotheby's Singapore) as saying, "There are many vibrant young contemporary artists in Hanoi, and people are definitely buying their work—hoping it will one day appreciate. . . . Contemporary [Vietnamese] art is very hot right now." Within a ten-year span, the late Lê Phổ's work (which combines post-impressionist, surrealist, and traditional Asian influences) surged at auction, from $300,000 to a record-breaking $1.2 million.[83] Lê's commingling of East and West fits into collectors' conceptions of Indochina: languidly elegant, exotified Edenic imagery.

Artists have varied artistic responses to what is expected of them. "Good" art is still measured by Western artistic canons. It is a form of cultural imperialism. Parallels can be drawn to the French colonial discourses about aesthetics, modernity, and authenticity. The complexities of positioning within a global economic order demand that artistic agency is seen from a variety of sociocultural perspectives. Museums, gallerists, and curators increasingly build shows and collections around the category "Southeast Asian," thematically highlighting flows among countries rather than focusing on lone nations. Art scholarship should also address this trend.

Critical and curatorial work on the artistic output of a single city or country is still important for a deep understanding of cultural influences and developments. For example, Taylor's *Painters in Hanoi*, as its title attests, homes in on different generations of Vietnamese painters within a specific geographic region. Ly Daravuth and his late partner Ingrid Muan[84] contributed to pioneering scholarship on Khmer contemporary visual art through research and through the Reyum Institute, an art center they cofounded in Phnom Penh in 1998 that houses exhibits, offers workshops (dance, art, music), and publishes books.[85] The cultural historian Ashley Thompson writes about the role of memory and the Cambodian state, ranging from ancient Angkorian temples to contemporary visual cultures (including the late painters Vann Nath and Rithy Panh).[86] This book continues to expand these parameters to include Vietnamese and Cambodian local and diasporic artists living in these countries who work in a range of media—video, works on paper, installation, photography. I highlight historical and sociopolitical connections that affect artists' relationships with their audiences.

My argument for transgressing national boundaries also applies to art history, which should continue to shift its Western-centric knowledge base to encompass visual cultures in myriad centers and peripheries. Art historians including Alice Yang,[87] Thomas Crow, and Patrick Flores, among others, note that contemporary Asian art histories are marginalized. I would further emphasize that Southeast Asian and Asian American art histories are marginalized. Addressing the void in Southeast Asian scholarship are a limited number of survey texts, such as *Reworlding Art History: Encounters with Contemporary Southeast Asian Art after 1990* (2014), by Michelle Antoinette, and *Modern and Contemporary Southeast Asian Art: An Anthology* (2012), edited by Nora Taylor and Boreth Ly. Apart from a few special issues of academic journals dedicated to Southeast Asian contemporary art, there is a dearth of sustained discourse, with the exception of *Southeast of Now: Directions in Contemporary and Modern Asian Art*, a peer-reviewed journal launched in March 2017.[88] Fewer than a handful of art historians are working on contemporary visual artists of Cambodian and Vietnamese descent— namely, Nora Taylor, Pamela Corey,[89] Boreth Ly, Moira Roth,[90] and me.

But art history is not enough. Art history's emphasis on fine art objects, biography, and national narratives cannot fully address affective dimensions of rapid sociopolitical shifts, mass media, and memory. In combining the approaches of visual anthropology with art history, I aim to shift the largely

Western focus of art history. In using art history's attention to close visual analysis of artwork, I further complement the insights I get from intensive fieldwork. To grasp the complexity of an artwork, I rely on close readings of the work combined with studio visits and interviews whenever possible. I also consider critics' and viewers' reactions to art pieces or films. My background in art history compels me to rigorously consider the link between form and content, materials and meaning. I also connect artists with the larger political and historical worlds they engage.

Following T. J. Clark and Thomas Crow's models of a "social history of art," I examine the social, historical, and political conditions in which artists' work is produced.[91] I focus on visual culture because it highlights social and individual visions of what is modern, traumatic, or desirable. Similarly, what is repressed and not seen on an everyday level may be represented. These representations make evident individual and institutional struggles.

Historicity and the Politics of Waiting

I maintain that narratives about the past and the future are mutable. The anthropologist Michel-Rolph Trouillot notes that "historical narrative [is] one fiction among others"—historicity and futurity get blurred.[92] Historical trauma is not a fixed event but an event that gets reinterpreted and reinvented with each recollection. These personal recollections have public and political dimensions. By the same logic, modernity is also not a static conception. Modernity is not a fixed linear project of progress but one that is constantly reinterpreted, reimagined by its architects and the populace.[93] Yet Dipesh Chakrabarty notes in *Provincializing Europe* that the teleological binary between European "modern countries" and those "stuck" in the past persists. Mimi Thi Nguyễn argues that the invitation to "catch up" to modernity, Derrida's "gift of time," has a catch.[94] The United States must push "liberal war"—promising liberal freedoms—to pull its invaded into modernity.[95] Derrida notes that this "given time" is a requirement and deferral of the gift: "There must be time, it must last, there must be waiting—without forgetting."[96] Here, I conceive of waiting and remembering differently—not as deferral and debt, but as defiance and solidarity. In terms of waiting, José Esteban Muñoz writes in *Cruising Utopia*, "Those who wait are those of us who are out of time. . . . We have been cast out of straight time's rhythm, and we have made worlds with our spatial and temporal configurations. Certainly this would be the time of postcoloniality, but it is also crip time, or like the old joke we still use, CPT (colored people time)."[97] Colored people time and colonial time—these contradictions, or clashes, in time are integral. Although they are in the same frame, their spatiality and temporality are anachronous. I think of "belatedness as opportunity," to echo Chakrabarty: postcolonial nations have a discrepant timeline that refuses, upends Western modernity's time-line of progress. In waiting, we are occupying, embodying different forma-tions of time and space outside of Bergsonian time of the clock. Muñoz notes, "Within straight time the queer can only fail; thus an aesthetics of failure can productively be occupied by the artist for delineating straight time's measure."[98] The *Merriam-Webster Dictionary* defines "straight time" as "standard working hours within a work week"; it can also be understood as heteronormative or homonormative temporalities of assimilationist mainstream timelines of "success."

I recall the images in *National Geographic* of "natives" under the watchful colonial gaze, waiting under the hot sun. I remember myself as a three-year-old refugee in a Thai camp, waiting, waiting, waiting. Flash forward to mass-media images of North African and Syrian refugees now, waiting, waiting. In linking passivity, failure, and shadow archives as geopolitical and temporal alternatives, waiting, too, becomes a component of return engagements. A return engagement also requires spatial and temporal lapse—a duration be-tween event and horizon.

Beyond breaking down distinctions in time—the past, present, and future—I challenge the parameters of place and belonging. I connect ref-ugees and returnees then and now and the highly political, personal acts of waiting (as subalterns, refugees, immigrants) and welcoming one an-other. This builds on the artist Faith Wilding's performance work *Waiting | Welcome* (as coalition building), as well as Derrida's insights on the wel-come. Derrida argues that the act of welcoming—of hospitality—requires asymmetrical power relations: the host has dominion over the guests. For example, one can think of host countries or host institutions (such as a museum inviting a guest artist for an art residency). He notes that the differences between pure, or "unconditional," giving and hospitality and "conditional" giving are in endless tension.[99] Specifically addressing immigrants and refugees, Derrida calls for "another international right, another politics of borders, another humanitarian politics, even perhaps a humanitarian engagement which would actually take place beyond the interest of nation states."[100] Toward this, one must radically reconsider identity and home—not an ethics of hospitality (welcome), but ethics as hospitality.

I now connect notions of ethical waiting and welcoming to my ideas on return and revolution—a turning of self and society. This turn is both disorienting and reorienting. The act of welcoming redefines who is host and guest and, ultimately, what subjectivity is. In his reading of Derrida's "'revolution' of the concept of subjectivity," the philosopher François Raffoul points out that the term *revolution* has to be understood also in the literal sense of a spatial turning around or reversal, the concept of the subject being "turned upside down," so to speak."[101] I stress again these ideas of spatial reversal, as well as subjective turning "topsy-turvy," in my earlier notes—return, revolution, and revolt as being cyclically interconnected. Revolution is not only a "turning around" (about-face—singular reversal), as Raffoul suggests, but a turning around and around (circle). Beyond losing distinction between self and other, the host is also "(g)host"—dematerialized, the site of a "visitation of a face," states Derrida.[102] Within Christian contexts, "host" refers to heavenly as well as military bodies (e.g., heavenly host: army of angels). The sacramental host, or bread of the Eucharist, comes from the Latin *hostia*, which means "sacrificial victim" (the gift, like hospitality, requires sacrifice). These links are not coincidental. Derrida notes that hospitality is always tinged with violence (again, in the same manner as the gift).

I suggest that face (self) and effacement (erasure of self) are coeval. For instance, "saving face" and "losing face" are sides of the same coin. (I elaborate on this in chapter 4.) Referencing Levinas, Derrida observes that the link between host and hostage "involves a paradoxical situation with respect to the status of the host, a peculiar reversal—*revolution*, once again—of the meaning of the host."[103] The subject (as host) is subjected—as hostage—to the other (guest). Finally, hospitality indicates "that originary dispossession, the withdrawal that, expropriating the 'owner' of what is most his own, and *expropriating the self of itself*, makes of his home a place of transit."[104]

These insights on the host and the gift are useful in thinking about historicity not as an end point, but as sites and times of return. In the conventional sense, time and property are subject to regulation. Both space and time are sites to come to: one "arrives at" a destination on time (hence, estimated time of arrival, or ETA). In another example, countries are expected achieve their gross domestic product (GDP) targets within a schedule. While one cannot "own" time, it is a condition of control (hence, "doing time"). First, the dissolution of self questions where subjectivity resides. The "expropriating the self of itself" is a deterritorialization (to borrow Deleuze and Guattari's description of the schizophrenic subjective conditions of capital). Returnees have no ownership of where they return to—they are dispossessed. Second, "home" is not a stable entity but constantly a "place of transit." Through return, polarities of ownership and dispossession (of oneself, one's place in the world) are broken: "If the at-home with oneself of the dwelling is an 'at-home with oneself as in a land of asylum or refuge,' this would mean that the inhabitant dwells there also as a refugee or an exile, a guest and not a proprietor."[105] Hence, a sense of home, oneself, is reached through motion and engagement.

With this reframing, the global South is no longer "stuck in time." For Bliss Cua Lim, fantastic cinema's "immiscible temporalities" evoke modalities beyond homogenizing modern time. Supernatural filmic narratives are untranslatable, unmixable, "immiscible" between two temporal frames: first, "the homogeneous time of Newtonian science and modern historical consciousness"; and second, "the heterogeneous times of the supernatural, the folkloric, and the popular."[106] Instead of reinforcing the opposition between homogeneous national time and the heterogeneity of transnational receptions, my artistic case studies—which deal with the haunted living and not the supernatural—reveal that translation is a strategic act. For artists wrestling with the long shadow of the politics of identity, art is a conscious negotiation between homogenous and heterogeneous rhetorical frames. The two temporal frames break down as the distinctions between local and diasporic, national and transnational collapse.

In this book I go back and forth in time and space to underscore this idea. The past and future—the weight of history and futurity—put us in an unmistakable and perhaps unbearable tension. For Walter Benjamin's angel of history, the tension is a storm blowing: "what we call progress."[107]

Time Lines

Challenging time and place while tracing significant ongoing economic and cultural shifts, I use several temporal anchor points in this book. The year 2008 is one anchor point, as it heralds what the Asian Development Bank calls the "first global financial crisis of the twenty-first century," arguably one of the greatest fiscal crises since the Great Depression of the 1930s.[108] Starting in 2007, the US subprime mortgage market crashed due to unstable investment cycles, eventually leading to an international banking crisis, with epicenters in the United States and Europe and shockwaves affecting the rest of the world. Yet within this economic downturn Asian economies survived largely unscathed.

In an article comparing the 1997 Asian financial crisis and the 2008 global financial crisis, the economists Donghyun Park, Arief Ramayandi, and Kwanho Shin observe that Asia "fared much better during the global crisis due to stronger fundamentals and better macroeconomic policies."[109] They note that "Asia's fundamentals [inflation rate, domestic credit expansion, the pre-crisis GDP rate] have strengthened further as a painful lesson of the [1997] Asian fiscal crisis."[110] Instead of constrictive macroeconomic policies of monetary and fiscal tightening, expansionary "countercyclical" policies (such as banks' supporting growth by providing liquidity for their systems) help cushion crisis and aid recovery.[111] The economists Margot Schüller and Jan Peter Wogart observe that Asian economies have responded to these fiscal crises by strengthening regional institutions and trying to shift international fiscal dominance: "Faced with the negative impact of regional and global financial crises, Asian countries have established joint-solution mechanisms over the last two decades in order to better protect themselves from short-term outflows of capital and from currency speculation."[112]

As Asian countries recovered from these fiscal crises and sought to strengthen their economies from volatile global market shifts, cultural spheres were also intrinsically linked. The years 2011–13 mark another turn and anchor point in my study: the art world's "global turn" directly spotlighting Southeast Asian contemporary artists, particularly Cambodian artists. Corey notes that this time frame heralds the rise of Khmer contemporary art's international visibility from exhibitions sponsored by East Asia and Southeast Asia (such as the Singapore Biennale and Fukuoka Triennale) to epicenters of Western art such as Documenta [Kassel] and the Guggenheim [New York]).[113] This shift from Eastern regional venues to Western stages is part of larger timelines linked to Khmer postgenocide socioeconomic redevelopment—or periods of "cultural restoration," as Muan terms it.[114] Corey "suggest[s] that from roughly 2003 to 2010, in the art world largely centered in Phnom Penh, there was a shift in the reception and discourse of contemporary art in alignment with growing international interest."[115] Cambodia is a compelling case study for the intertwined ways in which local postwar, post-fiscal crisis (re)development meshes with international institutional circuits of support and visibility.

I thus map these different nodal points—Southeast Asian wars, global fiscal crises, the "global" art turn—as palimpsest traces that inform and influence one another. In this rendering of "immiscible temporalities"— recalling again Lim's term to describe "that hint of untranslatable times, that trace of containment and excess"—I seek to draw out unexpected connections, affiliations, and responses.[116] These "untranslatable" temporalities are inherently tied to shifting geopolitics and the politics of translation. The legacies of such traumas have yet to be understood (or translated) beyond uplifting narratives of socioeconomic reconstruction. For instance, in the wake of the 2008 global fiscal crisis, unemployment in the United States rose 10 percent in 2010; it had fallen to 3.9 percent in 2018 and remained steady at 3.7 percent in 2019. Triggered in part by COVID-19, US unemployment is at 11.1 percent (affecting 17.8 million people as of August 2020), a decrease from previous highs at the outset of the pandemic (14.7 percent in April and 13.3 percent in May 2020, according to US Labor Department statistics).[117] This crisis still has long-term and far-reaching repercussions, despite positive state statistics. *The Economist* observes that this financial crisis has "evolved into the [ongoing] Euro crisis."[118] The economic historian Adam Tooze writes, "The financial and economic crisis of 2007–2012 morphed between 2013 and 2017 into a comprehensive political and geopolitical crisis of the post–cold war order"[119]—one in which increasingly nationalist right-wing power has coalesced in Europe and the United States (e.g., Brexit, Donald Trump). The Asia Development Bank observes two responses. The first response is a xenophobic, nationalist "'corrective' move toward greater domestic-led growth [in the West]—from an excessive dependence on export-led growth—particularly in the large current account surplus countries in Asia."[120] The second response sees the continued need for foreign investment and financing.[121] Although at odds outwardly, the two currents are still in play. As nationalist sentiment congeals, transnational coalitions realign. Against this backdrop, emerging Eastern countries align themselves with the West for cultural capital (hence, the emergence of Khmer contemporary art programs within art-world capitals). At the same time, Western countries try to stabilize their fiscal capital structures by tactically positioning themselves with Eastern superpowers, as well as the global South. I expand on these seemingly immiscible alignments later.

Another example of strategic cartographies: formerly economically and culturally aligned with Europe, Australia has shifted its foreign policies to embrace its position within the Asia Pacific and with Asia at large. In the 1960s, Australia's trade centered on Britain and the United States; today, it is focused on Asia, with four out of its top five two-way trading partners located in Asia, reports the Australian Department of Foreign Affairs and Trade.[122] In 2017–18, ASEAN was among Australia's top-three import- and export-trading partners, according to the Australian government's Trade and Investment Commission.[123] The East Asia Forum notes that Australia's trade with Asia is "bigger than with Europe and North America combined. Over three-quarters of Australia's commodity exports already go to Asia, and it draws close to 70 percent of its imports from this same region."[124] As with all strategic relationships, Australia continues to (re)position itself. Europe is vying for top partner status with Australia. On May 22, 2018, the Commission of the European Union (EU) opened up the renegotiation of free trade agreements, last visited a decade ago.[125]

As it turns out, the EU is also looking to the global South, having secured successful close trading agreements with Việt Nam, Singapore, and Mexico.[126] Part of the shift toward the global South and Asia may be an outgrowth of Asian economies' response to solidifying economic power since the fiscal crises. An *Asia Europe Journal* article notes that "European countries are supporting Asia's attempt to gain more weight in global financial governance. . . . and, thus, contribute to the acceleration of the power shift away from the USA toward emerging Asian economies in general, and China in particular."[127]

These Asia-centric statistics, press releases, and news headlines, however, may be misleading. Australia is facing both West and East: the EU is Australia's second-largest director and trading partner, behind China.[128] Chakrabarty reminds us that capitalism, Eurocentric knowledge production, and modernity are coeval and complicit. It is not "the West" versus "the Rest." Rather, the "West" is but one of many rest posts, a region among many. Western theory is both "indispensable and inadequate."[129] Whether this is the "American Century" or the "Asian Century," flows of culture, labor, and commerce are at once increasingly porous and policed—a paradox and a new paradigm.

The distinctions between "global" and "local" aesthetic practices and art histories are arbitrary and unnecessary. In an interview published in *Art Asia Pacific*, the curator and art historian Patrick Flores states, "I'm trying to get away from the local-global dichotomy, which doesn't hold, and to insist on an extensive locality or even an equivalent locality. It's not like 'you guys are the global and we are just a local articulation of the global.' No, we co-produce the global through our locality."[130] The global and the local are coterminous. As I have been asserting, the local and diasporic are also coeval concepts.

The issue of space and place—and, by extension, site specificity and locationality—is an underlying, unifying thematic of the book. Again, it is not about the outdated binary between the local and global. The art historian Miwon Kwon suggests that it is "not a matter of choosing sides—between models of nomadism and sedentariness, between place and space."[131] The fluidities of time and space in our digitized, global world call for a "relational specificity" that accounts for our proximities to, and distances from, one another. How do we critically engage "the visual turn" (to use Martin Jay's term) within contemporary culture, ranging from high art and couture to "lowbrow" pop entertainment?[132]

Kwon's relational specificity addresses the uneven formations "between one thing, person, one place, one thought, one fragment next to another." By placing these relationships, these conditions, side by side, the relationship becomes lateral, even, rather than horizontal, hierarchical. Kwon insists, "We need to be able to think the range of the seeming contradictions and our contradictory desires for them together; to understand, in other words, seeming oppositions as sustaining relations."[133] The local and the global mutually sustain each other; they are coproduced, as Flores points out. Similarly, history and modernity are not contradictory; they are produced in relation with each other. This is not a "relational aesthetics," an ending encounter (against which Claire Bishop has argued).[134] To conceive of no end is an endgame. This is not art about engagement (social practice) but the art of engagement. This is an art of multiple encounters, return engagements. These relationships are sustained only by returning again and again—gestures of reciprocity.

Return Engagements

"Return engagements" also evokes the term *return on engagement* (ROE), the social media version of monetary "return on investment" (ROI). Beyond short-term hard cash (ROI), soft influence (ROE) indicators are now seen as equally important as hard currency (ROI). Consumer participation (shares, likes, comments) builds long-term brand loyalty. According to *Forbes*, "Return on engagement can show you how well your brand is performing in terms of building and sustaining relationships with both consumers and influencers."[135] In contemporary art, who are the consumers and influencers, and what are the relationships in between them? Collectors and speculators see art as a lucrative return on investment. In this era, individuals market themselves as commoditized brands—the corporatization of identity (politics). The lines among audience and consumer, cultural production, and capital product are blurred.

Finance (ROI) and the terms *revolution* and *revolt* are linked by circular imagery: turns of stock portfolios or politics. As I outlined earlier, *revolt* and *revolution* connote looping cycles, not linear movement. Williams notes that the connection centers "the important image of the Wheel of Fortune, through which so many of the movements of life and especially the most public movements were interpreted. In the simplest sense, men . . . were revolved, on Fortune's wheel, setting them now up, now down." In fifteenth-century Europe, about-turns were expected—cycles of trade and trading sociopolitical places became enmeshed. The main emphasis was not "the steady and continuous movement of [Fortune's] wheel" but the idea of a reversal of fortunes—endless turning: the "top and bottom point [are] as a matter of course, certain to change places."[136] Instead of late capital's emphasis on economic upswings or metastatic growth, the original image of fortune's wheel focused on a downward spiral.

"Negative return" challenges the expectations of positive outcomes—return on investments. It is a divestment. Neoliberalism is tied to free markets, constant expansion. Trade expansion can hinge on control of land and lives. Halberstam argues that one must reject binaries of "freedom in liberal terms or death—in order to think about shadow archives of resistance, one that does not speak in the language of action and momentum but instead articulates itself in terms of evacuation, refusal, passivity, unbecoming, unbeing."[137] Here I connect the term *evacuation* to military evacuations—a dissolution. To disarm is to disengage.

The acronym ROE also stands for "rules of engagement," or military directives. Both return on engagement and rules of engagement pertain to the social. With the former, there are implicit rules on what will garner positive outcomes (likes and followers). The latter, rules of engagement, is a more formal code for social and military behavior. Both ROEs facilitate social and monetary exchanges (e.g., Instagram shopping, military spending). Finally, rules of engagement are internal to governing bodies, whereas the social media return on engagement is public-facing (for PLCs [publicly listed companies/public limited companies]). Rules of engagement pertain to a country's military forces (naval, air, army) and refer to "the orders issued by a competent military authority that delineate when, where, how, and against whom military force may be used."[138] For individual combatants, ROE is the intermediary between action and abstraction: when and how to kill, and for what causes; ROEs "have implications for what actions soldiers may take on their own authority and what directives may be issued by a commanding officer."[139]

Rules of engagement differ in each country and can shift in tandem with other countries and military contexts. The United Nations has a handbook for peacekeeping operations (published through the support of the United Kingdom and Germany) that states, "The use of force of any kind by a member of a peacekeeping contingent is defined by the rules of engagement (ROE). The ROE are tailored to the specific mandate of the mission and the situation on the ground."[140] Within this guidebook there are listings for sections on "Civil Affairs" and "Gender Mainstreaming," among other topics. While advocating for gender diversity in military and governmental posts, it also states that "gender roles are learned and are therefore, changeable."[141] On the surface the text comes off as forward-thinking, but it reinforces the rhetoric (oppression of gender/sexuality; human rights abuse) that leads to military occupation.

In the United States there are two types of rules of engagement. The first, a standard rule of engagement (SROE), operates when the country is not at war. It aims to limit armed fighting. The second, wartime ROE (WROE), attempts to moderate civilized, efficient combat. According to the Joint Doctrine for Military Operations Other than War, standard operating procedure (SOP), often culled from SROE and WROE, is a working "field list" of what is and is not acceptable behavior.[142] Despite these aims, ROEs have come under attack: "It was media exposure during the Vietnam War that highlighted the problems of requiring soldiers to fulfill *ambiguous* objectives."[143] On one hand, these rules were abused. The cultural critic Gina Marie Weaver argues that widespread racialized, sexual violence against Vietnamese women was "standard operating procedure." Weaver interviewed a veteran who calls this a "mass military policy," but this violence is erased from official narratives of the war. Military operations such as Richard Nixon's "secret war" on Cambodia and Laos (discussed earlier) also blurred the line between unofficial and official sanctions. On the other hand, pro-war supporters felt these rules were restrictive: "The standard operating procedures imposed on US troops during the Vietnam War resulted in accusations that domestic concerns were inhibiting the military's freedom of operation."[144] Standard operating procedure was also questioned during the Abu Ghraib scandal in 2004, in which US soldiers committed human rights abuses against Iraqi detainees.

In the American wars in Việt Nam and Iraq what I call "excessive images" triggered uncontainable outrage. These images are "excessive" because they embody a return of the repressed. The sexualized atrocities exceed conventions of civilized warfare: this was inhumane. Both ROE and SOP were supposed to control our basest impulses, unleashed in war. Although their intended audiences varied, both were a form of military documentation. What was normalized violence on-site seethed beyond the edges of their frames.

Television images of Việt Nam's "living room war" and photographs of Iraq's denuded male prisoners buttress empire's growing pornographic archives of violence. The abject spectacles of emasculation (sodomy, torture, rape) in the Abu Ghraib images are fueled by US sexual exceptionalism.[145] On US soil, figures of queer degeneracy threaten nationhood and must be policed and excised, then and now.[146] In Southeast Asia, the Middle East, and the United States, the menacing "Oriental as deviant" allows—and disavows—unethical behavior. Despite public shock and awe, all of this is business as usual.

I consider all types of ROES (rules of engagement, return on engagement) outlined earlier as *return engagements*: recurring and permeable structures for relations. Rules of engagement have similar criteria for return on investment (ROI). Both outline ways to collect data and report constituent information, whether they are target markets or military targets. Both ROI and ROE try to quantify socioeconomic and political commitments. Military, diplomatic, and business affairs all have degrees of investiture. These are enduring commitments. Both ROI and ROE qualitatively measure, and adjust for, failure and success. Return engagement invokes military engagements and the ties between geopolitics and economic development. For instance, despite close borders and ties, heated Khmer border disputes continue with Việt Nam and Thailand.

All three countries have set up shifting rules of engagement to respond to border issues. The Cambodian opposition party ruler Sam Rainsy has railed against Vietnamese border encroachments on Cambodian territory. Cambodia is also known as Kampuchea (កម្ពុជា). The Khmer press often refers to southern Việt Nam (formerly Cochinchina) as Kampuchea Krom (Southern Cambodia) because Sài Gòn and its vicinity were once Cambodia. Human Rights Watch has noted that the Vietnamese and Cambodian governments both abuse the Khmer Krom, the ethnic Khmer who live in Việt Nam. Regarded as Cambodian in Việt Nam, they have no religious freedom or land rights. If they take refuge in Cambodia, as some have, their neighbors see them as ethnic Vietnamese. As Human Rights Watch says, they are one of the "most disenfranchised groups" in the country, facing "social and economic discrimination and unnecessary hurdles to legalizing their status." Their case is just one example of the vexed contemporary relations between Cambodia and Việt Nam. Another is that the Cambodian minister of foreign affairs called on Việt Nam—in its capacity as the ASEAN chair in 2010—to prevent armed conflict between Cambodia and Thailand.[147]

Despite sensitive regional border issues, Việt Nam and Cambodia have a bilateral military relationship, including joint naval patrol and border cooperation. Honoring the fiftieth anniversary of the two countries' diplomatic relations, Cambodian Defense Minister Tea Banh and Vietnamese Defense Minister Ngô Xuân Lịch met in mid-January 2017 to review and outline their defense ties for 2018 and beyond. Among them, Việt Nam supplies the Royal Cambodian Armed Forces "with military equipment, infrastructure, and training," as *The Diplomat* notes.[148]

Clearly, Cambodia sees Việt Nam as an important ally. Việt Nam is one of the top five investors in Cambodia, with $3.1 billion in 214 projects (expanding the $2.83 billion invested in 183 projects in 2018), Quach Dư, Vietnam's ambassador to Cambodia, stated at a Cambodia–Việt Nam Trade Forum organized by the two countries in 2019 in Phnom Penh.[149] Việt Nam is Cambodia's third-largest business partner; bilateral trade between the countries is projected to reach $5 billion. Ambassador Dư also noted that Việt Nam is the top tourist spot for Cambodians.[150] To regulate external economic shocks, Việt Nam's foreign reserve was at an all-time high in 2019, at $63.75 billion. This upward trend was expected to continue in 2019–20 and beyond: in 2019, the State Bank of Việt Nam bought $8.35 billion from credit institutions to build up its reserve; by April 2020, its foreign reserve was noted to be at an all-time high of $84 billion dollars.[151]

Anthropology | Ethnographic Returns

Diasporic (dis)identifications are psychologically and physically uncertain: at once geographically intimate and distant. Simultaneous separation and closeness is a hallmark of return engagements. This "structure of feeling" has not been fully explored. As Williams notes, as an analytic frame it is "as firm and definite as 'structure' suggests, yet it operates in the most delicate and least tangible part of our activities."[152] My work moves away from the study of lived experiences of a specific generational place and time. Instead, the concept of return shuttles, shifts through varied spaces, times, and artistic cohorts—the living archives of memory and modernity.

My position as a researcher undoubtedly affects my relationships with my subjects. Within anthropology, as in other disciplines, self-reflexivity is crucial and increasingly challenged. I am indebted to the anthropologist Clifford Geertz's use of "thick description."[153] This interpretive approach delves into layers of mediated social meaning. Culture is a semiotic system, open to fissures and gaps. Geertz observes that "culture is not a power." It does not cause "social events, behaviors, institutions, or processes . . . ; it is a context, something within which [interconnected systems of meaning] can be intelligibly—that is, thickly—described. Culture is context."[154] Following this logic, I describe scenes in detail to give the reader an affective sense of the relationships among artist, art communities, and researcher. Although these personal anecdotes may appear casual, they convey the complicated networks that the artists and I write about must maneuver.

Unlike older anthropological models of immersive research for a year or two "in the field" and a return "home" to write up the findings, my return engagements are both intensive and sporadic. The traditional ethnographic divides between home and research abroad have been questioned for their hierarchical distinctions. Objects of inquiry (the field) and normative sites of knowledge (home institutions) are separated. For nearly two decades I have built my professional and personal archives. Like those of the anthropologists Anna Tsing and Christina Schwenkel, my "patchwork" ethnography embraces "long term and cyclical returns 'to the field.'"[155] Annual returns to Southeast Asia, which I also consider home, supplement my four plus years in "the field." Researchers such as Schwenkel and I challenge where fieldwork is and where home is. The continuing "return engagements" in which we participate are cyclical, sporadic, visceral experiences. Contrary to older models of diaspora, our movements reveal myriad subject positions. As transnational subjects, we do not experience a clear line between home and abroad.

Affective borders between here and there have become increasingly entrenched since the "ethnographic turn" of the 1990s in international exhibitions described by Foster. He notes that the "artist as ethnographer" role grew from attention in the 1960s to culture, media, and mediation in Western academia and art. This timeline can be traced back further. Anthropology serviced colonial aims; related fields such as area studies became institutionalized during the Cold War hysteria of the late 1940s. Knowledge of various cultures—and the production and dissemination of that knowledge—can serve political and military agendas. Who and what, then, are contemporary Southeast Asian artists in service of during this moment's ethnographic turn? Vincente L. Rafael, a historian of Southeast Asia, observes that "area studies not only reiterate different versions of Orientalism; they also produce by necessity multiple repudiations of these versions."[156] Following this argument, artists tied to Southeast Asia both reinforce and refute liberal pluralist institutions.

Foster, however, claims that institutions (academic, cultural, state) are no longer sites of inquiry (institutional critique). Rather, the artist becomes sited: "As the artist stands in the identity of a sited community, he or she may be asked to stand for this identity, to represent it institutionally. In this case, the artist is primitivized—indeed, anthropologized—in turn: here is your community, the institution says in effect, embodied in your artist, now on display."[157] For example, 1.5 generation Khmer American artists dealing with memory work are representatives of two communities by default: the United States and Cambodia. They must speak for—and embody—a double displacement. The traumas of assimilation to the United States are echoed by the more horrific traumas of the root of that displacement: the specter of genocide. These losses and this othering gets naturalized.

As Schlund-Vials notes the importance of who and what get represented, I assert that it is the who, what, and where that get conflated within a global art market. Thus, my work attempts to redefine relationships between "locals" (as "native informants") and locales. Regardless of terminology—"ethnographic turn" or "global turn"—the Southeast Asian art historian Michelle Antoinette argues that "international" shows from the 1990s to today still have decidedly Western-centric foundations, albeit with the gloss of artistic and theoretical diversity. Self-reflexive approaches by non-Western artists, scholars, and curators support, but do not supplant, institutional desires for counterhegemonic perspectives. How, then, can we tackle the paradoxes of representation?

My ethnographic training gives me another set of tools to engage creative producers—ways to think through authorship and authority. Through extended participant observation and oral interviews, I gain insight about each artist's unique process and the organizations with which each works. The Asian American art historian Margo Machida calls this process an "oral hermeneutics": an "exploratory form of dialogic engagement which seeks to share interpretive authority with artists by linking the use of oral history methods with a hermeneutical orientation toward textual interpretation."[158] This is simply ethnographic methodology applied to the analysis of art history. Although I do not refer to my approach as "oral hermeneutics," I also combine insights culled from conversations with artist-organizers with close readings of artwork.

Artists shift identities in local and international contexts. I use a range of methodologies to understand how artists and cultural organizers self-identify and are identified by critics, gallerists, and arts organizations in Cambodia, Việt Nam, and abroad. A work of art does not exist in a vacuum; neither do artists. It is my goal to both rethink and bridge the gap between transnational identities in Cambodia and Việt Nam. Currently, there is no conceptual art education or sustained contemporary cultural criticism in Việt Nam or Cambodia, yet there are vibrant cultural communities in these locales. Apart from text-based modes of interpretation and analysis, the intersections of ethnography and visual culture offer fresh insights into issues of voice and visuality. Through a combination of disciplinary approaches, the artist's perspective and working context become clearer.

Local and Diasporic

Although I focus on output by local and diasporic artists and filmmakers situated within Cambodia and Việt Nam, I am also attentive to work and networks outside of these nation-states, particularly in the United States. I focus on localized subjectivity and agency in both Việt Nam and Cambodia, thus decentering dominant US-centric discourse on the legacies of the war in Việt Nam and narratives that prioritize US military involvement. Cambodia's traumatic past is overdetermined. Social and political discourse—as well as artistic production and consumption—are not limited to specific national, ethnic, and diasporic boundaries; they traverse many disparate borders. These "contact zones" create unforeseen social, cultural, and economic interactions.[159] In the realm of cultural production, these unforeseen interactions can be the unpredictable strategic cartographies in which artists engage. How artists choose to self-identify and which facets of their identities get associated with their creative output are continually shifting, dependent on negotiations between individuals and institutions.

My work seeks to blur national and ethnic distinctions by drawing thematic comparisons between artists and artwork. The contested "contact zones" between identifications and geography, between "local" and "diasporic," make for uneasy, if convenient, exchanges and framings. Again, diaspora's fluidity unanchors the fixity of the nation-state and identitarian politics.

I define diaspora as a fluid process marked by continual encounters rather than as a fixed location. Diasporic crossings are return engagements—a continual crisscrossing between here and there, between now and then; a process of shape-shifting. Rather than seeing diasporic subjectivity—and identity at large—as stable positions, an "already accomplished fact, which the new cultural practices then represent," Stuart Hall conceives of "identity as a 'production' which is never complete, always in process, and always constituted within, not outside, representation."[160] This porous process is one that is at odds with the nation-state and the politics of identity, which the international

41

art circuit embraces even as it relegates artists of color to the margins. On the surface, the global art market embraces this flexibility while reasserting deeply entrenched hierarchical borders. Despite being challenged, national boundaries and the parameters of high conceptual art remain fixed.

A number of scholars in the humanities and social sciences have noted that migration, as a pressing geopolitical fact, has become a core focus of contemporary art and scholarship. The cultural critic and art historian T. J. Demos has outlined three overlapping concepts tied to migration in the humanities and social sciences over the past three decades: diaspora (referring to a collective geographic dispersal); nomadism (particularly "artistic nomadism," or unbounded creative movement); and refugees (those affected by forced displacement, persecution, or disaster).[161] Likewise, the anthropologist and art historian Saloni Mathur wrote in 2018 about a "mobility turn" in the arts and social sciences. In contrast to the celebratory discourse on nomadism that Demos traces in the West in the 1990s, Mathur argues that the migrant is not automatically a figure of resistance, echoing Hall's assertion that such identities are not a priori givens. Like Hall's figures in process and in "production," always founded within representation, Mathur sees the "paradigm of the migrant" as "ambivalent and indeterminate."[162] Hence, the geographic and historical specificities of migrancy "represent some of the most difficult forms of entanglement and separation."[163]

To grapple with the complexities of dispersal (without conflating lived realities) from the politics of creative representation it is important to parse out realpolitik and poetics yet still recognize their embedded ties. For instance, the art historian Anne Ring Petersen differentiates these two facets as "politics" and "the political." When migration becomes an object of politics, it "becomes an issue in some way—whether in national legislative and administrative immigration policies; in the ideological debates about multiculturalism and the recognition of minorities; in the image politics of news broadcasts about immigrants; or the strategies of cultural institutions vis-à-vis artists with a migrant background." However, Petersen asserts, the political is a sociocultural everyday lived framework as "migration and artistic representations of migrants' lives unfold": "The act of migration is usually followed by some kind of everyday life in another place where the migrant experience becomes an integral part of everyday practices and the social life and identity of the subject."[164] While the distinction between the objective of "politics" and subjective lived experience of "the political" is useful, I do not agree with Petersen's assimilationist framing. Rather, to echo Hall, this migrant subjectivity is eternally produced and reproduced through lived experience and through art. Through these various views on migration, I connect notions of entanglement, ambivalence, indeterminacy, and process.

In thinking through politics (as object of action) and the political (as lived sociocultural experience) I build on the writings of the art historian W. J. T. Mitchell and the artist-theorist Hito Steyerl on the relationship between migrants and images. Mitchell observes that migrancy has dual components: as theme and as image. In the first aspect, migration appears as a thematic within cultural production (as noted by Mathur, Demos, Petersen, and so on). Second, Mitchell states that the image of the migrant precedes the migrant's arrival. Images are by nature migratory. Yet Steyerl notes that, like classes of migrants that range from the privileged to the dispossessed, images are hierarchical. Her essay "In Defense of the Poor Image" observes that the global economy of proliferating pictures ranges from high-resolution limited-run and limited editions to viral, pixelated, and even pirated copies. Following these arguments that migration—as theme and as image—are in constant, enmeshed circulation, I assert that the migrant's image (as sociopolitical projection and as cultural production) is under constant negotiation.

Beyond parsing migration as a thematic (subject and subjectivity) and as a politic (object of action), it is difficult to account for its myriad manifestations. How does one group the proliferation of art addressing migrancy by artists who are "professional labor migrants"?[165] For a certain privileged class of artists, curators, and scholars within the globalized art market, itinerancy is a job requirement. Art history has long been preoccupied with categorization of genres (e.g., landscape, portrait, still life), yet migration as subjective experience and object of politicized action defies labels. Petersen writes that the "breadth of 'diaspora aesthetics,' or 'migratory aesthetics' . . . makes it clear that the category of genre cannot encompass it."[166] I want to address the divides between a "diaspora aesthetics" and shifting notions of diaspora itself. Just as images of migrants precede the migrant, as Mitchell notes, images of diasporic and local subjectivity precede the artist. The local and the diasporic are viscerally embodied, conjured, through visual cultures.

It is important that Asian American studies researchers reconsider our definitions of diaspora to make our focus truly transnational. The editors of *Theorizing Diaspora*, Jana Braziel and Anita Mannur, state that cultural critics, anthropologists, and literary scholars increasingly use the term *diaspora* to describe the twentieth century's mass migrations and displacements, including "independence movements in formerly colonized areas, waves of refugees fleeing war-torn states, and fluxes of immigration in the post–

World War II era."[167] This older view of diaspora emphasizes the boundaries of the nation-state. As a consequence of political or economic upheaval, refugees, migrants, and exiles flee one state for another. "There is no diaspora without borders and no borders without states," observes David Palumbo-Liu.[168] In crossing borders, diasporic subjects reinscribe the boundaries between home and exile.

The earlier meaning of diasporic movement referred to a diasporic population's dispersal from one location to a host of other places. The singular point of origin—former colony, war-torn nation, repressive regime, impoverished nation—ends in multiple possible destination points. Diaspora also "etymologically suggests the . . . fertility of dispersion, dissemination, and the scattering of seeds."[169] The seed-spore analogy has been widely used in Asian American studies in reference to talk about the Asian diasporas across the globe. Scholars describe communities that have settled and taken root in their new chosen homes. In this view, the homeland is a fixed entity, the essentialized site of origins.

More recently, scholars have veered away from simple constructions of nativist belonging to account for diasporic subjects' multiply situated identifications. Migrants, immigrants, and refugees often do not settle in one location; they take part in multiple movements, physical and psychological. Lowe, Paul Gilroy, and Rey Chow, among others, acknowledge that repeated geographic crossings, rather than binaries of home and exile, shape diasporic identities. The seed-spore model has ceded to frameworks that attempt to capture the "heterogeneity, hybridity, and multiplicity" of diverse diasporic experiences.[170] To return to one's homeland does not mean returning home.

Karin Aguilar-San Juan suggests that for many Asian American subjects, looking back does not mean returning to the mythic site of ethnic origins. Reversing the logic of returning to an Eastern homeland, she writes, "To go westward, is to go home, in the sense that many Asian Americans have family in California, Washington state or farther in Hawai'i." For Aguilar-San Juan, Asian Americans find home in America, not necessarily in Asia.[171] Palumbo-Liu's binary between the "memory of the homeland and the consciousness of the diasporic new land" is no longer a relevant distinction.[172] The immigrant's "new land" and old homeland are no longer distinct spheres. The old country is now a brave new world. Cambodia's and Việt Nam's breakneck growth ensures that the landscape of memory is altered. For some, the diasporic new land has been home for generations. Thus, heterogeneous diasporic frameworks must account for the different experiences of immigrants

44

who settled in the United States near the turn of the twentieth century, as well as more recent economic migrants and flexible citizens.

Digital Divides

In this digital age, borders are increasingly permeable. At the same time, borders are ever more vigilantly policed, fueled by anxiety over terrorism, global economic downturns, and the decline of US empire. The new diasporic subject questions these demarcations and fears. The anthropologist Ashley Carruthers observes that, for Vietnamese diasporic subjects, the distinction between homeland and diaspora collapses. Home is Việt Nam and abroad, and in between.[173] Overseas Vietnamese negotiate different ideological systems at once: capitalism, market socialism, democracy. The exchange of cultural goods such as music videos and films and repeated returns, both real and imagined, facilitate the breakdown of borders. What happens when the diasporic imaginary is distressing, as Khatharya Um asks, "signifying both an indelible connection and, simultaneously, a rupture?"[174] What does the current digital age mean for the making of the diasporic subject?[175] Diasporic and local communities are increasingly connected, as well as divided, by technology: YouTube videos and Facebook groups create a sense of shared commonality across space as online factions emerge. Again I stress the importance of envisioning diaspora as interactive processes and relations. Rupture, connection, and disconnection are part of the cyclical nature of return engagements.

This bond and split is the space of return, or lines of flight, to use Deleuze and Guattari's term.[176] "Line of flight" is translated by Brian Massumi from the French *ligne de fuite*, in which *fuite* refers not only to fleeing but also to flowing, leaking to a multiplicity of points.[177] One can think of a refugee fleeing from her home country, but also of the myriad movements, flows—actual and virtual—in which she engages. Here the subject is "leaky," unbound by infrastructure. Sara Ahmed suggests that "to leak is to lead"—a leak can cause damage, a rupture, but it can also radically transform existing structures from within.[178] The line of flight is the point of change in which two paradigms are transgressed. Here, the subject (I suggest the digital diasporic) shifts from actual to virtual conditions. I see transgressing local and diasporic distinctions as a line of flight: connection and rupture.

The lines between diasporic and transnational identities are blurred. Palumbo-Liu marks a distinction between a "cross-cultural" version of diaspora with "ethnicized" subjects and a transnational one of "transmigrant, multiply situated identities."[179] The cross-cultural diasporic subject has been incorporated by the state's multicultural logic, whereas the transnational subject refuses assimilation. This seems like the difference between racialized, settled Asian Americans versus more recent migrants who are in limbo, shuttling between identities. But this dichotomy may be a false one. One can be both a cross-cultural subject and a transnational one. The terms *diaspora* and *transnationalism* overlap, since both address movements across borders. Explicating the difference between the two terms, Braziel and Mannur note, "Diaspora refers specifically to the movement—forced or voluntary—of people from one or more nation states to another. Transnationalism speaks to larger, more impersonal forces—specifically, those of globalism and global capitalism."[180] They define diaspora as movements of subjects and transnationalism as movements of objects. The forces of global capital, however, cannot be decoupled from humans. I reframe transnationalism as a subject position, not an abstract force. Contrary to Braziel and Mannur's framing, diasporic movement from one state to another—and from one state of mind to another—is not only limited one-way crossings. Transnationalism accounts for myriad crossings.

Placing concepts of diaspora within transnational movements and moments grounds them. Much of Asian American studies inquiry has been focused on what happens in America and not Asia, since that was seen as the purview of Asian studies and area studies.[181] We must not overlook the links between Asia and America for diasporic subjects. Diasporic outlooks have long placed emphasis on zones of settlement, looking West, looking home, as Aguilar San-Juan muses. A transnational perspective focuses on movement rather than settlement. As transnational subjects, we are never truly settled. A transnational outlook is a return gaze, away from the West toward the East. But this differs from old homeland–new exilic land binaries and seed-spore metaphors.

Return engagements problematize the local-diasporic divide; the artists I examine use this very divide to strategically position themselves.[182] Looking to the East, Western-trained artists are essentialized as embodiments of the East by international art markets. Looking to the West, artists residing in the East (both local and diasporic) are expected to translate for hegemonic Western audiences. We must, once again, reconsider and redefine diaspora to account for new global realities.

As most Southeast Asian studies work focuses on Asia, and Asian American studies scholarship centers America, my project seeks to invert and question these lines of inquiry. Việt Thanh Nguyễn notes the "billions in overseas remittances, de facto nations in exile, and transnational traffic in ideas and people" as reason for looking at flows, leaks.[183] I also argue for a Southeast Asian studies attuned to larger diasporic movements—an area studies not focused only on local interactions. Most area studies scholarship focuses on a single nation-state, inattentive to regional and international interactions. Here I advocate for an Asia-centric focus (as Southeast Asian studies proper) yet with a diasporic outlook. For Southeast Asian subjects, the link between Asia and its diasporas is also important. Asian American studies should not only trace Asian American subjects transnationally. Transnational foci should lead, leak away from—not reinforce—American empire. Likewise, Southeast Asian studies can benefit from more research on Southeast Asian diasporas—not only to the global North, but to other axes and affiliations in the global South.

Relocations | Returns   CRITICAL REFUGEE STUDIES

The emergence of critical refugee studies reconstrues the affective borders of belonging and relationality. While much of this growing body of work focuses on the United States and its subjects, the locus of return engagements is firmly grounded in Southeast Asia, not the United States. This project unmoors the centrality and the mythos of Euro-America within the discourse on memory, trauma, and cultural responses. Furthermore, my work unfixes the preoccupation with US militarization through Southeast Asian (particularly Khmer, Vietnamese, and Lao) diasporic subjects. Beyond the aftermath of war and militarization, my book also looks to (post)modernity and its constituents as sites of inquiry. Examining relocations sparked by conflicts then and now is important. A critical look at returns is equally crucial in understanding the myriad manifestations of neo-empire and the postmodern condition.

Yến Lê Espiritu notes that America's rhetoric of refuge masks the perpetration and perpetuation of violence against its refugees, immigrants, and second-class citizens. In the aftermath of war, Espiritu highlights first- and second-generation Vietnamese refugees' counterhegemonic culture and knowledge production. She notes that American "military colonialism" in the Asia Pacific region lays the bloody path for the United States as sanctified "refuge."[184] The same routes of military personnel and weapons from the United States to Pacific Asia enabled the "return" of Southeast Asian refugees to US empire. This dynamic precisely exemplifies our troubled return engagements. These interactions constitute an interconnected, intimate web of social, cultural, and military relations. Espiritu states, "If you resurrect the history of the displacement and flight of the Vietnamese people, you will simultaneously call attention to other histories that have been systematically erased."[185]

This emphasis on buried narratives and revivification reinforces the refugee as liminal specter—half living and half dead—caught between memory and forgetting. The alignment with erased others centralizes US hegemony. Instead of highlighting one-way movement to the heart of empire, my work focuses on how artists displace and destabilize imperial cultural institutions through multinodal journeys. In addition to viewing Vietnamese refugees—and, by extension, other Southeast Asian refugees—as a "critical site of social and political critique," which places emphasis on disenfranchised bodies, I suggest artistic oeuvres open up other bodies of knowledge, other modes of (anti)sociality and unknowing. I see return and returnees as sites of critique. These returns do not unearth erasure—and reaffirm visible-invisible binaries—but, rather, question the hypervisible tethers and tropes of empire.

I maintain that through return engagements, this aesthetic and ethical entanglement is unending, and endlessly shifting. Việt Thanh Nguyễn's *Nothing Ever Dies* suggests memory and forgetting are coeval, asserting that "all wars are fought twice": once on the battlefield, and the second time through individual and social recollection (echoing arguments by Sturken and James E. Young). Nations and their displaced are not fixed discursive "sites." I trace how geography and subjectivity are constantly negotiated for transnational individuals and institutions. The crux is not what is remembered and forgotten within national agendas. The battle is over representation itself.

Addressing American wars in Việt Nam, Korea, and Laos, as well as the Cambodian genocide, Việt Thanh Nguyễn proposes a transnational purview, albeit through an American axis.[186] My earlier work with Yong Soon Min on Việt Nam and Korea also asserts that historical trauma and popular culture are deeply intertwined but argues for a Pan-Asian nexus.[187] Toward this I traced Korean and Vietnamese connections then (both countries were vassal states of China) and now (Việt Nam and Korea have significant bilateral economic exchanges). The basis for South Korean modernity—embodied through K-Pop (*hallyu*)—was founded and funded through war: the United States paid more than $2 billion to Korean mercenary soldiers in Việt Nam. Republic of Korea soldiers were brutal, slicing off ears, echoing earlier Japanese occupation in Korea.[188] I build on my earlier work to look at military

48

engagement and economic and cultural development from translocal and transhistorical perspectives.

In the chapters that follow, I intervene in anthropology, art history, and visual culture, as well as Asian American studies, American studies, and Southeast Asian studies, the boundaries of which are both permeable and patrolled.

Book Structure

Chapter 1 examines two documentaries: Rithy Panh's *S-21: The Khmer Rouge Killing Machine* (2003) and Spencer Nakasako's *Refugee* (2003). Both films focus on Khmer and Khmer American returns, confrontation, and silence. Revisiting David Eng and David Kazanjian's notions of loss as a productive space, I argue that these filmic subjects are melancholics unable to "successfully" mourn, whereas the spectators of these "trauma dramas" are exempt. Considering the Khmer Rouge tribunal verdicts and my stance on loss as nonproductive, I build on Schlund-Vial's call for a juridical activism and Việt Thanh Nguyễn's insistence on "just memory": recuperative cultural projects may aim to "produce" social justice, at the same time recognizing its impossibility. In contrast to conceiving refusal and silence as lack of voice—based on psychoanalytic loss, lack, and reclamation—these films serve as a Derridean *supplément*, both compensating and supplanting narratives of Khmer genocide. I propose silence and repeated gestures as alternate embodied and spiritual sites of intuitive comprehension, ambiguous and ambivalent.

Chapter 2 focuses on the Sài Gòn returnees Sandrine Llouquet and Tiffany Chung and how, as artist-organizers, they strategically position themselves as both Western-educated insiders and Southeast Asian outsiders on the global art market. I assert that artists, as well as national and cultural institutions, employ these strategic cartographies—shifting geopolitical identifications and affiliations. This critical process of reworlding (following Aihwa Ong and Rob Wilson) and remapping—reconfiguring oneself repeatedly—is in keeping with my frames of cyclical return and revolution. Late capital's ever-evolving demands for products and cheap (raced, gendered) labor and products dovetails with the strategies of internationally visible Việt Kiều (Vietnamese returnee) artists such as Jun Nguyễn-Hatsushiba, Đinh Q. Lê, Liza Nguyễn, and An-My Lê.

Chapter 3 explores the return to archives—personal, postcolonial, and spiritual—of the Cambodian collagist and painter Leang Seckon and the Vietnamese American experimental filmmaker Hồng-Ân Trương. Throughout the chapter, I assert that the reappearance of history's fragments—colonial and modern—as well as the formal use of fragmentation in their works rework Bergsonian notions of space and time. For instance, as nostalgic Americana and Indochina whets the appetite, Seckon's and Trương's fragmented appropriations of cadavers reinscribe this cannibalistic hunger within the fevered archive.

Chapter 4, the final chapter, deals with urban-rural development for economic return in Cambodia and Việt Nam through the work of the sculptor Sopheap Pich of Phnom Penh and the conceptual artist Phan Quang of Sài Gòn. I maintain that Pich's and Phan's translation of these issues are (self-) exploitative gestures. Similarly, Đinh Q. Lê's artwork on Agent Orange— first conceived in 1989 as kitschy souvenir objects sold in a Sài Gòn market stall and then presented again in 2009 for a group exhibition in Germany— pivots on the use of ongoing environmental and corporeal damage. By using the term *exploit*, I note that their strategic positioning proves both harmful and beneficial as they extract naturalized resources: nature (as art subject and art material), and their self-naturalizing stories.

The Gift   STRATEGIC GIVING AND TAKING IN RETURN

The stories one tells are an offering, a gift. I conceive of enacting strategic cartographies as tactical, reciprocal acts of giving and receiving. In giving oneself (via artistic representation), one also gains—receiving both real capital and cultural capital. In common understanding, to receive a gift is a choice. A paradox: to give is also to destroy, undo—themes on which I expand. Mimi Thi Nguyễn critiques the double-edged "gift of freedom" that US empire promises, exacting an eternal debt for refugees of its violence, ranging from wars in Southeast Asia to wars in the Middle East. Aesthetics and culture are core to this gift's contradictions: "We need not deny the violence and destruction that undergirds the gift of freedom to also take seriously its promise to reverence beauty, or respect aliveness, because these are part of its power."[189] In short, there is no choice in accepting the gift of freedom. For those constructed as subjects of freedom's benevolence and subjected to its brutality, strategic cartographies, and tactical alignments may be a means of achieving agency. Mutable freedom is given under the guises of free trade or freedom of expression—creative, sexual, political.

Part of this gift's debt is paid through economic capital, as well as cultural capital. In some instances, Vietnamese refugees become multicultural excuses for new abuses of ethnonational Others, renewed through the war on terror. A case in point: US Assistant General Việt Đ. Định, chief architect of the USA Patriot Act, was celebrated as a freedom-loving Vietnamese American immigrant who now worked to ensure counter-"terrorist" protection at home and dissemination abroad. In the age of "liberal empire," freedom is a gift housed in Pandora's box. Following Derrida's formulation of the gift, Mimi Thi Nguyễn notes that a gift always demands debt.

Giving presupposes taking in return—a reciprocal, if unbalanced, gesture. This relational act is a cycle, which I connect to circular movements of becoming, overturning, and undoing. Derrida asserts that a true gift builds to overcoming, as well as madness.[190] In contrast to Mimi Thi Nguyễn's framing of the gift as empire's rational, calculated one-sided domination of its subjects, I see artistic production as gifts that undermine (neo)colonial logic of eternal indebtedness.

The political theorist Kennan Ferguson notes that "to give" and "to take" have the same Indo-European roots: "In middle Dutch, the word *gif* meant both a gift and a poison; the German word *Gift* means toxin."[191] He elaborates, "From the gifts given by European explorers and colonists to native peoples . . . to the gift of economic development through industrialization and free trade, the poison has long been indistinguishable from the gift."[192] To recompense and to represent are also part of the dialogic of giving and taking, presents and poison. Representation is both form (in the case of art) and a formalized process (e.g., democracy). The gift can be both physical and figurative, simultaneously a realizable project and a projection.

Return engagements, while cyclical, rupture the giver-receiver dyad, asserting that the two roles are mutually constitutive. I draw another impossible aporia: the receiver is giver; the artist is audience; subjection is also dominance. The artist benefits and is bounded. She or he is the object of the gaze and its subjective maker. As artists enact strategic cartographies, they both reinforce and undermine the trappings of identity and nation.

Tracing thinkers on the gift—the anthropologist Marcel Mauss, the philosopher Georges Bataille, and Derrida, among others—Ferguson observes that obliteration of the symbolic gift is key in each of these analyses: "In the annihilation of the thing, the subjugation of the other is all that remains."[193] Seen in this frame, art can be both enactment and annihilation of subjecthood.

The idea of enactment and annihilation within gift giving connects with how artists within the "ethnographic turn" (or global turn) are at once "evacuated and elevated," to invoke Foster's phrase again. Minoritized artists simultaneously embody, bear, and receive the gift. They do this tacitly and tactically—there is no overt announcement of strategic cartographies at play. Within avant-garde conceptual art discourse, the "thingness" of an artwork (e.g., Duchamp's upturned urinal) is annihilated. The artwork is no longer an amalgam of found objects—the ready-made seeks to ultimately overturn institutional and art-history traditions. Thus, the subjugation of the other—in this case, hegemonic dictates of high art—remains, its annihilation figured as a leftover, a relic of industrialization. Within the lineage of conceptual contemporary (Western) art, thingness is effaced.

In another formalist art lineage, as espoused by the evaluative modernist art critics Clement Greenberg and Michael Fried, an art object's thingness is highlighted (e.g., paintings should only assert the medium's essence and not address sociopolitical concerns). In the essay "Art and Objecthood," Fried argues that art objects ideally are self-contained, timeless, separate from the world of everyday objects. Minimalist art foregrounds its status as material object, its "objecthood." Fried also plays semantically with the idea of "objecthood": "object" is cast as refusal, and an objection is defined in the *Oxford English Dictionary* as "a statement thrown in or introduced in opposition." As mentioned, the artist-giver both objects and accepts, receives. This objection can be the artist's interventions into a given medium or her critiques of the institution, or of society. Simultaneously, the artist knows that to make, to give to, is also to make up for—a lack. Lacan's *objet petit a* posits that our desire for knowledge of the Other remains perpetually unfulfilled. There will be no reciprocity.

Whether one straddles conceptual or formal camps, avant-garde art movements are claims for primacy—negation of one aesthetic paradigm over another. Cultural theorists such as Benjamin have speculated on how an artwork achieves its power, cultural resonance, or "aura." Thus, the art piece is remnant, remains—sign and signifier—that at once annuls and embodies dichotomies of subjugation and dominion. The art piece comes to signify the artist.

Beyond its materiality (and material conditions of production), art objects are symbolic gifts (that can create/destroy). Artworks are activated when exhibited, or "given" to the public. Bataille asserted that the crux of the gift was the metamorphosis of a thing into rank. The given/destroyed object transmutes into power (rank). I see this alchemy occurring in aesthetic realms where "prestige is power, this is insofar as power itself escapes the considerations of force or right."[194] Art—and artists—are transformable object-subjects circulating within and outside the logic of the gift. Within cultural diplomacy, art is both treaty and toxin, upholding and undermining infrastructures.

Antonio Gramsci's notion of the war of position (as opposed to the war of maneuver) situates cultural production as an active site of resistance and a space to question hegemonic structures. The war of maneuver is physical combat, whereas the war of position operates within the realm of culture.[195] In my earlier discussion of a revolution of culture—a turning of hegemonic discourse—I echo postcolonial theorists in noting that it is an ideological battle. As US wars on terror continue overseas, a longer, recurring battle over winning "hearts and minds" rages. Gramsci cautions that "one should refrain from facile rhetoric about direct attacks against the State and concentrate instead on the difficult and immensely complicated tasks that a 'war of position' within civil society entails."[196] One can see North American "culture wars" of the 1990s and of today—overlapping turf wars over religious, political, and aesthetic values—within this frame.

I read the war of position also as a war of positionality. Positionality theory posits that identity is fluid, not a fixed phenomenon but in constant flux, dependent on context and relationships.[197] I suggest that the war of position(ality) dovetails with Williams's Long Revolution, as both are directed toward tactical maneuvers over an extended period. Strategic cartographies also operate within this rubric. In this space, one can be camouflaged, a shape-shifter, a becoming. It is vital to be facile, porous as a way to concede and contradict institutional demands. It is a way to flexibly maneuver civil society's continual absorption of challenges to its structure. The counter-revolution already anticipates attacks, as I noted in my discussion of Williams earlier in the introduction. Gramsci echoes this idea: "When the state tottered, a sturdy structure of civil society was immediately revealed. The State was just a forward trench; behind it stood a succession of sturdy fortresses and emplacements."[198] Williams and Gramsci suggest that radical change within neoliberal democracy is possible only through culture.

What happens when one cannot fight back, speak back, look back? What happens when return is foreclosed? There may never be recourse, no true "just memory" or "belated" justice, as Việt Thanh Nguyễn and Schlund-Vials recognize yet still advocate for. For Mauss, the enemy can be vanquished only when the gift given "cannot be returned."[199] An asymmetrical relation of power is thus established. The cycle of giving and taking is both requirement and impossibility—forever recapitulated. Liberal empire promises to give vitality while taking life. Quoting Derrida, Mimi Thi Nguyễn notes, "Such violence may be considered the very condition of the gift, its constitutive impurity once the gift is engaged in a process of circula-tion."[200] Contagion is embedded within the gift's circular logic and cyclical movement, represented by the image of fortune's wheel I described earlier. Whichever direction the wheel turns, carnage is constant: "The violence ap-pears irreducible, within the circle or outside it, whether it repeats the circle or interrupts it."[201] As the wheel turns topsy-turvy, a system's fruition also lays the seeds for its dissolution. This violence is enacted through the gaze, through "scopic regimes" (to borrow Martin Jay's term). From the age of the world picture (Martin Heidegger) to the age of the world target (Rey Chow), circuits of looking are lethal. Through mapping, one is made and undone. Those who are targeted as objects of liberal empire's gaze, framed as gift, may not be able to return—overturn—its life-affirming and life-denying look. As the saying goes, an eye for an eye.

Stages (RETURN | GIFT | SACRIFICE)

I end this introduction by circling back to where I began: thinking of ges-tures of giving and what is expected in return—and of returnees—on local and international stages. The symbolic or real destruction of the gift—the sacrificial act—reveals the power of the giver. Also describing the United States' gift of freedom, Ferguson notes that "the bodily materialism of the armed forces themselves proves both symbolic and incontrovertible; the numbers of US soldiers wounded and killed constitute part of the cost of the [Iraqi] war."[202] If war dead are part of the material and symbolic price of freedom, how does one measure the value of this gift? Is it through com-parison of other sacrifices and losses? Việt Thanh Nguyễn quotes the war photojournalist Philip Jones Griffith: "The Washington DC memorial to the American war dead is 150 yards long; if a similar monument would be built with the same density of names of the Vietnamese war dead in it, [it] would be 9 miles long."[203] What, then, are the real wages of war? As we see in the examples of wars in the Middle East and Southeast Asia, "The gift stages the circulation of persons and things (in the case of war, troops and arma-ments) to bind a relation of giver and recipient across the globe."[204] Within this frame I come back to my idea of return engagements as stage, staging, repeated enactment—repayment of an offer to perform. The act of giving (offering and receiving, in turn) is performative.

In addition to being a poison, the performance or ritual of gift giving can also be a salve, restorative. Derrida states, "The performative that comes on the scene here is a 'restoring of sight' rather than the visible object. . . . Truth

54

belongs to this movement of repayment that tries in vain to render itself adequate to its cause or to the thing."[205] In returning the favor, repaying one's blood debt, the eternally grateful refugees must be able to see the benefits they have been granted (the "visible object," the American dream). The "restoring of sight" Derrida refers to is internal vision (intangible faith, belief) rather than external vision (external materialist modernist objects). As an act of performative resistance, one can turn a blind eye, reject offering in vain "adequate" payment. To turn a blind eye to empire's binds is to embrace the invisible, the negative, the shadows. The ritual of return requires engaging the unseen, the unforeseen. To our blind hearts we now turn, again.

What Remains

Silence, Confrontation, and Traumatic Memory

remains (plural noun):
  1. the part which is left after
    e.g. the ravages of time, weather or destruction
    2. the part which is left over
      3. a dead human body
        —*Merriam-Webster Dictionary*

THE OPENING SCENE of the documentary *Refugee* (Spencer Nakasako and Mike Siv, dirs., 2003) features Mike Siv and two of his friends zigzagging in a small wooden vessel over milky-brown river water.[1] Close-ups of the three Cambodian Americans, all of whom are in their early twenties, alternate with shots of the gaggle of vendors on the river: women and men hawking fruit and other goods on an unnamed waterway in Cambodia. Excitement and bewilderment show on the young men's faces. Mike's voice-over states:

> My name is Mike Siv. I am twenty-four years old. At about the age of three my mom and I escaped to America. I don't remember anything about the war, about how me and her escaped, about my dad and brother staying behind. As far back as I can remember . . . I only remember coming out of an airplane and being in America. I just wanted to know what it's like to be a son and what it's like to have a father.

This chapter examines *Refugee* and a documentary that features a Cambodian subject who relate to Siv's story: Rithy Panh's *S-21: The Khmer Rouge Killing Machine* (2003). *S-21* revisits the site of the infamous Tuol Sleng prison, a former high school where seventeen thousand Cambodians were executed, with the two remaining survivors of the prison, who were liberated when the invading Vietnamese army removed the Khmer Rouge. It also documents these survivors' confrontation with men who had served as guards at Tuol Sleng.

Refugee and *S-21* at once displace *and* reify standard Western mainstream representations. The films were made to draw attention to narratives that public memory in the global North has largely elided.[2] Meanwhile, images of starved, desperate Syrian and Vietnamese boat refugees (among other huddled masses) have become clichéd, ingrained in popular consciousness. We are objects, not subjects. Both films center their Southeast Asian protagonists' subjectivity within the frame. Tropes make these refugee arrivals, the Khmer Rouge genocide, and other traumatic events in Southeast Asia simultaneously invisible and spectacular. Third World others (Cambodians, Vietnamese) are mute, marginalized, and rendered as suffering spectacles within mass-media depictions of American military involvement in Southeast Asia.[3]

In contrast to tropes of refugee arrival and hypervisible yet mute spectacles of trauma, my focus on departure, return, and silence lead to alternative pathways and subjectivities. Although *S-21* and *Refugee* perform both a testimonial and a pedagogical role, critical readings often reinforce their silent voids. For example, the media studies scholar Deidre Boyle champions *S-21*'s response to "speechless horror" as "shattering silence."[4] I argue that the filmic subjects' silence marks agency beyond language—persisting moments of deferral, contemplation, and even refusal—that mainstream Hollywood productions deny. Through silence the filmmakers allude to the fact that the subjects' trauma is unpresentable, whereas traumatic representations serve the spectator. When the subjects in these two films choose not to speak, I propose, their silence is key to an ethics of witnessing and confrontation, both of which require sustained engagement.

In these films, quietude marks what remains—unexplainable, unfathomable, untranslatable. With "remains" I refer to real and spectral bodies, alive, dead, and in between. Remains are also the traces of what is left behind, resuscitated in collective and individual memory and history. In both films, scenes of return and confrontation mark agency and refusal. By returning to "what remains" time and again, the filmmakers, their subjects, and audiences meet deep silences and ambivalence. I explore the unspoken moments and repeated gestures that are central in understanding these films. The protagonists of these documentaries, both "victims" and "perpetrators," are haunted.[5]

Both the filmmakers and the subjects of *S-21* and *Refugee* are eternal melancholics; only the neoliberal, First World audience is exempt from endless mourning.[6] Reconsidering David Eng and David Kazanjian's notions of loss as a productive potentiality, at once "hopeful and hopeless," I assert that these filmic subjects are melancholics unable to "successfully" mourn, whereas the spectators of these "trauma dramas" are exempt.[7] First I provide a brief history to situate the films.

Shared Histories

Cambodia and Việt Nam have a long history dating back thousands of years, outlined later, that undergirds some current tensions. This shared regional history is often lost in mainstream and mass-media discourse (including in *Refugee* and *S-21*). Cambodia's powerful past includes the Hindu state of Funan and, later, the fabled Kingdom of Angkor. At its twelfth-century zenith, the Khmer empire encompassed Việt Nam, Laos, Thailand, and Myanmar, among other territories. In the seventeenth century, Việt Nam annexed an area of the Mekong River and continued to expand. As Việt Nam and Siam (Thailand) grew in strength, Cambodia increasingly lost territory and power.[8] By the nineteenth century, the Vietnamese and Thai dynasties had brought Cambodia to the brink of dissolution. Cambodia repeatedly sought French assistance in resisting this and became a protectorate in 1864. Within twenty years, it was practically a colony in terms of French presence and political control. In 1887, France had forced Cambodia to join the Union of French Indochina, with Tonkin, Annam, and Cochinchina (North, Central, and South Việt Nam, respectively). Laos joined after the Franco-Siam War in 1893.[9]

After "Pol Pot Time": A Brief Historical Tracing

Cambodia's traumatic past is overdetermined. In Western consciousness, it is a country synonymous with genocide—psychic images of bloodshed and terror. Cambodia is thousands of black-and-white photographs of the dead, civilians staring ahead blankly past the shutter click into their uncertain future, which is now the undeniable past. Much scholarship has addressed the Khmer Rouge and Cambodia's troubled past and present and the connections in between. Partly for these reasons I sketch only a brief outline of events and factors that inform the documentaries I discuss in this chapter. Histories reflect hierarchies. The postcolonial cultural theorist Michel-Rolph Trouillot points out that the construction of historical narratives "involves the uneven contribution of competing groups and individuals who have unequal access to the means for such production."[10] Hegemonic history and social memory reflect power and the lack of power. The testimonials to Cambodia's past and present lay different claims, depending on who is telling the story. Some discourses are privileged, while others are erased. Cambodia's ancient and contemporary histories are interrelated stories of regional territorial struggles, from the growth of the Angkorian Empire to French colonial protection of a vanishing kingdom and today's border skirmishes with Thailand. Khmer history looks vastly different from the perspective of the Vietnamese, Cambodians, and Americans.

Western historians often categorize the twentieth-century conflicts in Southeast Asia into three Indochinese wars. The First Indochina War (1946–54) began with French decolonization in Cambodia, Laos, and Việt Nam, which ended with the Geneva Conference. The Second Indochina War (1954–75)—also known as the Việt Nam War or, to the Vietnamese, the American War—consisted of Vietnamese unification and US attempts to stop the "domino effect" of communism; fighting also occurred in Laos and Cambodia. The Third Indochina War (1975–91) was over who would govern Cambodia and how.[11] This strife provoked regional and international attention.[12] The historian Craig Etcheson notes, "Thus what historians characterize as distinct wars with distinct protagonists appeared to many Cambodians to be simply one long war, with one central protagonist—the Khmer Rouge—driving the entire conflict."[13] A saying captures Cambodian sentiment about this horrific past: "We are all conspirators, we are all victims."[14] By this logic, the United States, the loser of the Second Indochina War/Việt Nam War, is also a conspirator.[15] In this book, I refer to these latter military engagements variably as the American War in Việt Nam, as well as the Việt Nam War, to underscore the shifting geopolitics of naming.

Because of the long shadow of the Việt Nam War, the general American populace does not know about the depth of US involvement in Cambodia. In the story of contemporary Cambodian civil strife, Western historians such as Etcheson often downplay US complicity. US involvement in Cambodia and Laos was directly tied to the US military presence in Việt Nam.[16]

The North Vietnamese transported supplies via the Hồ Chí Minh Trail. The Vietnamese referred to it as the Trường Sơn trail, after the neighboring mountains, which bordered Cambodia and Laos. In a controversial article published in the *Los Angeles Times* in 1997, the journalist Robert Scheer notes that in 1969, Richard Nixon and Henry Kissinger launched "Operation Breakfast" in Cambodia, a fourteen-month carpet-bombing assault that led to the overthrow of the anti-imperialist Prince Norodom Sihanouk and the installment of Lon Nol. Scheer states that Lon Nol was a "U.S. puppet who could not hold power. The legacy of U.S. policy, including the 600,000 dead and many more maimed, created the conditions for the Khmer Rouge's seizure of power in 1975."[17] During Nixon's "secret war" in Cambodia and Laos from 1969 to 1973, 2.7 million tons of bombs exploded in Cambodia. According to the historian Marilyn Young, the 150,000 tons of bombs dropped in Laos from 1964 to 1969 were meant to wipe out civilization in the Plain of Jars, an archeological landscape in Laos's Xieng Khouang Province.[18] Failing in Nixon's intention to quickly end military engagement in the area, the four-year carpet-bombing campaign was a disaster for all involved.

The US bombings paved the way for anti-US, anticapitalist, anti-imperialist sentiment nurtured by the Khmer Rouge, also known as the Communist Party of Kampuchea (CPK).[19] The Asian studies scholar and historian David P. Chandler explains that the air attacks, which "destroyed a good deal of the fabric of Cambodian pre-war society," verified the CPK's claim that the United States was the main enemy and encouraged thousands to join the anti-American struggle. After the bombings, thousands flocked to US-financed Phnom Penh.

On April 17, 1975, the Khmer Rouge, a Maoist-inspired group of rebels headed by the French-educated leader Pol Pot, took hold of Phnom Penh, which was then evacuated. Declaring 1975 "year zero," the CPK aimed to get rid of the existing hierarchical power system and was intent on "reconstructing society from ground zero."[20] It pitted people who had taken refuge from US bombing in metropoles such as Phnom Penh—typically urban professionals and white-collar workers—against people who had been unable, typically for economic reasons, to take such refuge, typically peasants. The CPK charged what it called the "new people" siding with the United States against the "base people."[21] During the repressive four-year regime known as Democratic Kampuchea, in which dissidents, ethnic minorities, and religious followers were killed, approximately 1.7 million Cambodians— one-quarter of the population—died of torture, illness, starvation, or mass executions. Under the banner of an agrarian, communist revolution, production and consumption was collectivized. Under the same utopian fervor, urban areas were evacuated, religious worship was banned, and education was eradicated.[22]

In December 1978, North Vietnamese troops invaded Cambodia, driving the Khmer Rouge into the jungle and putting Hun Sen into power. During the Vietnamese occupation, 600,000 refugees fled to camps on the Thai border. The Vietnamese government left in 1989; civil war persisted for nine more years.

Scheer notes that the Hun Sen government discovered the infamous "killing fields" instigated by Pol Pot. However, China and the United States protected and financed Pol Pot as a means to oppose the Hun Sen coalition in Thailand. Scheer indicts the US government for meddling in Cambodian political life; he makes a connection between US foreign policy in Indochina and the past and current political violence in Cambodia.[23]

Providing more background to the current political climate, the American journalist Karen J. Coates states that in 1993 the United Nations administered democratic elections, with Prince Norodom Ranariddh's Funcinpec Party receiving 45 percent of the votes. However, she notes, "Hun Sen refused defeat. He and his cronies intimidated the nation and threatened to secede several Cambodian provinces. In the end, he was given a power-sharing post with his rival. Ranariddh was installed as first prime minister, Hun Sen as second prime minister."[24] Since the formation of the coalition government in June 2004, Funcinpec has not been an independent political party. Hun Sen has been Cambodia's prime minister since November 30, 1998.[25] On July 28, 2013, Hun Sen won the national election against the opposition Cambodian National Rescue Party.[26] By July 30, 2018, when Hun Sen was reelected in a landslide, he faced no opposition, since his most significant rival—the Cambodian National Rescue Party—had dissolved. In power for more than thirty-three years, Hun Sen is one of the world's longest-serving prime ministers. In a written statement, he declared, "Cambodia has successfully decided the nation's fate through a free, just, and fair election with the preliminary result showing 82.89 percent of registered voters showed up."[27] Hun Sen "is credited with helping achieve economic growth and peace after the devastation caused by the Khmer Rouge regime," notes the BBC, yet he "is also seen as an authoritarian figure with a poor human rights record and the resources and will to thwart any real political challenge."[28] Much of the artwork in this book was made against the backdrop of this continuing, vexed history pivoting on narratives of loss.

Film as *Supplément*

This chapter makes the case that cultural production serves as a supplement to psychoanalytic theories that pivot on loss and lack.[29] In keeping with my premise that loss interpreted through art is not a rehabilatory site, I borrow Jacques Derrida's term *supplément*, and the related *suppléer*, which means "to supplement" (compensate) or "to supplant" (replace). It is the latter connotation—to supplant—implying an overturning, in which I am most interested, as it connects with my theory on the connections between cyclical movements, return, and sociopolitical revolutions. In the Derridean sense, supplementarity has two divergent meanings: (1) replacement (e.g., replacing a void, loss); and (2) addition (e.g., adding new structures). The lost object can never be replaced, but that should not matter (in both material and political senses of the term "matter"). The question is not *what* was lost, but the sociopolitical, cultural, and metaphysical conditions of what remains.[30] I assert that the supplement is "what remains" after loss: how grief becomes political, economic, and cultural artifacts. The supplement, then, is not an object but a process—a trace, under erasure. For instance, documentary film is not only a medium but a tool for mediumship, a convening with the dead. Cathy Schlund-Vials also notes that art can be part of "melancholic movement from grief to grievance, from suffering injury to speaking out against that injury."[31] We are not delimited by mourning. Eng and Kazanjian note a "melancholic excess—an abundance implicit in the very notion of remains that exceeds the restrictive enclosure of melancholia as a pathology, negativity or negation. [Thus] bodily, spatial and ideal remains are linked, overlapping and affecting one another."[32] Remains, like the overlapping flickering individual images that constitute film, are ghostly palimpsests.

I see the supplement as "melancholic excess," an addition (supplement), as well as a negation (to supplant). Following this, film as a supplement does not need to add or name but can index abyss and apprehension. Thus, film and art (e.g., the late Khmer Rouge survivor Vann Nath's paintings) at once fills the void in representation and points to its impossibility. The deviating connotations of supplement as replacement (of a loss) and addition evokes Roland Barthes's insights on photography (to this I add film) as both presence and absence. Film, as supplement, is a conjuring. Documentary film, as it attempts to fix meaning, also unmoors narratives.

In "Freud, Jung, and the Dangerous Supplement to Psychoanalysis," the psychology theorist Gord Barensten notes that Sigmund Freud's and Carl Jung's deviating takes on repetition and trauma can be viewed "otherwise" through Derrida. Toward this reworking of prevailing views on Freud (repetition compulsion) and Jung (return to the shadow as process of individuation) I add Derrida's ideas on repetition to my own concepts of return. In dealing with wounding, return—whether compulsive (Freud) or recuperative (Jung)—largely occurs below rational thought, at the level of the unconscious. Both also view repeated returns as a precondition to work through trauma; once reconciled (successful mourning via Freud or successful individuation and integration à la Jung), there is no need to come back to darkness. It is a logocentric working through by convening and connecting—speaking to one's psychoanalyst (anterior); speaking to one's shadow selves (interior). Within a psychoanalytic frame, the compulsive repetition of the traumatic past can be stopped only through representation. Derrida refutes Freud's claim, asserting that repetition allows for reinvention. This does not mean producing new subjectivities or reiterating tropes but, rather, a process of difference, or differentiation, as Jung would describe it.[33] This fits with my larger proposal of an ethics of return that is not productive—a negative return. The art of loss is neither productive nor a product, easily commodifiable nor legible. "What remains" can include film, art, and literature, as well as the silences and gaps inherently embedded within these forms.

In contrast to conceiving silence as lack of voice, I propose silence as alternate embodied and spiritual sites of intuitive comprehension, ambiguous and ambivalent. This framing builds on the art historian Ashley Thompson's notion of silence and passivity as strategies of Khmer Buddhist (non) engagement.[34] Intentional silence and passivity do not reproduce karmic action or language or the logic of all-encompassing categorical knowledge.

In contrast, officious talking-head documentaries—reflecting longstanding regimes of rationality and totalizing representation—strive to explicate, make issues clear for the viewer. Western philosophy's emphasis on language, particularly speech, has been described by Derrida as logocentrism.[35] First coined by the psychologist and theorist Ludwig Klagesin in the 1920s, logocentrism privileges speech above all forms of (self-)representation. Logocentrism can be traced within Western thought from Plato (literary *diegesis* [narration] versus artistic *mimesis* [imitation]) to Freud (the "talking cure") and Ferdinand de Saussure (semiotic sign and signifier), among others.[36]

The emphasis of contemporary identity politics on enunciation, corporeality, and fixity (versus silence, absence, and unknowability) is founded on logocentric Western philosophical traditions that prioritize what Derrida calls a "metaphysics of presence."[37] Within traditional Western metaphysics, a God-like, all-knowing consciousness is prescient about all that is present, without ambivalence or ambiguity—an objective "truth." This infinite knowledge is outside the realm of finite humans yet something that humanity arguably strives for in science, philosophy, and art. For instance, during the Renaissance beauty was seen as an expression of truth, and vice versa. Deconstructionism has questioned these objective assumptions, but this legacy lingers. What does Derrida deride and define as metaphysics? He identifies it as "the enterprise of returning 'strategically,' 'ideally,' to an origin or to a priority thought to be simple, intact, normal, pure, standard, self-identical. . . . All metaphysicians, from Plato to Rousseau, Descartes to Husserl, have proceeded in this way, conceiving good to be before evil, the positive before the negative."[38] Following this familiar terrain, minority artists also return "strategically"—evoking strategic cartographies—of standardized originary points. Within this process they cast negative traumas into positive valences. Likewise, curators, critics, and theorists do the same. If cultural production is a *supplément* to psychoanalytic loss, then it always already bears the trace of void. A useful bridge for philosophy and media theory, Derrida's insights on the trace questions the inherited binaries between loss and gain; "real" and referent; conscious and unconscious. One aspect inherently bears the mark, the trace of the other. Echoing Barthes on photography, film is both absence and presence.

Recalling that the supplement is a contradictory replacement *and* an addition, the "productive"—the addition from outside—is also a negation from within. For example, for artists engaging in strategic cartographies, the addition of simplistic geo-biographical framing by institutions also requires artists' (self-)effacement of their complicated transnational identities. In short, the familiar refrains of identity politics is also a self-refraining, a complicit silence. The philosopher Robert Bernasconi thus notes that the supplement is an "addition from the outside, but it can also be understood as supplying what is missing and in this way is already inscribed within that to which it is added."[39] Silence precisely enfolds a present absence, the palpable auditory addition of nothingness. Within this context, one is uncertain whether silence "is a plenitude enriching another plenitude, the fullest measure of presence" or "the supplement supplements . . . adds only to replace . . . represents and makes an image. . . . [I]ts place is assigned in the structure by the mark of an emptiness."[40] Silence is presence and void.

Silence disavows demands for narrative and political cohesiveness. For filmmakers and audiences alike, individual and institutional demands are at once inward-facing (in terms of the story within the film) and outward-facing

What Remains

(in terms of the story framing the filmmaker). First, within the narrative of the films, the subjects strive for ethical witnessing (*S-21*) and familial closure (*Refugee*). Second, outside the narrative structure of these films, sociopolitical agendas motivate the two projects. *S-21* seeks juridical justice; *Refugee* aims to complicate Asian American identity politics.

Audiences and critics also have expectations—dictated by geopolitics—of the filmmakers and their subjects. For instance, the filmmakers of *Refugee* and *S-21* are often categorized as diasporic: their works fit within Western moving-image history and discourse that is different from the development of fine arts in Cambodia and Việt Nam. Despite varying artistic lineages, however, these cultural producers get bound up in local-diasporic binaries. For instance, Siv and Nakasako are situated as distinctly Asian American. Panh, however, ruptures this local-diasporic dyad: residing in France and Cambodia, he was Cambodia's first-ever Academy Award nominee.[41] This historic nomination was heralded by the *Japan Times* as a "victory for Panh and for Cambodia," illustrating my earlier point that minority artists variably become representatives for their country of origin.

In addition to geographic divides, there are also generational divides—that is, those who experienced genocide directly (*S-21*) and indirectly (*Refugee*). Seemingly insurmountable geographic and generational gaps can be addressed through unspoken encounters rather than didactic attempts. My aim in discussing Panh and Siv and Nakasako alongside the other artists and filmmakers analyzed in this book is to draw parallels in the shifting strategic cartographies they employ in their practice and across a range of international institutions, from film festivals to galleries—spaces that demand that these artists give voice across the voids of trauma. Hence, artists expected to speak on behalf of their ethnic communities chose to be tactically silent internally (within their artworks) and externally (facing the outside art worlds) as a means to further amplify their power.

Confrontation and Deferral

Opposing frames—such as local and diasporic, silence and voice—cannot coexist within metaphysics' long-standing "pure, standard, self-identical" representational hierarchies. Thus, in *The Margins of Philosophy*, Derrida notes, "An opposition of metaphysical concepts (speech/writing, presence/absence, etc.) is never the face-to-face of two terms, but a hierarchy and an order of subordination."[42] I read this "face-to-face of two terms" as a confrontation—both metaphorically embodied and literally enacted in *Refugee* and *S-21*.

I selected *S-21* and *Refugee* because they are among the most visible documentaries on Khmer and Khmer American traumatic memory that address confrontation, return, and silence, the key themes in this chapter. Scenes of return and confrontation—between victims and perpetrators in *S-21*, and between a son and his long-lost father in *Refugee*—are unique to these films and are my main focus. Adding another facet to my framework of return engagements, I assert that these scenes of return and confrontation blur the lines between testimony and witnessing, victim and conspirator, human and animal.

When confronted, one is expected to reply in return. What happens when there is no response from the individual or institution? Works such as *S-21* are seen as seeking "justice-oriented" juridical activism by scholars such as Schlund-Vials, which manifest in the Khmer Rouge tribunal, discussed later in the chapter. The tribunal process has been long delayed, as Schlund-Vials points out, with defendants denying and deterring accusations, resulting in what amounts to institutionalized silence.[43] Recognizing that state-sanctioned justice may be an aporia, she views cultural production as "alternative sites for justice, healing, and reclamation."[44] Rather than seeing this as a failure of international and local legal systems, or a failure of representational politics, I view these demands and expectations as multifaceted. This "failure," thus, is not a letdown but a letting go. Following work on queer failure by Jack Halberstam, José Esteban Muñoz, and Lee Edelman, among others, the challenge to "successful" outcomes and an enunciatory politics opens up larger questions about the very possibility of reconciling ever-present traumas. In keeping with my stance on loss as nonproductive, art cannot inherently "produce" social justice or juridical activism.

With the delayed process of the tribunal and other extended processes of mourning, confrontation, and witnessing, I link Freudian notions of deferral ("deferred action"), Derrida's ideas on difference and the law, and Michel Foucault's insights on violence. Although central to his theories on trauma, Freud's concept of *Nachträglichkeit*—roughly translated as "deferred action"—has been neglected within current trauma studies discourse. In short, this theory describes a forgotten initial event that registers only after a second event—a delayed "trigger"—retroactively conjures the first event as traumatic. Freud notes that "a memory is repressed which has only become a trauma" through a subsequent encounter.[45] The psychoanalytic theorists Gregory Bistoen, Stijn Vanheule, and Stef Craps observe that "*Nachträglichkeit* thus refers to a mechanism that literally alters the subjective interpretation of the past, in such a way that this altered memory causes new and unexpected effects in the present."[46] I suggest that this present "mechanism" can be a mediated public-facing encounter such as a film or a tribunal. Freud stresses that the original event was not aggravating; it was the memory that *became* traumatic, only after the secondary encounter. For audiences in the global North, the original traumatic event, such as the Khmer Rouge genocide, is only remembered—and only registers as traumatic—through a secondary encounter that makes the first event legible. Similarly, for Mike Siv in *Refugee*, the original traumas of displacement and the horrors of war do not fully register affectively until his subsequent encounters with his family in Cambodia.

Derrida's différance comments on identity and difference and is related to the concept of the *same*. His term evokes the French word *différence*, playing on the auditory slippage between "differ" and "defer." Textually, différance points to how meaning is constructed through the erasure of other meanings, leaving only traces or deferrals of other identities. Within the context, and letter, of the law, repetition is a requirement for justice to be enacted. Thus, Derrida writes, the "law is always a law of repetition, and repetition is always submission to a law."[47] Linking this with Freud's melancholic repetition compulsion, then, seeking retribution within the law's formal channels is a constant deferral, a wounding that will never fully heal. Tying it to nachträglichkeit, the original event (e.g., crime, trauma) is not recognized until the secondary event (trial, memory) officially recognizes it, calling it into the present. Hence, tribunals and cultural production are always already "deferred actions" that register the original wounding in the present, in the eyes of the audience (or jury). This requires a participatory, binding relationship that is mutually constitutive (victim and perpetrator; defendant and accuser; artist and audience; global North and global South)—a "double participation." Derrida writes in *Dissemination* that this "double participation . . . does not mix together two previously separate elements; it refers back to a *same* that is not identical, to the common element or medium of any dissociation."[48] In this light, art and identity are always a repetition of the same, which demands different modes of dissociation.

Boyle reads dissociation psychoanalytically in *S-21* as symptomatic of survivors' inability to reconcile these past traumas. Focusing on the former prison guard Peouv (Khieu Ches), Boyle argues that compartmentalization causes him to reenact his experiences (following Freud's compulsion to repeat) rather than verbalize them.[49] Thompson intervenes in Boyle's analysis, noting that it is difficult to "isolate perpetrators from victims," actions from language.[50] Double participation, in essence, cannot reconcile disconnects ("[It] does not mix together two previously separate elements"). Complicating art, identification, and traumatic violence, Thompson asserts, "Insofar as the core of psychoanalysis involves close examination of the irrepressible expression of the physical symptom at the expense of discursive narration, and it formulates the cure as the gradual transformation of the former into the latter, the film director [Panh] would seem to play the role of the analyst here. Though, in Peouv's case, in the frame of the film, at least, the cure remains elusive."[51]

I agree with Thompson's implication that film directors (such as Panh or Nakasako and Siv) cannot presume the role of the analyst in facilitating catharsis;[52] artists should not be held responsible for healing for their subjects, themselves, or their audiences. There is no productive cure through logocentric measures. I read this double participation as the blurred bonds between perpetrators and victims, artists and audiences, gift and toxin— bound by complicity—no matter the degrees of dissociation.

Trauma Dramas

Collective trauma and cultural trauma are related yet separate concepts. A sense of collective trauma precedes cultural trauma. The sociologist Jeffrey Alexander argues that events are not "inherently" traumatic—trauma is a "socially mediated" phenomenon.[53] Individual ordeals become a collective issue if they affect a significant number of people. The events can touch people directly or indirectly. Trauma is socially mediated through film, political discourse, and popular culture. Through public discourse, a collective's sense of injury congeals as cultural trauma. Alexander notes that cultural trauma occurs "when members of a collective feel that they have been subjected to a horrendous event that leaves indelible marks on their group consciousness, marking their memories forever and changing their future identity in fundamental and irrevocable ways." Wounds form scars. Some cultural scars fade while others remain.

What society constructs, remembers, and represents as a wounding event depends on many shifting political, cultural, and even economic variables.[54] The sociologist Neil J. Smelser observes that "collective coping" is an "ingredient of cultural traumas. Representations, to be collective, must be understood and shared."[55] Film is an agent that affirms collective pain and constructs cultural trauma. These "trauma dramas" are mass-media narratives in film, television, and newspapers that cast particular perspectives on a tragic event, thereby contributing to how the trauma is subsequently constructed.[56] Memory and forgetting are complementary processes linked to mass media.

Mass media's production of traumatic narratives creates a shared sense of cultural trauma. After being disfigured, society must reconfigure itself. Part of this reconfiguration is representing the harm inflicted on the body politic. To recall Elaine Scarry's work on pain, the world is "unmade," undone through instances of individual or collective trauma. Horrific instances shatter an individual's or group's world, and sense of the world, beyond comprehension. The world is eventually "remade" after the traumatic fact through articulation, language, and art—through culture.[57] Different collectives manufacture and contest cultural trauma.

The individual stories in *S-21* and *Refugee* are case studies of cultural trauma.[58] Although the youth of *Refugee* did not experience genocide firsthand, they grapple with its aftereffects through secondhand narratives and the firsthand shocks of familial separation, US assimilation, and homeland return. The survivors of S-21 share their grief because they want justice. Through trauma the world is unmade; through filmic testimony the world is remade.

Other collectives make culture-specific traumas as object lessons, as cautionary tales: consider the overdetermined connotations of Hiroshima and the Holocaust. In *S-21* and *Refugee*, the world of Khmer atrocity remakes itself for a sympathetic audience.[59] This global North viewership is horrified by human rights violations and touched by tales of separation and loss. As far as the "developed" world is concerned, the sites of horror in this small developing nation did not exist, were unmade from the start. To put it another way, Khmer horrors exist at a safe remove—the pornography of genocide does not really matter politically unless you were directly affected. The Cambodian genocide became hypervisible for the first time for the First World only when German documentary crews, who translated it into digestible snippets (e.g., *Kampuchea: Death and Rebirth*, dir. Gerhard Scheuman, 1979); international news coverage; and US feature films such as the Oscar-winning *The Killing Fields* (Roland Joffé, dir., 1984) drew attention to it.[60] This illustrates my earlier discussion of delay and Freud's nachträglichkeit (deferred action), in which the initial trauma (e.g., Khmer genocide) registers only through a secondary event (documentary or mainstream film) that renders its shocks in the present. Today, Cambodia still exists in the world imagination through the topography of trauma and temples, then and now conflated.

S-21 and *Refugee* translate Cambodian local and diasporic traumatized narratives for different audiences. They serve as an important resource for diasporic Cambodians who are coming to terms with the genocide, particularly young generations who doubt that the genocide even happened. A key audience for *Refugee* is college-educated Asian Americans, a largely neoliberal demographic. A main target for *S-21* is the international community, Western policy makers, and, to a lesser extent, Cambodians (although the film is in English). As mentioned, one of *S-21*'s goals was to bring about a Khmer Rouge tribunal. Films such as *S-21* and *Refugee* gratify the need of largely neoliberal audiences to understand the world through a certain lens. The (Western) neoliberal audience discovers "truths" about traumatic Cambodian pasts as the filmmakers (and the films' subjects) grapple with this history. The painful scenes that these films conjure both build up and break down barriers between the First World and the Third World.

"Ethical" spectatorship and trauma studies scholarship are complicit in maintaining structural inequities. Again and again *we*, the neoliberal audience—largely sited in the global North—witness the traumas of war and displacement on small and large screens. Part of this "audience" consists of refugees, migrants, and exiles whom the military engagements in Southeast Asia and elsewhere directly or indirectly affected. These audiences and endless mourners are not mutually exclusive as populations; they may even be mutually constitutive. The audience may include those who were affected by the traumas of history and assimilation featured in the films. Nonetheless, I maintain that the spectator's position is a privileged one. The films, including fictionalizations such as *The Killing Fields*, as well as documentaries, address an exalted audience. Even those of us who have endured traumas depicted in them are the spectators of suffering, *not* the spectacles of suffering. Our empathetic and varyingly critical viewing practices, however, still help maintain the racial, class, and gender hierarchies at which we gape. We watch in horror, in sadness, in disbelief. Above all, we watch in silence.

As Scarry points out, silence and inarticulateness mark the undoing of the world through pain, torture, and trauma. Articulation and, perhaps, action signal the remaking or the reconstitution of one's world. Other than doling out awards, however, the First World audiences of these films largely remain silent. Critical commentary about the issues that the films present has been sparse. The consciousness-raising spectatorial exercise does not lead to action. Empathy and apathy can go hand in hand.

The limited distribution of *S-21* and *Refugee* hinders them from influencing Western cultural memory. They are not mainstream films but independent documentaries screened at international festivals and academic conferences. The audiences at these events are often urbane, if not urban, middle-class, educated white-collar workers. Their cultural memories are the communal recollections, both triumphant and tragic, of a society. Similar to cultural trauma, these memories are a collection of individual stories or singular events that become a larger part of public discourse. Unlike cultural trauma, not all collective memories are painful. Building on Freud's concept of the "screen memory," in which benign memories displace difficult ones, the cultural theorist Marita Sturken notes that "cultural memory is produced through representation—in contemporary culture, often through photographic images, cinema, and television. These mnemonic aids are also screens, actively blocking out other memories that are more difficult to represent."[61]

Panh's and Nakasako's work displaces Hollywood screen memories of Southeast Asian trauma and US involvement memorialized in films such as *The Killing Fields* and *Apocalypse Now*. They create an alternative cultural memory. Yet the screen still exists, no matter how seemingly transparent.[62] Neither work indicts US foreign policy, which had a role in creating political instability in the region. Neither film mentions President Richard Nixon's secret bombings, which led to the rise of the Khmer Rouge and the eventual exodus of refugees. Instead, both films focus on providing a subtle spectacle of suffering and healing, if not reconciliation, of survivors of the Pol Pot regime. Through the filmic lens they translate individual agony into collective memories of cultural trauma. Both films fulfill their intended functions of representing specific wounds that were previously unseen or acknowledged. In this process, Khmer and Khmer American traumas become a small part of international cultural memory. In the space between screen and spectator, many worlds are unmade and remade. The screens showing *S-21* and *Refugee* reveal worlds of pain worlds apart, but they do not fully reveal their intimate causes and conditions.

Viewers are haunted by cultural memory. Sturken notes that memory is "a process of engaging the past rather than a means to call it up."[63] *S-21* and *Refugee* invoke personal and collective memories to engage the past and present. In the remainder of this chapter, I explore issues of loss, witnessing, and the politics of representation to understand this engagement.

Rithy Panh's S-21: The Khmer Rouge Killing Machine

The diasporic filmmaker Rithy Panh was born in 1964 in Phnom Penh and survived the Khmer Rouge regime, although his parents, sister, and other family members did not. He escaped Cambodia to the Thai border at fifteen and eventually settled in France.

In 1985, he started studying at the Institut des Hautes Études Cinématographiques, France's national cinema school.[64] After Panh first settled in France, he rejected all ties to his homeland.[65] He has noted that he gave up speaking his native language for a long period because he wanted to forget the past: "I had been uprooted and I felt somehow incomplete, torn between forgetting and remembering, between past and present, always ill at ease. . . . And when you've survived genocide, you always feel guilty about being a survivor."[66] Panh realized that he had to confront his traumatic past and has therefore produced several features and documentaries mainly about life in Cambodia and genocide, which have garnered numerous prestigious international awards. His 2013 film *The Missing Picture* (*L'image manquante*)— also about the Khmer Rouge and the limits of memory and representation— won the top prize in the "Un Certain Regard" section at the Cannes Film Festival in 2013 and a nomination for the Oscar for Best Foreign-Language Film in 2014. In 2020, Panh won the Berlinale Documentary Award for *Irradiated* (2020), a film that positions Khmer genocide alongside Hiroshima, the Holocaust, the Việt Nam War, among other global atrocities. Although he tried to erase his past, he came to the conclusion that "we can't build our future by forgetting. The survivors must tell their stories and ensure that the memory of what happened is handed down from the past to the present. We owe a debt to the dead and we have an obligation to our children."[67] Panh sees the importance of linking the past and the future, recognizing they are not made up of discrete, unrelated events. While there is much academic scholarship and film criticism on Panh's work along the lines of giving voice,[68] I do not recite them in detail in this chapter. Instead I choose to focus on scenes of silence as a counter-reading and counternarrative to prevailing discourses on art addressing trauma.

In *S-21: The Khmer Rouge Killing Machine* two survivors confront the guards who worked at the prison centers more than twenty-five years ago. "S-21" is the code name for Tuol Svay Prey High School, which the CPK converted into a center for torture and imprisonment after it closed all schools in the city. All prisoners who entered S-21 were marked for death. The prisoners were tortured to extract "confessions" about their bourgeois lives and their activities against Ângkor (the Khmer Rouge). After their confessions were meticulously recorded, the detainees were killed. It was a deadly ironic situation: to prolong their lives, the prisoners refused to confess, which only extended and exacerbated the level of their torture.

According to the Documentation Center of Cambodia (DC-Cam), The S in S-21 stands for "*Santebal*, the Khmer word meaning 'state security organization'"; "21" was the walkie-talkie number of the former prison chief Duch.[69] In Khmer, *Tuol Sleng* means "Hill of the Sleng Tree"; the sleng tree bears poisonous fruit. Mass killings were done in the countryside, "off-site," after victims were tortured and interrogated. Of the seventeen thousand prisoners admitted to S-21, only seven reportedly survived.[70] This number has been widely accepted and mythologized by Western media over the past thirty years as indicative of the brutality of the regime. According to Dacil Keo, a DC-Cam researcher based in Phnom Penh, the number came from one of the first documentaries about the Khmer Rouge, *Die Angkar* (*The Angkor*), produced in 1981 by Studio H&S of the former East Germany which shows photographs of seven S-21 survivors. Keo suggests the number was used for its symbolic power and alignment with the date of the overthrow of the regime, January 7, 1979.[71] The official number from DC-Cam is 179 prisoners (of whom one hundred were soldiers) who were released from 1975 to 1978. Twenty-three survived after the Khmer Rouge regime was toppled. As of December 2018, five out of 202 were still living.[72] S-21 became the Museum of Genocidal Crimes in 1980.[73] In Sài Gòn, the former Museum of American War Crimes—renamed the War Remnants Museum in 1995 as a concession to good relations with the United States—served a similar political function of evoking horror, pity, and outrage at past atrocities, as well as support for the current regime.[74]

The fact that the Museum of Genocidal Crimes and the War Remnants Museum echo each other is not coincidental. The Vietnamese government created them both under the leadership of Mai Lam, a historian and Vietnamese colonel fluent in Khmer with experience in legal studies and museology.[75] (East Germany also had a role in creating the Museum of Genocidal Crimes.) The day after Vietnamese soldiers drove the Khmer Rouge from Cambodia, Vietnamese photojournalists discovered the torture site by following the stench of decay emanating from the grounds. The Vietnamese government closed and cleaned up the site with Cambodian colleagues. Its ample archives were the source material for the museum. The trauma studies scholar Lisa Moore notes that it was created with the aim of appealing to the international community for aid and to recognize the new Vietnamese-backed government in the People's Democratic Kampuchea. The museum, as "objectively" as it appears to present the crimes of the Khmer Rouge, is a propaganda tool.

Lam hoped to craft a narrative that served the People's Democratic Kampuchea and the Vietnamese government's agenda, as well as address the future needs of Cambodians.[76] Lam told interviewers in 1994, "In order to

understand the crimes of Pol Pot [and] Ieng Sary, first you should understand Cambodians, both the people and the country." Chandler charges that
the biased history he constructed in the S-21 displays "denie[s] the leaders
of the CPK any socialist credentials" and compares Tuol Sleng to Auschwitz.[77]
The analogies between Auschwitz and Tuol Sleng, like other sites of trauma,
are overdetermined today. Both sites draw legions of trauma tourists. Visitors are at once compelled and repelled by the specter of what remains and
the spectacle of remains. Within this narrative, the communist Vietnamese
government is portrayed on the international stage as heroes who successfully stopped unfathomable evil.

Tuol Sleng was a secret operation, known to very few. Now it is infamous the world over. Interviewed in 1997 by a journalist, Pol Pot claimed, "I
made only big decisions on big issues. I want to tell you—Tuol Sleng was a
Vietnamese exhibition. A journalist wrote [about it]. . . . When I first heard
about Tuol Sleng it was on the *Voice of America*. I listened twice."[78] Thus, Pol
Pot suggested that the Vietnamese government invented the story.

While the testimony of survivors does not encourage those who might
believe Pol Pot, the charge of propaganda gains fuel from the fact that Cambodians were denied access when the museum first opened on January 25,
1979.[79] A 1980 document from the People's Republic of Kampuchea (PRK)
Ministry of Culture, Information, and Propaganda states that the site aims to
show "international guests the cruel torture committed by the traitors to the
Khmer people." Tuol Sleng was finally opened to the public in July 1980.
The first week the museum was opened to the general populace, thirty-two
thousand people came. The cultural anthropologist Judy Ledgerwood wrote
that survivors came "searching for meaning, for some explanation of what
had happened. A visit would not have been an easy task; people who went
through the museum in the first year said that the stench of the place was
overwhelming." We also witness these scenes of painful discovery in Panh's
documentary. Early in *S-21*, images of the mundane fill the screen, everyday
life in a contemporary rural household in Cambodia: a farming family seeds
rice under azure skies; a wailing infant receives a bath. The family has a
small, wooden house. One of the family members, Him Houy, a small, thin
man in his forties, served as a security deputy at S-21. The banality of his
surroundings raises the question of how genocide and mass terror can arise
in the quotidian. His father urges him, "Tell the truth. Then perform a ritual
asking for forgiveness to get rid of the bad karma." But the former guard is
weary and remorse-stricken. He states, "I am sick all day. I have a headache
when I think about it." In a close-up, his mother, Yeay Cheu, states bluntly,

"They indoctrinated him, they turned my son into a thug who killed people."
Featured in a medium-shot, three-quarter profile with his mother sitting in
the background, the son dejectedly stares off into the distance and responds
calmly, "If we killed people of our own free will, then that's evil. But I was
given orders. They terrorized me with their guns. That's not evil. The leaders
who gave the orders are evil. Deep down, I was afraid of evil. I was afraid
to die." Later in the documentary, the other former guards and staff—all
similarly ordinary and unassuming—also claim that they were terrorized
by fear and intimidation. Their statements echo other perpetrators of other
crimes in other infamous contexts who claim that they were "only following
orders," evading agency and moral culpability. Echoing the anthropologist
Alexander Laban Hinton, How does genocide come to take place?[80] The film
asks its subjects, "How do you survive absolute horror? How do you become
a killer?"[81] *We are all conspirators, we are all victims.*

There is a fine line between victim and perpetrator, civility and barbarism. Hinton warns that genocide, as a floating signifier, is semiotically
linked within twentieth-century discourse on violence to "barbarism." "Barbaric" acts are antithetical to enlightened, rational "civilization." Mass violence is construed as "primitive." As an example, Hinton notes how violence
in Bosnia and Rwanda is represented as the "primordial clash resulting from
a seething cauldron of 'ancient tribal hatreds.'" He also cautions against universalizing moral rhetoric that champions "modern" morality, embodied by
"a type of 'civil society' governed by international law."[82] Much of the current
literature on international human rights, and human rights violations, operates on the implicit binaries between civility and barbarism, morality and
inhumanity. It draws distinctions between modernity and savagery, universal and particular.

According to this patronizing logic, the natives are not fit to govern
themselves and need intervention, constant supervision, or they will revert
to their uncivil/savage ways. The long, troubled case of the United Nations–
backed Khmer Rouge tribunal is a telling example. After five years of negotiations, the tribunal consisted of a hybrid Cambodian-international court.
Phnom Penh has stated that it will allow only two cases to be tried out of a
total of five against former Khmer Rouge cadres. So far, only Duch, who ran
S-21, has been tried; he was convicted on July 26, 2010. An article published
in *Time* magazine in November 2009 quotes an international law monitor
accusing the Cambodian government of obstructing the tribunal. The New
York–based monitor, Open Society Justice, claims that "political interference . . . poses a serious challenge to both the credibility of the court and its

ability to meet international fair trial standards."[83] International news outlets and human rights organizations continue to voice concerns over corruption and political pressure interfering with the court proceedings.

Thompson critiques the international demands Khmer subjects and cultural producers (such as the painter Vann Nath and the filmmaker Rithy Panh) have to address, writing, "Much of Cambodian art of the past decade has been produced, in one way or another, in response to more-or-less external demands that Cambodians assume responsibility for the Khmer Rouge as both an historico-political event and traumatic experience. These demands are transmitted to Cambodia through numerous means, but perhaps most broadly through international initiatives for democracy and justice."[84] Thompson notes that Euro-American notions of justice, democracy, and commemoration (based on Shoah politics of reconciliation and memorialization) may not be suitable to Khmer Buddhist sociopolitical contexts founded on other frameworks of (non)self, society, and culpability.[85] The burden of responsibility and representation rests on a metonymic relationship: one accounts for the whole—the impossible contradictions of Western justice and democracy.

Beyond legal protocol, Cambodia and Việt Nam, among other Asian countries, are constantly criticized for failing to meet international human rights standards and, by extension, moral standards. For instance, Western mass media often chastise China, Việt Nam, India, and Cambodia for subhuman working conditions. These criticisms ignore the role of international conglomerates that benefit from sweatshops, such as Nike, Old Navy, and Walmart, all of which depend on exploited labor in developing countries to maximize their profits.

International corporations and intergovernmental organizations significantly impact the lives and livelihoods of the Third World. Deterritorialized organizations such as the International Monetary Fund, World Bank, and nongovernmental organizations (NGOs) are indirectly influential in determining political and moral agendas in developing countries.[86] As the anthropologist Lisa Rofel writes, NGOs may "provide moral justification for the spread of empire" through their vision and implementation of universal rights and needs.[87] It seems innocent enough: these organizations are there to help these developing countries economically, politically, and culturally.

Significant (imperial) violence has been waged under the rhetoric of civilizing and moral missions. The nomadic, rhizomatic flexibility of deterritorialized institutions (and their flexible rhetoric) is the hallmark of empire, and of late capitalism.[88] Rofel notes that an empire "regulates not just territory but social life in its entirety; and thus a major mode of rule is biopower; and though bathed in blood, empire always presents itself, in the guise of the concept of a just war, as dedicated to peace."[89] International military interventions—such as the Iraq War, the Việt Nam War, and the Persian Gulf War—are waged in the name of transcendent peace, human rights, and modernity. Yet these "just wars" are seen as having different means and ends from other forms of military action instigated by other nation-states.

The Animal in You

Explaining how guards were able to torture and kill prisoners, a guard interviewed in *S-21* is matter-of-fact: "We saw them as animals." Another guard says, "Torture was something cold and cruel. I didn't think. I was arrogant. I had power over the enemy. I never thought of his life, I saw him as an animal."[90] The philosopher Theodor Adorno describes this dehumanization as typical of genocidal regimes. It echoes the strategy used by most "in" groups against their chosen "out" group. For instance, propaganda by the US government during World War II often depicted Japanese people with animal features. Adorno traces the curve of this dehumanizing and ultimately murderous logic: "The possibility of pogroms is decided in the moment when the gaze of a fatally-wounded animal falls on a human being. The defiance with which he repels this gaze—'after all, it's only an animal'—reappears irresistibly in cruelties done to human beings, the perpetrators having again and again to reassure themselves that it is 'only an animal,' because they could never believe this even of animals."[91] Part of the function of documentaries such as *S-21* is to humanize Cambodians; to put a human face, as it were, to such atrocities seen as monstrous. Adorno elaborates on the difference between the civilized and the savage: "In repressive society the concept of man is itself a parody of divine likeness. The mechanism of 'pathic projection' determines that those in power perceive as human only their own reflected image, instead of reflecting back the human as precisely what is different."[92] The self-same image is considered human. The image of difference marks the nonhuman, the "animal." *S-21* provides an image of difference to those in power (Western hegemony) yet also reflects back the human. The humanity of the faceless cogs—"screws" within the Khmer Rouge "killing machine"— is revealed. The film both challenges and reinforces the victim-perpetrator binary. The workers at Tuol Sleng are variably featured with family members or as young adolescents following a brutal regime; they do not merely come to represent the face of evil or of animal barbarity. Panh reverses the question: "Who are these animals that could commit such atrocities?" In interrogating the torturers, he gives them a degree of human agency by letting them voice their stories, after years of silently following orders. The former prisoners and their torturers have chosen to be part of this filmic dialogue. The victims and the perpetrators reflect each other.

"I saw him as an animal," the torturer says. That utterance and that "pathic projection" disavows human agency and subjectivity, initiating a psychic and real space in which violence can be enacted on a subject construed as a nonsubject, ultimately rendered as a nonentity.

Disavowal, displacement, and effacement. "I was only following orders," the guards individually echo each other in defense. The disavowal of human subjectivity, and of a subject's humanity, allows for the displacement of responsibility, the displacement of emotions and ethical judgment. And it allows for the effacement of their offense. As the critical theorist Akira Lippit interprets Adorno's passage, "The ethics of murder is made possible by seeing the animal first as nonhuman, then inhuman. If one's victim can be seen as inhuman, the aggressor reasons, one is justified in performing acts of violence, even murder upon that body, since those acts fall beyond the jurisdictions of anthropocentric law." The circuitous logic and circuits of power in which men are rendered inhuman, allowing for inhumane treatment, is not outside the realm of rationality; it is the result of deductive reasoning that effaces agency and culpability.

Being a responsible worker precludes ultimate responsibility. Or does it? "I was only following orders." "I saw him as an animal." In identifying with the killing machine, the perpetrators also become dehumanized. As they argue, they are only nuts and bolts, willingly blind to the Khmer Rouge's machinations. In bloodlessly following commands, the guards participate in cold-blooded crimes. Scared like animals, they diminish other humans to animals. Still later in the film, Vann Nath, the survivor, admonishes the guards, bitterly, "We distinguish humans from animals. If we turn men into animals, that's not right."[93] Once more, the divide between human and non-human is evoked. For both victims and perpetrators, survival is an ethical dilemma. "The leaders who gave the orders are evil," decries a peon. By this logic, obedience to authority is not evil. Deference to power is a rational act. If the leaders are evil, those in control are supra-human—they are above humans; they have transcendent power over life. If the leaders are evil, those in control are at the same time sub-human—they fall below humane behavior. What is moral? What is the nature of evil? Is it human or animal?

The director asks the question whether the torturers could themselves have been victims, caught up in a cruel regime. They were in fact teenagers.

But Vann asks a former staff member, "If you are victims, then what are we?" This question harks back to the dividing line between humans and animals, between victims and perpetrators. The executioners were also treated like animals by their own regime, coerced and threatened with death for themselves and their families. The film asks the neoliberal audience the same question about accountability and victimhood: by structural inequities and invasive foreign policies, are the viewers implicated in these crimes? *If you are victims, then what are we?*

Melancholia and Memory

His back to the camera, a diminutive man clad in a green long-sleeved shirt and gray pants stares up at a three-story building, which takes up most of the frame. The nondescript, faded yellow building with cracked plaster framed by palm trees is S-21. He starts crying. The camera zooms in slowly. Vann Nath, who is a painter, appears with Chum Mey, an engineer, one of the two other survivors who remained at the time. Mey continues sobbing, his face in profile. "If I hadn't been imprisoned in Tuol Sleng, I wouldn't have lost my family. Nath, why did it happen like that?" That question continues to haunt. Each prisoner was forced to "confess" his or her crimes against the party and produce a lengthy list of suspects—friends, neighbors, relatives. Many confessions and lists were pure fabrications, a brief respite from the bloodletting, water torture, and electrical shocks.

Vann, a handsome man with white hair, survived S-21 because of his skills as a painter—his jailers kept him around to paint flattering images of Khmer Rouge leaders. After the Khmer Rouge regime ended, the Vietnamese-backed PRK requested that his subsequent paintings document the crimes he witnessed at S-21 for the Tuol Sleng Museum of Genocide.[94] The film shows him working on such a painting as the camera shifts between close-ups of Vann and details of a painting that depicts blindfolded and shackled prisoners being led to S-21 for the first time. The camera zooms in on the canvas, focuses on the paint being applied. The painting, however, remains unfinished throughout the film. Vann's grief is palpable, and unresolved.

The prisoners *and* the guards of S-21 are both melancholics (in the Freudian sense)—the scene and site of trauma is ever present. In Freud's essay "Mourning and Melancholia" (1917), there are two different forms of grief in response to loss. The first response is "normal" mourning; the second type is "pathological" melancholia.[95] They display similar symptoms: "profoundly painful dejection, cessation of interest in the outside world, inhibition of all activity."[96] Nonetheless, mourning is a natural, healthy process—the mourner grieves for a period of time and then recovers. The lost object is eventually replaced, substituted. Noting that grief eventually subsides, Freud states, "After a lapse of time, it will be overcome."[97] In contrast, melancholia does not have resolution. It becomes a pathological affliction. The melancholic cannot overcome grief. It is endless; the lost object/subject cannot be substituted, replaced. In mourning, the "world becomes poor and empty; in melancholia it is the ego itself."[98] The melancholic identifies with the lost object. Freud states, "The free libido . . . was withdrawn into the ego . . . to establish an identification of the ego with the abandoned object. . . . The ego wishes to incorporate this object into itself, and the method by which it would do so, in this oral or cannibalistic stage, is by devouring itself."[99]

The melancholic subject is ambivalent toward the lost object, simultaneously feeling love and hatred. The melancholic experiences nostalgia, guilt, and rage. The melancholic *consumes* these conflicting feelings, feeds on himself or herself. This is a form of self-punishment. Stuck in eternal limbo, the melancholic cannot reconcile these contradictory impulses—desire and disgust, reverence and resentment. What is a melancholic to do?

In Chum Mey's inconsolable cry "Why did it happen like that?" is the constant return to the site of loss. Clearly this is a question that Mey has pondered over and over again, unable to deal with the grief of his losses. In *Beyond the Pleasure Principle*, Freud mentions that the "compulsion to repeat" is the patient's impulse to return again and again to a distressing situation, although he or she no longer recalls the origins of the compulsion.[100] The repetition compulsion is an endless loop, a psychic return to the site of trauma. Vann's paintings of terror and torture can be seen within this framework. One painting features rows and rows of prisoners lying on the floor, stacked head to foot. His constant short, steady brushstrokes and the slow buildup of paint translate trauma, revive scenes of pain. In the film, both the "victims" and the "perpetrators" are subject to revisiting sites of trauma. Panh states that the Khmer Rouge regime survivors' inability to mourn produces a "massive collective wound" that "will not heal."[101]

Reconsidering Freud's conception of melancholia in the *Loss* anthology, Eng and Kazanjian propose that this melancholic position is a productive one, a space in which individual and collective guilt, shame, love, rage, and hope can be articulated through ethical responses and aesthetic production that highlights ambivalence and loss. In short, loss is "counterintuitively" recast as a "creative" rather than a negating force.[102] Eng and Kazanjian note that the melancholic is not pathologically fixed in space and time but, rather, in "continuous *engagement* with loss and its remains." This is what I call return engagements. This repeated "engagement generate sites for memory and history, for the rewriting of the past as well as the reimagining of the future."[103] The remnants of traumatic loss—what remains (through cultural production)—allows for ongoing, open-ended encounters, at once "hopeful and hopeless."[104]

Within this light, can Vann's paintings be seen as a generative space? Beyond grief, the depictions of blood, bones, and brutality become a site of witnessing. Panh's corpus of work can also be viewed through this lens, as an attempt at healing, justice—sites of discourse. Both Vann's and Panh's melancholic life's work examines painful pasts to fully engage—poetically and politically—the now. Eng and Kazanjian characterize such efforts as "an ongoing and open relationship with the past—bringing its ghosts and spectres, its flaring and fleeting images, into the present."[105] What are the limits of representation, particularly "flaring and fleeting" representations of the horrific, of the unrepresentable?

Both Panh, the filmmaker, and Vann, the painter, push the boundaries of representation and narrative. They question the limits of banality, beauty, and the horrific. The art historian Pamela Corey discusses the reception of Vann Nath's images as being both "real" representations of trauma and surpassing its limits, encompassing formalist modernist concerns of "high art" (medium, color, line, and so on).[106] Tracing assertions by Thompson and the artist Sopheap Pich that Vann's images are more than documentary images, Corey states, "Vann's portraits of historical episodes reveal visual representations of agency and resistance, as Thompson argues, exceeding the act of documentation, and as Pich suggests, a mode of artistic practice committed to painting as method."[107] Beyond the rhetoric of resistance and refusal, Vann pays close attention to composition, architectural planes, forms. Vann's focus is also on the art of painting, of making beautiful marks. This is often overshadowed by international and academic discourse highlighting the marks of damage, physical and psychological, depicted in his images. For Thompson the paintings embody a "self-mastery." The works "render . . . a determination to overcome as they did the torture experienced there."[108] This interpretation echoes Freud's notion that, for grieving survivors, "after a lapse of time, it will be overcome."[109] To render also invokes surrender, at once conjuring and losing one's sense of self. To render an image (of oneself, of an event) requires revisitation. Traumatic acts are reenactments—the "delayed action." Referring to Derrida's *Freud and the Scene of Writing*, Thompson notes, however, that "repetition is at the heart of the experience 'itself'; we all act ourselves."[110] Vann's and Panh's traumas are experienced by proxy only through repetition—the experience "itself" is the repeated viewing (by various observers, local and international) of the paintings and film, each rendition, each iteration heartrending.

Return Policy

Traumas are mediated, remembered; there is a compulsion to revisit the trauma. The trauma theorist Shoshana Felman writes, "Trauma never happens once."[111] Trauma repeats itself, returns; trauma is a specter. Former prison guards reenact the day-to-day activities of S-21 in empty spaces, empty rooms—formerly full of prisoners—in the film. They, too, have returned to acknowledge the dead. At age twenty-two or twenty-three or even younger, thirteen or fourteen, they were tiny cogs in the death machine, the ones who followed and implemented the Khmer Rouge's ruthless policies. In several scenes, groups of guards recount various torture rituals. Black-and-white photographs leave traces of maimed bodies, gnashed visages, upturned eyes, pools of blood, the almost dead.

Guards individually pantomime their duties twenty-five years ago, voicing their daily routine: "I unlock, lock the door. I bring them their water. *You shut up! Or I will kick you!* I close the door. I go to the next room." Prisoners' food and water rations are kept to the minimum; because of the malnourishment, they need to relieve themselves only every few days. Twenty-five years have passed since the guards performed these routinized rituals, but their gestures seem so effortless. Their individual bodies each uniquely remember the intimate, mundane contours of the torture center.

In one scene, the camera remains static—a wide shot of a large, empty yellow room—as two guards enter a room, check it, and yell at imaginary prisoners, then leave. As viewers, we assume the position of the camera—distanced, unmoving (perhaps unmoved), mute—as these beings torture and are tortured by their invisible ghosts. Daily, these ghosts distress the survivors. These ghosts are victims and conspirators alike, just like their living counterparts.

Our field of vision is incomprehensible (what is this abandoned room?) until the protagonists, the "actors" within the documentary, play out the scenes before our eyes, embodying the terror we have only heard and read about or have seen splayed in black and white. Yet within these reenactments there is a silence, a void. Of course, one of the voids are the vanished victims, whose spirits are conjured through these rituals. The empty rooms signify the unfathomable terror. Their emptiness also points at the gaps between the subjects and their audience—the gaps in history, memory, and translation.

What Remains

Why did the conspirators and the victims agree to walk these halls again? Perhaps because they never left; perhaps because they want to exorcise their ghosts. They, too, are returning to remember, or perhaps to forget. Ghosts—of the tortured and of torturers—continue to torment the living. The guard's enactments of their duties perhaps also bear their "compulsion to repeat"—they are also witnesses to trauma. Perhaps they return again and again psychically—and return physically this time—not to absolve their crimes, but to acknowledge them. *We are all conspirators; we are all victims.*

I asked Panh during an interview about his process of working on the film. As he described, he built trust and rapport with the few former guards over the course of three years. Eventually he persuaded several prison guards to talk candidly on film about their experiences there. When Panh asked the former guard Khieu Ches to explain his daily activities at the prison, he had difficulty expressing himself verbally. He was twelve when he was a guard. As Panh described the scene to me: "It wasn't pre-scripted. . . . The guard couldn't describe [what he did] because the nature of the violence was beyond verbalization. . . . He had difficulty speaking it. He started gesturing. I said that he could show us instead. . . . Then it came automatically, these actions he did day after day. He didn't have to think about it, it was ingrained. It was his body's memory, deep in his muscle."[112] Again, language fails. It is only the body's silent memory that can fully recall and articulate the past, blood memories etched in marrow. In the scene that Panh refers to, the camera does not remain static but follows Ches, who shows how he circulated among prisoners on the second floor of Tuol Sleng. The camera does not follow him as he enters the former classrooms where prisoners were once shackled side by side. The camera is pressed up against the bars of the classroom; the guard is now at a distance. It is once more a visual metaphor for the distanced, mediated vision the audience can access. Some film critics such as *Variety*'s Derek Elley have called these "reenactment" scenes overly repetitive. Others say these scenes are ineffectual because, from the viewer's point of view, they may have been scripted; the viewer does not know the filmmaker's intent.[113] I contend that these points do not matter. Even if, contrary to Panh's statements, these scenes were scripted, it would not diminish their power. The viewer does not need to know the director's intent through heavy-handed voice-over explanations or edits. The stagings come off as part theater of the absurd, part flashback, part performance art. I concur with Boyle, who calls the scene of Ches reinhabiting his brutal twelve-year-old self one of the most powerful in the documentary. As she says, it straddles the line between the past (the inner rooms of Tuol Sleng) and the present (where the camera is stationed, on the periphery), with Ches as an intermediary. To echo Feldman, trauma never happens once. Every day the conspirators and the victims, these living ghosts, wander the halls of Tuol Sleng.

Traumatic memories come flooding back for the torturers and the survivors, uncontainable. Panh's representational strategies highlight ambivalence and silence even as they interrogate and confront perpetrators. "The idea of putting victims and executioners together is very seductive, but it's also tricky," Panh notes. "You don't want to be a voyeur. You kind of have to develop an ethic of the image."[114] Clearly, Panh has an agenda, but his strength as a filmmaker lies in his willingness to let his subjects speak for themselves.

S-21 functions as a form of testimony because both the conspirators and the victims bear witness in it. Panh is a witness, as is the film's audience—a very different thing. Yet the two are often conflated. For instance, the media studies scholar Annette Hamilton calls Panh's oeuvre a "cinema of witness."[115] In a similar vein, the Washington Post writer Ann Hornaday commends Panh for knowing that the "proper role of an artist in the face of unspeakable acts . . . is fulfilled by choosing simply to bear witness."[116] Thompson notes that Vann Nath, the painter who became the international embodiment of a Khmer Rouge survivor through Rithy Panh's lens, bore his fellow prisoners' pledge: "Whoever survives will bear witness."[117] This begs the question of what is "proper" witnessing (and invokes again Freud's "proper mourning"). Instead of a proper witnessing or mourning, I propose that ethical witnessing and mourning may not and should not end; this is a politics of vigilance. To witness may just be a single act of ingesting, observing, and it does not necessarily require repeated moral action. Bearing witness requires agency and responsibility. To witness is merely to be a voyeur, but to bear witness requires an ethical framework.[118] To bear witness is a social act; to simply witness is not.

Testimonies and testimonials are social acts; they require witnesses. The psychoanalyst Dori Laub writes, "For the testimonial process to take place, there needs to be a bonding, the intimate and total presence of an *other*—in the position of one who hears."[119] In a sense, this other "who hears" is the dialogue initiated by Panh between inmates and captors. The former inmates and their captors bear witness for one another. The other who hears is also the filmmaker and his implicit audience. The guards' reenactments are testimonies, just as Vann's paintings are testimonies. His paintings appeared in 2000 in the landmark exhibition *The Legacy of Absence: A*

What Remains

Cambodian Story at Reyum Gallery in Phnom Penh. Works by a total of seven Khmer artists were shown, with various approaches to "bearing witness."[120] The curators, the artist Ly Daravuth and the art historian Indrid Muan, who founded Reyum Gallery, pointed out that refusing to testify is also a means of dealing with the past.[121]

Works that engage testimonies, however, are also marked by silence, refusals. Silence belies knowledge as well as voids. These testimonies are a form of grieving, but to follow Eng and Kazanjian's formulation about loss as a productive space, what is gained? Perhaps in this return Vann can better understand his torturers, and vice versa. And the audience can better understand the whole situation. But to what ends? For compassion, for healing, or for justice?

Thompson suggests that Vann Nath received international attention through *S-21* because, as a witness, he "stands up for himself, he stands up to the Khmer Rouge and to the painful past. In this action, he stands, at once, out from and in for the millions of Cambodians who suffered under Khmer Rouge rule."[122] In contrast to expected ideas of testimonial standing up for oneself, Thompson argues that Vann is actually at once "resolved and resigned."[123] I have argued against an enunciatory politics of voice ("stand up for") and for a poetics of silence. Thompson states that the confrontation between survivors and conspirators belies a Buddhist Khmer cosmology, which reframes silence, justice, and action. She writes, "To what extent self-affirmation is expressed through 'standing' in a Cambodian context remains a question for me, as does the very import of the notion of self-affirmation. If the Buddha is to be taken as a model for dignified behavior—and in Cambodia he frequently is, implicitly or explicitly—any challenge to affirm the self would likely be met with unmoved *silence*. We do not, in fact see Vann Nath stand."[124] Whether we valorize those who "take a stand" or celebrate sit-ins, these models of self-affirmative politics may be at odds with culturally specific concepts of the self as empty or of silence as both passive and proactive response.[125] Thompson further argues that Vann Nath's "artistic power was profoundly Buddhist. . . . [His self-mastery] served to efface the ego, or to more precisely put [it], to eliminate attachment to the self as a psycho-material reality." Instead of seeing control over oneself as enunciation, a proclamation, it is an erasure. Hence, Vann's "self-affirmation went hand in hand with exemplary retreat."[126] Instead of forwarding a political agenda and proclaiming an identity, there is an evacuation.

To claim that loss and trauma are productive, generative spaces (to use Scarry's framework) is to follow a teleological model of progress and growth.

These frameworks hinge on the assumption that there is a "moving beyond" to the next stage, that "healing" may help instigate growth. But for melancholics, there is no such thing as productive, conclusive mourning, only a perpetual grief, a continual return to the site of trauma. As postcolonial scholars have argued, notions of progress and growth are all relative. Modernity itself also is a traumatic process, a site of loss and trauma. Development and transition leave wounds.

The melancholic's obsession with his or her wound mirrors the (post)modern's obsession with development. The melancholic's gaze is fixed on the past, whereas the (post)modern's gaze is steadfastly locked on the future. Underlying both obsessions is fixity: both inhabit the present but are mired in another moment in time and space, stuck. The postmodern melancholic demands an audience: the pain he or she has endured (because of historical trauma, because of the shocks of modernization) is real. The postmodern melancholic is caught in an endless loop, waiting a long time for an other to witness his or her suffering, to hear.

Laub observes, "Testimonies are not monologues; they cannot take place in solitude. The witnesses are talking to *somebody*: somebody they have been waiting for a long long time."[127] Indeed, it has been a long time. The empty rooms in Panh's film stare blankly through the decades of denial and silence following the Pol Pot regime. It has taken about forty years for justice to attempt to intervene. The hybrid tribunal has cost more than $300 million. It is marred with allegations of corruption, which, Human Rights Watch notes, have not been sufficiently addressed by the tribunal: "Ongoing political interference by the Cambodian government in the work of the Khmer Rouge tribunal . . . seriously undermined the court's integrity, independence, and credibility."[128] Corruption is a fact of life in Cambodia. Indeed, Transparency International reports that Cambodia is seen as the most corrupt country in Southeast Asia and one of the most corrupt in the world.[129]

Allegations suggest that interference with the tribunal goes up to the highest levels, to Prime Minister Hun Sen, a former Khmer Rouge leader.[130] In repeated national forums, Hun Sen expressed his "concern" about national stability, warning that another civil war could break out again if the tribunals continue, essentially demanding that the tribunal not call any leaders beyond the five who have been detained thus far. Pen Sovann disputed Hun Sen's prediction in an interview with Cambodian newspaper *Khmer Machas Srok*.[131] A former Khmer Rouge propaganda official who defected, then served as prime minister of the Hanoi-backed PRK for almost six months of its ten-year existence, he called Hun Sen's claim a "personal opinion" based on the prime minister's desire to "protect persons of the former the Khmer Rouge Regime."[132] Today, people associated with the Khmer Rouge and those the regime tortured are both invisible. As films such as *S-21* suggest, only scratching the surface of their ordinary lives reveals their part in history.

Panh sees scratching the surface to reveal complicity within the Khmer Rouge machinery as a step toward acknowledging the past. Coincidentally, I interviewed Panh on the day the United Nations tribunal announced its first sentence. Kaing Guek Eav, known as Duch, was a mid-level leader but the head of Tuol Sleng prison and the first Khmer Rouge brought to trial.[133] His conviction was the first significant verdict of the tribunal, but the announcement that he would serve thirty-five years and that his sixteen years of imprisonment prior to sentencing would be part of that number disappointed many observers. Many people in the courtroom and overcrowded public gallery wept. Duch, who turned sixty-seven in 2011, is said to have overseen seventeen thousand deaths at Tuol Sleng. Unlike some other cadres, Duch expressed remorse; in November 2009 he stated in court, "I am psychologically accountable to the entire Cambodian population for the souls of those who perished. . . . I am deeply remorseful and profoundly affected by destruction on such a mind-boggling scale."[134] However, he also maintained—like so many of his colleagues—that he was merely a "cog in a running machine" and had made a naïve choice.[135] Prosecutors maintained that he was responsible for devising many of the torture techniques used to extract "confessions" from S-21's inmates. He countered that he was also a victim: "I was completely terrified at this destruction, but I just did not know what I could do about it. The only option available to me was to devise a proper interrogation tactic."[136] The Tuol Sleng Genocide Museum is a gruesome display of these "proper" interrogation tactics—ghastly spectacles of rusted metal and dried blood.

Panh's films have been instrumental in focusing international attention on the Cambodian genocide and in getting the tribunal started. *S-21* premiered at the 2003 Cannes Film Festival, winning the Prix François Chalais. It also received best documentary honors at the European Film Awards, the Valladolid International Film Festival, and the Chicago International Film Festival, among other international awards. The Khmer Rouge leader Khieu Samphan—who succeeded Pol Pot as Khmer Rouge intellectual head (chief ideologist) when the latter became Cambodian prime minister in 1976—claimed during his November 2007 pretrial hearing that he first learned about his regime's atrocities on viewing Panh's film in 2003.[137] Second in command to Pol Pot, Khieu Samphan accepted no accountability for crimes committed, but acknowledged that there was a scheme for the mass killings and that Tuol Sleng existed because of the facts presented in the film. He had publicly denied both points for decades, including in his 2004 memoir.[138]

Khieu Samphan's example shows that the film bears witness, providing irrefutable evidence of genocide despite denials. The documentary medium can have an immediate visceral impact; it can point and say, "Look there, this happened." Panh recognized the importance of this at the outset; as he told me, many people in Cambodia don't believe the genocide occurred: "Some young people don't think the genocide happened; no one tells them about it, usually none of their family members. They say, 'There is no evidence.' They see the film, and then say, 'I believe.'" Seventy percent of Cambodians were born after the Khmer Rouge's fall from power. While the film's audience has largely been an international one, Cambodians increasingly see it. The tribunal has driven this to an extent. Yet distribution channels in Cambodia remain limited. The highly regulated television channels in Cambodia will not air it. I have been unable to find a pirated DVD of it inside the country among the thousands of pirated Hollywood DVDs and politically charged documentaries on sale in local markets, DVD stores, and malls. The presence of *Burma VJ*, which depicts protests in Burma by monks in 2007, in these outlets suggests an appetite for documentaries that would surely be larger for *S-21*, given its local relevance.[139] It has been screened in the country on rare occasions. The Bophana Audiovisual Center in Phnom Penh, a non-profit resource center cofounded by Rithy Panh, showed it on International Human Rights Day in 2014. The projection room at the Bophana Center can seat about forty at maximum capacity; at most screenings there are approximately twenty people—mostly a mix of expatriates and local Khmer high school and college students. International film festivals, special screenings in urban Cambodia, and accessing the Bophana Center archives in person are the only other way to see *S-21* in the country.

Surveys show the suppression has been successful. In January 2009, the Human Rights Center University of California at Berkeley reported that 85 percent of Cambodians had little or no knowledge of Duch's trial. Yet Youk Chhang, director of the Documentation Center of Cambodia, suggests this will change, saying the tribunals will "spark" interest and that "the whole country [has become] aware" because of the release of a textbook and classroom education on the period of the genocide.[140] More than twenty-eight thousand people attended Duch's trial at the Extraordinary Chambers in the Courts of Cambodia (ECCC), the official name of the tribunal, and millions feverishly tracked the trial on television, radio, and newspapers in Cambodia in 2011. Through mass media, what was unknown or willfully forgotten is now unearthed, remembered.

For local and diasporic Cambodian audiences, as well as for international viewers, *S-21* serves as a reminder that horrific events happened, a way not to forget. As a pedagogical tool, the film unspools the past that was hidden in Cambodia. For those who are already familiar with the events, it puts a contemporary face (literally) on those who remain, reminding the viewer that past is still present. Yet Panh notes, "Documentary is subjective; it is not fact. Many still cannot believe this happened. They cannot imagine the Khmer Rouge time."[141] While *S-21* works as a pedagogical and testimonial tool, Panh's approach is not overly didactic but evocative. Still, it is clear that Panh's agenda is a political one; he aims to preserve cultural memory and seek justice.

Referring to the Duch verdict, Panh said, with a tinge of sad irony, "Until today we didn't know who is perpetrator, who is victim. We just learned officially today that Duch [was] a perpetrator and the commander of S-21."[142] What he meant was that, before the verdict, there was no official recognition of the crimes by the Cambodian government or any other nation, apart from the Tuol Sleng Genocide Museum first established by Việt Nam, discussed earlier in the chapter. Acknowledging Duch's "shocking and heinous crimes" on February 3, 2012, the UN-backed war crimes tribunal extended his sentence to lifetime in prison, with no chance for appeal.[143] On September 2, 2020, after ten years in prison, Duch died at seventy-seven years old in a Phnom Penh hospital of a lung disease.[144] The end of Duch's life and the conclusion of the tribunal, however, will not provide resolution for Khmer people.

The tribunal is nonetheless significant. Chum Mey, the other survivor featured in *S-21*, proclaimed in an interview during Duch's trial, "I cry every night. Every time I hear people talk about the Khmer Rouge it reminds me of my wife and children." As we learn in the documentary, he lost his entire family during the genocide. He often visits the former prison. As he says, "I come every day to tell the world the truth about the Tuol Sleng prison . . . so that none of these crimes are ever repeated anywhere in the world."[145] While this may seem like a positive sequel to devastating losses, he is still a melancholic, forever grieving, continually returning psychically and physically to his site of trauma. In his act of bearing witness, he is also enacting a "compulsion to repeat."

Panh echoes Chum Mey's sentiments in an essay he wrote before he filmed *S-21* entitled "Cambodia: A Wound That Will Not Heal": "I lived with memories of my relatives, with the anxiety—the certainty—that the same tragic story would repeat itself."[146] Perhaps Panh, too—as "productively" as he has dealt with loss—is a melancholic. It is telling that Panh's article names the wound that will *not* heal as Cambodia, a country, a people. The melancholic will not heal from his wounds. Both Panh and Chum Mey are concerned that these tragedies will *repeat*. Panh is certain that "the same tragic story" will recur while Chum Mey is committed to preventing similar crimes from reoccurring "anywhere in the world." Again, the obsession with repetition, the repetition compulsion—the constant return, the constant grief—marks the delay of mourning.

Even though Panh's earlier statements imply that a level of healing and mourning has taken place because of his subjects' involvement in the film (as well as for the varied audiences of the film); the film itself does not attempt to depict any resolution or reconciliation. The film's subjects may have "changed," according to Panh, but we do not know whether for better or for worse. Both torturers and survivors are presented in the film as melancholics to the rest of the world. For viewers of the film who identify with the survivors, there has been a "bonding" (to use Laub's terminology) or a sense of recognition. It is the film that serves as "the other who hears." As I have argued, the film serves a testimonial function. These viewers/survivors are finally able to talk about their experiences, but that may not necessarily be the path to effective mourning. I would venture to say that the only ones who are able to "mourn"—following Freud's framing—are the members of the international audience (but not the filmmaker) who have the luxury of safe emotional, psychological, and physical distance from the subject matter. The "lost" object/subject for these viewers, including me, is not directly experienced as "real." It is a representation that points at the lack of representation. Perhaps it is not even mourning that occurs but, rather, pity or, at best, empathy.

The final scene of *S-21* features an old, empty classroom—a blank gaze, a hollow wound, now familiar, its victims gone. Also gone are the guards, whose long, lonely shadows filled the hallways and whose voices echoed in the chambers. The camera is low to the ground, unmoving; an eddy of dust fills the air. Once again silence and void. As with other moments in the documentary, this absence makes its presence keenly felt, a mute witness. After returns and confrontations, only ashes remain.

Justice and Just Memory

What remains for the subjects and viewers of *S-21* and *Refugee* are memories—memories mediated through institutions such as film festivals, academia, and legal structures. Asian American studies and postcolonial scholars ask, Which memories get reinscribed, and toward what ends? Việt Thanh Nguyễn argues for a "just memory," an ethics of representation that neither valorizes state agendas nor pities wartime victims and postwar generations. An "unjust memory," by contrast, "limit[s] empathy and compassion to those just like us" and "terminate[s] empathy and compassion for others."[147] In short, this ethical memory holds all participants of war accountable and complicit, although certain national cultural "war machines" (such as the United States) have more global influence.

I maintain that the oscillation and ambivalence of return engagements exceed ideas of limit. I evoke both the *supplément* (addition, replacement) and the "melancholic excess" discussed earlier in this chapter, uncontained by psychoanalytic frames of pathological loss.[148] This "madness" (to borrow from Derrida) challenges the narrative and representational tropes demanded by memory work. In Derrida's later works, true forgiving, mourning, hospitality, and gift giving are at once possible and impossible aporia—all hinged on irrationality, madness.

A just memory entails an endless, unjust forgetting. As justice is blind, just memory itself may also be blind to its goals. To render is to omit. In *Memoirs of the Blind*, Derrida observes that, in attempting to draw an image (literal and metaphorical), traces of all other images are conjured: the "memory," "history," and "story" of all past, present, and future images. Thus, just memory is a drawing, or a redrawing, a trace of genocide sites and memories in all of its potential possibilities. This *tracé* comprises insight and blindness: recognition and ruin, the possible good and its impossibility. Derrida observes, "The *just* measure of 'restoring' or 'rendering' is impossible—or infinite. Restoring or rendering is the cause of the dead, the cause of deaths, the cause of a death given or requested."[149] Việt Thanh Nguyễn notes that Southeast Asian American writers and artists fall within multiculturalist narratives of grudging American acceptance and are expected to make work as witnesses to war—frames that delimit their possible output. Yet these frameworks could be without boundaries. He instead argues for an "alternative" and "complex ethics of memory" composed of a "just memory that strives both remember one's own and others."[150] To remember "one's own," it is vital to engage with others unjustly forgotten. The dialectic of just memory and forgetting includes expanding "the definition of who is on one's side to include ever more others."[151] This is humanity, equanimity writ large. But how do we inscribe our wishes, prayers?

Derrida notes that all writing is *sous rature*—under erasure, bearing the trace of all other texts (just as drawing bears the stain of all other imagery).

I parallel this with Yến Lê Espiritu's observation that Vietnamese refugees bear the mark of all others displaced: "As you trace their lives, other erased histories will become visible, like the history of US colonialism."[152] Likewise, Schlund-Vials champions a juridical activism discussed at the beginning of this chapter—and recuperative visibility—traumas traced through cultural production. Schlund-Vials observes that Cambodian American artists "take on the responsibility of reassembling—or recollecting—communal memory without the luxury of justice at the level of the nation state."[153] Thus, artists can reenvisage justice, beyond legislative limits. I underscore the urgent claims of Espiritu, V. T. Nguyễn, and Schlund-Vials that agency, in all of its memorializing messiness, can lie within the hands of cultural producers and their communities.

As Nguyễn, Schlund-Vials, and Espiritu, among other Asian American and postcolonial scholars, simultaneously question and seek to *restore and render*, I argue (following Derrida) that these frames of visibility may be blinders, offering limited sight and insight. "Just" measures—and just memories—are both "infinite" and "impossible" as they reinforce *and* undermine structures of violence, pathways of seeing and telling. This pathway is both literal and metaphorical: one-way displacements without return. Even with a return to the site of trauma or one's homeland, the initial displacement—the site of loss—figures most prominently. As global North multiculturalist identity politics has shown, recuperative, additive models tell the same stories, only slant. Following Rey Chow, Việt Thanh Nguyễn keenly notes that, within identity politics, the minoritarian Other is both "idealized and victimized."[154] Such adherence to adding "just" stories and images only grounds more social deaths, as these postcolonial and critical refugee studies scholars also warn.

"Return engagements" calls for micro- and macro-level perspectives. As outlined earlier, a revolution, a cycle, a revolt calls for things becoming off-balance, a disequilibrium in which positions are overturned again and again over the long term, not just now. The concept of "just memory" invokes justice as well as connotations of the word "just": balance and fairness; swiftness; recentness ("just now"). The term *just* also invokes "only," as in just enough. Yet "just memory" also draws "attention to the lifecycle of memories and their industrial production, how they are fashioned and forgotten, how they evolve and change."[155] Art, as cultural artifacts, trace competing geopolitical imaginations over time.

To read culture as text, however, without institutional context, is not enough. Việt Thanh Nguyễn observes that national "industries of memory" (e.g., Hollywood films, Khmer and Vietnamese trauma tourist sites) are still powerful. To this cultural-industrial complex I add museums, galleries, artist-run spaces, and foreign embassies and their attendant cultural spaces and programs. Yet transnational exhibitions and venues have differing frameworks on what constitutes the global, national, and regional. To attend to these transregional nuances, sociological and anthropological approaches supplement how the critic reads these spaces and narratives. Yet to apply largely sociological lenses to interpret movement of bodies—as Espiritu does—is also not fully just, not enough to encompass the range of metaphorical possibilities and futures envisaged by cultural production. Largely absent from these analyses is a deft grasp of visual culture, which combines sociopolitical, economic, and aesthetic (and art-history) considerations.

Forwarding an ethical stance grounded in the past, or recapitulating memories (just memory), reinscribes teleological damage. Presentist attempts to "restore" and "render," redress, past wounds demand infinite remediation. A critical fixity on trauma and its sites (whether refugees, trauma tourism, or mass media) is a melancholic position. As Freud, Cheng, and others suggest, melancholia is driven by compulsion, individual or structural. Return engagements and eternal returns (Nietzsche), however, are driven by choice. Citing Laub, Schlund-Vials states that "yet another repetition of the experience of separation and loss . . . allows perhaps a certain repossession of it."[156] Whereas possession conjures involuntary seizure (physically or by a spirit), this "repossession" reevaluates and reanimates the terms of loss. Likewise, Eng and Kazanjian note that the "politics of mourning might be . . . *animated* for hopeful and hopeless politics."[157] Here I want to underscore the uncanny connections between animate (alive) and inanimate (deceased); self-possession and spiritual possession (losing oneself); and political choice—hopeful and hapless.

Spencer Nakasako's *Refugee*

After the ashes of the Việt Nam War settled, a different set of confrontations ensued as Southeast Asian refugees "returned" to the heart of Western empire, as Espiritu observes, without real choice.[158] In the 1980s, an influx of Southeast Asian refugees resettled in America, displaced by violence in their own countries. In the Reagan era, against the Cold War backdrop of anti-immigrant and anti-Asian sentiment, Spencer Nakasako sought to give voice to these diverse communities. He founded the Media Lab at the Vietnamese Youth Development Center in the Tenderloin District of San Francisco and worked with disadvantaged Southeast Asian youth in the Bay Area to document their lives for seventeen years. Currently, Nakasako teaches documentary film courses in the Journalism Department at the University of California, Berkeley.[159] His documentaries have been screened widely at national film festivals, within and outside Asian American contexts. His workshops and collaborations have yielded several documentary projects—notably, *A.K.A. Don Bonus*, a Cambodian teenager's video diary about his coming-of-age struggles (which won a National Emmy award), and *Kelly Loves Tony*, an Iu Mien refugee couple's video diary about love and young adulthood in Oakland. Mike Siv, the protagonist of *Refugee*, a college student and coach for an afterschool youth basketball program, proposed to Nakasako that he lead a summer video workshop for Siv's students; the partnership led to the documentary. Nakasako and Siv worked together to edit the final film.[160]

Many Cambodians were displaced several times: first by the US bombings in which many fled to Phnom Penh, then the evacuation of Phnom Penh by the CPK, and then, finally, escape and resettlement in other countries. Although Khmer refugees arrived in the United States after the fall of Cambodia in 1975, the decline of the Khmer Rouge in 1979 marked the mass migration to America. The biggest wave of immigrants came in the 1980s, when 114,064 refugees were admitted, according to the US Citizenship and Immigration Services.[161] According to 2017 data from the Pew Research Center, there are approximately 330,000 Cambodian Americans, up from 206,052 in 2000.[162] To put this in a larger context, there are 14.7 million people of Asian heritage in the United States, of whom 3.3 million are Chinese, according to the 2010 US Census. Vietnamese are the fourth-largest community, at 1.5 million. The largest Khmer American community in the United States is in Long Beach, California (50,000), followed by Lowell and Lynn, Massachusetts.[163] Cambodian Americans are a comparatively small segment of Asian America.

For many Khmer immigrants, the cultural and psychological adjustments were difficult, at best, partly because of different conceptions of social regulation, different articulations of biopower. In *Buddha Is Hiding: Refugees, Citizenship, and the New America*, the anthropologist Aihwa Ong examines Cambodian communities in America (mainly Oakland and San Francisco) and how citizenship, race, and cultural and political structural differences affected these new immigrants.[164]

The refugee, the immigrant, and the exile are eternal outsiders within the matrix of freedom, liberty, and citizenship that rhetorically embraces but realistically excludes and occludes difference, producing grieving subjects. In *The Melancholy of Race: Psychoanalysis, Assimilation, and Hidden Grief*, the literary theorist Anne Cheng notes that histories of socioeconomic exclusion become real and psychic loss.[165] Hence, Cambodian refugees grapple for survival and success on the outskirts of American cities and American consciousness.

Refugee introduces us to Mike Siv and his friends within the context of the urban ethnic ghetto of the Tenderloin and within the larger marginalization of Cambodians. In an early scene, Mike seems to think the return will be fun: "Me and my homies, David and Paul, we're going to Cambodia. We'll see the sights, visit family, have some fun." But all parties know that this will be an emotionally difficult journey. This site of return is a liminal space, an in-between state. David and Paul were born in the States and have never visited Cambodia; Mike fled as a young child and has never returned. Their connection to Cambodia is a psychic one. Their only memories of Cambodia are mediated: family stories and photographs, popular songs, films—cultural artifacts. The political scientist Khatharya Um observes, "Diaspora is thus a site inhabited simultaneously by continuities and discontinuities—ghosts, memory fragments, interruptions, and contradictions."[166] Mike and his friends grew up with this sense of disjointedness, which they hope their trip will help reconcile.

Mike remembers the transition to America, the liminal space of transit, a dead zone of despair and desire. His earliest memory is of coming off a plane. Trying to remember "as far back" as he can, he realizes his only connection to Cambodia is a tenuous one. He also wants to make connections to another tenuous relationship—the one with his absent father. These are both sites of lack and loss, the nonexistent relationship with one's country of origin, the missing father.

Even though the journey the film depicts is Mike's first physical return, he has returned to the site of loss many times before that. As he tells his father, tenderly and bitterly, "Every day, for twenty years, I thought about you, about what it's like to have a dad." Mike occupies the position of the melancholic several times over, caught in an endless cycle of mourning—for a lost but living father, for a living but lost country. He also experiences what Anne Cheng calls "hidden grief" over living in a country where he feels displaced, lost. As Cheng notes, socioeconomic exclusion becomes real and psychic loss. Mike's constant return to the site of familial trauma and lack fuels a repetition compulsion, marking a constant loss—*every day, I thought about you*. His statement is also a testimonial. *The witness has been waiting for this moment for a long, long time.* He meets decades of silence. Later on, we learn that the truth about his father's life in Cambodia has been shrouded in silence; similarly, stories about the lives lost in Cambodia have been silenced. In a way, the loss of the father—in real and symbolic terms—is the loss of *logos*, of law in a Derridean sense.[167] Mike's relationship with his father becomes metonymic for his relationship with his homeland—it was the very loss of law, the displacement of order, the failure of language that caused the original traumatic separation from both father and fatherland. Yet as Eng and Kazanjian point out, from this melancholic loss perhaps something can be gained. The past and future become not a fixed problem but an "open question." Loss becomes not only a negative space but a creative one.

After shots of a long flight, sightseeing in Angkor Wat, and partying in Phnom Penh, Mike, David, and Paul meet their families. The scenes consist of handheld shots that give a sense of immediacy and intimacy. Speaking about the filming technique, Nakasako mentions that it involves both "subjective" and "objective" viewpoints. Mike is reunited with his father and brother first. Spotting them by sight, perhaps by the images he has seen in family photos or videos, he takes a deep breath and says, "It's my family, I know it's them." After a family banquet at the home of Mike's aunt, David meets his sister for the first time. Holding him, she cannot stop crying. "Brother, I missed you so," she wails in Khmer. *Logos*, language, loss. David cannot respond, as he forgets the little Khmer he knows. "When she gets emotional, I forget how to speak," he complains to Paul later. The failure of language. Yet it is language that allows Mike a space to engage with his family and his past. His mastery of Khmer allows Mike to bridge barriers that his friends cannot, or will not. Paul refuses to see his family until the very last day of their journey, perhaps because of the divides in language and culture. He is afraid of dealing with the emotional toll.

The audience witnesses the failure of language on multiple levels. Mike's friends find it hard to communicate in a virtually alien tongue. There are gaps in translation and cultural gaps. For Mike, David, and Paul, English is their native language, and Khmer is a foreign language. They struggle. This lack of facility with Khmer further contributes to their liminal position, as second-generation refugees, between countries and cultures. Another failure of language is the Derridean one in which even mastery cannot overcome language's inherent lack. In this case, there is always a void, a gap. Meaning is not fixed; language is ultimately an insufficient means of communication.

David's sister is struggling to survive in Cambodia. David says off-screen, "I knew they weren't well off, but I didn't know it was like this. They live

97

beneath someone's house. They don't even have walls." His mother has given him $1,000 to give to his sister to build a new house. Although Mike, David, and Paul are impoverished by American standards, they are struck by the level of subsistence in rural Cambodia. Poverty and dirt.

Mike Siv's younger half-brother Nang, who grew up with their father in Cambodia, stays with him in a hotel. Paul catches them both on-camera waking from an afternoon nap as he enters the room. The wide panning shot shows the brothers on twin beds in the white-tiled room. The television's white noise drones in the background. Mike asks his brother about what he thinks about staying with him. In a framed close-up, Nang grins widely and scans the room. He says, "It's a nice room and has everything you need— a fan, a refrigerator, a television." A close-up shot of the swaying white ceiling fan follows, then a quick cut to the television screen, which features a young woman singing. A medium shot shows the two brothers sitting on the edge of their beds. Nang explains, "At home there's none of these things. . . . It feels comfortable sleeping in the same room as my older brother. It feels like a dream. . . . It's more like I don't want us to be apart again." The fan whirs. No one speaks. This scene illustrates the tremendous distance between the brothers. My heart sinks when I watch this scene because of what is not expressed. The hotel is not a home; it is a temporary shelter, an in-between space. They both know they will be separated again, that this sense of home and ease is fleeting. Perhaps it is the material comfort of this space—apart from the relative poverty they each experience in Cambodia and the United States—that affords them this moment. Briefly, they are at home in the world. It is impossible to sustain. The sense of comfort is possible precisely because it is a liminal space and moment: these brothers will continue their separate lives on opposite ends of the world.

Mike Siv is immediately comfortable with his brother and his aunt, but he is still not quite at ease with his father. He hears from his aunt that the reason his father stayed behind was because he had another wife. After a family birthday party, Mike Siv confronts his father about betraying his mother, asking, "When did you meet your new wife?" Squatting on Mike's left, his father replies, "When I had to escape concentration camp, I had to go into hiding to stay alive. I heard [that] you, your mom, and Nang were all burned to death. I felt all alone and had no one to depend on. This woman helped me out; she practically helped me stay alive." Mike's voice-over states that his father learned that he and his brother and mother were still alive after es-caping from the camps after the Vietnamese invasion. His father continues, "Your mom didn't want us to separate, and she cried and cried. I told her to escape for your future. That persuaded your mom to escape." Mike stares directly at his father, silent. He looks angry. But his voice-over accedes, "His decision was right, in a way, because everyone is still alive."

The scenes in which Mike confronts his father can be read as sites of revelation and testimony. Both the father and son share what they have witnessed through the decades of separation; they want to share their losses. To quote Laub again, "Testimonies are not monologues; they cannot take place in solitude. The witnesses are talking to *somebody*: somebody they have been waiting for a long, long time." Mike's confrontations can also be read as a return to traumatic sites, a compulsive repetition, revisitation of loss.

Before he is about to leave Cambodia, Mike confronts his father again. In an upstairs room, in a medium shot, they circle each other on a mat, like wrestlers, then sit down to have a chat. Mike cuts to the chase: "I want to know why I grew up without you. Every day I thought about you and Nang and what happened to our family." The melancholic subject is ambivalent toward the lost object (or subject), simultaneously feeling love and hatred; nostalgia, guilt, and rage. The melancholic's relationship to the aggrieved is one of love and resentment. After a pause, his father responds, "I understand, but that's the way it happened. I decided for you to escape. You were too young. All I wanted was for you to be alive. The reason we're not together is because of Pol Pot and the Khmer Rouge." Clearly angry and hurt, Mike retorts, "You can blame it on the war, but if a family wants to stay together, they could. You did it with your family. Why couldn't you do it with ours? If I had to choose, back then, I'd choose to stay together. I would've chosen to stay together as a family." The camera zooms in on his father's face. His father remains silent. He cannot explain. Perhaps he does not understand, either, why they are so divided. The poverty of words. Between them is an unbridgeable gap, inconsolable grief. Their silence slices the room like the afternoon sun illuminating the room, leaving sharp shadows on their faces. The viewer does not know why the father is silent and the son, enraged. Perhaps the camera's presence interferes with any intimate communication between the two. Perhaps the father is *unwilling* to speak. Perhaps the father realizes that explaining is impossible. The camera's mediation further complicates the mediation of language. There is an act of double witnessing: the son attempts to find the "truth" that evades him. The audience witnesses the subjects creating a documentary and is also privy to the documentary medium's shortcomings. Mike attempts to engage in testimony's "double function" of initiation of recovery and social discourse. Through his act of testifying his hurt and pain to his father, he hopes to initiate recovery of years of loss.

What Remains

Through collaborating with Nakasako on the documentary, he hopes to have his experiences become part of larger discourse on Asian American (particularly Khmer American) experience and the afterlife of trauma. Yet his attempts partly falter. He cannot recover his lost father and "the years living without him" or make his sense of family complete.

Silence and void. This scene once again illustrates the failure of language. "All I wanted was for you to be alive." "I would've chosen to stay together as a family." Between the two utterances is a world of loss. The father's and his son's intentions to communicate their personal truths falter. I highlight this scene because the moment when communication and language breaks down captures the ambivalence that both protagonists embody. This moment disrupts the desire for resolution. This scene, out of all the scenes in the documentary, distills the incommensurability of experiences *not* through narration or voice-over but through simple silence. The father's shocked, sad silence, his act of refusal, encapsulates so many things in an instant. The father's expression conveys weariness, survivor's guilt, and frustration. The son looks on. The film's first-person narration primes the audience to identify with Mike. After all, the documentary is seen (sometimes literally) through his eyes. But the point of identification splits. The viewer may also more readily identify with the father and understand his choices.

In the final scene of *Refugee*, the three friends end their journey with a visit to the "killing fields." Usually boisterous and charming, the three are solemn as they look at the open mass graves. The camera pans across the wooden signs, which recount in English the number of dead executed at each plot.[168] As they pass a golden stupa, Mike's voice-over states, "Being at [the graves] and saying goodbye to Nang, I've been thinking about the idea of separation and *real* separation. My dad couldn't say he was sorry because that meant he was wrong. Because I'm his son and he wants me to be proud of him. Even though I was disappointed he wasn't the man I wanted him to be, I've got to accept that because he is my dad." Mike Siv expresses his lifetime of hurt and rage in *Refugee*. In contrast to Panh's documentary, *Refugee* features first-person narrative, a self-reflexive narrator. While Panh's masterly film *shows* the audience the effects of trauma, Mike Siv tells the audience his ambitions and disappointments. *S-21* may be more "sophisticated" in terms of its presentation and deft touch, but *Refugee* has a candid directness.

While *S-21* and *Refugee* address gaps in representation, they challenge, yet unwittingly, reinscribe certain binaries, including peace and war, First

World and Third World, and victim and perpetrator. For instance, *Refugee* presents San Francisco's Tenderloin neighborhood as a contemporary war zone, connecting it to past wars in Southeast Asia. Cambodia cannot escape the specter of its civil war. War is the reason for the Khmer diaspora's dispersal. While *S-21*'s subjects live in a time of peace, they still suffer from the effects of war. Although Vann questions the distinctions between victim and perpetrator, these categories are upheld throughout the film. In a different manner, Mike and his father both claim victimhood. Both films contrast appeals to "universal" ideals of responsibility with the particulars of Cambodian history.

Nakasako's and Panh's documentaries, as well as Vann's devastating paintings, raise the question, What is the relationship between ethics and aesthetics? In what follows, I ponder the role of academic translation, or interpretations of trauma, and of trauma texts.

Silences

In the article "Consuming Trauma; or, The Pleasures of Merely Circulating," the literary scholar Patricia Yaeger self-reflexively questions the field and the object of trauma studies.[169] She states that liberal academics exist in a dialectic between pleasure and pain: we foster and facilitate the circulation of painful narratives and concomitantly partake of the pleasurable academic economies afforded by those narratives, such as conference papers, publications, and careers. We seek the pleasures of "merely circulating" and "consuming trauma." The academic's consumption of trauma may be related to the melancholic's self-devouring. The melancholic *consumes* these conflicting feelings, feeds on himself. Academic discourse feeds on itself, is self-referential. In consuming trauma, in the feeding frenzy of traumatic narratives, there is both pleasure and pity, reverence and revulsion.

The Cambodian genocide, and historical trauma in general, has fueled a cottage industry of artists, writers, filmmakers, and academics who produce works and engage in dialogue at a reasonably comfortable remove.[170] Conferences, film festivals, publications, and art exhibitions may be "safe" spaces to engage these horrors. The very hierarchies and state policies responsible for such terror may not be effectively challenged or ever changed. The fact that an audience is more knowledgeable about an issue does not mean it will take action. Testimony and pedagogy may not be sufficient. Witnessing and bearing witness are not enough.

What Remains

Cultural productions such as *S-21* and *Refugee* function as a form of witnessing in the global North and of testimony in the global South. The editors of *Cultural Trauma and Collective Identity* argue that, through political and representational hierarchies, certain traumas and places become more legible than others.[171] But who is listening? The cultural critic Kelly Oliver notes that witnessing involves not only an empathetic response but also a deep recognition of structural injustice—beyond specific cases. Again, witnessing bears a double meaning: eyewitness and bearing witness. Oliver observes that witnessing consists of "ongoing processes of critical analysis and perpetual questioning that contextualizes and recontextualizes what we see and how we see." Moving beyond mere recognition, she urges the viewer to "witness the subjectivity of ourselves and others, which takes us beyond mere eyewitness testimony or images."[172] In this framework, witnessing is a process, not an act. Witnessing allows us to begin to comprehend complicated actions and reactions.[173]

Both *S-21* and *Refugee* present scenes of return and confrontation that mark agency, refusal, rage—responses that are highlighted by ambivalence and silences. Mike Siv's "acceptance" of his father's refusal to apologize and his ultimate disappointment just reconfirm his self-justified worldview. Mike's collaboration has assuaged his own ache, but there is no real recognition of his father's guilt and pain. In using, or perhaps cannibalizing, Mike's narrative (among other disadvantaged Southeast Asian youth), Nakasako has built a successful career as an independent filmmaker. I do not doubt Nakasako's sincerity or his intensions. *Refugee*'s audience is primarily a college-educated (or college-attending) Asian American who may consume this documentary like any other insightful cultural text. Having understood something new, the audience moves on to the next thing.

S-21 has achieved much recognition for shedding light on a period of Cambodian terror. "Local" Khmer filmmakers would not be able to get the same message about the Khmer Rouge across to the rest of the world. They do not have proper access to international networks, funding, and cultural capital. The film had to play the game of international festivals and prizes to get its message across because the distant echo of genocide was not sufficient or important enough. Finally, after decades of silence, something reverberates across the distance. The one who hears must take witness. The diasporic filmmakers had to return to their site of loss.

In the singular return, the moment of confrontation, there have already been many psychic returns, many repetitions that have preceded to make this single act possible. The return encompasses the repetition compulsion, to revisit the wound again and again. Regardless of the number of times, to return is a melancholic gesture. Lot's wife looked back and turned to salt. Both Panh and Nakasako urge us to look back, however, to return to a place we might not remember or recognize. Look again. *The witness has been waiting for this moment for a long, long time.* How does one remember Tuol Sleng, its survivors and perpetrators? What questions openly engage the future and past? What remains?

Silence remains. But silence is not a void. It is a witness. Silence is a space for contemplation, reconsideration—unutterable and unfathomable depths. Quiet depth is not death. *What are our responsibilities when we write about the dead?* In *The Work of Mourning*, a collection of essays honoring his beloved deceased friends, Derrida notes that the dead live on *in* us. We are haunted. Derrida writes, "Ghosts: the concept of the other in the same . . . the completely other, dead, living in me."[174] We are left with interiorized images. "We are speaking of images. . . . [The other] appears as the one who has disappeared or has passed away, as the one who, having passed away, leaves 'in us' only images."[175] How do we deal with these images that we have inherited? We have incorporated the corporeal. Oliver suggests that we move beyond merely recognizing these images, these ghosts. We must acknowledge the structures of injustice that produce them. We are haunted within and from outside. We see and are seen. The gaze is not one-way; it is reciprocal, yet not symmetrical. Derrida observes that there is a "dissymmetry that can be interiorized only by exceeding, fracturing, wounding, injuring, traumatizing the interiority that it inhabits or that welcomes it through hospitality, love, or friendship."[176] The images alive and dead within us—the specters that live on—must be embraced. These images live on in memory and mass media through films such as *S-21* and *Refugee*, in memorials and museums such as Tuol Sleng. Vann Nath writes in his memoir, "Nowadays there is talk about closing the Tuol Sleng Museum of Genocide. There are those who argue that this will help heal the wounds and bring our fractured nation back together. . . . However I feel very strongly that the museum should stay open. . . . [If the museum is abandoned], it means that those men, women, and children who died there were simply eliminated; that their deaths were meaningless."[177] Vann knows that the images must live on for true healing to take place. They must remain. The men, women, and children who died at Tuol Sleng are not "simply" eradicated. The dead live *in us* only in images, to echo the grief-stricken Derrida. Yet the construction of meaning and memory is a complex, uneasy task. *Why did it happen like that?* In many ways *Refugee* and *S-21* are fragments—fragmented stories, memories, lives. *We are all conspirators; we are all victims.* I am haunted by the guards' melancholic expressions; Vann's silent paintings; a father's silence; the piles of written "confessions" in thin, yellowed notebooks; the oscillating ceiling fan and flickering blue television screen in Mike and Nang's old hotel room; the bloodstains on the prison walls—what remains.

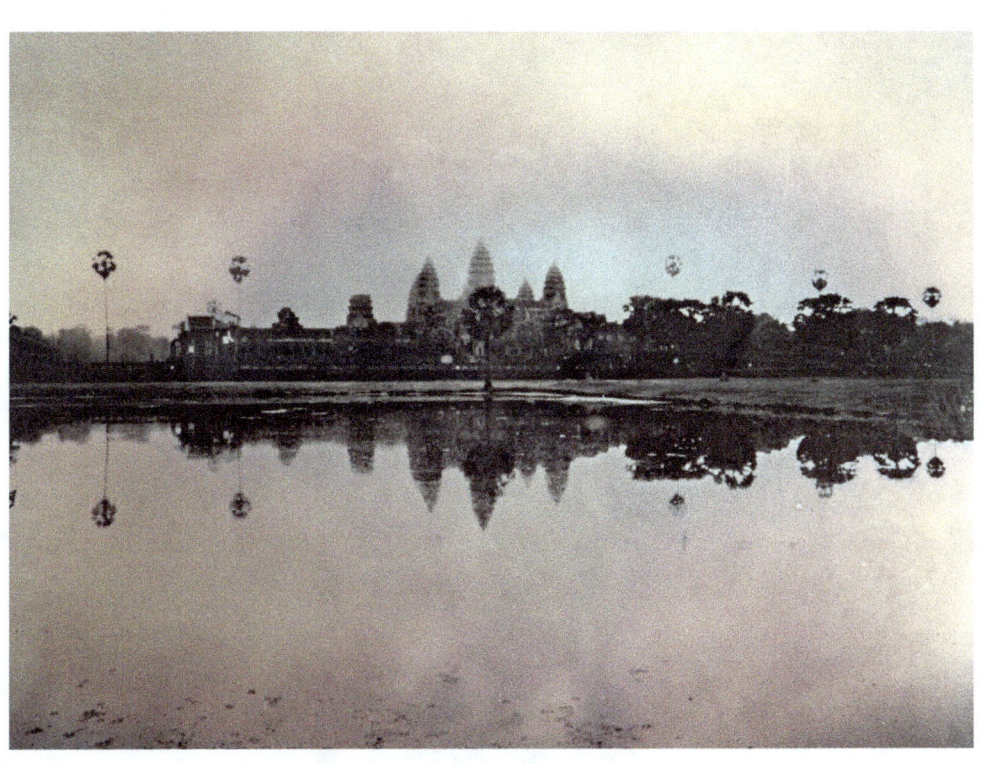

PLATE 1 Binh Danh, "Divinities of Angkor #1," 2008,
daguerreotype, 13.25 × 16 inches, from the *In the
Eclipse of Angkor* series. Courtesy of the
artist, Haines Gallery, San Francisco,
and Lisa Sette Gallery, Phoenix.

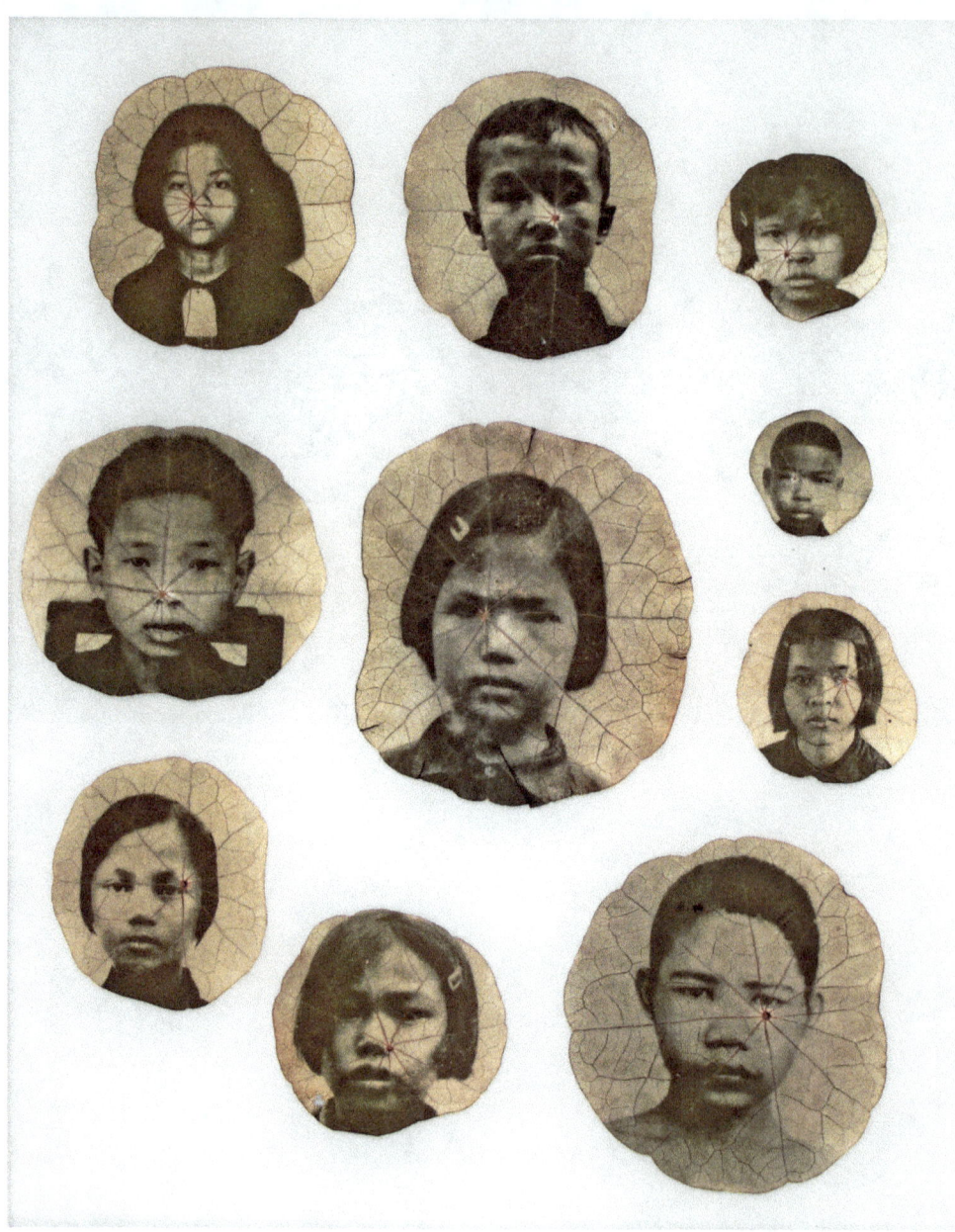

PLATE 2 Binh Danh, "Memories of Tuol Sleng Genocide Museum #1," 2008, chlorophyll print on nasturtium and resin, 12 × 10 inches, from the *In the Eclipse of Angkor* series. Courtesy of the artist, Haines Gallery, San Francisco, and Lisa Sette Gallery, Phoenix.

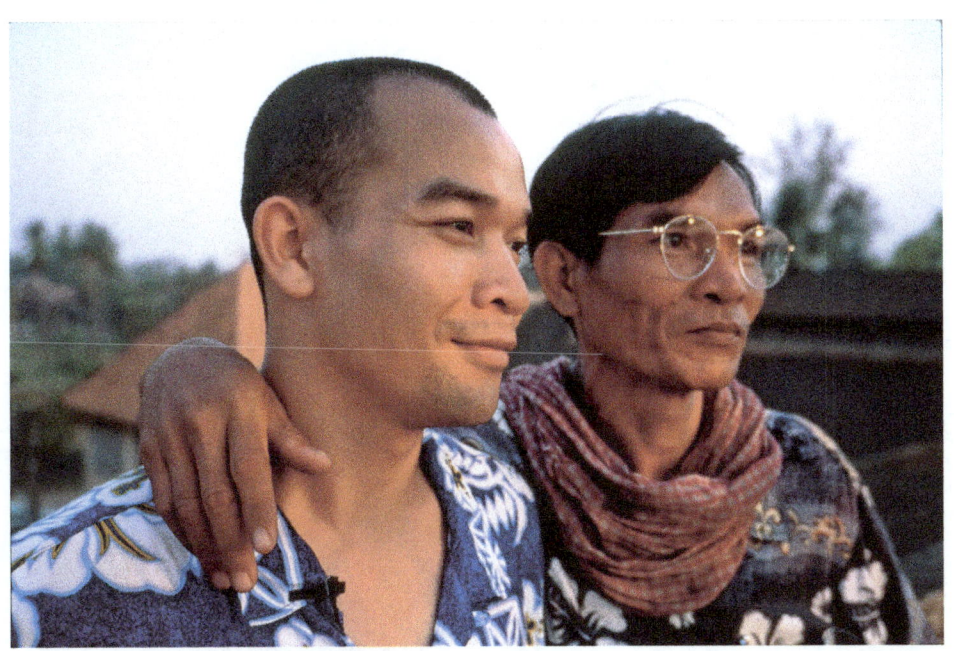

PLATE 3 Spencer Nakasako, *Refugee*,
film still of Mike Siv and his father.
Photograph by Scott Tsuchitani.
Courtesy of the filmmaker.

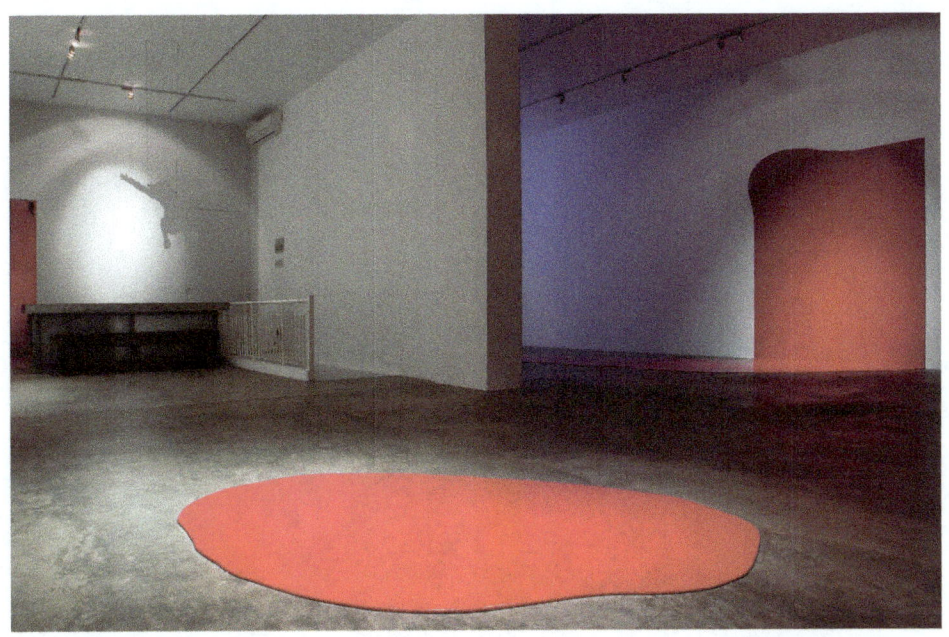

PLATE 4 Sandrine Llouqet, *Milk*, 2008,
installation view. Courtesy of Galerie
Quynh and the artist.

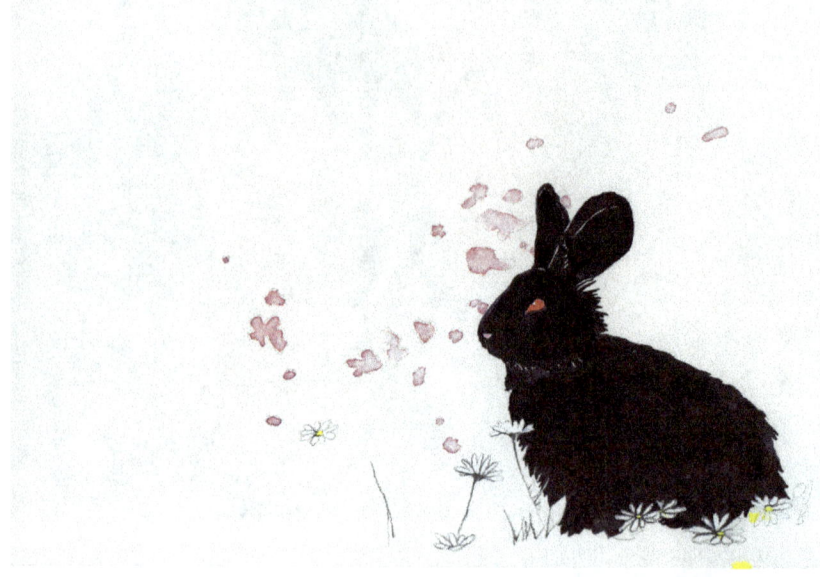

PLATE 5 Sandrine Llouquet, *Milk*, 2008, detail. Courtesy of Galerie Quynh and the artist.

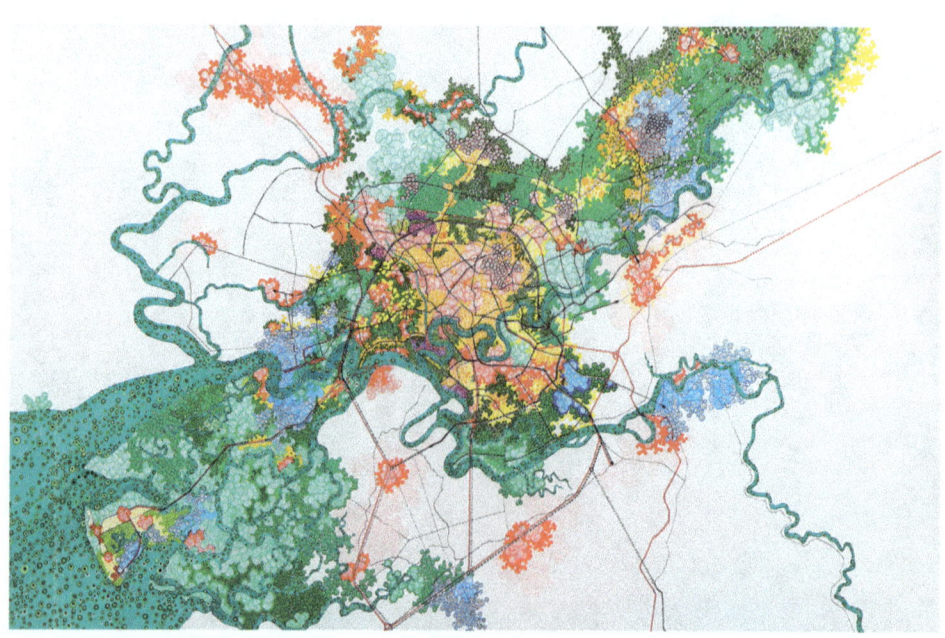

PLATE 6 Tiffany Chung, *10.75ºN 106.6667ºE 1867/2007*, 2007, oil- and alcohol-based markers on paper, 135 × 90 cm. Courtesy of the artist and Tyler Rollins Fine Art, New York.

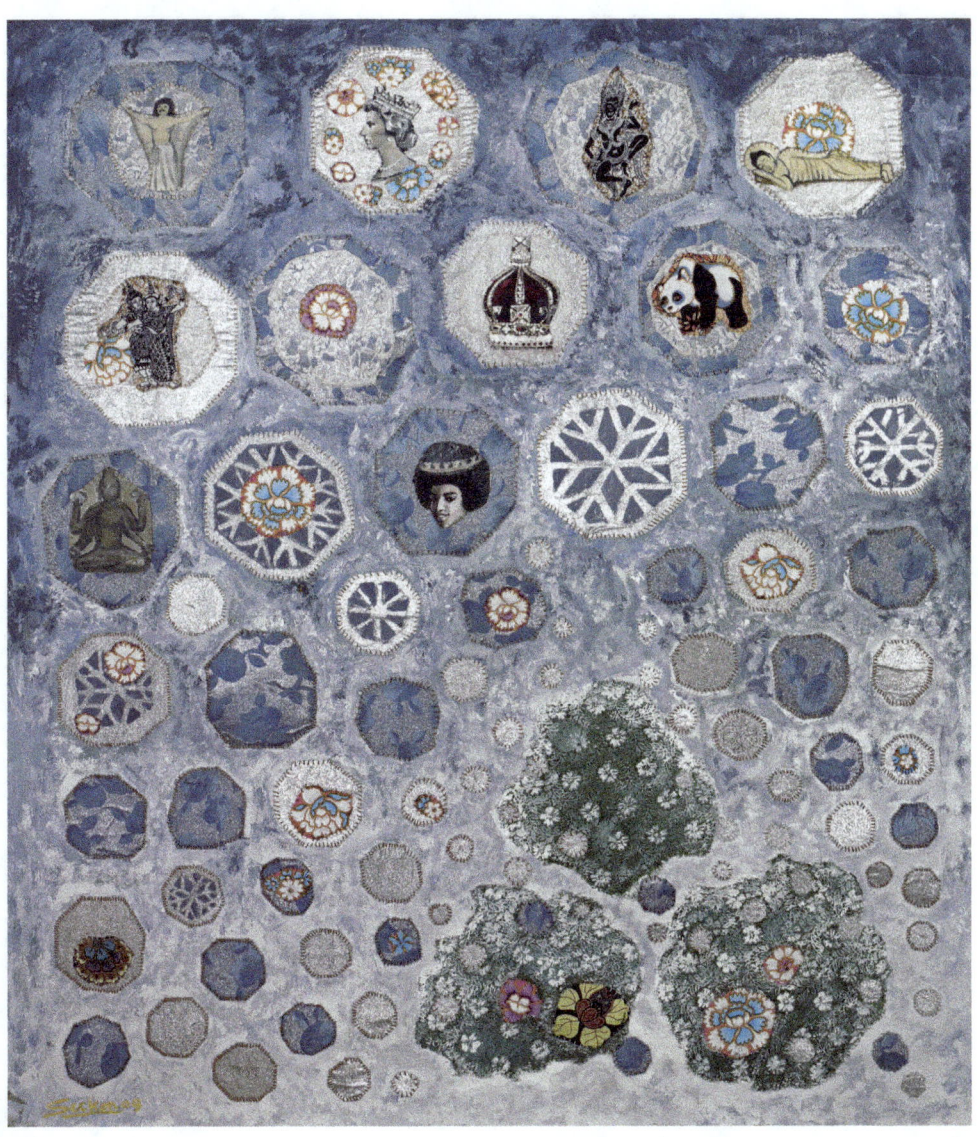

PLATE 7 Leang Seckon, "Snowflower Skirt (Somphut
Picar Brille)," 2009, mixed media on canvas,
150 × 130 cm (59 × 51 inches), from the
Heavy Skirt series. Courtesy of
Rossi & Rossi and the artist.

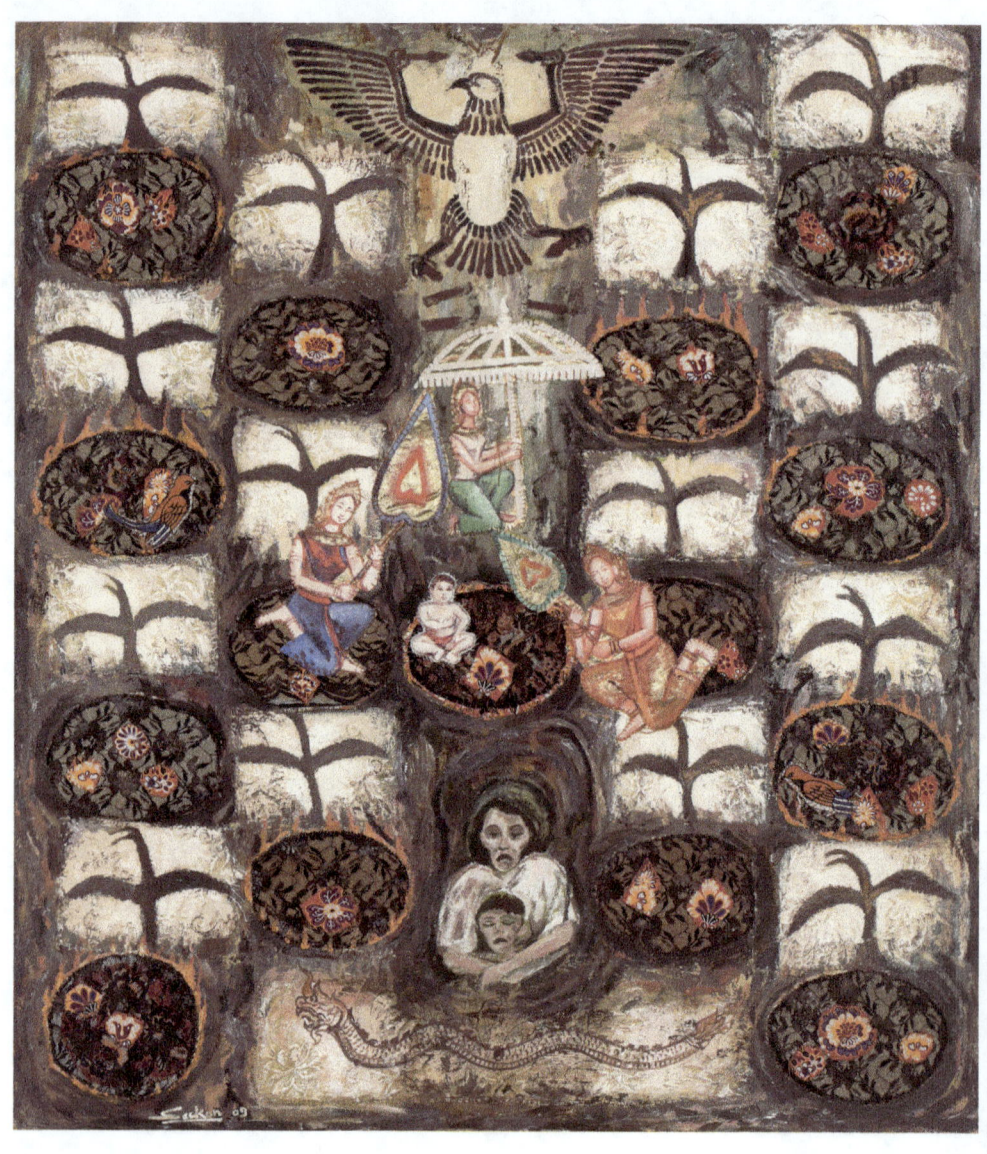

PLATE 8 Leang Seckon, "Flicking Skirt (Somphut Bohbaouey)," 2009, mixed media on canvas, 150×130 cm (59×51 inches), from the *Heavy Skirt* series. Courtesy of Rossi & Rossi and the artist.

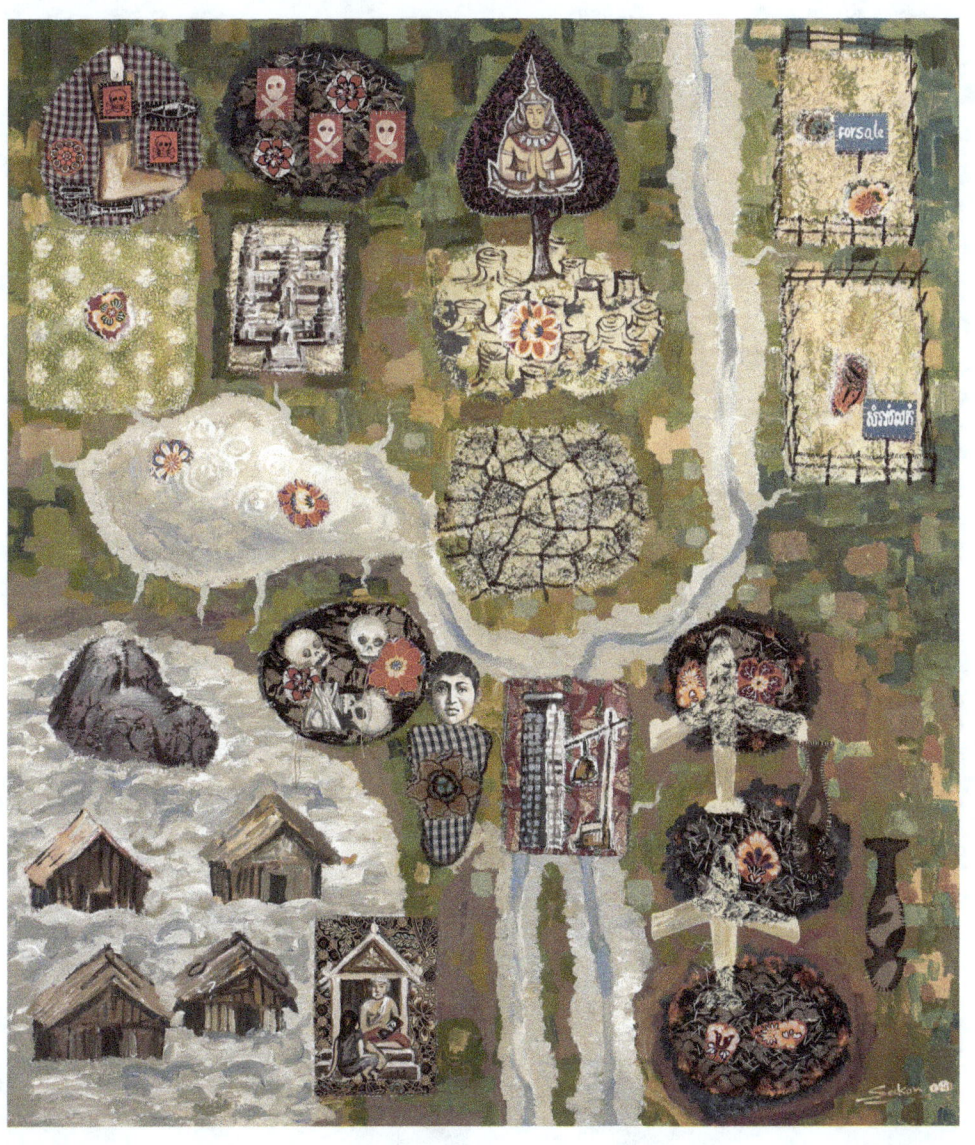

PLATE 9 Leang Seckon, "Salty Flower Skirt (Somphut Picar Ompul),"
2009, mixed media on canvas, 150 × 130 cm (59 × 51 inches), from
the *Heavy Skirt* series. Courtesy of Rossi & Rossi and the artist.

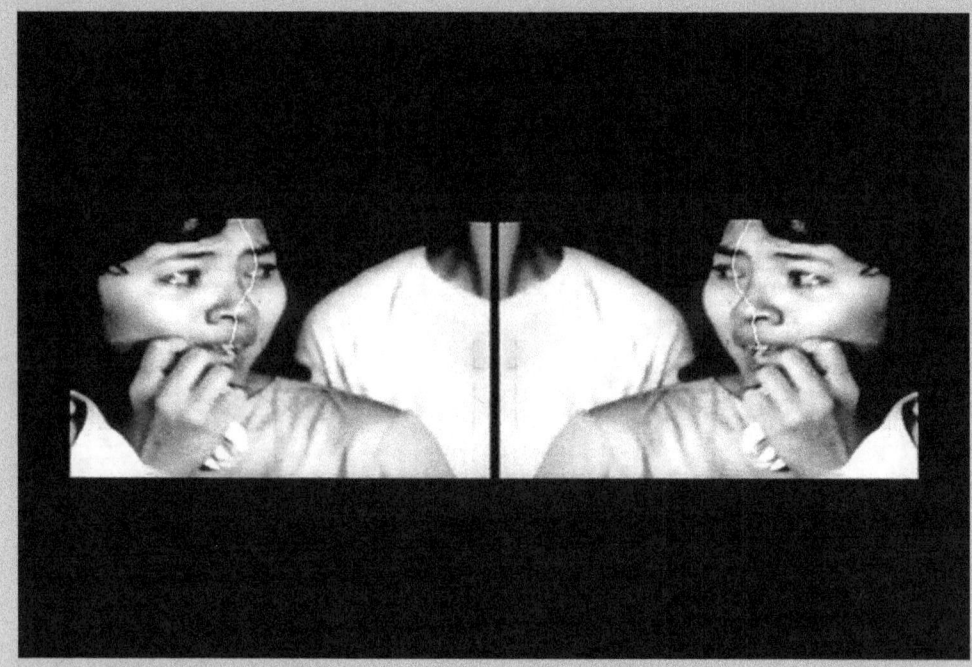

PLATE 10 Hồng-Ân Trương, "The Past Is a
Distant Colony," 2007, still image.
Courtesy of the artist.

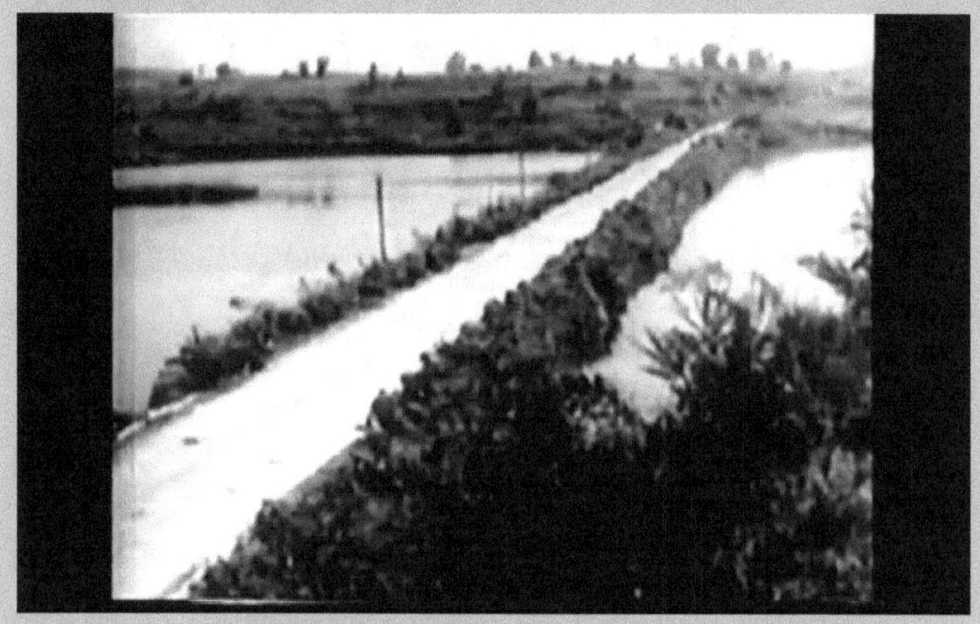

PLATE 11 Hồng-Ân Trương, "It's True because
It's Absurd," 2007, still image, *Adaptation
Fever* trilogy. Courtesy of the artist.

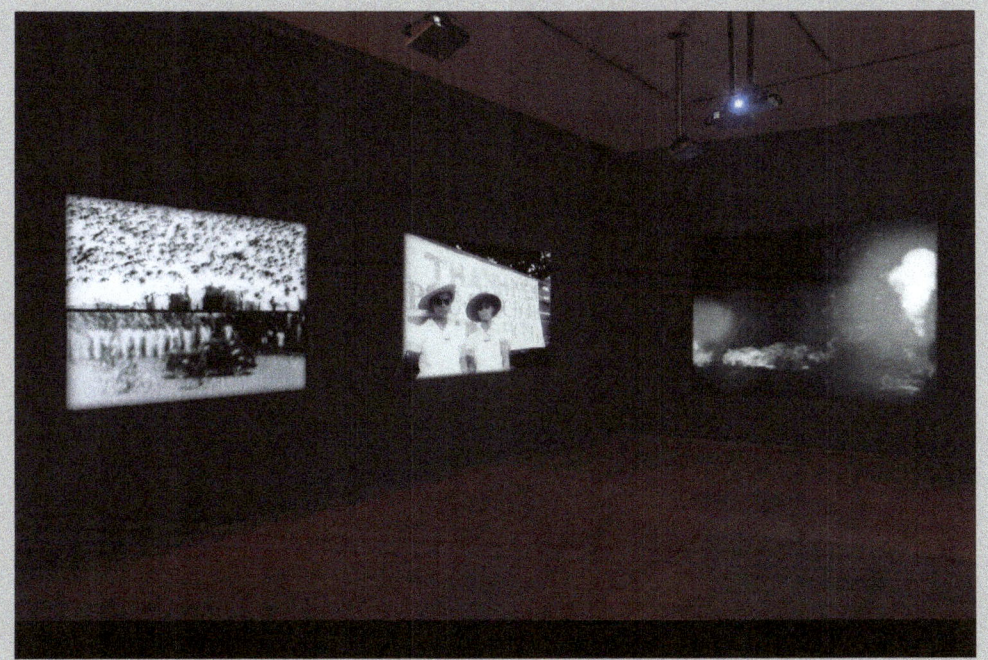

PLATE 12 Hồng-Ân Trương, *Adaptation Fever* trilogy, 2007, installation view. Courtesy of the artist.

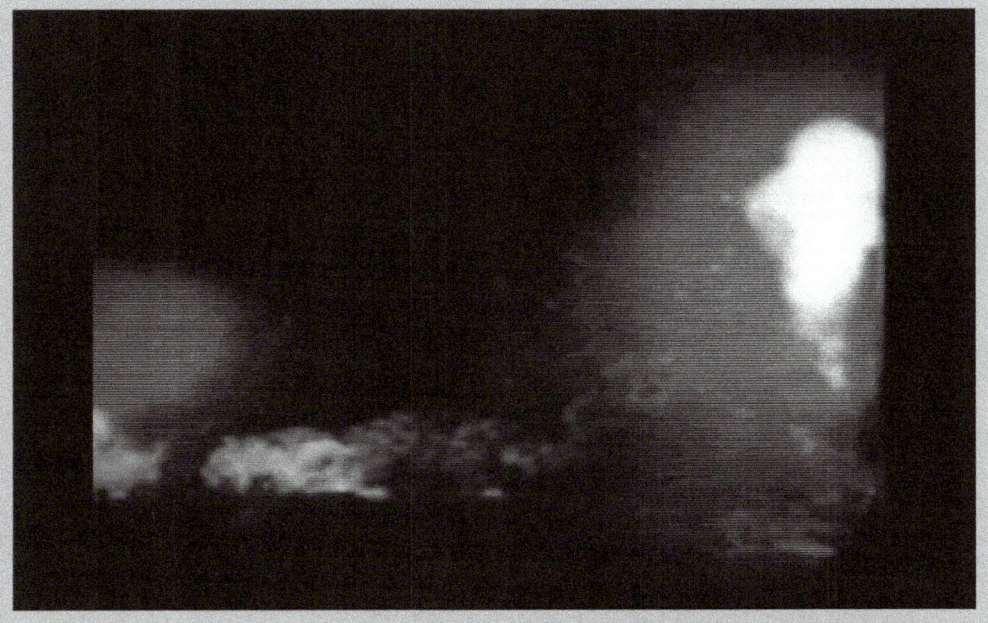

PLATE 13 Hồng-Ân Trương, "Explosions in the Sky (Diên Biên Phu 1954)," still image, *Adaptation Fever* trilogy. Courtesy of the artist.

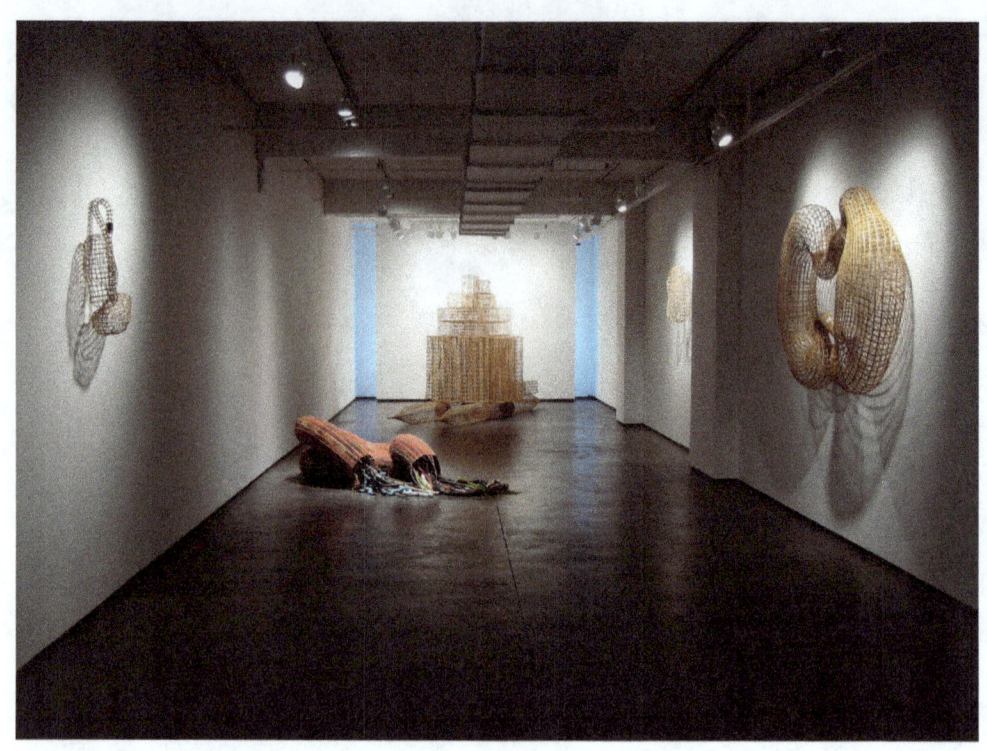

PLATE 14 Sopheap Pich, *Cycle*, 2004–2008, at far right with
in installation view of *The Pulse Within*, Tyler Rollins Fine
Art, November 12, 2009–January 9, 2010. Courtesy of
the artist and Tyler Rollins Fine Art, New York.

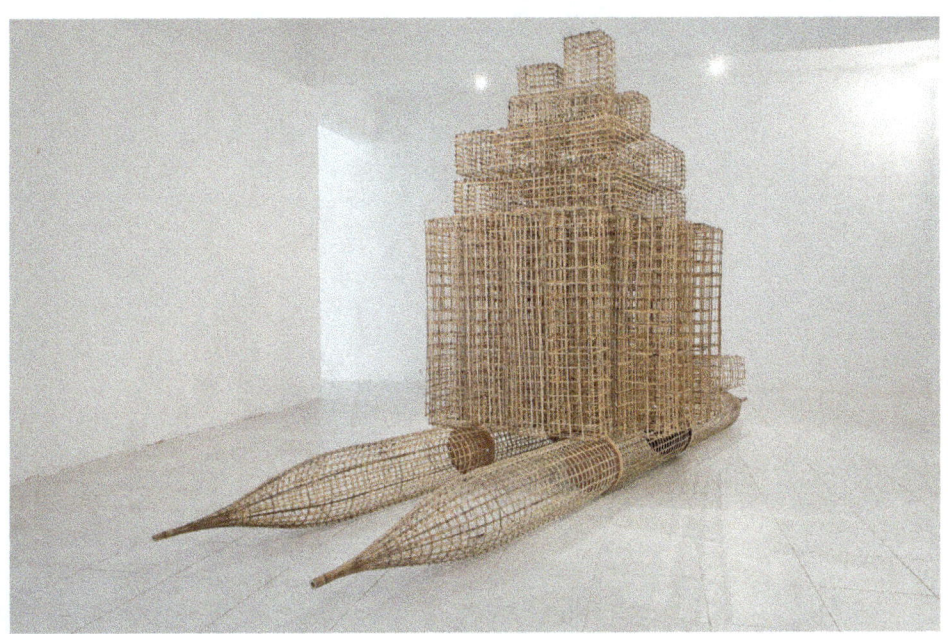

PLATE 15 Sopheap Pich, *Raft*, 2009, bamboo, rattan, wood, wire, and metal bolts, 226 × 450 × 132 cm (89 × 177 × 52 inches), site-specific installation. Courtesy of the artist and Tyler Rollins Fine Art, New York.

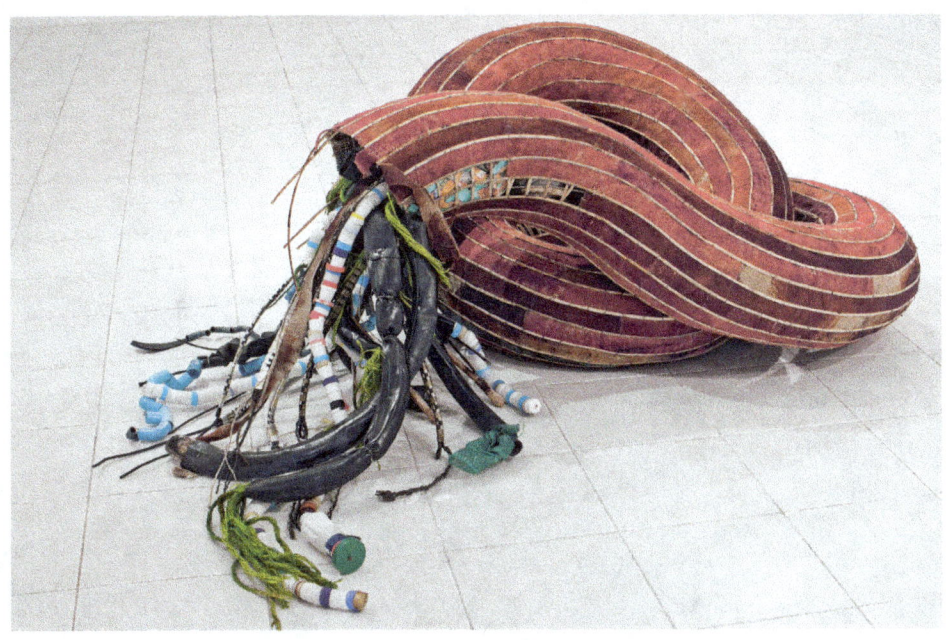

PLATE 16 Sopheap Pich, *Junk Nutrients*, 2009, bamboo, rattan, wire, plastic, rubber, metal, cloth, and resin, 165 × 124 × 74 cm (65 × 49 × 29 inches). Courtesy of the artist and Tyler Rollins Fine Art, New York.

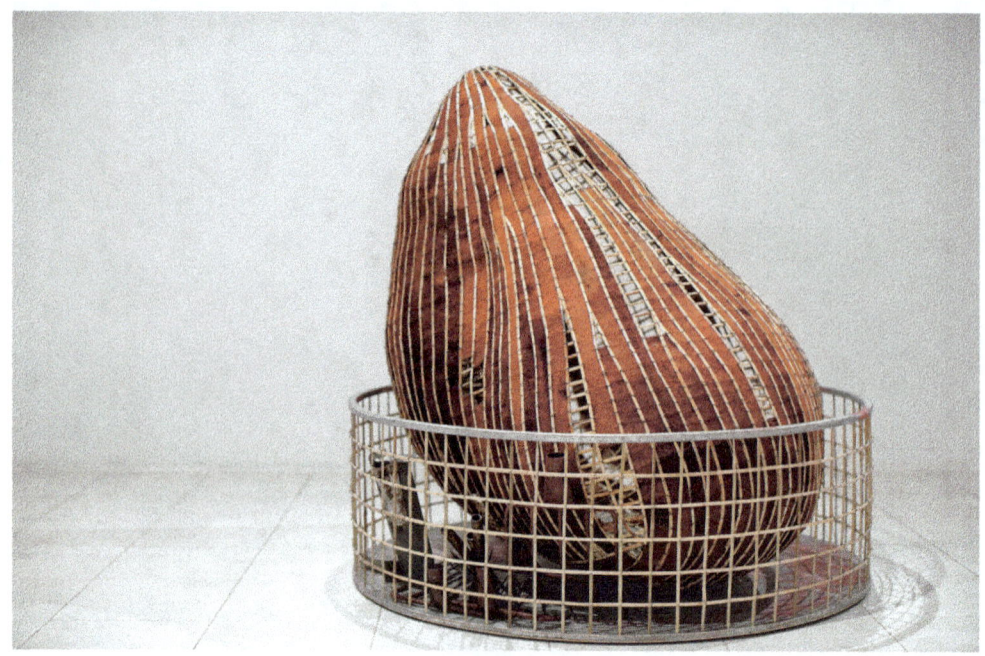

PLATE 17 Sopheap Pich, *Caged Heart*, 2009, wood, bamboo, rattan, burlap, wire, dye, and metal farm tools, 130 × 117 × 119 cm (51 × 46 × 47 inches). Courtesy of the artist and Tyler Rollins Fine Art, New York.

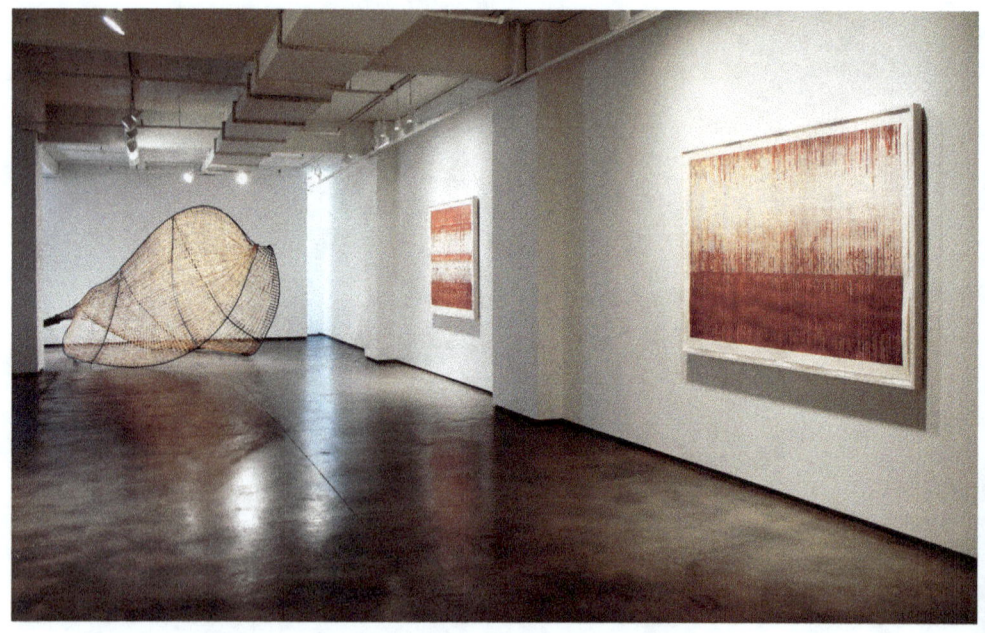

PLATE 18 Sopheap Pich, *Expanses,* installation view, Tyler Rollins Fine Art New York, November 1–December 21, 2018. Courtesy of the artist and Tyler Rollins Fine Art, New York.

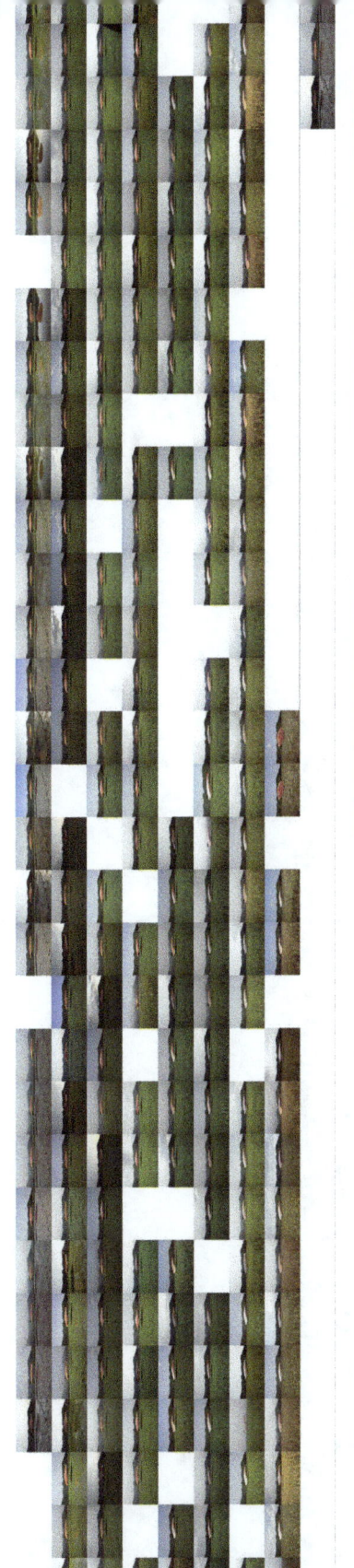

PLATE 19 Phan Quang,
The Umbrella, 2010, photographic installation comprising
204 digital C-prints, 100 × 1,100 cm
(39.37 × 433 inches). Image courtesy of the artist.

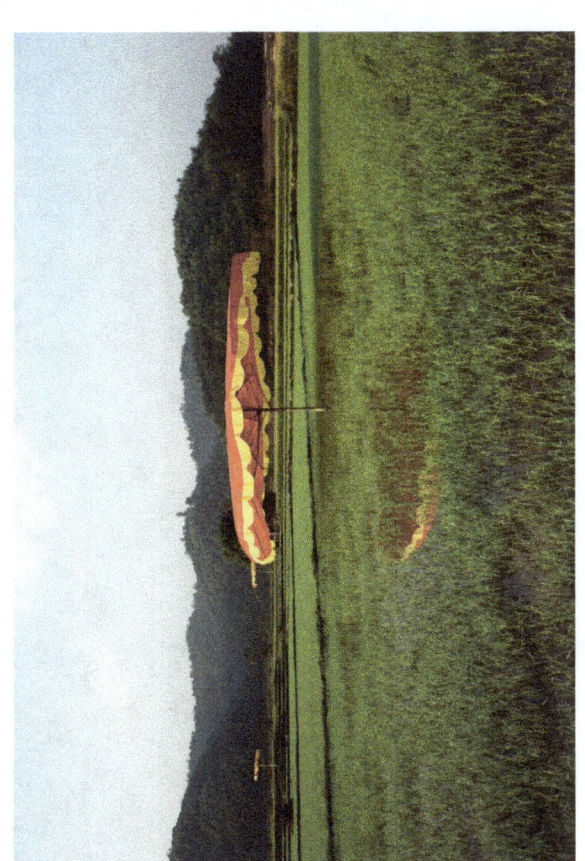

PLATE 20 Phan Quang, detail from *The Umbrella*,
2010, chromogenic print on archival paper.
Image courtesy of the artist.

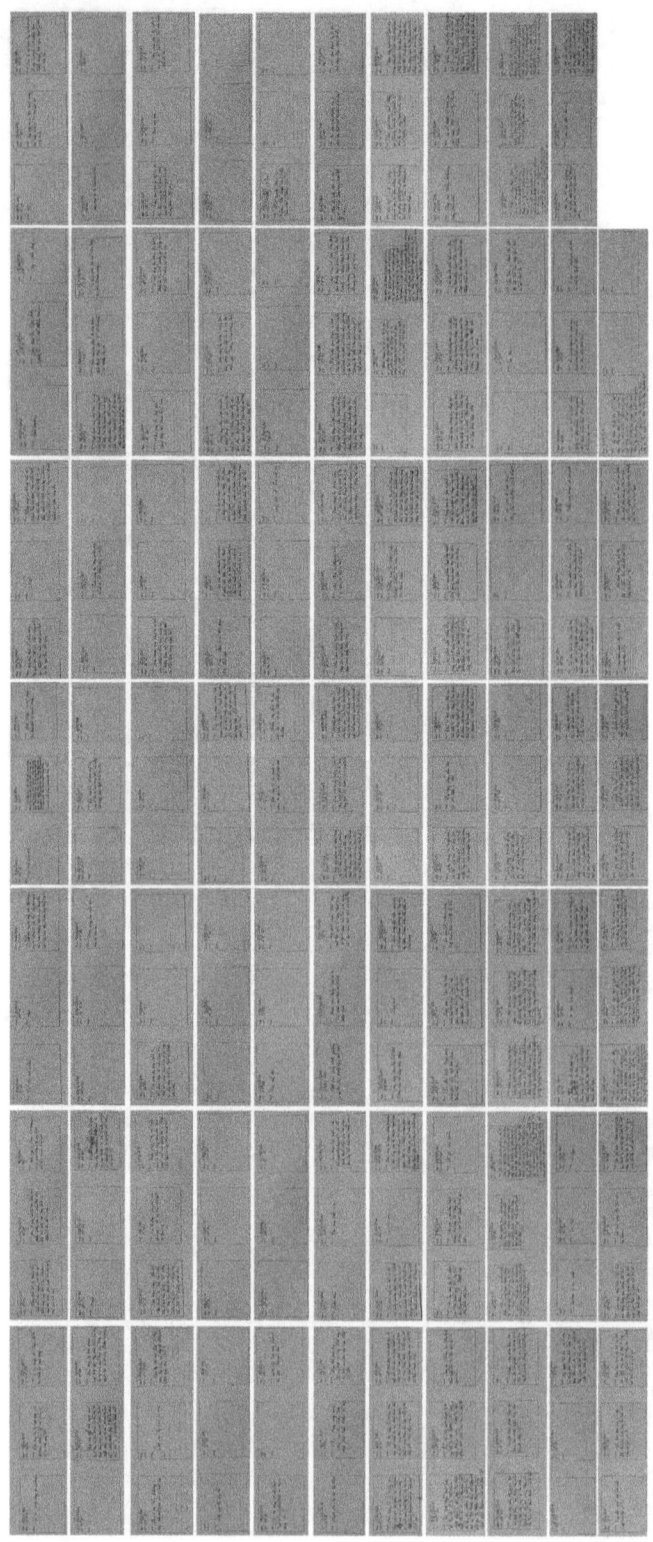

PLATE 21 Phan Quang, "Life of a Farmer," 2010, ink on paper mounted on board, 90 × 480 cm (35.43 × 189 inches), from *The Umbrella* diptych. Image courtesy of the artist.

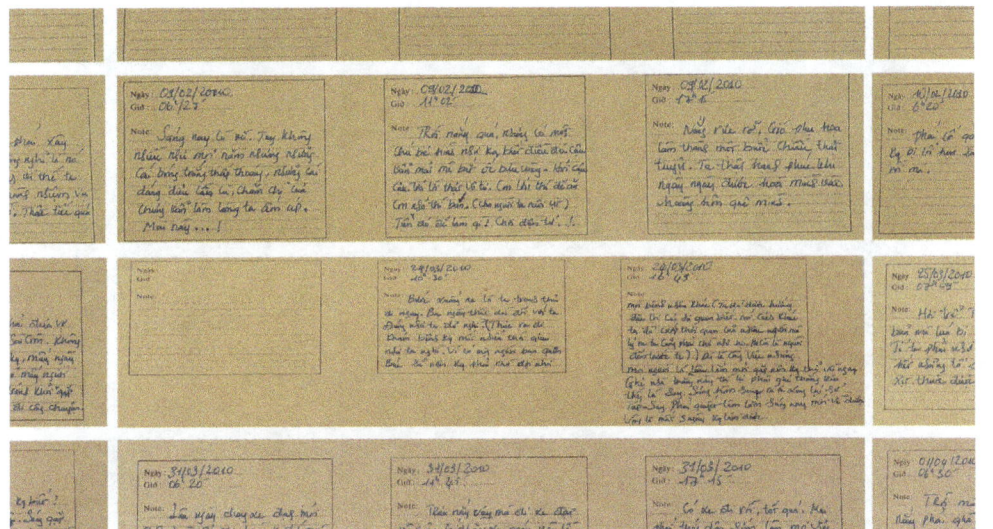

PLATE 22 Phan Quang, "Life of a Farmer," detail, 2010, ink on paper mounted on board, 90 × 480 cm (35.43 × 189 inches), from *The Umbrella* diptych. Image courtesy of the artist.

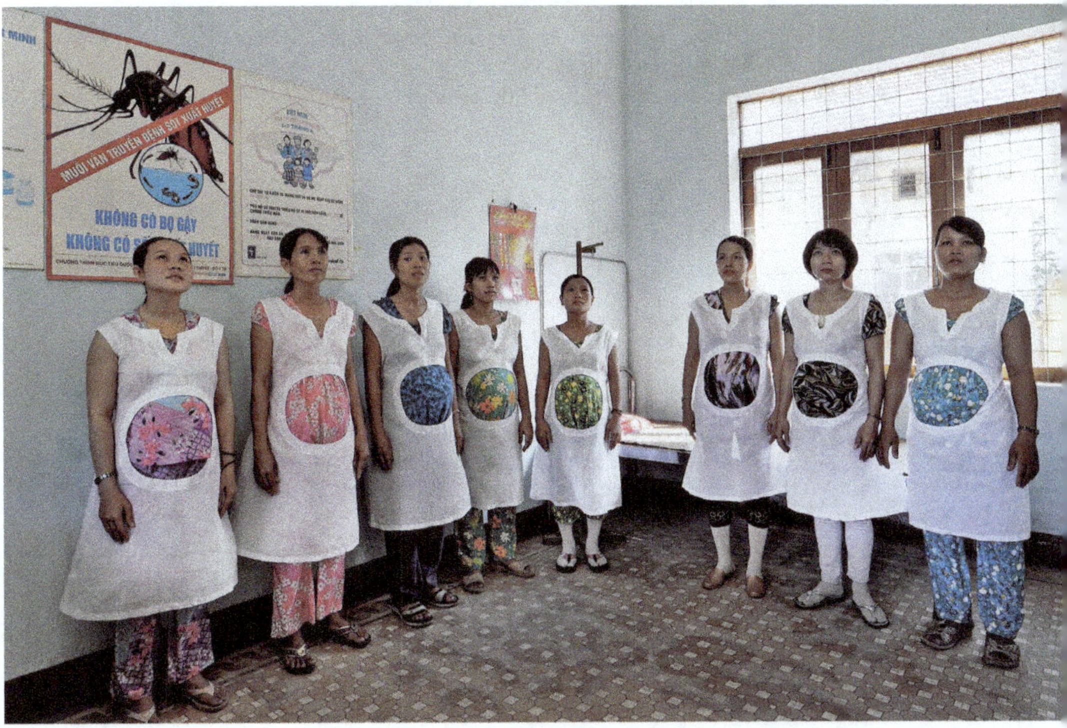

PLATE 23 Phan Quang, *Dream*, 2010, archival pigment print on aluminium, 70 × 105 cm (27.55 × 41.33 inches), ed. 4 + 1 AP. Image courtesy of the artist.

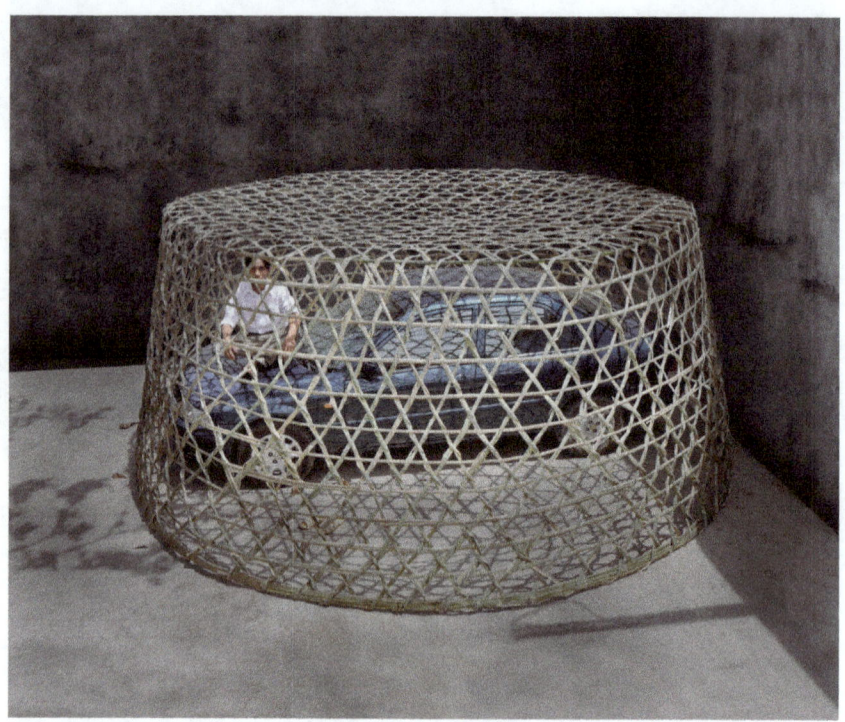

PLATE 24 Phan Quang, "Nouveau Riche," 2011, archival pigment print on aluminium, 100 × 150 cm (39.37 × 59 inches), ed. 5 + 1 AP, from the *Space/Limit* series. Image courtesy of the artist.

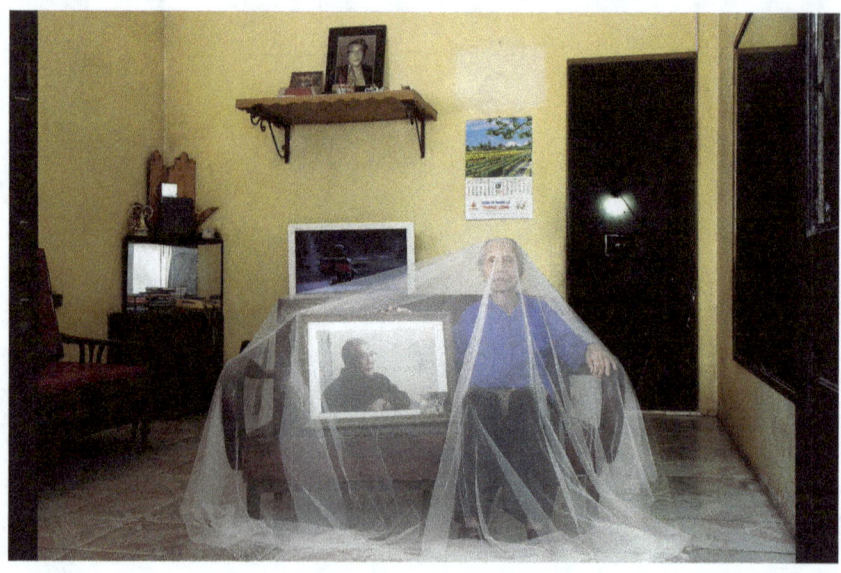

PLATE 25 Phan Quang, "Re/Cover No. 5," 2013, digital C-print, 100 × 170 cm (39.37 × 66.9 inches), ed. 5 + 1 AP, from the *Re/Cover* series. Image courtesy of the artist.

The Art Part

Việt Kiều Artists, Divides,
and Desires in Sài Gòn

THE LINKS BETWEEN CAPITAL AND WAR are dissociated. In chapter 1, I connected capital and war machines (the state, media). In this chapter, I
write about the double dissociation—and double participation[1]—of
art and capital, diasporic artists and location. As the theorist Michel Foucault has outlined in his musings on biopower, regimes of
knowledge and institutions of discipline justify power rationally
by disguising violence and coercion under the screens of modernity.[2] The trauma studies scholar Alexander Laban Hinton
stresses the "deep and complex relationship between genocide and modernity, which [is] bound by tropes of 'progress,'
projects of social engineering, the reification of group difference."[3] Indeed, Democratic Kampuchea justified its reforms as advancing progress and social betterment; it was
creating a just, ideal world where social inequities did not
exist. Its utopian communist vision was a critique of the
violence of capitalism and empire; the Khmer Rouge's
rhetoric was also one of civility and humanity. The
revolutionary leaders did not intend for such devastating losses.[4] I do not endorse the Khmer Rouge
leadership's claims of fending off US imperialists
and purifying society. Nor do I support America's past and present foreign policies. On either

side of capitalism and communism, and in between, progress is the justification for barbaric, civilizing violence. In sweatshops, torture chambers, detention centers, and fallow fields throughout the First World and Third World, this violence is both mundane and murderous.

This chapter focuses on Vietnamese diasporic artists who returned to Hồ Chí Minh City and the local and international networks and negotiations they must maneuver. I highlight Sandrine Llouquet and Tiffany Chung because they are among the most internationally visible diasporic artists connected to Việt Nam.[5] Llouquet's and Chung's artworks use formal strategies of assemblage to speak of doubling, the uncanny, and palimpsest sociopolitical identities. I link these themes to the critical and commercial circuits that make their work legible and saleable.

Both Llouquet and Chung have considered Việt Nam home; each has lived in Sài Gòn for more than a decade. Chung relocated to Houston, Texas, in September 2017, and Llouquet relocated to Lisbon in August 2019; both moved to be closer to immediate family. Their itinerancy embodies the myriad return engagements that are the focus of this book. These artists are "returning" to the global centers where they grew up and were educated—the United States and Europe—yet will forever be tethered in terms of their careers to Southeast Asia. This is a "negative return," as I outlined in the introduction. As Yến Lê Espiritu argues in *Militarized Refuge(es)*, the rhetoric of return was used for Southeast Asian refugees to Western countries in the 1970s who had a role in their wartime displacement, places where they had not been to before. Llouquet's and Chung's journeys, however, inverse this logic: their returns to Việt Nam, Europe, and the United States are not of dispossession. Yet their self-possessed moves bear the multiple dimensions of return engagements: creative, fiscal, metaphysical, and, yes, militarized.

Llouquet and Chung have ambivalent subject positions, representative of Việt Kiều artists tied to Việt Nam. The term *Việt Kiều* (overseas Vietnamese) itself is a fraught term: once considered pejorative because of its use by the Vietnamese government to refer to diasporic Vietnamese, the term has been embraced variably by its constituents. The anthropologist Charles Keyes traces the first instances of Việt Kiều to the eighteenth century in Siam (now Thailand), then during French colonialism, with a critical mass in the early 1980s (in the United States, France, Australia, and Canada). The Vietnam Studies scholar Ivan V. Small notes, "Though the term *Kiều*, from the Chinese word root *Qiao* meaning sojourning overseas, is often rejected among resettled Vietnamese immigrants abroad, it is more generally embraced by those returnees or transnational who have chosen to return to Vietnam from the West for long-term employment or resettlement."[6] Although not etymologically related, the term is a "homonym for bridge (Kiều, Qiao, Cầu)." Small states that Việt Kiều metaphorically embody continual return engagements: "Transnational mobility does reflect a bridge like identity, in that the return 'bridge' is two-way: they retain foreign passports meaning that the possibility of crossing back to the other side is never foreclosed."[7] In this context, I use the term Việt Kiều (as opposed to người Việt hải ngoại, which also translates as "overseas Vietnamese"), because, as Small observes, it is a commonly used "informal term." It is used casually by expatriates and locals alike, including by my own family, colleagues, and friends in Việt Nam and abroad. In a Việt Nam Studies Group discussion thread, the historian Hồ Tài Huệ-Tâm nonetheless suggests that perhaps it is "the ambiguous position of individuals of Vietnamese origins vis-à-vis the Vietnamese state, Vietnamese society and the country of their new residence that is the source of discomfort."[8]

I assert that this "ambiguous" subjectivity functions as both burden and cultural bridge. It enables greater visibility within the international art circuit and constrains the ways in which Việt Kiều artists negotiate their multiple identities as "local" and "nonlocal," a part of—and apart from—artistic and social communities in Việt Nam and abroad. Writing about Việt Kiều contemporary artists residing in Việt Nam, the art historian Nora Taylor suggests they are seen by local Vietnamese artists as "both foreign and familiar."[9]

These tensions and contradictions allow an international art market that fetishizes the politics of location to read these artists as "local" while valuing the cultural capital they amassed through Western education. Sue Hajdu, an artist, critic, and organizer based in Sài Gòn, calls this "strategic global positioning." Hajdu is also critical of international "instant noodle curators" who "drop in for twenty-four hours, meet a few familiar names, then just add water." She notes that double-edged curatorial criteria are often at play: "more articulate" returnee artists may overshadow their "local" counterparts, or "the standards of complexity, conceptualism, criticality and originality de rigueur for overseas-educated artists [are more] leniently applied to locals, or trumped by market forces."[10] Curators rely on local specificity to counteract critiques of homogenizing tendencies in the art world.

Strategic Cartographies ART MAKERS AND WORLD MAKING

I argue that artists and curators, as well state and cultural institutions, employ strategic cartographies—tactical, shifting geopolitical affiliations and identities. I use the term cartography to emphasize the process of mapping identity within the world and as an act of world making. Hajdu's "global positioning" implies premeditated moves across a predetermined map of global art-world dominance—a play into power. My formulation, however, sees the process of dealing with hegemony as negotiating discrepant mappings that are at once legible and illegible to dominant forces. This follows the anthropologist Aihwa Ong's concept of "worlding" to envision alternative mappings. The cultural studies scholar Rob Wilson sees worlding as a "tactic," which the art historian Michelle Antoinette considers a "reworlding," or repositioning the axes of Southeast Asian art histories. In keeping with my stance against additive models, worlding or reworlding does not mean charting another terrain, discipline, or methodology to usurp the existing hegemonic structures and discourses that appear naturalized. According to Gayatri Spivak's concept, worlding is a process that is interior and anterior, within and without. Using literature as an example, Spivak notes, "To consider the Third World as distant cultures, exploited but with rich intact literary heritages waiting to be recovered, interpreted, and curricularized in English translation fosters the emergence of 'the Third World' as a signifier that allows us to forget that 'worlding,' even as it expands the empire of the literary discipline."[11] Western cultural hegemony relies on "peripheral" geographies and knowledges to define and centralize itself and parasitically grow while disavowing and incorporating its other. This expansion and parasitic growth of disciplines and knowledge structures, as well as bodies to be disciplined, ties into my earlier discussion of host, hospitality, gifts (signifying knowledge, freedoms), and poison. Referring to Lisa Lowe's *Intimacy of Four Continents*, Mimi Thi Nguyễn warns us about the "politics of knowledge," a historicism, a story of empire that erases its deathly structural demands. Lowe observes, "What we know as 'race' and 'gender' are traces of this modernist humanist forgetting."[12] "Another name for these traces," Nguyễn states, "is debt."[13] What we "owe" our sense of self and place hinges on a willful amnesia.

If disciplines are empires of knowledge, which bodies of knowledge are subjugated? We can extend Spivak, Lowe, and Mimi Thi Nguyễn's insights to art history and contemporary art practices. The contemporary global art market, criticism, and scholarship all celebrate and critique the global turn. As "a signifier" for socioeconomic development, these "distant cultures" and artists are highlighted—hospitably hosted—in biennales and triennales, naturalizing and perpetuating continued violence and erasures. Through various worldings, subaltern artists tactically engage the global art world, recalling and forgetting the conditions of their emergence.

For example, the art critic and archivist Sharon Mizota's *Los Angeles Times* review of *Where the Sea Remembers*, a group show of "contemporary Vietnamese art," connects emerging Third World art scenes with economic ascendancy. Following Mizota's narrative, the fifteen artists in the show are emblematic of a region that is waiting to be discovered, interpreted, and, perhaps, curricularized—in translation—by the so-called First World. Mizota writes, "An ambitious project at the South L[os] A[ngeles] gallery the Mistake Room seeks to introduce local audiences to contemporary Vietnamese art. . . . [The show] is no doubt an indicator of the economic rise of Vietnam. As we've seen with China and India, a strong contemporary art market definitively marks one's arrival on the international cultural scene."[14] Yes, Việt Nam is a rising economic power, but as I have discussed—contrary to Mizota's claim—there is no significant local art market and collector base in Vietnam, unlike in China and India. In the review, the artists' divergent backgrounds are acknowledged, even foregrounded, yet conflated. The show's title, *Where the Sea Remembers*, conjures the famous composer's Trịnh Công Sơn's song "Biển Nhớ" (The Sea Remembers). The curatorial statement, written by the artistic director César García-Alvarez, with the staff members Nicolas Orozco-Valdivia and Kris Kuramitsu, notes that this song "was often sung as a farewell by those staying behind in the refugee camps to those who were discharged and relocated."[15] The exhibition temporally straddles "after the end of the war in 1975" (curator's statement) and "after 2007," which Mizota says is "when communist Vietnam entered the World Trade Organization and relaxed its borders, allowing for greater exchange with the rest of the world." On the world stage, Việt Nam's return engagements are bookmarked by the traumas of history and modernity.

These framings exemplify Spivak's critique of "the 'Third World' as a signifier"—subject to forgetting and erasure—within the process of worlding. For instance, Vietnamese diasporic artists in the show such as Llouquet and Thinh Nguyễn (b. Bảo An, Việt Nam, 1984), who have spent the majority of their lives in the West (and currently reside there), signify "contemporary Vietnamese art." Both embody the "Vietnamese art scene," although Thinh Nguyễn has no real sustained professional or personal connections with their birth country, having fled the communist regime as a teenager. Thinh Nguyễn is best known for their work focused on, and in, the United States, *Across the American Plains, 2013–14*, in which they were nomadic for a year, hosted for up to four nights at a time by strangers and friends. The artist deals with trans as well as transitional identities, intimacy, and alienation. Describing this installation work, the art critic Catherine Womack of *Los*

Angeles Magazine observes, "Framed photographs feature blurry images taken from the windows of cars . . . and could be easily be mistaken for images of Vietnam."[16] To echo Spivak, the "Third World" as signifier is recovered, if only through blurry images and by blurring identifications. Thinh Nguyễn's *Across the American Plains* recalls Tehching Hsieh's *Outdoor Piece, 1981–82*, a yearlong, roving durational "homeless" performance on the streets of New York. Tellingly, in their highest-profile shows to date, both Asian American artists are framed by their country of origin. Hseih had a retrospective commissioned by the Taipei Art Museum, curated by Adrian Heathfield, at the Taiwan Pavilion—a temporary satellite venue off the main permanent national pavilions in the Giardini—at the fifty-seventh Venice Biennale in 2017. T. Nguyễn and Hseih, as an emerging and a senior artist, respectively, are tactically positioned by institutions. Los Angeles and Taipei both continue to unsteadily forge themselves as formidable international art centers, combating the notion that they are "distant" hubs of creative activity. In doing so, institutional legitimization via individual legibility comes to the fore through geopolitics—a worlding.

Let me return briefly to *Where the Sea Remembers* to wrap up my discussion of intelligibility, worlding, and strategic cartographies. After being "introduced" to the "local [Los Angeles] audience," the "local" Vietnamese artists must also be "recovered, interpreted" (per Spivak's framing) in order to become worldly—global citizens and art-market players. Inversely, through the "Third World," Los Angeles gains significance: the local becomes international. Only now is Los Angeles arguably gaining traction as New York's dominance of the art world wanes, so such positioning is timely and crucial. Echoing Homi Bhabha's third space, the Mistake Room curators write, "It is here between the countries we knew and the homelands we choose to inhabit that [the show] locates a contemporary experience of nationhood." Although liminality is celebrated, the nation remains a dominant albeit destabilized rubric. Thus, the nation-state becomes a state of mind. In closing, they note that this transitional (if not truly transnational) subjectivity is "always forged by partial choices, acts of distancing and affiliation, and creative tactics of world-making." This partly dovetails with my concept of strategic cartographies as a worlding and its coterminous, contentious aspects of remaking and unmaking. Yet, as Spivak warns, it is precisely the framing of emergence (an "in between . . . contemporary experience of [Vietnamese] nationhood"; "[the show] is no doubt an indicator of the economic rise of Việt Nam") that obscures the violence of naming, visibility, and translation. Mizota notes in her review that while the "multi-faceted survey [attempts to] reach beyond works that are easily legible"—inadvertently evoking Asian stereotypes of unintelligibility/inscrutability—certain works "require no translation at all."[17] These translations (or lack thereof) indeed allow us in the global North and South "to forget that 'worlding'" that expands neo-imperial frameworks we all complicitly perpetuate.[18]

Art making itself is a forgetful, expansive process of translation and, as I have argued, a world making and unmaking. In an early interview with Elizabeth Grosz, Spivak defines worlding as "a texting, textualizing, a making into art, a making into an object to be understood."[19] Abstract concepts— self, nationhood, disidentifications—become art objects that transcend their materiality. At the same time, artists' mutable, myriad subjectivities become objectified, fixed, understood.[20] The phrase *a making into*, however, suggests ongoing engagement. Likewise, the evocative "to be understood" also requires vigilance, vulnerability, and empathy on both sides—artist and audience. Worlding as "textualizing" demands constant contextualization.

Spivak's conception of worlding builds on the philosopher Martin Heidegger's essay "The Origin of the Work of Art" and his concept of worlding. For Heidegger, "The world worlds, and is more fully in being than the tangible and perceptible realm in which we believe ourselves to be at home. World is never an object to be seen."[21] Worlding is phenomenological rather than empirical—affect over objects. Worlding ultimately is not its material conditions but, rather, a process—the shifts of "in being" and becoming. We cannot objectively study the world; instead, we experience the world as a set of significations from birth to death. These sets of shifting meanings continue after we die. He notes that "projective saying (poetry), in preparing the sayable, simultaneously brings the unsayable into the world."[22] To follow Spivak, this process of "making into art"—of worlding—and entering comprehension is inherently unknowable, unspeakable.

Strategic cartographies are thus a critical process of worlding, unworlding, reworlding, and remapping—reconstituting and relocating oneself again and again—in line with my ideas of cyclical return and revolution. Maps both reflect and create power. Among its earliest usage, a map (*chorographia*, Latin, sixteenth century) was a "portrait of a place."[23] As contemporary minoritized artists are "evacuated and elevated"—their subject and geographic positions are conflated as a site. Thus, artists and their works are also portraits of places. Instead of viewing this as a bind, I connect artists' tactical negotiations of sites as a continual process of becoming, morphing.

Adopting Gilles Deleuze and Félix Guattari's concept of "becoming" (as well as Heidegger's worlding as "in being" and Spivak's worlding as "a making into"), I engage ethnography and art history to chart cultural and sociopolitical changes in Việt Nam. Discussing political flux and potential, the anthropologists João Biehl and Peter Locke use Deleuze's theoretical frame to open up ethnographic approaches. Biehl and Locke note that "the anthropological venture has the potential of art: to invoke neglected human potentials and to expand the limits of understanding and imagination—a people yet to come."[24] Likewise, Antoinette uses the concept of "becoming" to evoke "ever-renewable subjectivities" and art histories to replace "static notions of a fixed, 'territorialized' space called Southeast Asia."[25] Deleuze and Guattari make a distinction between molar and molecular identities. Molar identities are stable constructs, "fixed in being, able to be grasped as a whole, recognized within the current social formation."[26]

Diaspora and citizenship—even dual citizenship (which I address later)—are molar identity formations. In contrast, molecular identities are in constant fluctuation and "offer the possibility for transforming identity and society" because of its shifting nature.[27] Molecular identities are becomings—they exist in a liminal state. Becomings emerge on a molecular, not molar, level. Within a modernizing state, new identities, new ways of being within a global economic order, are forged.[28] These changes occur on a molecular level. Việt Nam's market socialism is a dramatic mutation from its earlier socialist genetic codes. Vietnamese locals are no longer represented as a molar, unified proletariat fighting for a common good. They are becoming individual consumers with discrete desires and wants. Case in point: throughout the country, billboards targeting various market groups have largely displaced propaganda posters. The distinct demographic desires are manifest in emergent molecular identities and evident in the traces of feminist discourse and queer representation in literature, online, and in movies. Ambivalence, varyingly embraced and abhorred in popular discourse, marks these metamorphic identities.

Both diasporic and local denizens are constructed as liminal subjects by cultural and state institutions. Local and diasporic artists are caught between history and modernity, psychic and real space and place, through shifting state policies and political rhetoric. I extend Deleuze and Guattari's notion of "becoming" to Vietnamese local and diasporic subjects, as well as to Việt Nam as a nation-state. Since the first đổi mới (renovation) market reforms in 1986, Việt Nam and its denizens are also in the process of becoming, transforming, mutating, healing. As Việt Nam changes, categories such as diasporic, local, and foreigner are no longer constructive. The trope of "becoming" more accurately pinpoints the changing identities of local and expatriate subjects. Becomings reject "the supposedly fixed terms through which that which becomes passes."[29] The terms *diasporic* and *local* are no longer fixed. A multiplicity of migrations—physical and psychic—destabilize these terms. Instead of a local-diasporic dyad, strategic cartographies are more becoming.

The Art Part   DISCURSIVE DIVIDES

Strategic cartographies operate as Việt Nam, and its artists pivot between neoliberal and socialist ideologies. For example, the Vietnamese government promotes (free-market) economic development while maintaining a socialist ideological stance. The West's desire for continually new economic and cultural commodities mirrors Việt Nam's entry in 2008 into the World Trade Organization (WTO), which marked its desire to further engage in capitalist enterprise. Shifting art markets in which Western economic and cultural dominance no longer prevails (but still holds sway) reflects the shifting geography of global capital and labor. Now multiple centers and its attendant peripheries mark new modes of economic accumulation and exploitation, mirrored by cultural accumulation and exploitation. The rise of new bull markets (such as China, India, and Việt Nam) builds the foundation for the rise of new art markets. Việt Kiều artists exploit the desire for new cultural "products" and producers to their advantage by using their liminal positions as both "Vietnamese" and Westerners (with attendant economic and cultural capital) in Việt Nam.[30] Part of their privilege is being able to "pass" at will.

As new art markets evolve, outdated canons persist. Asian art scholars such as Alice Yang question the parameters of art-history inquiry (which often privileges Western academic and artistic canons), seeking instead to find resonance among myriad localized perspectives. In the essay "Why Have There Been No Great Vietnamese Artists?" Taylor notes that "artists from peripheral loci of art production—that is, outside the Western art market centers in places such as Việt Nam—often 'exist' or are known only because Western galleries, art auction houses, or even art historians have situated them."[31] Indeed, the "art world"—including the system of art scholarship, galleries, and art fairs, as well as the recent explosion in international biennials and triennials—is tied into market economies and reflects aesthetic, economic, political, and cultural hierarchies. To echo Taylor, the desire to discover a "great" Vietnamese—or any—Vietnamese artist is a moot point. It just reinforces binaries of universal and particular, center and periphery, visible and invisible, the West and the rest. Interweaving and interdependent historical, social, and political variables affect any given artist's relationship with her or his audience(s). These factors in turn shape legibility and intelligibility (which "local versus universal" themes easily translate for an international art audience), visibility (scholarship, discourse, access to art venues, promotion, publications), and marketability (art market). The consumption of art is tied to economic development. The Vietnamese government's 1986 open-door đổi mới policy has spurred vast socioeconomic changes. The state has gradually shifted over three decades from a communist to a socialist-capitalist political economy. Việt Nam has now embraced globalization—advertisements are everywhere. Foreign investment fuels the changing infrastructure of urban and rural areas. In cities such as Sài Gòn and Hà Nội, construction is nonstop. The emerging middle class's hunger for commercial products grows. There is not yet a significant local collector base for contemporary art. I expect this to change in time. The Post Vidai collection, started in 1994, claims to be "the only collection in the world" focused on contemporary Vietnamese art. Its collectors envision "a new Vietnam as a diasporic community"; local and nonlocal are no longer relevant in this new world order.

Despite the global economic crisis and the country's own recession, Việt Nam has been one of the fastest-rising economies in Asia.[32] Lê Xuân Nghĩa, deputy chairman of the National Finance Supervision Committee, stated that stimulus packages have helped curb the country's recession and that the global slump may actually help boost the country's gross domestic product (GDP): "As people in the world have seen their income go down, governments in the world have encouraged importing cheap products, including ones from Việt Nam. This really serves as the opportunity for Việt Nam to push up exports in the time to come."[33] Việt Nam's entry into the WTO promises that trade expansion will continue.[34] The increased international flows of tourism, commerce, and culture in Việt Nam have profoundly affected the growth of contemporary art.[35]

Coinciding with đổi mới in the late 1980s, Vietnamese artists began to cater to foreigners by producing Fauvist interpretations of serene landscapes, occasionally populated by women in *áo dài* (traditional flowing dresses).[36] These lush palette-knife paintings still dominate commercial galleries in Sài Gòn, Huế, and Hà Nội. Artisans readily cater to collectors' desires for "authentic" Vietnamese art. Nonetheless, the state primarily recognizes socialist realism and silk and lacquer paintings; the national museums feature these genres. Conceptual contemporary art has little government institutional and fiscal support.[37] Government cultural committees screen and approve all cultural productions and events prior to public viewing. The government must balance its own desires for rapid modernization with the need to control political and cultural representations. The tension between capitalist market reform and socialist ideology become manifest in the kinds of imagery the government permits. Censors do not allow galleries, artists, and curators to show politically sensitive artwork.

Việt Nam's university system has no conceptual art education. Only academic lessons—formal training on line, composition, and color—based on those that the French colonial art system established exist. This framework still dominates art school curricula in the country's education system. Contemporary Vietnamese artists who grew up in the country have had to rely on their own research, study, or residencies abroad and a mostly informal network of salons and workshops to learn about global art history and art theory. This network is particularly active in Hà Nội and Sài Gòn, the two largest urban centers in Việt Nam, and Llouquet and Chung are among the artists who contribute to the growing community dialogue about contemporary art in these places.

North, South; East, West

Most official government and cultural institutions are located in Hà Nội, the political capital of Việt Nam. It is medium-size leafy city with a population of 7.94 million.[38] A large scenic central lake, Hồ Hoàn Kiếm, serves as a focal point for denizens. In the mornings and evenings, locals and tourists can be seen strolling, exercising, or flirting on benches on the lake's perimeters. The huddled warren of little shops and homes flanking the lake in the historic Old Quarter contrasts with the rising skyscrapers on the outskirts of the city. The state's plans to expand Hà Nội would double its current area. Meanwhile, cultural organizations and galleries are sprinkled throughout the city. Foreign cultural institutions such as L'Espace (the French cultural institute), the Goethe Institute, and the British Council have a range of cultural programming, including a regular showcase of Vietnamese contemporary visual art.[39] The students, both adults and children, see attaining foreign language and cultural fluency as positive investments in their futures. These institutions often support and show socially engaged work. They offer local and foreign artists a degree of artistic freedom from state censors during exhibitions and related programming.[40] Foreign investment in these cultural spaces is a form of neocolonial enterprise aimed at creating positive public relations with locals and expatriates. The institutes offer foreign-language classes, and they encourage students to study or work in Việt Nam. Their well-intentioned leadership shares Việt Kiều organizers' impulse to build an artistic community and scene. They all aim to develop cultural discourse, to bring a bit of their Western home to Việt Nam, to educate the locals, and to make space for nonlocals and locals to network. It is a civilizing mission, although no one couches it in such loaded terms, as they might have in decades past.[41] For some artists, organizers, and members of the general public, these spaces are oases of cutting-edge culture. Through exchange programs with international artists and organizations, creative experimentation is often encouraged. The presence of these foreign cultural institutions is also a diplomatic tool to foster positive relations between Việt Nam and the given cultural embassy—good for trade, commerce, and political relations.

Galleries and artist-run spaces are a vital component of the cultural scene in Hà Nội. The artist Vu Dân Tân (b. Hà Nội, 1946; d. 2009) and his partner, the scholar and curator Natalia (Natasha) Kraevskaia (b. Astrakhan, 1952), opened the pioneering Salon Natasha in 1990 in their studio/home. Although no longer active, it was the first private independent art space in Việt Nam to promote artistic experimentation.[42] Now other spaces and activities spearheaded by artists form a rich network. Trailblazing activities include workshops organized by the local artist and organizer Trần Lương (b. Há Nội, 1960); Đào Anh Khánh's (b. Hà Nội, 1959) performance extravaganzas; and Nhà Sàn Đức (also known as Nhà Sàn Studio, established in 1998 by the artists Nguyễn Mạnh Đức's [b. Hà Nội, 1934] and Trần Lương), the artist Đức's "house on stilts," which has served as a performance and exhibition space and a local artists' hangout for more than a decade.[43] Since 2013, the younger generation of artists from Nhà Sàn Studio regrouped in another location as Nhà Sàn Collective.[44] Commercial galleries such as Art Vietnam Gallery (www.artvietnamgallery.com), established in 1992 by Suzanne Lecht, and mixed-use café/art spaces such as Manzi and Tadioto, opened in 2008 by the former Vietnamese American journalist Nguyen Qui Duc, add to the breadth of work on display in the city.[45] Affiliated with the Hà Nội Fine Arts University, the Việt Art Center (www.vietartcentre.vn) opened on July 13, 2006, has hosted exhibitions and events for contemporary Vietnamese and international artists, designers, musicians, and architects. The university has also added video courses to supplement its retinue of academic art lessons.

Sài Gòn's contemporary art scene began far more recently than Hà Nội's. Sài Gòn is the economic center of Việt Nam. Commercial galleries include

Galerie Quynh (www.galeriequynh.com), opened in 2003 by the Vietnamese American Quỳnh Phạm, and Salon Saigon (www.salonsaigon.com), a gallery, library, and permanent collection that also hosts not-for-profit professionalization workshops and critiques for artist. Salon Saigon, formerly directed by Sandrine Llouquet, was founded in 2017 by the private art collector John Tuệ Nguyễn, chief executive of the high-end travel company Trails of Indochina.[46] Alternative spaces—such as Sàn Art Independent Art Space (cofounded by the artist Đinh Q. Lê [b. Hà Tiên, 1968]), the Factory Contemporary Arts Centre, A. Farm (a residency program founded in 2018 as a collaboration of Sàn Art, MoT+++, and Nguyễn Foundation), and Zero Station (www.zerostation .vn), founded by the artist, scholar, and curator Nguyễn Như Huy (b. Hà Nội, 1971)—provide a diverse array of art exhibitions and programming. Himiko Visual Café (http://www.himikokoro.com) and L'Usine (lusinespace .com/category/gallery), a "lifestyle" store and cafeteria with a separate gallery annex, combine commercial space with gallery space. The Vietnamese American artist Rich Streitmatter-Tran's (b. Biên Hòa, 1972) dia/projects functions as an art archive and gathering space, as well as the artist's studio.[47] Foreign cultural institutions such as the Institute of Cultural Exchange with France (IDECAF) and the British Council occasionally do cultural events, including a film series at IDECAF and concerts through the council. These institutions have fewer programs in Sài Gòn, however, than in Hà Nội.[48]

Gender/Wars

As contemporary art spaces grow in Việt Nam, these places and the artists connected to them reflect rapidly shifting political policies and cultural attitudes. Vietnamese women bear the brunt of society's ambivalence about its brisk cultural changes. The historian Estar Ungar notes that military socialism "de-gendered" Vietnamese women (starting in 1954 in the north and 1975 in the south), and market socialism "re-gendered" them (1986 to today). During the war years, women filled typically male-dominated leadership, production, and education roles, due both to socialist policies that stressed gender equality and the exodus of men to the war front. As men returned to the workforce, the state has refocused on traditional, Confucian-based gender roles. However, this rhetoric is rife with tensions and contradictions within a liberalized marketplace. The reemphasis on femininity takes on different classed valences in agrarian and urban areas. The state encourages rural women to embrace domestic and farming duties, while men may seek more profitable industrial jobs in the cities. For their educated urban female

117

counterparts, new bourgeois identities attest to a wider range of occupational and consumer choices.[49]

The cultural critic Nguyễn-võ Thu-hương points out that the global market demands—and exploits—differentiated gendered and raced labor. This feminized workforce consisting of marginalized Third World Others is relegated time-consuming and monotonous tasks, such as low-paying factory garment and electronics work. Thus "traditional" feminine traits become "worker attributes of docility, dexterity, and tolerance for tedious work on the global assembly-line."[50] Asian female workers bear the burdens of a deterritorialized global economic system on a constant quest for high yields and low overhead.

Vietnamese women are exemplars of the nation.[51] Vietnamese womanhood is mythologized in eras past and present as long-suffering or tragically heroic. For example, the national pantheon includes the Trung sisters, first-century anti-Chinese resistance fighters who killed themselves after defeat. Việt Nam's most famous work of literature, *Tale of Kiều*, is an eighteenth-century epic poem about a beautiful, talented, and educated woman named Kiều who sells her body to save her father and brother from prison. As in much of Vietnamese literature, she is an object, not a subject. These narratives also continue in contemporary films.

In Việt Nam, highly successful "commercial" films since the 2000s such as *Long Legged Girls* (Những Cô Gái Chân Dài, dir., 2004) and the box office record-breaking *Bar Girls* (Gái Nhảy, dir., 2003), among others, signal a new genre: productions dealing with sex, drugs, high fashion, homosexuality, prostitution, AIDS, and other topics previously unaddressed in public discourse.[52] These Hollywood-inspired, government-sanctioned films mix propaganda and entertainment by introducing sensational, titillating story lines with subtle moral messages in what film scholars calls "propatainment." They are a radical break from earlier government-funded propaganda films, which were commercially disastrous. In these local and diasporic films, such as *A Scent of Green Papaya* (Trần Anh Hùng, dir., 1993), women are still objects of a masculine gaze. In cultural productions, women embody the tensions between tradition and modernity.

Within the Vietnamese art world, female artists have had to take a back seat to their male peers for a variety of reasons. To be a Vietnamese female artist is to be in a "triple bind," according to the postcolonial theorist Trinh T. Minh-ha.[53] Vietnamese are already marginalized within international art circuits; a female artist's subject position further isolates her in Việt Nam and abroad. It is difficult to negotiate a hierarchical global art scene thrice alienated as a woman, an artist, and Vietnamese, or any combination of the three: artist of color, woman of color, female artist.[54] These artists also operate within Vietnamese patriarchal society, where masculine conceptions of success and art dominate.

Vietnamese modern art marginalized women and modes it considered feminine. Victor Tardieu opened the first official art school of Indochina, L'École des Beaux-Arts d'Indochine (EBAI), in 1925 in Hà Nội. Its mandate was to teach Vietnamese locals "modern" fine arts techniques. This art education was entirely European. It neglected the folk art woodcuts, calligraphy, ornate embroidery, silk painting, and abstracted painterly techniques inherited through centuries of Chinese domination.[55] At EBAI, renamed Hà Nội College of Art in 1975, new oil-painting techniques following European masters emphasized the illusionistic depiction of space and figures. Illusionistic rendering expressed modernity rather than abstraction.

Western academic techniques displaced Vietnamese traditional arts and handicrafts. This approach is still taught in arts universities today throughout Việt Nam. A large number of nationally prominent artists graduated from EBAI. The distinction between "high art" and "craft" increasingly became a gendered and geographic divide: predominantly male artists were enrolled and indoctrinated in modern painting techniques at the EBAI in the north, whereas schools emphasizing craft emerged in the south, including the École des Arts Décoratifs.[56]

After communist independence, both the north and the south followed government dictates to produce propaganda that merged European techniques with Chinese socialist realism. Socialist egalitarian policies allowed women greater opportunities to produce and exhibit artwork during this period. The then newly formed Artists' Association provided studios, exhibition venues, and prizes; half of its members were women.[57]

From the 1950s to the 1980s, artist-workers fueled artistic and cultural production, which blurred the previously held distinctions between high and low culture, artisan and fine artist, men and women, intelligentsia and worker.[58] All art was for the nation. The "re-gendering" shift from a domestic local market in which the state was the primary patron of the arts to a foreign market geared toward private collectors and an international audience has been both a boon and a burden for artists. Male artists who produce paintings of peaceful landscapes and women in áo dài dominate commercial galleries in Sài Gòn and Hà Nội. These palatable, creamy concoctions evoke early through mid-twentieth-century Western painting movements (Impressionism, etc.), and artists have made millions on the art market with them. They continue their careers producing derivations of vibrant, poetic images that made them successful: empty streets, sensuous ingénues.

Commercial galleries generally exclude Vietnamese female artists doubly. Socialist realism and lacquer paintings encouraged by the French during the colonial period (also images of foliage, fauna, and females) remain the dominant genres featured in the national museums and officially recognized by the state. Women who paint lacquerware or in socialist realist styles are relatively rare. "Boundary-pushing" male artists who eschew this mode and have become versed in conceptual, performance, and video art regard the work of female artists recognized by the state, such as Bé Ký, as staid. Male Vietnamese artists have had the luxury of focusing on their work, experimenting with styles and media, and establishing networks in cafés as their spouses take care of domestic duties. Despite being assimilated into the world of the Artists' Association during the 1950s–80s, female artists—during the military and market socialist eras—have had little time for networking, as they have had to worry about making a living and tending their children. The combination of Confucian ethics, a patriarchal society, and masculine national art discourse compels many Vietnamese female artists to choose between artistic careers and family. The work that certain international collectors seek—which, unlike depictions of idyllic scenes and innocents, criticizes Vietnamese society—is often the domain of male artists who have the time and resources to experiment with form and content.[59]

Of course, there are exceptions to the rule. Female Vietnamese artists such as Ly Hoàng Ly (b. Hà Nội, 1975), Đinh Y Nhi (b. Hà Nội, 1967), Đinh Thi Tham Poong (b. Lai Châu Province, 1970), and Phan Thảo Nguyễn (b. Hồ Chí Minh City, 1987), among others, have had some commercial and critical success in Việt Nam and abroad. Early performance installations by Ly Hoàng Ly, who holds a bachelor in fine arts from Hồ Chí Minh Fine Arts University and a master's from the School of the Art Institute of Chicago, dealt with themes of domesticity and cultural and social constraints. Ly's solo exhibition at The Factory, *0395A.ĐC*, in 2017 featured an overview of her work, including repeating motifs of the house, boat (as a reference to Vietnamese "boat people"), and water (*nước* means "water" and "nation").[60] Paintings on canvas and traditional *do* paper by Đinh Y Nhi, who has a bachelor in fine arts from Hà Nội Fine Arts University, often feature flattened, elongated "child-like stick figures, or cartoon faces,"[61] according to the former journalist Nguyễn Qui Đuc, who also owns Tadioto. The figures and faces are presented frontally, either as a single portrait or as repeating figures—perhaps a commentary on social and political anonymity and alienation within a one-party system. Đinh Thi Tham Poong, who also has a bachelor in fine arts from Hà Nôi Fine Arts University, creates medium-size patchwork pattern-inflected watercolors on handmade *do* paper that deal with her mixed heritage as Thai and Muong (two of Việt Nam's ethnic minorities).[62] The surreal images feature men and women in traditional garb juxtaposed with imaginary natural landscapes. Often, layered silhouettes are "cut out," revealing a landscape, shifting the relationship between figure and ground, positive and negative space, nature and humanity. The work illustrates Tham Poong's belief that "everything contains each other, is intertwined with each other."[63] Asia Art Archive Hong Kong states that the artist's exhibition *Emigration*, installed at Salon Natasha, Hà Nội, in 1997, "drew attention to the position of ethnic minorities in Vietnam's rapidly modernizing society."[64]

Phan Thảo Nguyễn, whose degrees include a bachelor of arts from Hồ Chí Minh University of Fine Arts; bachelor of fine arts from Lasalle College of Arts, Singapore; and master of fine arts from the School of the Art Institute of Chicago, paints in oil on X-ray film backing sheets and creates multichannel video installations that deal with history, literature, national narratives, and the lines between fact and fiction. Nguyễn was the recipient of the prestigious Rolex Mentor and Protégé Award in 2016 (her mentor was the acclaimed artist Joan Jonas); her winning entry for the Signature Art Museum's $44,000 Signature Art Prize in 2018, *Tropical Siesta*, is based on observations written by the first Frenchman to visit Việt Nam, the Jesuit missionary Alexandre de Rhodes (1591–1660), who romanized the Vietnamese alphabet. Nguyễn states that the work, which consists of two-channel video and six paintings, explores the "hidden histories of Việt Nam" as contemporary rural schoolchildren imaginatively reenact de Rhodes's musings.[65] Many of these artists wrestle with the intersections of personal and national Vietnamese identity, embodying the artist-as-ethnographer/artist-as-ethnographic subject's "return to the real."[66] Local Vietnamese women have also forged successful art venues, including Himiko of Himiko Visual Café and Mai of the now defunct Mai's Gallery, but their activities are generally limited to the local sphere.

Vietnamese female diasporic artists residing in Việt Nam potentially face a triple bind—as women, as producers of art the government does not endorse, and as Việt Kiều. But they also have greater flexibility to navigate gendered hierarchies and, by extension, greater visibility within and outside Việt Nam. Llouquet and Chung also have more financial resources than many artists, which gives them greater freedom to produce and exhibit work.

The politics of identity and buyers' markets impose essentializing gendered and geographic categories on Vietnamese artists. Other diasporic Vietnamese female artists have dealt with the legacies of war, most visibly the Vietnamese American An-My Lê (b. Sài Gòn, 1970) and the Vietnamese French Liza Nguyễn (b. 1970). Gender appears unexpectedly, however, in both artists' work, in overdetermined ways.

An-My Lê, based on the US East Coast, is a photographer. Her black-and-white *Small Wars* series documents Việt Nam War reenactors in Virginia—history fanatics, veterans, and young men role-playing their fathers' war (figures 2.1–2.2). She also appears as a subject within the frame, variably playing a translator or the "enemy" Charlie: a Việt Cộng female guerrilla soldier.[67] She plays both sides. It is uncanny, this doubling of representation. She is caught between history and memory, the shutter click of the camera. The artist mentions in an interview that the reenactors urged her to participate to provide a missing component: a real, not imagined, Vietnamese other in this mock war, her ethnicity "presumably adding an element of authenticity to the make-believe."[68] Thus, she highlights her ambivalent subject position, simultaneously owner and object of the gaze. Jacques Derrida notes the slippages of translation. Lê's role falters as a translator, as a photographic subject, and as the photographer. In the photographic frame, she is a mutely unstable subject—a diasporic subject who escaped communism, her posturing as a threatening Việt Cộng soldier evokes again the mythos of Việt Nam as a threatening feminine entity. She is caught in a triple bind. As a "becoming," Lê is presented simultaneously as a guerrilla, an artist, and the embodiment of Việt Nam.

Liza Nguyễn, by contrast, appears nowhere in her own work. Yet she is everywhere in it.[69] The young photographer, who splits her time between Paris and Düsseldorf, is an archivist of sorts. In her formally stunning *Surface* series, stark white backgrounds frame clinical shots of differently hued round mounds of dirt, culled from infamous sites of American and French military aggression in Việt Nam, including Mỹ Lai.[70] Nguyễn documents what remains: soil (*Surface* series); military relics (*Postcard* series); her late father's possessions (*My Father*, an artist book). These disparate projects serve as personal monuments to loss and memory. Nguyễn's output, like that of An-My Lê and Jun Nguyễn-Hatsushiba, exemplifies the counter-monument impulse—multivocal, multivalent, polysemic. As Marilyn Young points out, (counter-)monuments are also telling of their creators' preoccupations.[71] Đinh Q. Lê's work may seek redress; Nguyễn-Hatsushiba's videos deal with the weight of trauma; An-My Lê's images point at the gaps between

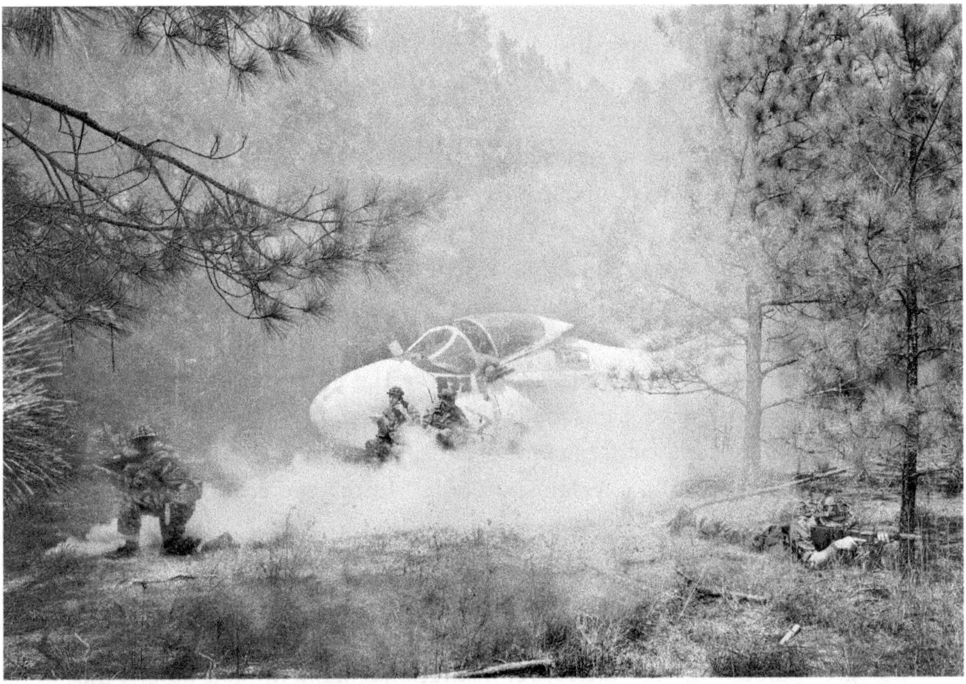

2.1 An-My Lê, "Rescue," 1999–2002, gelatin silver print, 38 × 26.5 inches, from the *Small Wars* series. Courtesy of the artist.

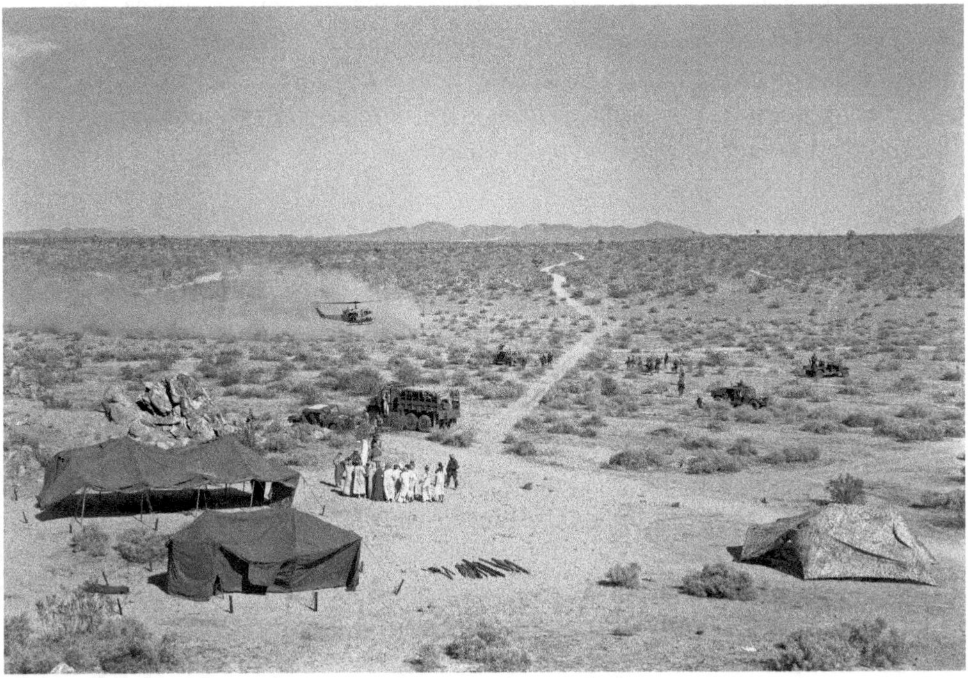

2.2 An-My Lê, "Resupply Operations," 2003–2004, gelatin silver print, 38 × 26.5 inches, from the *Small Wars* series. Courtesy of the artist.

fact and fantasy; Liza Nguyễn's photographs straddle absence and presence. In the international art world, all four artists are tethered to a traumatized topography, as well as to their minority identities—and celebrated for it. Only Nguyễn's *My Father* series has a trace of overtly personal narrative—a daughter's coming to terms with a lost life, a lost history, through the depiction of her father's intimate, mundane objects (false teeth, an old hair comb, Wrangler jeans), edifices, and friends' written recollections, accompanied by their portraits. Ghostly matters. Object lessons of small objects.[72] These haunted objects are uncanny, familiar in their banality: they serve as memory's living doubles for a dead father.[73] The figure of the father is estranged from language. He is mute figure, marked by void and silence. The secondhand stories form fragments of a life, point to the failure of language and representation, not a reclamation of it.[74] In this project, the Derridean father, logos, is absent.

The global North often sees the public realm as "masculine" while coding the private sphere—and personal matters—as "feminine." An-My Lê's work questions these distinctions. Đình Q. Lê and Jun Nguyễn-Hatsushiba do not foreground their life narratives, yet institutions highlight their biographies when presenting their work. They stake their claims on the battlefield of public memory. In contrast, Liza Nguyễn's private grief is evoked by signifiers of a domestic life. Trinh's "triple bind" could also apply to Vietnamese male artists. In the Western public imaginary, their masculine identity is as overwrought as Vietnamese female subjectivity. In various ways, all four diasporic artists bear—and question—the burden of representation of a people, a country, a war, a wound, a mistake.

Saigonistas

As female artists tied to Việt Nam, are Llouquet and Chung affected by the same constraints as their local peers? The shift to market socialism has left artists without government support, to compete among themselves for shows and collectors. Despite overall increased national economic prosperity and higher standards of living, Taylor notes, women have had to endure social setbacks: "The rise in prostitution, domestic violence, and inequalities in the workplace made the late 1980s a considerably less prosperous time for women than men, which extends to women artists as well."[75] Fast-forwarding to 2021, the inequity Taylor mentions still pervades. The "re-gendering" of the country has reinforced patriarchal values and inequities.[76]

Llouquet's and Chung's status as Việt Kiều forms a buffer zone for gender, generational, and class divides. These Saigonistas have cultural capital and class position that puts them in an elite position within Vietnamese society. Their cosmopolitanism still allows them to transcend geographic strictures and social mores. Because of their greater facility with language, greater fiscal resources to produce work, and extended international networks, diasporic artists such as Llouquet, Chung, Đinh Q. Lê, and Jun Nguyễn-Hatsushiba emerge as standouts from the sea of local artists. Occasionally, "diasporic" artists are excluded in favor of "local" artists by foreign curators and institutions, but this is the exception to the rule. Often they are lumped by institutions and individuals under one category: "Vietnamese artist."

Chung's numerous international residencies attest to her ease with dealing with cultural institutions and negotiating difference. An American passport also allows for ease of travel. Vietnamese nationals have to go through more hurdles—permits to travel, invitation letters—when traveling overseas. Perhaps generational differences overshadow gender differences. Female artists in their fifties and older may feel more bound by gender hierarchies than younger cohorts. Although gender divides exist, younger artists appear to have more ease of movement and choices to create work, as long as they have the resources to support their practice. They feel less torn by the pull between tradition and modernity; after all, they are modern subjects.

Llouquet's contacts abroad, as well as her "foreign" contacts at "home" in Sài Gòn, have given her exhibition and organizational opportunities that are not available to many "local" artists, male or female. In October 2008, the French Consulate teamed up with the Wonderful District arts initiative (of which Llouquet is half), Sàn Art, Galerie Quynh, and the Fine Arts Museum to present *Le Mois de l'Image*, a series of exhibitions and performances highlighting the work of more than twenty Vietnamese and French artists, DJs, and VJs.[77] Llouquet used her ties with the French Embassy and her art world contacts in Việt Nam to facilitate these exchanges and ensure its success. From 2017 to 2019, Llouquet was the artistic director of Salon Saigon, which still holds regular artists' workshops, talks, screenings, and exhibitions focused on contemporary art.

Sandrine Llouquet and Tiffany Chung are artists who have had exhibitions in significant international venues, predominantly in Asia. Their work has not reached the level of visibility and given the same critical attention that Đinh Q. Lê, Jun Nguyễn-Hatsushiba, and An-My Lê have been afforded. Perhaps this is because the work addressed in this chapter does not overtly address historical trauma. Thus, it is more difficult to categorize Llouquet's and Chung's practice. Chung's work references Vietnamese pop culture, but it speaks of a Pan-Asian sensibility. Llouquet's work evokes her position as a cosmopolitan subject: at home everywhere and nowhere.

Relatively recently, Chung has addressed war, migration, and refugees in her work. Consequently, she has gained greater international prominence. Her war-related works were shown at the 2015 Venice Biennale (one of the most prestigious venues on the international art scene) and the 2018 Sydney Biennial, among numerous other museum exhibitions and biennials on four continents. Continuing her interest in critical cartographies, Chung debuted *Vietnam Exodus Project* in 2016 at Art Basel in Hong Kong. The series focuses on Vietnamese refugees in Hong Kong through a series of cartographic drawings, installations, and videos that use demographic data on refugees, interviews, and archival materials on asylum seekers. Connecting her firsthand experience as a refugee to the global Syrian refugee "crisis" now, Chung's *Syria Project* (2011–15) features abstract maps of meticulously researched data: the growing number of internally displaced people, refugee camps, and war dead, including children killed in different areas of conflict.

In 2019, Chung had a solo exhibit at the Smithsonian American Museum of Art entitled *Vietnam, Past Is Prologue*. The show's promotional material highlights her father's history as a war pilot and her own migration as starting point for her investigations of other histories of the Vietnamese diaspora. Chung was invited by the museum to exhibit work that "responds to the Vietnam War, and its legacy on the culture and population of the United States."[78] Demonstrating the claims of Asian American studies scholars such as Sylvia Chong, Yến Lê Espiritu, Mimi Thi Nguyễn, and Việt Thanh Nguyễn that the specter of the Việt Nam War continues to "return" to haunt the American public, the exhibition "probe[d] how the America we know today was shaped by Vietnam."[79] The show was held in conjunction with a group exhibit *Artists Respond: American Art and the Vietnam War, 1965–1975*. In all of these projects, Chung uses her signature stylized maps. Later in the chapter, I trace Chung's initial use of these maps, which originally include overt references not to the traumas of war and displacement but, rather, to the traumas of development. This illustrates my point about the legibility and fetishization of traumatic narratives within the global art scene.

Diasporic artists take advantage of the cheap labor available in Việt Nam to create their work. In a way, they have outsourced their production. Chung makes full use of a feminized Vietnamese workforce: many of her sculptural pieces are painstakingly handcrafted by hired help. For instance, thousands of pink pom-poms were glued to the surface of a giant bullhorn. Llouquet's work often relies on local craftspeople to construct (e.g., the Plexiglas playground, the reddish-pink giant ooze in *Milk*, and so on). Đinh Q. Lê has used local sculptors (*Lotusland*), embroiderers (*Texture of Memory*), and so on to create works for different projects. Nameless laborers do not make Jun Nguyễn-Hatsushiba's work; they often *are* the work. In his underwater videos, manual laborers such as cyclo drivers pantomime their earthbound duties. The work is more a reflection on progress and modernization than a critique of global/local circuits of gendered, classed labor.

In certain instances, artists must engage in "tedious work" themselves. Chung has rendered thousands of tiny circles for *Maps*, performing extensive, monotonous work. Similarly, Đinh Q. Lê's photo weavings are meticulously fabricated using a traditional grass matt-weaving technique learned from his aunt. Although Lê has considering hiring help, the complex montages require him to create each piece alone, a monotonous and physically laborious task.[80] Blurring the line between high and low, Lê appropriates a traditionally female mass-produced "handicraft," such as grass mat weaving, to create individual works of "high art" that feature collages of common photos and mainstream films. Llouquet's most commercially successful works are her drawings and paintings. These artists are merely rarefied versions of laborers on the global assembly line: artists and workers churn out products through time-consuming and monotonous tasks. In military socialism, artist and worker are one, but this is the era of differentiated gendered labor. The "traditionally feminine" attributes of "docility, dexterity, and tolerance for tedious work" applies to both the feminized Third World labor force and the artists.

In the global art market, are "Vietnamese" artists feminized and fetishized for a certain kind of labor-intensive work? The higher demand for works that feature the artist's physical touch and labor may illustrate this point. Yet the parallels do not sustain: the low-wage laborers' physical work is replaceable; they are expendable, anonymous. In contrast, artists' physical and mental labor are placed at a premium; their names become marketed, recognized global brands. Following the cultural theorist Walter Benjamin's insights, more than half a century later, the art world still places high value on "originality," aura, and (ethnic?) authenticity.[81] The artist's labor—whether manual or intellectual—becomes a prized commodity. Pierre Bourdieu notes a marker of class is the connoisseurship of creative originality and innovation.[82] The artist and her output (and their aura) becomes a synonymous object, a "unique" product—painstakingly produced, packaged, and ultimately endlessly reproduced in this age of media and migration.

It's a Wonderful World | Sandrine Llouquet

Sandrine Llouquet creates unassuming drawings, site-specific installations, and Flash animations that are simultaneously playful and evocative, hinting at wonder and wounds. Her practice embraces these contradictory impulses, culling images and references from mass media, her personal narrative, collective memory, and literature. Her images are at once familiar and unsettling— disjunctured, surprising, decontextualized. The presentation of her drawings and animations within complete installations point at the complexities of memory and representation, desire and lack, jouissance and despair. This part of the chapter examines Llouquet's "flexible citizenship" by focusing on her solo exhibition *Milk* at Galerie Quynh in 2008. A brief discussion of trauma studies discourse helps frame Llouquet's artistic strategies.

Referring to her body of work, Llouquet writes, "Each piece is a tentative . . . combination of the contradictory feelings which animate me, particularly violence and sweetness."[83] Violence and sweetness, ambivalence and liminality are at the heart of her practice. Trauma and kitsch, play and pathos are not polar binaries for Llouquet; they inform and transform each other. Perhaps this ambivalence occurs in her personal life, as well. Her daily interactions in Việt Nam reinforce the liminality of her subject position in that after more than ten years' residency in Sài Gòn, she is constantly reminded that she is not a "local" because she grew up France.

Llouquet's parents emigrated to France when she was a child; she has lived in Việt Nam sporadically throughout her adult life. She told me that she has always felt like a nomad, occupying an in-between space, constantly reinventing herself. In addition to immigration, her parents' divorce when she was a child made her feel as if she is in a state of "permanent detachment," forever in flux. As an undergraduate, she enrolled in the Hồ Chí Minh City Fine Arts University for a year (1997–98) because she wanted to learn lacquer painting techniques. But the university segregated her from the other students, as she noted with dismay:

> I don't know why. [The administration] never told me why. But I couldn't take classes with the other students. Maybe because then I couldn't speak Vietnamese that well; maybe because I was a foreign student. They let me

enroll in all the classes I wanted, but they gave me my own instructor, my own classes.[84]

Perhaps because of Llouquet's initial language difficulties, the school thought it made sense to give her separate instruction instead of having a potentially disruptive interpreter within a group class setting. Academic art lessons do not require extensive language-based instruction, however, as they are intensive hands-on studio sessions, either drawing and painting for hours from still life or nudes. "What I really wanted to do was to take the same life drawing classes, sit in on the rest with the students," she said. "At first I didn't have any friends, I did my own thing. But then the more curious ones came by, said hello. Then we had conversations."[85] An institutional decision to give her differential—perhaps deferential—treatment constrained her ability to belong and integrate. This exclusion suggests the ways overseas Vietnamese become assimilated yet segregated within the larger social fabric. Ong has used the term *flexible citizenship* to highlight how transnational subjects strategically position themselves within their chosen residence (whether temporary or permanent), maintaining privileges yet eliding full responsibilities as a citizen subject. For example, Ong notes that the Chinese government hails its diasporic subjects with patriotic, "prodigal son" rhetoric.[86] The Vietnamese government uses similar rhetoric, encouraging the 3.2 million overseas Vietnamese to resettle in Việt Nam to help build the country's infrastructure and future. It marks these transnational subjects as a desirable Other with valuable skills and foreign expertise yet also welcomes them as a "natural," and perhaps in time, naturalized extension of the national body politic. Việt Nam's Deputy Prime Minister and Minister of Foreign Affairs Phạm Gia Kiêm issued a statement in 2007 that highlights connections to homeland and minimizes political, generational, and geographic divides: "Wherever they are and irrespective of generations, young or old, male or female, political views, religions, ethnicity, and stories of the past, Vietnamese expatriates always turn to their country of origin."[87]

The Vietnamese government, however, has not always been so welcoming of Việt Kiều. In the 1990s, as the first waves of overseas Vietnamese returned, the state treated with them suspicion, as potential "traitors."[88] It harangued them at the workplace, conducted additional or more invasive inspections of Việt Kiều business owners, and immobilized diasporic and foreign investors via red tape.[89] Government red tape affects not only expatriates but also locals, the anthropologist Ken MacLean suggests, and has a much longer history. In *The Government of Distrust: Illegibility and*

Bureaucratic Power in Socialist Vietnam, MacLean argues that systemic mistrust stemmed from the creation and misuse of government documents in the 1920s. Surveys and decrees from high-level officers in Hà Nội to rural low-level cadres were intended to provide accurate documentation to better regulate citizens. The flurry of paperwork and audits, however, created bureaucratic confusion—its legacies still affecting locals and expats alike. Official reports reflected not on the ground realities but, rather, on a "papereality" between fact and fiction: "Consequently, living conditions in rural areas were neither fully legible . . . nor fully illegible to high-level officials. Instead they were somewhere in between."[90] In spite of the distrust, MacLean shows that all participants (bureaucrats, low-level officials, peasants) have been able to interact efficiently through continual compromise. Yet this is another example of strategic cartographies—flexible negotiations between official and unofficial frames of operation: "Amidst the resulting mistrust and ambiguity, many low-level officials were able to engage in strategic action and tactical maneuvering that have shaped socialism in Vietnam in surprising ways."[91] Ambiguous legibility, then, is both a challenge and a working solution: spaces of suspicion and surveillance also create counterhegemonic gaps.

The state's substantive control over the political economy and its constituents, native and foreign, hinges on apprehension. For example, Thu-hương Nguyễn-võ notes that the culture of state suspicion is also linked to perceived alliances during the Việt Nam War and today: Vietnamese ethnic minorities such as the Bahnar are distrusted because of their Roman Catholic religious affiliations, history of autonomous organizing, and ties to coreligious groups abroad.[92]

The "in-between"-ness of the state's subjects (rural citizens, ethnic minorities)—their simultaneous legibility and illegibility as native and Other—also extends to the Vietnamese diaspora. In this light, liminal Vietnamese subjects are seen as a part of the state but also separate. Thus, Hồ Chí Minh City Fine Arts University welcomed Llouquet as a potentially productive citizen-subject but also quarantined her. She was both legible and illegible as a Vietnamese subject—at once foreign and local. What she describes as her own "permanent detachment" may be her way to resolve this, a refusal to be placed, confined, defined. It is also a mark of cosmopolitanism: "home" is nowhere and everywhere. In her *Milk* exhibition, what Llouquet describes as the "tentative combination" of sweetness and violence takes on complex, disquieting permutations and themes through seemingly simple, disparate elements. On the ground floor of the gallery lies a cluster of individually framed, tenderly executed drawings with touches of watercolor. There is also a "playground" of five large, freestanding objects that the artist refers to as hybrids between sculpture and drawing—white silhouettes painted on clear Plexiglas supported by white framed boxes. The whole effect resembles large vitrines, perhaps a parody of Damien Hirst's disconcerting formaldehydes; instead of suspended animals, there are children.

On the second level, the viewer sees an ersatz red/pink puddle; enigmatic medium-size drawings on Plexiglas hang at eye level (plate 4). An almost life-size Plexiglas cutout of a girl jumping, arms akimbo, is suspended from the ceiling. Turning the corner into an enclosed gallery space, one is affronted by another giant red/pink puddle cascading down the walls, oozing diagonally through the space. Within the same space, there is a nearly life-size graphite drawing on the wall of a seated human figure with a jangled black-and-white video projection for a head. In a separate area upstairs, an intimate red/pink-colored room features another medium-size Plexiglas drawing, a desk lamp taped to the floor, and a small window that emits an eerie twilight. In the lower diagonal corners of this room the paint has been chipped off, resembling gaping wounds. An ambient, ominous soundtrack by the artist Thierry Bernard-Gotteland envelops the upstairs gallery like fog.

The title of the exhibition, *Milk*, conjures a host of associations: dairy milk, mother's milk; extraction and exploitation ("to milk a situation"); opaqueness ("milky"). "Milky" is also a synonym for spiritlessness, tameness, timidity. As a new mother, Llouquet may be covertly addressing childhood wonders and maternal preoccupations in her work. A tenuous combination of wistfulness, foreboding, and childlike awe tinges the work. As Sigmund Freud noted, tenderness and trauma underscore familial relations (think Oedipal drama, family traumas). Violence and sweetness, trauma and tenderness oscillate here, as elsewhere in Llouquet's oeuvre. Transformation and adaptation are recurring motifs in her work, as well. Her installations "adapt" to the strictures of a given location. The work also transforms the locale through interventions in the physical space (e.g., drilling a "river" into concrete gallery floors, as in *Bleu presque transparent* at the Cortex Athletico Gallery, Bordeaux, France, in November 2004, or painting directly on windows, as in *Trời Ơi!* at Galerie Quynh, Hồ Chí Minh City, in November 2005—all examples of the artist's site-specific work).

Llouquet's work process is spontaneous and intuitive, responsive to the physical space. She writes, "Adaptability to a place and to a context is not only a quality necessary to a person in their daily life, but also to the contemporary artist in their work."[93] Nonetheless, her adaptation and transformation of a space shifts that environment, causing the viewer to feel simultaneously at ease and out of place, out of bounds, an uncanniness. This divided or doubled self is the local-diasporic divide that the artist embodies, at once insider and outsider. Her French connections also mark this familiarity and distance. French colonial conditions mark different historical waves of "local" and "diasporic" movement. Militarized and intimate relations marked the path for postcolonial Vietnamese subjects emigrating to—and living in—France (including Llouquet's parents), as well as for Vietnamese with French citizenship now living as expatriates in Việt Nam (such as the artist and her peers).

Llouquet is a longtime fan of Lewis Carroll's *Alice's Adventures in Wonderland*, a tale in which ridiculous juxtapositions of the familiar abound. Within this childhood classic, the protagonist Alice undergoes repeated change and transformation. Llouquet's work conjures this state of limbo and disorientation. *Milk* is a surreal wonderland of sorts. The name Atelier Wonderful, an experimental artists' space in Hồ Chí Minh City that Llouquet organized with her former partner Bertrand Peret, references Carroll's novel. Every week for five months in 2005–6, Atelier Wonderful showcased a different project by visual artists, architects, graphic designers, and musicians.

Strangeness, surprise, and curiosity underlie wonder. Suspension of disbelief may be another facet. During the Renaissance, *Wunderkammern* (wonder cabinets) were immensely popular. Wunderkammers were collections of curiosities, microcosms of the known world; they were the predecessors to contemporary natural history museums. They were also wonderlands, miniaturized, contained. However, their purpose was to present a controlled, rational universe that its owner surveyed and controlled. The "wonder cabinets" and "wonder rooms" (rooms instead of cabinets filled from floor to ceiling with artifacts) of the European gentility expressed a curiosity about the known world and its dark recesses, a wanderlust to explore and exploit. The cabinets inspired wonder and morbid fascination. Llouquet's Plexiglas playground (as well as the other components of *Milk*) can also be seen as a contemporary wonder cabinet, although a postmodern disbelief, a questioning of (meta)narratives, has displaced the belief in a rational and moral order.

The art historians Martin Jay and Anne Friedberg have noted that Enlightenment rationality and the quest for truth through categorization and representation—as exemplified by the Wunderkammers—has been upended since the postmodern turn. During the Renaissance, paintings were seen as truthful windows on the world. The views from these "windows" were from a single vantage point.[94] Using linear perspective, generations of artists attempted to faithfully represent three-dimensional reality on a two-dimensional plane.[95]

Llouquet's playground formally resembles freestanding windows (if not cabinets or vitrines). Conceptually, however, they do not provide accurate "truthful" representations of the world at large; any notion of Cartesian truth is called into question. Linear perspective is merely a game. The lines on which some of the playground figures rest (conjuring a road, a perch, a horizon line) are actually three-dimensional elements. The viewer's initial grasp of the image becomes altered as these lines shift in space; the original image cannot hold, things fall apart. Trauma fragments any rational order.

With deft visual wit, Llouquet plays with form and content. She views the exhibition space as a blank space, a piece of paper. In the *White Noise* series of drawings on white Plexiglas presented as part of *Milk*, she deals with spatial relations. Using the planar surface of paper as a subject matter within the drawings, Llouquet cleverly comments on representation and reality. The surface of paper becomes a subject within the drawings, transforming within the series into a platform, a ledge with which human subjects interact. Llouquet is interested in visibility and invisibility, voids and gaps. Negative spaces within a picture plane or empty spaces within the gallery are also important.

The "white noise" of the projection also signifies a breakdown of representational logic. Linear perspective, linear logic, and linear narratives are scrambled. The teleological logic of modernity in Việt Nam is also scrambled. Llouquet's subtle, contemplative work straddles—and questions—the borders between sweetness and violence, form and content, fantasy and nightmare. Việt Nam's communist utopia, a proletariat fantasy, for some devolved into a nightmare realm of physical and psychic privations.

The two dominant colors of the exhibition—white and a reddish-pink (*màu đỏ đỏ*)—take on different registers within *Milk*. The gallery walls are painted white and light gray. One is not quite sure whether the light-gray areas are architectural shadows of the white walls; this subtle intervention adds to the sense of unease. Within both Western and Asian contexts, white often conjures innocence and purity. However, within Asian cultures white is the symbolic color of mourning. The recurring reddish-pinkish blobs on the floor and walls register as syrup or melted candy, an otherworldly waterfall, anthropomorphic shadows. The shiny blobs could also be outsize pools of nail polish or blood. The saccharine becomes sinister. The red/pink room with the gash in the paint—perhaps these are traces of trauma, abuse. The stains can also be read as sexual, a public display of private matters: menstrual blood, birth, sexualized violence. There are monsters outside (and inside).

The monstrous and mundane are inexplicably bound in Llouquet's work. At first glance it appears lighthearted; the subject matter, banal. On closer inspection, the mundane becomes monstrous, mutating as the viewer's perception shifts. In the cluster of small framed drawings a black rabbit with red eyes stares balefully out from among the other mostly "sweet" yet mysterious images (plate 5). Figures throughout the exhibition are in some way injured, or perhaps they are mutants. In the playground of white silhouettes, figures are disfigured, disjointed, limbless, headless. White upon white. The limbless, disfigured figures throughout the show bring to mind the spectacularized images on display at the War Remnants Museum in Hồ Chí Minh City of those affected by Agent Orange doing everyday activities, or of victims of war one encounters in urban and rural Việt Nam. The specters of historical trauma become contained within Llouquet's shadow boxes. The caricature-like white silhouettes in *Milk* recall Kara Walker's fantastical/nightmarish room-size black-paper cutouts, which reference the psychological, physical, and sexual violence of the antebellum South and its aftermath. Like Walker's work, Llouquet's work references gender, sexuality, and violence, but in a more obtuse vein.

The anomalous, anonymous figures in Llouquet's work are in the process of becoming, transforming, mutating, healing. Deleuze and Guattari conceive of "becomings" as mutants. (They use vampires and werewolves as examples.) Llouquet's humans are also mutants, "becomings." A "becoming is not a correspondence between relations. But neither is it a resemblance, an imitation, or, at the limit, an identification," Deleuze and Guattari write. "To become is not to progress or regress along a series. . . . [B]ecoming does not occur in the imagination, even when the imagination reaches the highest cosmic or dynamic level. . . . [Becomings] are perfectly real."[96] Llouquet's silhouettes and figurative drawings of "becomings" are not merely figments of the imagination; they are real, archetypical. They are uncanny: familiar and unsettling. Elaborating on the uncanny, Freud states there is a "doubling, dividing, and interchanging of the self."[97] These human representations are neither progressing nor regressing within fictional, scientific, or historical narratives. They simply are.

Việt Kiều are ambivalent subjects. Uncanny presences, returnees are both foreign and familiar. We are reminders of painful pasts and embodiments of hopeful futures. Freud states that "the uncanny [*unheimlich*] is something that is secretly familiar [*heimlich-heimisch*], which has undergone repression and *returned* from it."[98] Many overseas Vietnamese left in dire circumstances, only to return as unattainable visions—and, at times, false caricatures—of success and achievement. First rejected as traitors and then ambivalently embraced by the Vietnamese government, Việt Kiều embody the uncanny aspects of repression and return. They are increasingly a part of the national Vietnamese imaginary yet remain set apart. Việt Kiều disrupt the molar binary poles of local and foreigner.

In personal interviews, several Việt Kiều expressed dismay over double standards: foreigners received better service. At the same time, they experienced criticism from locals for not being "Vietnamese" enough. They must negotiate their dual molar identities: expatriate and Vietnamese. Doubling is also a hallmark of the uncanny, the same but not quite. Việt Kiều are the same but not quite. Local and overseas Vietnamese mirror each other with parallel histories, parallel lives. We are doubled and divided. We are a part of each other, yet torn apart.

Citizenship

New forms of citizenship encourage Việt Kiều to settle in Việt Nam, to officially become part of the nation-state to access property and voting rights, among others. We are encouraged to adopt molar identities and become "recognized within the current social formation."[99] Migrants are hailed as subjects, indoctrinated/interpellated, and enfolded within the nation-state's molar logic. Việt Kiểus' unstable position, however, mark them as the ultimate "becomings."

Transnational capitalism demands strategic subject positions that transcend geopolitical boundaries—strategic cartographies. Việt Nam's citizens, regardless of whether they are returnees, foreigners, or locals, must constantly reshape their molecular identities as the country reinvents itself. Becomings are shape-shifters, as Deleuze and Guattari assert. These becomings include foreign investors, intelligentsia, government officials, and Vietnamese local and diasporic entrepreneurs. For returnees and select foreigners, the government's offer of dual citizenship is an extension of flexible citizenship, in theory and practice.[100] Through shifting đổi mới policies, the state vacillates between allowing free rein and controlling its excesses. As Ong presaged, "New strategies of flexible accumulation have promoted a flexible attitude toward citizenship."[101] Vietnamese elites use flexible citizenship to their advantage. In short, those with real and cultural capital benefit on the new economic frontier.

The Art Part

Eva Cherniavsky uses the term *neocitizenship* to grapple with how political, economic, and affective notions of citizenship have radically shifted within neoliberal globalization. The biopolitical state can no longer adequately regulate its subjects to fit within a homogenizing imaginary. I counterpoise this with Deleuze and Guattari's claim that "becoming does not occur in the imagination. . . . [B]ecomings are perfectly real."[102] Cherniavsky's description of a homogenizing state imaginary also evokes MacLean's work on top Hà Nội officials who ineffectually tried to implement master plans on rural peripheries. In the 1920s, during the first stages of centralized Vietnamese government control, the state tried to mold exemplary model citizens.[103] Now the state no longer makes citizens in its image. Cherniavsky asserts that top-down practices have changed: "Contemporary flowering of civil society corresponds to the eclipse of normative vertical cultures in the emergence of the citizen as a kind of hologram or simulacrum."[104] The World Bank refers to civil society as a "wide array of organizations: community groups, non-governmental organizations [NGOs], labor unions, indigenous groups, charitable organizations, faith-based organizations, professional associations, and foundations."[105]

Within the frame of cyclical revolution I discussed in the introduction, political action and mobilization are no longer achieved from the top down or, from the upturning of society, from the bottom up. Intervening with the centralized state may not yield direct results.[106] The "flowering" of diffuse civil society purports to serve a multiplicity of sectors from the ground up but may be similarly ineffectual. Like the "papereality" of Vietnamese bureaucratic documentation that MacLean describes, citizens within society are now rendered unreal. Today's simulacral citizen-subject—no longer uniformly hailed by the state, now hyperindividuated (think target marketing)—is constantly shifting. What, then, "becomes" of the diasporic citizen-subject?

Following the logic of becomings being perfectly "real," this can be realized only in the realm of repeated return: the space of shuttling back and forth, an oscillation, "neither a progression nor a regression."[107] Within this new global order, standard geopolitical coordinates no longer make sense. Critical theory and analysis alone does not suffice in addressing neoliberalism's fractured states. Hence, acknowledging its limits is not a "turn away" from critical inquiry, Cherniavsky asserts, but a "return to theory through the byways" of lived experience, as well as cultural production.[108] This echoes Hal Foster's characterization of the art world's turn away from poststructuralist theory and the "return to the real" in the late 1990s, which marked a new phase of neoliberal subject making. Cherniavsky calls for "partial and improvised reckonings," what I call the space of return engagements. Knowledge production, she notes, should also encompass unknowing, an "impossibility of thinking the changing present."[109] I circle back to my ideas of the "negative return" as a space of unknowing, a challenge to positivism's classificatory rhetoric. Within the changing present, what are the parameters of dual citizenship for overseas Vietnamese?

Effective July 2009, the Vietnamese government approved dual citizenship for overseas ethnic Vietnamese and certain categories of foreigners who benefit Việt Nam through their work in science, national security, defense, or economic development.[110] The amendment revokes the Nationality Law of 1998, which banned dual citizenship.[111] Dual citizenship applies only to expatriates and the foreign-born offspring of a Vietnamese parent or of Vietnamese parents, granting them "all rights of citizenship," and requiring those who return to Việt Nam to "obey all citizens' duties toward the state and society according to its laws."[112] It sounds straightforward enough. Dual citizenship for nonlocals is an outgrowth of the overseas Vietnamese visa exemption decree, launched September 1, 2007. Trần Thất of the Ministry of Justice stated that "the new law meets the desire of many overseas Vietnamese to retain Vietnamese citizenship."[113] The new legislation affirms the logic of flexible citizenship: Việt Nam's (elite) citizens are afforded even more mobility of movement and leeway for capital accumulation and investment.

Return Investments

Why do Vietnamese who fled the communist regime decades ago desire to be a part of it now? Why would a cosmopolitan desire dual citizenship? Many expatriates retain close ties to their homeland, sending remittances to relatives in the country. Even those Việt Kiều who do not have blood relations now have business relations.

Dual citizenship mitigates the hassle of reapplying for visas and visa extensions and allows for greater levels of investment and property ownership. In 2006, Việt Kiều could own only one house and had to reside in the country for six months, although the law had a few exemptions.[114] Dual citizens face no such restrictions and can own more than one house.[115] Yet the government still owns the land. The government has reversed some older policies to build and maintain strong connections with overseas Vietnamese because of their monetary power. As of July 2015, restrictions were relaxed under the revised Law on Housing, with a caveat: total expatriate ownership was limited to "30 percent of the total units in one condominium complex, a maximum of 250 houses in a ward, or 10% of the total landed property units in one residential compound" with a fifty-year lease. In 2008, only 150 returning Vietnamese (citizens and noncitizens combined) bought homes in Việt Nam.[116] In 2015, 205 out one million Việt Kiều who wanted to buy homes in Việt Nam were able to obtain property rights due to continued difficulty in getting loans and approval. The overseas Vietnamese Nguyễn Trí Hiếu stated in a 2017 newspaper interview: "Unlike many Vietnamese who buy a house with their savings, foreigners buy homes using bank loans and only pay 15–20 percent with their money. However, foreign banks only offer a mortgage if the customer has property title insurance, which is now unavailable in Vietnam. So they are unable to obtain loans."[117] Despite these difficulties, developers are trying to keep up with demand. From 2015 to 2018, thirty-five thousand new high-end apartments were for sale (listed at $1,500 per square meter, at minimum). In comparison, in 2012–14, fewer than ten thousand units were listed.[118]

In 2015, Việt Kiều sent $12.5 billion in remittances to Việt Nam, more than twice the $6 billion sent in 2008.[119] This number continues to rise: in 2017, $13.8 billion was sent in remittances, growth of 16 percent from 2016.[120] In 2018, the number grew to $16 billion, "more than 100 times [Việt Nam] had received 25 years earlier," declared the newspaper *VnExpress International* in January 2019.[121] Ivan Small notes that in 2019 the country was among the top ten to receive remittances from its diaspora, and "international remittance flows are higher than overseas development assistance."[122]

Remittances illustrate the many return engagements returnees profer. Among the fiscal returns of remittances are also "social remittances," or "gray matter," which, Small states, are "the ideas and knowledge the diaspora bring home from elsewhere." The government enthusiastically encourages remittances, foreign investment, resettlement, and tourism.[123] In response, more than half a million Vietnamese expatriates visit Việt Nam a year, up from eight thousand in 1987.[124] The expertise and capital of overseas Vietnamese are now viewed as integral components of the country's modernization. These moves strengthen nationalist sentiment and ties to the "motherland."

Dual citizenship is also a way to further stimulate economic growth and draw diasporic Vietnamese into the country's nation-building project. It both reaffirms the psychic and geopolitical bounds of the nation-state and recognizes the borderless flows of capital. Former Foreign Affairs Minister Phạm Gia Kiêm stated, "No matter where, all the sons and daughters of the Vietnamese nation long to be back to their motherland and reunite with family, friends to engulf themselves in and share all the successes of the country's cause of 'đổi mới' (reform and renovation) [*sic*]." But just exactly how the "sons and daughters of the Vietnamese nation" from afar will "share" and participate in "success," and the terms of their participation—framed by regulations and laws—is still being debated, point by point.

Despite attempts to incorporate Việt Kiều, their status is still uncertain, open to dispute. These returnees defy fixed molar positions in Việt Nam's social order. New forms of belonging and citizenship entail new responsibilities. With the privileges of citizenship—including voting—also come banal duties such as conscripted military service for men of a certain age. Việt Kiều's offspring could also be conscripted.[125] The law provides exemptions for overseas residents who live in particular places. Dual citizens' right to vote and in which elections is yet to be decided. Trần Thật, the director of the Department of Justice Administration of the Ministry of Justice, has said that the state will be "flexibly regulat[ing]" these rights.[126] Details have yet to emerge. Thật told the newspaper *Tuổi Trẻ*, "We have to accept the reality that a Vietnamese citizen overseas cannot carry out the same obligations as those in Việt Nam." Similarly, Deputy Chairman Nguyễn Đục Kiên stated in March 2009, at a National Assembly meeting concerning new laws for Việt Kiều, that they were "an indispensable part of the nation," but that they would have different "responsibility, duty, rights and benefit[s]" from resident Vietnamese. He decried proposals to have Việt Kiều receive equal property benefits. Thus, we are a part of the social fabric yet set apart. The position of Việt Kiều within Vietnamese society is unstable. Their economic and educational privilege is welcome in certain instances but must be curtailed, contained, and controlled. Negotiations continue over the stipulations governing both dual citizens and noncitizens—legal acts becoming lived actions. Legal strictures and state structures define molar identities.

In doing so, they contain internal politics and external market forces. Deleuze and Guattari note that molar subjectivities are segmented to "ensure and control the identity of each agency, including personal identity."[127] Việt Kiều problematize this equation since they are domestic and foreign figures. Their uncertain status reflects Việt Nam's ongoing uncertainty on how to balance domestic concerns with foreign influence.[128] Việt Nam is in precarious shape.

The Art Part

Born in 1969 and raised in Đà Nẵng, Tiffany Chung received her bachelor of fine arts from California State University, Long Beach, and her master of fine arts from the University of California, Santa Barbara. She returned to Việt Nam in 2000 and has lived in Sài Gòn for more than seventeen years. She moved to Houston, Texas, in 2017 to be closer to her parents. During her time in Việt Nam, Chung identified as local. She often uses a pop sensibility to capture the essence of the vibrant city life of an increasingly urban—and urbane—Việt Nam. Her pastiche installations combine photography; sculptural elements often made of foam, wood, or fabric; and, at times, video. Highly stylized sculptural objects reference street vendors' carts, gas stations, and so on. Her work offers a new vision of space and place—a candy-colored utopic and hyperreal fantasy that displaces the historical documentary images of a traumatized topography. Chung foregrounds excess, consumer culture, and surface and questions the distinctions between public and private space, (cultural) adaptation and (economic) aspiration, performativity and pleasure.

Chung's *Maps* series comments on what Việt Nam and its citizens are becoming. My analysis of this series questions the logic of progress and connects cartographic and colonial impulses. I also critique the manner in which "Vietnamese" artists such as Chung gets fetishized within a global art market.

Maps is the title of Chung's 2008 series of works on paper. She uses urban planning and subway maps as a starting point to create abstract, intricately detailed, large-scale renderings. The images consist of colorful dots and lines that form patterns, shapes. The forms almost morph before one's eyes, turning and turning. Mapping is a form of knowledge, a way to exert control over the known universe, a way to chart development. The cartographic gaze extends the limits of human vision, makes the unknown known.

The cultural theorist Graham Huggan notes, "Maps are neither copies nor semblances of reality but modes of discourse which reflect the ideologies of their makers."[129] I connect the process of a critical mapping as a manner of becoming. A becoming is not a "resemblance, an imitation . . . an identification" in the same fashion that maps are neither "copies nor semblances" of the real.[130] Although Cherniavsky argues that neoliberal citizens now are holograms or simulacral,[131] I assert that mapping as becoming envisions and embodies multiple realities at once—both "foreign and familiar," as in the case of diasporic artists. In this way, rather than merely reflecting ideology (as Huggan suggests), cartography also creates reality.[132] Strategic cartographies, beyond just reflecting given, mapped identities, forges other possibilities. Mapping is a mode of being, becoming. The urban planner and theorist Annette Miae Kim underscores this process: "Maps do more than represent points of view; they play an active role in constructing them."[133]

Chung's *Maps* is a project aligned with critical cartography's aims at thinking through affective, biopolitical, and spatial relationships charted by maps. Chung notes in a written artist statement that the project aims "to examine the cultural and spatial transformations linked to economic development that are taking place in the outer areas of Sài Gòn where rural and urban intersect. I'm interested in observing the urbanization process that is going on here while relating it to some new cities developed in the past twenty years in other Asian countries."[134] Indeed, Việt Nam is in the midst of historic, breakneck development; the country is transitioning from a largely rural economy to an urban one and shifting from a state-run economy to a market economy. Following China's urbanization, Việt Nam's infrastructure is increasingly decentralized.[135] Urban sociologists such as J. John Palen also note that center-periphery models of settlement and development do not account for the organic, multicentric growth and decline of urban, suburban, and rural zones (financial districts, residential areas, commercial centers, and so on).[136] Sài Gòn is currently planning its decentralization, charting new financial, residential, and educational zones.[137]

Chung's "maps" resemble organic growth, perhaps mold or microorganisms growing in a petri dish. For the artist, Việt Nam's rapid economic development is both bounty and blight. Chung presents a candy-colored utopic universe as a veneer for dystopic realities. She occasionally culls images from Ebenezer Howard's book *Garden Cities of To-morrow*. Howard is the founder of the English garden-city movement, which sought to incorporate expanses of green within urban networks.[138] This movement had long-lasting effects on urban planning throughout the world. Perhaps Chung's organic maps wryly comment on these utopic garden cities. Garden cities are exemplars of controlled growth. However, in Chung's vision this organic growth is overripe, perhaps decaying or festering. The maps also look fungal. Fungi are parasitic organisms that lack true root and stem structures; they reproduce by spores. Perhaps Chung is noting that this rapid urban development is parasitic; it lacks depth, roots, sustainability, and structure. Parasitic or paradisic, the center cannot hold.

To continue the discussion of spores, representations of diasporic communities often use seed/spore analogies and imagery. On closer inspection, Chung's maps consist almost entirely of circles and dots. These dots can be viewed as spores, diasporic seeds scattered. While discussions of diasporic communities have been conceptualized along home-exile or center-periphery axes (in which a community moves from a "homeland" to settle in other territories), more recent discussions of diasporic communities have shifted away from this home-displacement binary to account for the complexities of multiple diasporic identities (in which one's subjectivity consists of multiple movements and affiliations).[139] Chung's own identity as a "diasporic" artist is questioned: yes, she emigrated from Việt Nam and settled in the United States to live and study, but she has since lived in Japan, among other locales. Older models of diaspora would not be able to "map" her movements and identifications beyond simple conceptions of home and abroad. The overlapping dots in Chung's maps may speak of these ongoing movements and patterns of settlement, metaphorically and, perhaps, literally represented by the overlapping patterns.

The Empire's New Clothes

The system of economic exchange and development that fuels growth is fungus-like—opportunistic, parasitic, but not necessarily fungible. Goods and services are not equally exchanged. The cultural anthropologist Lisa Rofel has argued for a framework of "discrepant modernities," which challenges universal-local dichotomies in rhetoric on modernity, subject formation and identification, and consumption. Being attuned to the fact that modernity is not a singular, uniform destination point can provide a richer conception of uneven and parallel socioeconomic developments of nation-states across the globe. For instance, Third Worlds exist in First Worlds, and vice versa, as Trinh has noted. Rofel questions discourses pertaining to modernity and its Eurocentric, homogeneous, and teleological assumptions; she advocates a conception that does not reify binaries between universalism and cultural pluralism. Instead of viewing modernity as "a singular certainty" or separate cultural space, Rofel acknowledges "discrepant modernities"—localized psychic and real spaces and places in which relationships to modernity are articulated and contested.[140] Chung's work also comments on the rhetoric of modernity and its elisions. Urban planning, various maps, and utopic visions of development (including garden cities) all forward particular visions of controlled progress and order.

Chung's large drawing *10.75°N 106.6667°E 1867/2007* (plate 6) acknowledges these discrepant modernities. It layers a 2007 Seoul subway map, a Tokyo Metro transportation map, and an urban planning map for Sài Gòn made in 1867, when the city became part of the French colonial empire. Kim's practice of critical cartography, like Chung's artistic practice, puts in conversation distinct temporal moments. Kim traces two generations of critical cartography. The first, colonial mapmaking, sought to affirm an empire's power and marked its colonies. Serving primarily an economic function, these maps were used in resolving property and legal disagreements. The second generation of critical cartography aims to "move beyond mapping the edges of physical mass in favor of time, social relations, and economic activity."[141] What is officially known as Hô Chì Minh City originated as two separate cities, Cholon and Sài Gòn, which grew under different regimes: French colonialism, Chinese regulation, the Việt Nam War, and socialist reunification. Each of these historical moments has influenced the city's design and left affective legacies, shaping how people relate to one another and move through contemporary Sài Gòn's spaces. Although invisible on a single map, these discrete sociopolitical moments and movements can be discerned by looking at different maps and city systems. Hence, Chung layers different historical timelines and cities. Each heritage—the imperial, colonial, modern—informs the others. It is neither "progression nor regression," as Deleuze and Guattari observe of becomings. Whichever way one moves on a subway map, one does not progress or regress. One simply circulates among rhizomatic nodes, coming, going, and back again.

Chung's use of the 1867 colonial French map of Sài Gòn suggests that this historical moment also informs the present and future experience—and development—of the Asian metropolis. The Tokyo and Seoul subway maps point at possible modes after which contemporary Sài Gòn, and Việt Nam at large, may "map" itself. As an example, Việt Nam is currently building two subway systems. One, in Sài Gòn, is being built by the Japanese conglomerates Japan International Cooperation Agency (JICA), Sumitomo Corporation, and Shimizu-Maeda, with Korean, French, and Italian subcontractors.[142] The other metro system, in Hà Nội, is being built by the China Railways Sixth Group. *Scientific American* notes that these two historic projects "have the potential to transform Saigon and Hanoi into modern cities with efficient, clean, and accessible mobility for all."[143] Plagued by delays, both projects were set to be completed by 2020, but are still in progress. JICA first conducted a feasibility study in Sài Gòn in 2006, whereas Hà Nội's project broke ground in October 2011.[144] The energy and policy adviser Tali Trigg claims in a 2018 op-ed that the problems are not technical but due to improper "administrative planning, technical cooperation and effective implementation."[145] Overall, the projects suffer from inadequate "mapping"— a clear, unified overview.

Mapping—apart from legal and logistical parameters (as in the first generation of critical cartography Kim outlines)—registers on a social, everyday level (the second generation of critical cartography). Kim notes that maps chart "the important ways the space is used, negotiated, and experienced."[146] In addition to the purported public confusion over the overarching Việt Nam metro plans, the everyday lived experience of major urban restructuring can also be frustrating. The official guidelines and plans of the metro projects do not reflect daily negotiations, the fact that Sài Gòn street "maps created just a year ago [in 2017] are largely useless, and getting around can be a nightmare."[147] Critical cartography, such as Chung's and Kim's interventions, addresses the tensions of space, especially of spaces and people in flux.

Việt Nam's having different foreign partners for the metro system project (Japan in Sài Gòn, China in Hà Nội) echoes Chung's layering of the different subway maps. In addition to being "models" for development, comparative Asian modernities can serve as cautionary tales. Trigg warns that Việt Nam's metro projects' "lack of proper planning and enforcement," mirroring the Bangkok metro's recent (2016) Purple Line "debacle."[148] Among other issues, the cost of the Sài Gòn metro system has tripled over initial estimates, and the construction of Hà Nội's metro has suffered from a series of accidents, including the death of a civilian in 2015 after a metal beam fell onto a passing car.[149] The accident-ridden Chinese collaboration versus the accident-free Japanese partnership feeds into "longstanding assumptions in Vietnam about the perceived superiority of Japanese workmanship and engineering."[150] As Việt Nam forms international partnerships, it continues to align itself along strategic cartographies—drawing and redrawing itself after multiple geopolitical possibilities. In the case of the fraught metro projects, Việt Nam is aligning itself with both Japan and China, leading embodiments of Asian socioeconomic and cultural power.

Chung's *10.75°N 106.6667°E 1867/2007* looks to the future but also to the past. Sài Gòn's colonial development also shapes its current footprint. Kim asks rhetorically, "Can alternative maps effectively reconstruct power relations? Or is this form of representation inescapably bound to reproduce hegemonic epistemologies of knowledge?"[151] Chung's "alternative" maps reveal shifting power relations by using mapmaking's existing representational tropes. She makes a connection between imperial violence and the contemporary processes of globalization. The postcolonial critic Gerry Turcotte writes, "Mapping and imperialism are linked. One is a signpost of the other's presence, a signal of ownership as resolute as a planted flag. . . . The cartographer's gaze is a totalizing one, naming and organizing a 'blank' space into knowable spheres. . . . The cartographer's eye/I is invisible, concealed, transparent, just as the language of imperialism is presented as natural and universal. . . . Maps are re/presentations, palimpsests, forgeries."[152] Is globalizing rhetoric regarding development another echo of imperialist discourse? Is this the empire's new clothes? Việt Nam's current shifts echo past patterns of displacement, racialized hierarchies, and socioeconomic disparity. As noted previously, First World economies such as Japan, Korea, and the United States, as well as multinational corporations, have funded its infrastructural development.

Other works in the series also layer different maps from different eras. The palimpsest layers reveal the underlying foundations and assumptions of urban progress. The layering of maps and diagrams to form a disorienting topography challenges the "singular certainty" of the original maps.[153] Colonial ideology is overlaid with visions of modernity. There is no single, coherent vision, just cryptic terrain. The work's intricate details sprawled seemingly endlessly render this composite geography simultaneously tender and terrifying—a brave new world.

Super Markets

The international art markets in which Tiffany Chung's work circulates highlight the politics of difference. Chung's rise on the international circuit was marked by the exhibition *Play*, a photographic series from 2008 featuring Vietnamese cosplayers[154] (not discussed here). This was her first solo show in New York; it was held at a gallery in the downtown Manhattan Chelsea neighborhood, a highly competitive art market. Home to more than fifty high-end galleries, Chelsea is known as the center of the New York gallery scene. Since the center of the Western avant-garde art movement moved from Paris to New York after World War II, Chelsea is now arguably the "center" of the dominant art world.[155] Postcolonial critics such as George Yúdice argue that the idea of a single center is outdated.[156] Now there are multiple commercial and cultural centers, with attendant peripheries. The United States' post–World War II status as the financial and artistic leader of the modern world is now questioned. It has become a faltering empire, and new economic giants have emerged from its long shadow.

Art and economics are linked. The World Bank predicts that India and China will be the two top economic superpowers within the next few decades. China is currently the second largest economy in the world.[157] The power of art markets and art stars in both countries reflects this economic growth, and the art world is shifting again. New York, Paris, and London are no longer the purveyors of what is considered "hot." Hong Kong and Dubai have become major players and purchasing sites, with auction houses holding regular shows in these locales. The journalist Matt Miller notes, "The art market has gone global. . . . Russian oligarchs, Chinese property developers, and Indian industrialists are becoming as critical to the upper reaches of the international art scene as American hedge fund heads."[158] These ascendant economic powerhouses have fueled the development of cutting-edge art scenes and profitable art markets. Art markets follow bull markets. The art world is similar to any other marketplace.

Competition drives market economies and art markets. Bourdieu links economic and cultural development: capitalist desire for new commodities and consumers parallels the art world's desires for new cultural commodities and collectors.[159] Other New York gallerists such as Ethan Cohen Fine Arts (www.ecfa.com) have cornered the market for "niches" such as contemporary avant-garde Chinese art.

High-profile living Chinese contemporary artists have fetched millions for a single work of art. Case in point: The Beijing-based "cynical realist" Yue Minjun's self-portrait sold for $7 million at Christie's first Hong Kong auction in May 2008.[160] His contemporary, Zeng Fanzhi, is now the top-ranked artist living Chinese artist in terms of sales: *The Last Supper* (2001), featuring identical seated youths wearing red scarves (indicating membership in the communist Young Pioneers, sold at Sotheby's Hong Kong on October 5, 2013, for $23,269,070. In 2019, Yue was still among the ten top-selling living Chinese artists; his sales have totaled $148,545,080.[161] In his cartoon-like paintings he is cloned endlessly in a single image. The bubble gum-pink clones all wear the same grin, which can be read as a mocking response to China's historical traumas such, as the Cultural Revolution and Tiananmen Square.[162]

The art historian Karen Smith, a critic of contemporary Chinese art, notes that Yue's signature smile does not signal irony. Rather, it masks "real feelings of helplessness." Smith also suggests that the grin has a long history within Chinese traditional art, particularly the Maitreya Buddha ("laughing Buddha"), "who can tell the future and whose facial expression is a laugh. Normally there's an inscription saying that you should be optimistic and laugh in the face of reality."[163] By removing the spiritual inscription as well as propaganda slogans, Yue makes room for a host of associations.

Both Yue's pink and Sandrine Llouquet's *Milk* installation of reddish+pink (*màu đỏ đỏ*) may evoke the "communist red" associated with socialist China, Việt Nam, and Russia. The art historian Tingting Dai connects

Yue's red-pink and his figures' outsize, "swollen" heads to injury, bruising, a physical metaphor for trauma. Furthermore, Dai notes that Yue's paintings (e.g., *Garbage Hill* [2009], a pile of smiling pink heads) refer to propaganda photographs from the Cultural Revolution, in which masses of male and female Red Guards are pictured uniformly smiling.[164] Minjun's and Zeng's works are popular among foreigners looking for "political" art that would make a return on their investments. Within the past ten years, the prices for contemporary Chinese art have skyrocketed. As a result, collectors' interest has reached a plateau. This once emerging market has reached a saturation point. The *Atlantic* suggests that a younger generation of Chinese artists are no longer making the "political" work popular from the mid-1990s to the early 2000s. They prefer abstraction and to explore "[twenty-first]-century themes such as urban malaise and the digital era, rather than narrowly Chinese [sociopolitical] concerns."[165] Yet these trends still fall into my larger argument about how the traumas of history and modernization ("urban malaise") get fetishized and consumed by a global art market. Regardless of creative shifts, Chinese art is still breaking records due to the nation's economic ascendance and a growing local collector base. For example, the Chinese modernist painter Zhang Daqian (b. Sichuan Province, 1899; d. 1983) is the artist whose work has sold at the highest price ever at an auction, eclipsing Pablo Picasso (who is second on the list) by $31 million annual sales in 2017.[166] Significantly cheaper, Southeast Asian art has been hyped as the next "hot thing." Southeast Asian trade lays the foundation for Southeast Asian high art.

Over the past decade, articles from the *International Herald Tribune* to the *New York Times* have trumpeted the rise—and rising prices—of Vietnamese contemporary art.[167] Anticipating the surge of interest in Southeast Asian art, gallerists such as the New York–based Tyler Rollins and Valentine Willie, who has had a virtual empire of galleries in Singapore, Yogyakarta, Kuala Lumpur, and Manila, have chosen to specialize in Southeast Asian artists. Valentine announced his partial retirement from commercial art in September 2012 to focus on consulting for regional museums and not-for-profit art institutions.[168] Rollins's roster includes Vietnamese, Thai, and Cambodian artists. "After many years of travel in the region," his description of his gallery states, "we have identified an impressive group of emerging and mid-career artists whose work we feel privileged to present to New York audiences, in many cases for the first time."[169] Thus, it represents the gallerist as an expert anthropologist or archaeologist of sorts, discovering works from the exotic margins of the (art) world to share with a rarefied New York clientele "for the first time." This hints at neocolonial discovery and conquest, the unveiling of previously unknown cultural riches. Echoing the rhetoric of fin-de-siècle World's Fairs, the gallerist is both scavenger and cartographer, mapping out unfamiliar terrain and identifying the best specimens from far-flung locales. It may just be Rollins's goal to discover—or establish the market for—a "great Vietnamese artist." Bourdieu notes that a work of art is created "twice over": first by the artist, and then by the spectator (gallerist, critic, collector, museumgoer, etc.) and his society.[170] A given art world confers value on artists and their artworks (which reflects that fickle audience's aesthetic, cultural, and class interests).[171] Rollins and those who agree with him—myself included—evaluate and translate artists and artwork the (Third or Second) world over for an international art audience. Again, the question is one not of discovering a "great" artist, but of acknowledging the cultural assumptions of what constitutes greatness and the systems that occlude certain gendered, raced perspectives.[172]

Many diasporic artists, including those residing in Việt Nam, take advantage of the opportunity to get more bang for their buck. Producing artwork in a developing country costs a fraction of what it would take in First World countries. For instance, the large-scale prints Chung makes for her photo-based work cost about $100 to produce in Việt Nam. In the United States, such prints would cost ten times as much to make. Her photographic prints are listed at around $9,000, and drawings start at $15,000. Chung hires professional photographers, models, photo retouchers, videographers, and film editors for her video projects in Việt Nam for far less than their American counterparts would charge. It takes a proverbial Vietnamese village to make an art video. I have taken advantage of the cheap, highly skilled labor available in Southeast Asia for my own art. As artists, we become middlemen. We must know the local language and customs or have a translator to manage an ambitious art project. It is impossible to produce the same quality and quantity of work at the same low rate in the United States.

Conclusion

Most local artists and organizers I asked said there was no difference between Việt Kiều artists and Vietnamese artists who had been born and raised in the country. Some cited collaborative efforts. Perhaps this was in deference to the fact that I am a Việt Kiều artist myself. Perhaps this was in keeping with mass-media and government rhetoric. But others gave varied answers. Some Việt Kiều had advantages: an artist's legibility, visibility, and marketability hinge in part on language and access, in addition to talent. Nonlocal artists have more leeway.

Divides still exist. A part yet apart. Many local artists recognize that if they learn English and overcome language barriers, there will be greater opportunities. Grants, residency, and exhibition opportunities are often available only in English, increasingly the global lingua franca. Artists who do not have some grasp of English are disadvantaged when accessing information about grants. They also are deprived of vital conceptual information about international art movements and theory. However, diasporic artists residing in Việt Nam may be overlooked because they are not authentically "Vietnamese." International collectors and curators often conflate local and diasporic categories, to the chagrin of some local artists. Jun Nguyễn-Hatsushiba and Đinh Q. Lê's primacy in gaining international attention reflects the advantages of Việt Kiều artists.[173] Some in the local art community were dismayed that the government selected Nguyễn-Hatsushiba—and not a "local" artist—as the official representative of Việt Nam at the 2005 Venice Biennale, one of the international art world's most significant exhibitions. This situation speaks to the politics of representation on various levels.

In the course of this chapter I have examined Tiffany Chung's and Sandrine Llouquet's artistic concerns, as well as the art markets in which they operate. I have argued for complex considerations of local-diasporic binaries and identifications, troubling simple categorizations while recognizing the usefulness of such distinctions.

Both local and diasporic Vietnamese artists desire success and visibility within international art circles. But the Vietnamese government's contradictory desires to encourage and curb economic growth and creative expression constrains their output. The ongoing quest for the next hot market/trend fuels the desire of collectors, auction houses, and gallerists to commodify complex Vietnamese subjectivities and identifications into marketable entities. And our conceptions of what is avant-garde limit curators' and critics' desire to fully understand and contextualize these movements. The art communities of Việt Nam lack governmental support and infrastructure—education, exhibition venues, grants, and art criticism. Yet they are thriving. Artists such as Sandrine Llouquet, Tiffany Chung, among many others continue to blur and shift boundaries. As increased international and regional interactions within and outside Việt Nam continue, new identities are forming, "becoming."

Personal and
Public Archives

Fragments and
(Post)Colonial Memory

THIS CHAPTER LOOKS AT the return to historical archives evident in the contemporary artwork of both the Cambodian painter and collagist Leang Seckon and the Vietnamese American experimental filmmaker Hồng-Ân Trương. Throughout the chapter, I make the case that the reappearance of history's fragments—colonial and modern—as well as the formal use of fragmentation in their works question the spatial and temporal contradictions of modernizing projects.

Time and space are compressed, congealed within the archive. In this enclosed space, the past is unearthed in the present. Trương and Seckon engage archives in different ways. Seckon is creating an artistic archive, a public statement culled from his personal collection of memories and mass-media remnants. Trương uses archival footage to point at the gaps in national identity and representation.

Jacques Derrida notes that the Greek etymology of the word *archive* entails both "commencement" and "commandment," evoking authenticity *and* authority. The archives, or *archons*, of the Greek superior magistrates embody authority. But it is also concealed, sheltered. Thus, the archives are visible as authoritative sites, yet they are also hidden and therefore conceal authority. Reflecting on

Freud, as well as technology and memory, in *Archive Fever*, Derrida muses that the interior psyche is reflected in external, public archives. Yet both are mere traces.[1] There is no inside or outside, only difference.[2] The inner world of the mind and the archive of the outer physical world imperfectly mirror each other. The notion of authenticity is questioned. Again there is a doubling: the interior, invisible private realm of the psyche, site of hidden "truths" for psychoanalysts, and the visible public collection, the site of "authentic" and originary data for archivists.[3] Both are flawed constructions. Just like his earlier insights on the inherent lack within language, Derrida notes that the archive—the site of the inscription of collective memory and official history—is imperfect.

Derrida's insights on the archive take into account Freud's pleasure principle and death drive—*Eros* and *Thanatos*—two conflicting motivating forces. The pleasure principle is linked to an archive or conservation drive. In this capacity, the "archive affirms the past, present, and future; it preserves the records of the past and it embodies the promise of the present to the future."[4] The death drive, in contrast, is "archive destroying."[5] Not only does the death drive "incite forgetfulness, amnesia, the annihilation of memory"; it also forcefully propels the "eradication" of "the archive, consignation, the documentary or monumental apparatus."[6] Trương and Seckon mine the oscillation between remembering and forgetting, between eros and Thanatos in their work. Seckon fights against historical amnesia and cultures of indifference through his testimonials of collage and paint. His *Heavy Skirt* series is the promise of the present and the past to the future. Art and beauty survive. This is not to valorize his efforts at a commercial art space. His autobiographical series becomes a portable archive, a time capsule delivered to a different (if not parallel) universe.

Seckon's archive is read as authentic, for he is "authentically" Cambodian, telling "true" stories from the deep recesses of his inner psyche. But as Derrida would point out, these attempts fail. It is all a mere trace. And Seckon knows this. His pieces cobble together what resembles autobiography (*Heavy Skirt* references his poor mother's mended skirt) but stitches it into a larger myth about Cambodia, nationhood, and survival. He cobbles together stories Cambodia tells itself about its golden past and stories that have been told about Cambodia's traumatic past into a textured fable. It is a collective memory, not only an individual one. Memory is part reality, part mythology.

Autobiography can encompass fact and fiction. I assert that Seckon is strategic when he claims he is only telling personal stories. This tactic serves a double function. First, it gets him out of trouble with the Cambodian government; he does not make *overt* political critique. Second, his personal narrative is the "difference" the international art market craves: a Cambodian artist *must* speak his or her "local" experience of suffering and survival, of the double traumas of history and development.

The doubling continues: archive fever is the desire to preserve memory *within* a person ("to save") but also the yearning for this information to be public ("to print out").[7] It is the fever to maintain cherished, perhaps secret, knowledge for oneself, but it is also the fever to share it with others. Instead of embodying an intimate personal archive, Trương overloads the viewer with national representations. Her aim is to deconstruct identity and nationhood, not to reconstruct it, as Seckon does. Fever is both passion and symptom. For Trương, *Indochine* is both desire and illness: love unto death. The desire of colonial possession bears the trace of death and violence.[8] Colonization encompasses both the pleasure principle and the death drive. It is both eros and Thanatos. The colonial archive is writ large on its subject's psyche and bodies. In a sense, the colonies are the archive, the public manifestation of an interior drive. The archive is the warehouse, the repository of its master's innermost desires. In the creation of its own colonial vision and archives, the center attempts to eradicate peripheral history and memory. In her use of mirror images, Trương comments that the inner and outer worlds have no real bearings. There is no center, no periphery; they are mutually constitutive. The external institutions of discipline penetrate the interior psyche. The truth claims of the state compete with the will to truth of its subjects.[9] This is the "archival violence" Derrida speaks of, the omissions and repetitions. The collapse of memory—the impulse of the death drive—are the prerequisites of the archive: "the archive takes place at the place of originary and structural breakdown of the said memory."[10] Memory and history falters; the archive aims to take its place. As Trương demonstrates, the interior colony of the mind is where things break down. Her endless loops and her breakdown of narrative and images all point to the effects of archival violence. There is no cohesive memory, no coherent identity.

Epistemic breakdowns occur in multiple locations. Writing about the possibilities and limits of postcolonial archives, Sandhya Shetty and Elizabeth Jane Bellamy state, "Archival violence occurs within the purview of colonialist power/knowledge, but it also occurs 'at the home' of the *archons*— or as Derrida would emphasize, '*there*' in the liminal space where the law meets writing."[11] The letter of the law is written, inscribed on colonial bodies and minds. This is where the liminal archive, the colony, reveals itself to be the place of both "commencement" and "commandment," simultaneously a beginning and a mandate. The rule of the law starts here. Imperial decrees are instituted, tested, revised here. In the beginning there was the Word.

The archival primacy of text and image erases other situated knowledge. To alleviate archival violence (and its omissions), it is crucial to feel and listen to embodied—and geographically embedded—sites of comprehension. Boreth Ly argues against the logocentrism of Southeast Asian studies archives—founded in colonial scholarship—as well as the primacy of the visual within visual studies as a field.[12] Verbal and visual objects of study are not objective. They are geopolitically subjective. Ly notes that, "unlike in the West where there is an understanding of pure, objective and empirical vision, local Southeast Asian perspectives on objects and visions are more embodied and multi-sensorial."[13] Yet I caution against Ly's partitioning of "local"-nonlocal, East-West embodiments. To be attuned to translocal subjectivities, I champion sonic and spiritual modalities of knowing. In this chapter, I pay particular attention to the metaphysical and tactile registers of Seckon's oeuvre, as well as the sounds and silences in Trương's output.

The immaterial and the material continue to be coeval aspects of the archive, whether the archive is embodied, at a physical institution, or dispersed virtually. *Archive Fever* was first presented as a lecture near the dawn of the internet age in 1994, two years after the phrase "surfing the internet" was coined and four years before Google's search engine was launched.[14] The analogy of "saving" virtual files (input) or "printing" them as documents (output) is still apt. To imprint and to inscribe are related processes. For Freud, what individuals inscribe or make public is really a screen for another, more private scene of authentic "writing." Of course, Derrida would challenge the lines between authentic and false, inside and outside, original and copy.[15] "Writing" and its corollary, witnessing, are faulty processes. While Seckon inscribes his story, half hinting at an a priori scene of authentic reflection, Trương comments on the process of inscription itself through her faulty and incomplete translation of *L'Amant* and other cinematic and literary texts. While the painter/collagist "saves" and safeguards memory through internal processes, the filmmaker looks at the residual collective "printed" output. Some of her source material is literally "printed": the aging analog films she works with, as well as the photographic prints. Both media—film and photography—have shifted from the analog to the digital realm. The very materiality of the archival films and photographs—now perhaps digitally remastered and stored in a virtual database—contributes to a mournful sense of nostalgia and distance in Trương's work. Her uncanny experimental videos, digitally edited, evoke the look and feel of film. They are works of art in the age of digital reproduction; their elegiac aura captures a sense of loss and bewilderment: the demise of empire, the demise of analog technologies. The modern shifts to the postmodern. I do not delve into this further, as Susan Sontag and Roland Barthes have written famously and extensively about the pathos inherent in photography. A twilight art captures the twilight empire, now vanished but not without traces.

"The medium is the message," Marshall McLuhan famously observed. Echoing this claim, Derrida notes that technology defines the archive. The technology of "archivization" shapes the very memory and history that is to be stored. In another of twist of inside-outside categories, he also states that the structure of the archive determines it. The outer configuration of the collection determines what goes into it. Technology is the archive. "Archivization produces as much as it records the event," Derrida observes.[16] For instance, documentary images often constitute the event for the global community, who often do not experience it firsthand. The atrocities of the Khmer Rouge regime are constructed by its artifacts. Nhem En, who took thousands of infamous black-and-white photographs of Tuol Sleng prisoners, stated that the world had him to thank for leaving a trace or else the world would not know anything had ever happened.[17] The Việt Nam War was fought not only in the jungle but on the television screens and newspapers of the United States. It was the first televised war, a war of representation. Trauma is rendered legible, digestible through its representations.

If the medium is the message, what are Trương's and Seckon's messages via their chosen media? The very materiality or immateriality (in Trương's case) defines in part the kind of audience that will view this work. Trương's video installations are ephemeral, seen as film screenings or installed in institutional or gallery spaces. They do not go well with your living-room couch. Her experimental videos have cultural cachet as avant-garde pieces with a limited audience. Trương plays the game of high conceptual art, eschewing any pretense of commercial gallery sales. The medium of video installation is about an engagement with time, space, and narrative (or lack thereof). Her work deals with the ghosts of history and modernity, so the spectral nature of the flickering image is apropos. She assaults us aurally and visually and deftly conjures up the echoes (haunting songs and voices) of the past. Trương knows that technology constitutes the archive. Her series is called *Adaptation Fever*, after all, perhaps a sly nod and wink to *Archive Fever*. Speaking about her thought process in relation to the archive and artistic media, Trương says, "I just think in moving images; I am thinking in time-based images. I think electronically! In both sound and image—I am always thinking of movement. Part of it is because I am drawn to the archive, the digital archive, the photographic and filmic archive, and so I am just working in the medium in which I find my source material."[18] The *Adaptation Fever* trilogy is about the technologies of biopower: the bombs, propaganda, and letter of the law. The frenzy of the visible is at a fever pitch. In playing with different representational technologies—photographs, *cartes postales*, film, and video—Trương remarks on how histories and memories are constituted. The subjects and content produced by propaganda film are very different from the subjectivity recorded by the video camera. Post-card images of the colonies are for the cosmopolitan eyes of the colonizers. Family photographs present an entirely different archive, a different history. Through technologies of discipline, citizen-subjects are produced, documented, mapped, and catalogued by the state.

Seckon, who has worked with performance and large-scale, sculptural community-based installation, chose to work with paper, canvas, and paint. His choice to make large-scale paintings and small collages makes his work very collectible for international art connoisseurs. Seckon's two-dimensional still images do not engage the viewer the same way video does. Although the *Heavy Skirt* series presents narrative, the nature of the medium renders it silent. The touch of the artist's hand and his signature lines mark the work as "authentic." It is handcrafted, "folksy," raw. These works are rough-hewn; they do not have the pristine billboard polish of a Jeff Wall painting. The imperfect lines, scribbles, and torn edges deliver the message of poverty and pride.

Heavyweight | Leang Seckon

In November 2009, just before Seckon's solo show in London, he and I caught up at a restaurant next door to his studio, then returned to his studio so I could see his work in progress. I assert that Seckon's 2010 show in London marked a significant international "turn" in his career, so I focus part of this chapter on the works and themes that emerged from this pivotal moment. Based on the success of this first solo exhibition in London, Leang Seckon had a second solo show at Rossi & Rossi London in 2014. His work was subsequently featured in high-profile international group exhibitions, including the 2012 Shanghai Biennale and the eighth Asia Pacific Triennial of Contemporary Art (APT8), in 2015, at the Queensland Art Gallery and Gallery of Modern Art, Brisbane.

Back in his studio before his first UK premiere, Seckon was excited and anxious. An aunt helped him sew finishing touches as his mother looked on. Although he had participated in high-profile exhibitions in Japan, China, and Burma, among other locations, he was uncertain about how his work would be received in London. At first glance, it looked as if he was making large quilts. Upon closer inspection, the large canvases, each measuring approximately 59 × 51 inches, consisted of patches of fabric with painted images—a patchwork of references. His hand-embellished collages of archival photographs; stickers; cigarette boxes; and cutouts from magazines, leaflets, and newspapers were smaller, about 16 × 20 inches. The title of his first "autobiographical" series of work, *Heavy Skirt*, refers to the skirt his mother wore when she was pregnant with him. She had only one skirt that she mended and patched, which made it heavier and heavier. Similarly, Seckon's canvases are patched, stitched, embellished with images and stories and memories, real and imagined, individual and collective, until they become heavy, ripe with associations. Throughout this chapter I put the word "autobiographical" in quotation marks to refer to Seckon's work because the series merges historical and mass-media fantasies, stereotypes and fact. An unlikely cast of characters and symbols appear in his art: Cambodian rock-and-roll stars from the 1970s, flowers, fields, Khmer Rouge cadres, Elvis, zombies, snowflakes, and bombs.

The patched images and references make perfect sense for a disjointed life. "Collage is the only [term] to capture it," the artist-activist/writer Anne Moore observes about Seckon's work. Collage, sewing, stitching, and patching—all techniques of culling fragments—are the only way to capture life's incredible splendor and, for survivors, its "black lace destruction."[19] Seckon was born in Pier Reang, Prey Veng Province, forty-five minutes from Phnom Penh, in 1974 amid heavy American bombing of Việt Nam and Cambodia. Rural Pier Reang, a farming community, is close to the Việt Nam border. Speaking of his childhood, Seckon said, "My mom, she was confused by the bombs from the sky. . . . The Vietnamese soldiers came to Cambodia with tanks to scare people."[20] He grew up in a period of confusion, uncertainty, and instability, with competing Vietnamese, American, Chinese, and Khmer ideologies at war. Richard Nixon's secret, illegal bombing was aimed partly at defeating Việt Cong nestled on the eastern border of Cambodia. *The bombs from the sky.* While US officials avoided discussing Cambodia and Laos at the time, the domino theory was at work.

The Pet Shop Boys recorded a song in the late 1980s titled "Domino Dancing"; part of its lyrics read, "All day, all day, watch them all fall down. All day, all day, domino dancing." Although the Pet Shop Boys are singing about tainted love and, perhaps, war, the song was on Seckon's playlist, along with music by the Khmerican (Khmer American) band Dengue Fever, Kylie Minogue, and 1960s Khmer rockers such as Sin Sisamouth and Ros Serey Sothea. This soundtrack, with an additional dose of hip hop, can be heard in the high-rise malls and traditional markets of Phnom Penh. Cambodian rock-and-roll reached its zenith during the 1960s and early 1970s, combining American and English influences with traditional Khmer melodies and rhythms, and often upbeat vocals, for a unique sound. Seckon's collage *The Soldier Singing* (*Thiehien Jrieng Jomrieng*) captures this mood. A cutout of a young Elvis Presley is in the center of the composition, framed by floating flowers and a guitar, with another reproduction of the singer Jeff Buckley with a guitar at the far left, a "Live from England" logo below his navel. A Khmer sticker reads, "A good story for kids." A Mercury Records album and painted vinyl record anchor the image. Perhaps these are the "good" stories of the past with which Seckon grew up. The other figures are drawn in with accent colors: male and female Khmer singers with red lips, a machine gun, and the singing soldier, whose song conjures up this brew. Looking at Seckon's pastiche images of singers, soldiers, and saints, I can hear Khmer rock-and-roll reverberating from decades ago, from the then pristine white modernist buildings, bombs illuminating the urban night sky.

During a visit to his studio I asked Seckon about the singer featured in *The Soldier Singing*. Perhaps it was a relative or his father. "The singer is me," he said, grinning. He is a well-known singer who has performed on Cambodian national television several times. Hollywood, indeed. He has sung on different stages in different stages of his life. When he was conscripted to military service for a year in 1990, he stated that he did not want to "carry guns. I only want to put them down and sing." And sing he did. He described his taste this way: "I love Khmer music from the sixties and seventies. I also listen to Indian music when working. I like pop music, too, fun to dance and listen for short time. But when I want to go deep, deep with my thoughts in the studio, I listen to Indian music. I listen to Khmer music."[21] Similar to his images, Seckon's taste in music spans many cultures and eras. Instead of a hierarchy of cultural references, he uses collage, drawing, and sewing to stitch together seemingly disparate views.

Sew What?

We cannot put things into perspective. Like the African American feminist artist Faith Ringgold (b. Harlem, 1930), Seckon uses fabric and paint to tell complex stories using a flat "folk" painting technique that disregards perspective. Ringgold's large painted "story quilts" critique race and gender issues within dominant Western society with wit and humor, often referencing art history. For instance, her large 1991 story quilt *The Sunflower Quilting Bee at Arles* (acrylic on canvas, tie-dyed, pieced fabric border, 74 × 80 inches) depicts a group of African American women holding up their sunflower quilt in a vast field of sunflowers as Vincent Van Gogh stands in the background to the left, holding a bouquet of, yes, sunflowers. They are framed by buildings of the village of Arles, the famous artist's refuge (he created more than three hundred images of it), rendered in Van Gogh's signature vibrant blues and yellows. Ringgold was among the first Western female artists to use women's "craft," blurring the line between high and low art, challenging long-held masculinist traditions of what is considered fine art. Through her work she has questioned art institutions, which often omitted minority perspectives.

Quilting has a long history for African Americans. African women adapted quilting from men's traditional weaving in Africa as they entered America as slaves. The slave community used quilts for various purposes, including the conservation of individual and collective memories, warmth, storytelling, and as message guides for the Underground Railroad to direct slaves north to freedom. Inspired by Tibetan Buddhist *tangkas*, Ringgold started sewing borders around her paintings, which led to her first story quilt.[22] The portable tangkas—often depicting deities, Buddha's trials and tribulations, and the Wheel of Life—are usually painted on cotton duck or silk and quilted or embroidered. Ringgold mixes Eastern and Western traditions and "highbrow" and "lowly" visual references in her contemporary work.

Seckon also blurs the boundaries between craft and fine art, combining sewing, collage, stitching, and painting. He heartily embraces sewing and patching, dismissing the idea that it is mere women's work. Here, gender boundaries are fluid. Cambodia, like the rest of Indochina, has already been seen as feminine entity by its colonizers, by the rest in the West. Akin to Ringgold's early artistic sewing collaborations with her late mother, Seckon's work gains inspiration from his mother's sewing and patching. Her heavy skirt still weighs heavy on his mind. Patching is a spiritual activity; mending is meditation—cobbling tattered pasts, collaging blood-stained painful fragments into a semblance of hope.

A country torn asunder can only scramble to patch, sew together its future, regardless of how bleak. Basic sewing employs approximately 700,000 of Cambodia's fifteen million people, many of whom work forty-eight-hour weeks and send remittances to family members in the countryside who survive on less than a dollar a day. In October 2010, thousands of Cambodian garment workers went on a weeklong strike in Phnom Penh for higher wages. My trilingual friend Socheat earned about $60 a month working in a factory. He had to quit his studies to support his widowed mother; his father and brother were casualties of the civil war. But this is not a sob story. He is lucky. Many workers get paid $50 a month. That extra $10 allows Socheat to eat out several times (an average restaurant meal costs $2) or to buy necessities.

In 2013, Phnom Penh factory workers waged a three-month protest to increase the minimum wage from $61 to $80 a month.[23] The Coalition of Cambodian Apparel Workers Democratic Union, which represents about forty thousand workers, aimed for $93 a month so employees can cover their basic living expenses. Anna McMullen, a campaign coordinator for the nonprofit garment workers' rights cooperative Labour behind the Label, states, "There's a huge gap between what [garment workers] are being paid and what they need to be paid to live with dignity."[24]

In addition to wages, working conditions are an ongoing, sensitive issue. The apparel industry is Cambodia's largest formal employer, generating $7 billion annually (2017–18).[25] It is the third-largest source of foreign income in Cambodia. Well-known brands such as Gap, H&M, Benetton, Puma, and Adidas take advantage of the cheap, skilled (largely female) labor force. Harsh (and costly) public lessons learned, mainly through litigation, have changed the policies of a few companies, such as Walmart and Nike; many continue to operate in the manner those companies did a decade ago. In 2015, the international organization Human Rights Now! called out Marks & Spencer, H&M, and Uniqlo, among others, for "serious human rights abuses," including "low average salaries, forced and unlawful overtime work, long work durations that sometimes amount to mandatory twenty-four-hour shifts, unpaid overtime work, manipulation of workers by inducing a fear of contract non-renewal, infringement of freedom of association, and lack of protection for female workers such as maternity leave."[26] Some workers have been threatened with physical assault if they go on strike.

A rash of mass fainting at factories occurred in 2011. The real cause is undetermined. On August 25, 2011, nearly three hundred employees (out of four thousand total) fainted in an H&M factory in Kampong Chhnang, a province an hour away from Phnom Penh. On August 25, 2011, 198 employees were hospitalized for fainting at the same factory due to an "overpowering smell."[27] Mass fainting incidents occurred at a Puma factory in July and

August 2011. After an inspection on August 23, 2011, the m&v company representative Un Chhan Teak claimed that there was no connection between a mass fainting incident there and working conditions. "After one or two women collapsed, the others panicked and followed suit," he said. "We will allow them to stop working for two days."[28] Reports suggest there have been other such incidents.

The International Labour Organization attributed the fainting spells to nutritional deficiencies. Workers cannot afford to feed themselves properly on the wages they earn. Ath Thorn, the president of the Cambodian Labour Confederation, pointed to missed meals and long working hours as inflation eroded the value of workers' salaries.[29] It seems possible that fainting is a form of protest. Human Rights Watch observes, "These problems have been caused by the fact that Cambodian Labour Law has not yet sufficiently implemented in work settings; laws on short-term contract have been misused to dispose workers who speak up for inadequate treatment at workplaces; and lack of an effective mechanisms to redress the violations."[30]

The protests continue. Short-term contracts are common. These contracts leave workers in a continually precarious state: workers have no continuity or stability when a company relocates, expands, or shuts down. In 2014, three people were killed and several others were injured after "police opened fire on textile workers protesting in Cambodia"[31]—the workers demanded that the minimum wage (then $61) be doubled. In February 2018, two thousand workers protested the sudden shutdown of the Yu Fa Garment Industry, Yu Da Garment Industry, and sre Garment Company, three sister factories that supply the US companies Walmart and JC Penney. These workers did not receive severance pay or their January wages. In a similar vein, in September 2018, five hundred workers (of 2,500) working at the Ghim Li Factory, also in the Por Sanchey district of Phnom Penh, blocked National Road 4, a major transport artery, as part of a strike for missing wages when a factory relocated.[32] Although the Khmer government paid $22 million toward missing wages for the Ghim Li Factory workers a month before their protests, detractors say short-changing workers is endemic. In an interview in 2018 with the *Phnom Penh Post*, William Conklin of the Solidarity Center, a workers' rights organization, noted that when a factory closes, the government steps in to sell its remaining assets and divide the proceeds. "The amount," he said, "is often less than what workers are legally owed."[33]

Since the garment industry is big business in Cambodia, Prime Minister Hun Sen has been seen on social and mass media interacting with workers—including having lunch with them, posing for photo opportunities, and addressing them in public speeches. These public displays before and after the July 2018 elections (which Hun Sen won) were also a response to the prime minister's detractors who have formed unions in coalition with government opposition parties.[34] Perhaps the result of years of protests and local and international lobbying, wages for workers increased 150 percent within five years (2012–17). During minimum wage negotiations in 2019, Hun Sen requested that workers halt their protests (again blocking a major road). Addressing thousands of workers on September 18, 2018, in Kampong Speu Province, he stated, "Last year [the minimum wage] was $153 [2017] and this year's is $170 [2018], so your wages will increase in 2019."[35] Labor Minister Ith Sam Heng announced on October 5, 2018, "The minimum wage for textile, garment and shoe workers [effective January 2019] is set at $182 per month." Although an increase of 7 percent, this falls short of the major unions' proposal of $189. Echoing Labour behind the Label's statement four years earlier, Yang Sophorn, president of the Cambodian Alliance of Trade Unions, responded, "I am not satisfied with $182, because it does not allow workers to live with dignity."[36]

Whether it is a living wage or not, the current wage of $170, some employers argue, already makes Cambodia undesirable and uncompetitive. Kaing Monika, deputy secretary general of the Garment Manufacturers Association in Cambodia, bemoans, "We can't anymore say we are a cheap hub for labor."[37] The fear is that Cambodia may be outpricing itself. In another statement, Kaing Monika said that the rising minimum wage was "beyond the affordability of some of our members and the competitive level of the country."[38] Việt Nam, another global leader in garment manufacturing, has more competitive minimum-wage rates, ranging from $114 to $165.[39] Đặng Phương Dung, a former official of the Việt Nam Textile and Apparel Association, states, "Of course if companies move, Việt Nam might benefit a little bit."[40] Cambodian factory closures—and related protests over lack of pay and other working condition violations—may be a continuing problem. Of 579 factories approved and tracked by the compliance and transparency monitor Better Factories Cambodia (BFC) since 2014, 114 factories have closed (roughly 20 percent). The remaining 465 factories that meet BFC's transparency standards make up fewer than half (roughly 42 percent) of all the garment and shoe factories in Cambodia. Out of the active 465 factories tracked by BFC, 59 percent (275 factories) had critical compliance issues.[41]

Cambodia's garment industry is torn by international and internal pressures. On one hand, the demand to be a "cheap hub for labor" comes at the cost of laborers' lives. Yet, on the other hand, to be an "ethical sourcing destination" (to use BFC's terminology) may mean becoming a nondestination—a nonplayer in a market dominated by fast fashion's cut-throat, bargain-basement dictates. Apparel Resources, another garment industry transparency monitor, observes, "Cambodia, home to 1,100 garment and footwear factories, pays higher than Bangladesh, Sri Lanka, India, Myanmar, Indonesia, Laos and Pakistan to its workers."[42] The pressure mounts: the European Union (EU), Cambodia's largest trading partner, warned in 2019 about punitive trade measures and tariffs in response to the nation's move away from democracy. A Reuters article notes, "Some Western countries have criticized a July election won by Prime Minister Hun Sen, calling it flawed, because of a campaign of intimidation by his allies, and the lack of a credible opposition dissolved by the Supreme Court."[43] Exports to the EU in 2017 under the special "Everything but Arms" (EBA) trade partnership with Cambodia were worth $5.8 billion (or five billion euros).[44] With these penalizing tariffs, Western countries demand democratic processes and transparency. Yet the West's paradoxical desire for ever-cheaper outsourced subhuman labor now supplied by Khmer factories means shifting to cut-rate, cut-throat operations elsewhere in subaltern Asia.

Cold War politics, pricing, and ethics are enduring battles. From the highest government conference rooms to the factory cutting floor, the garment worker is caught in the crosshairs. The workers continue to sew, and Seckon continues to stitch together these stories.

The Realm of Hungry Ghosts

In dealing with the traumatic stories of history and modernity, collage, fragmentation, and beauty are artistic strategies. In Seckon's universe, karma and kitsch go together. "Snowflower Skirt (Somphut Picar Brille)" (plate 7) may be the most outlandishly joyful work from the *Heavy Skirt* series. In "Snowflower Skirt," the viewer sees an icy blue sky with an informal grid of snowflakes framing portraits of what appear to be Michael Jackson wearing a crown, Queen Elizabeth in profile, a reclining Buddha, a panda, and peonies galore, among other symbols. Seckon created this work for his London debut. When I asked him about the piece, he replied that it is his imaginary image of the United Kingdom. "I [have] never been to England before," he said, laughing. "I think there is snow. Of course, celebrities. The Queen is there, too."[45] His playful comment underscores the media's construction of national stereotypes, a fact he is keenly aware of since he uses mass-media fragments such as magazines, newspapers, and postcards in his collages. This work is a vision from the Orient of the Occident, a *cool* place, both cold and "hot."

Seckon is sincere and ironic. The surface shimmers like glitter. I think of the Royal Palace in Phnom Penh and its glitter and glamour. Some of the interiors combine Cambodian wooden intricacy with French Baroque gilded grandeur. Cambodia has always been a cosmopolitan hub in Southeast Asia, an Angkorian empire, the Pearl of the Orient. Mosques, boulangeries, missionaries, malls, and golden *wats* are all part of Cambodia's landscape. Phnom Penh and London are diverse global cities—in both locales, the sacred and profane go hand in hand. So it makes sense that British royalty shares a constellation with multi-armed Shiva, a panda, and resurrected Jesus in this composition. In other works, spiritual images also emerge. Speaking about religion, Seckon states, "For me, I know I'm very active with art, but I still pay respect to religion, especially Buddha. I find peace for life in my artwork but there is a fire inside sometimes, burning me and hurting me. At those times my art is not enough support for me and I need more, so I think on the Buddha's words saying something about how to dampen this fire inside."[46] Spirituality's calming presence cools. As I meditate on a floor cushion in Wat Langka, the brightly hued tiles morph in front of me: the circular, organic patterns interweave, becoming trees, flowers, humans. The effect is similar in "Snowflower Skirt": individual fragments merge and morph, shifting the affect of the total composition. Silhouettes of flowers look like a blue china pattern or an aerial view of Earth. It is a blue world, a blue sky, a blue constellation, but it is not sad. It is intimate, intricate, and full of humor. Some snowflakes resemble flowers or are embedded with flowers. Others snowflakes look like the Buddhist Wheel of Life or Wheel of Becoming (often found in Tibetan art), *bhāvacakra* in Sanskrit. The Wheel of Life depicts the cycles of samsara, the cycles of suffering. It is a sort of map of the inner and outer worlds, of six different realms, among them the realm of the gods, the realm of the jealous gods, the human realm, the realm of the hungry ghosts, and the hell realm.[47] They are metaphors for states of mind. For instance, the hell realm is the manifestation of anger, a warring state, whether it is the rage of an inner war or hot combat. In the realm of hungry ghosts, the ghosts have giant bellies and tiny pinhole mouths. A novice asked the Zen Buddhist monk Thích Nhất Hạnh to describe this insatiably hungry world. He answered with a single word: *America*. It could easily be England or any other materialistic consumerist nation.

In Seckon's renderings, gods, monsters, and people inhabit the same realm—different worlds in one. The art historian Ashley Thompson's insights about Angkorian-period artwork give context for this. She writes that the figures of portrait statues simultaneously embody gods and humans;

there is no separation between the divine and the everyday.[48] Seen within this longer trajectory, a universe inhabited by anthropomorphic deities is both microcosm and macrocosm. Thus, Seckon's miniaturized landscapes and magnified symbols are part of a larger Angkorian Buddhist world-view in which the cosmos, spirituality, and art are intertwined. Divinity and destruction—*apsaras* (celestial nymphs) and bomb flowers—mutually constitute this kaleidoscopic map. "Mappings" of the Wheel of Life or the universe also appear in Western traditions. Ancient Greek astronomers grouped the heavens into a star-bearing circle. Western astrology depicts the twelve celestial signs in a ring; its counterpart is the Asian zodiac. William Blake often used circular imagery in his renderings of the universe. In "Snowflower Skirt," the spiritual and cultural icons East and West merge. The East and West are not polar opposites. They inhabit the same (visual) plane. The snowflake "frames" also look like medallions, military medals of honor. In other paintings, soldiers wear medals, symbols of honor and horror. "Snowflower Skirt" is the artist's projection of a future time and space (his future trip to England, which is now past), just as some of his works reflect past geographies and memories, jubilant and tragic, stitched together.

In contrast to *Heavy Skirt*, "Modern Skirt (Somphut Sivilay)" references the buoyancy of the era before the American bombings, before the Khmer Rouge regime. It depicts a garden, a pattern of spade-like trees on which grow vignettes and portraits of smiling, elegantly dressed couples, foliage and apsaras playing musical instruments in the clouds. Their music inspires rain, which fills the lakes teeming with fish; the rice fields are abundant from the downpour. Flowers are everywhere. "Modern Skirt" is like an upturned deck of playing cards or Tarot cards: the King of Spades, the Queen of Hearts, Death, the Lovers. The 1950s–60s in Cambodia is seen by historians as a golden age. King Sihanouk declared independence from French colonial rule in 1953, and the country embarked on projects aimed at crafting a strong modern national identity.

Cultural production flowered. Film, modern fashion, and music bloomed. A building boom from 1953 to 1970 known as Cambodian Modernism or New Khmer Architecture flourished under Sihanouk's patronage. This brand of modernism, championed by the Cambodian architect Vann Molyvann, combined Cambodian traditional aesthetics and details with Corbusian high modernism. Is it ironic that a name synonymous with modern nationalist Khmer architecture was trained in France, the country's recent colonizers? All of these activities were part of the nation-building project after independence. Through an ambitious public works project, the nation sought to create itself anew, a modern nation full of confidence, no longer hindered by the shackles of imperialism. King Sihanouk is a filmmaker and composer. His films show Phnom Penh in its modern glory: a happy, orderly citizenry; angular, state-of-the-art architecture.

Molyvann's famous buildings can still be seen in Phnom Penh today, including the iconic rounded cheese-wedge shape of the Chaktomuk Theatre; the angular, impressive eighty thousand-seat National Sports Complex; and the recently refurbished yellow art deco-esque dome of Pshar Thmey. "Modern Skirt" is a nostalgic painting. Some of the portraits are rendered in black and white, preserving the sentimental affect of old family photographs in albums. This work also recalls the branching hierarchies of family trees, except there are multiple trees, multiple connections. A small collage, misleadingly entitled *Soldiers Arrive at the Palace (Tiehien Mok Dol Veang)*—one thinks of invasion!—evokes the period in which the king leads this cultural renaissance. Perhaps the soldiers are there for a peaceful state ceremony, full of pomp and circumstance. Color cutouts of traditional Khmer dancers are interspersed with black-and-white photographs of men in uniform. I am not sure whether the images are from Seckon's family archive, and I am reluctant to ask. Over these images are pencil drawings of architecture and painted flourishes. Space and time collapse. I ask Seckon whether this collage depicts a particular incident. He replies, "In my work many things are combined, many times at once. . . . These dancers are there but they do not know the soldiers come. It is another time."[49] This work speaks of the transitions of different eras, different states of mind. The grandeur and glory of the palace and Sihanouk's reign are abruptly interrupted. Still, one is not entirely sure whether this is the past or the present. Speaking of his smaller collages and the collage-like effect of his larger paintings, Seckon says: "When we look at collage, we see the image is not far away and not close; there is no perspective like in a realistic rendering of something. But collage has its own perspective, with its own logic or lack of logic. Just like nature and our lives make sense and they do not, we understand and we do not."[50] "Modern Skirt" is not painted from a singular perspective with a single vanishing point. Similar to Sandrine Llouquet and the scrambled lines in her video (discussed in chapter 2), Seckon does not use the logic of linear perspective. He does not subscribe to Enlightenment views of progress. This painting is an aerial view of a garden, but there are also portraits. It collapses space and time. The cycle of rain and growth is represented in the same patterned manner as the trees. Further elaborating on his layered work, Seckon says, "In my collages I use not only old things, but new things too—just whatever

165

Personal and Public Archives

I feel to use at the time. Cambodian people when they see my collages feel: 'Oh this looks very old, like something secret' and they feel a bit strange. Sometimes they feel it is very interesting."[51] Looking at Seckon's paintings and collages feels very intimate, regardless of the size. It feels as if he is sharing a secret with us, whispering in our ears, telling us a meandering, riveting narrative full of laughter and heartache. I did not ask him who the soldiers were in *Soldiers Arrive at the Palace* because I want to only half-know. I want for the secret to remain his.

And some things are open secrets or still-kept secrets. Seckon's personal narratives are a strategy of discussing sensitive matters. He is simply telling stories from his life, both factual and fantastic, not making overt political critique. But Seckon is not a mere chronicler. He is critical of the present state of Cambodian affairs. He observes, "People nowadays give many offerings and make many ceremonies but don't seem to really make other connections about their personal behavior and its effects."[52] Seckon acknowledges and embraces the many contradictions of his country—corruption and generosity, historical amnesia and tribunal testimonials, landmines and resorts, Lexuses and shantytowns.

The Cambodian government, like Việt Nam's, controls all television stations and has a firm grip on the media. The Hun Sen government commonly threatens, bans, or sues publications and journalists that criticize the government. Human Rights Watch notes that the state has bullied publications into firing opposition reporters or directly attacked or killed them. In a 2015 report based on Khmer, English, Vietnamese, and Chinese materials, Human Rights Watch states that "during [Hun Sen's] time in power, hundreds of opposition figures, journalists, trade union leaders, and others have been killed in politically motivated attacks. Although in many cases the killers are known, in not one case has there been a credible investigation and prosecution."[53] For instance, on March 23, 2017, the Phnom Penh Municipal Court convicted Oueth Ang of the premeditated murder of the well-known political commentator Kem Ley. Although Oueth Ang was sentenced to life in prison, the International Commission of Jurists, Amnesty International, and Human Rights Watch all maintain that the trial was not credible.[54]

Many citizens refuse to speak on the record for fear of repercussions. In October 2009, a new penal code was passed that lists disinformation and defamation as criminal offenses. Citizens can be prosecuted for peacefully criticizing government institutions or individuals. In July 2009, the editor Dam Sith shut down the long-standing opposition newspaper *Moneaksekar*

Khmer under threat of imprisonment.[55] In this climate, beauty is a survival strategy.

To speak about damage, Seckon uses splendor in his art as a strategy and as subterfuge. The *Merriam-Webster Dictionary* defines splendor as "a great brightness or luster: a brilliance," and "magnificence, pomp." In dealing with dark chapters of the past, both personal and communal, Seckon incorporates lighter elements such as elaborate, colorful patterns and visual layering of references to vernacular and popular culture. For example, there is still beauty in the shadow of warplanes in "Golden Flower Skirt (Somphut Picar Mier)." The painting is a large, checkered grid of green fields of color, again resembling a giant quilt. Traditional rural Khmer wooden homes on stilts, pagodas with peaked roofs, a bridge, stupas, and large and small flowers fill alternate squares. Look again. There is an ominous airplane near the center of the composition, almost hidden in plain sight. The large sunflowers simultaneously resemble palm trees, dahlias, children's pinwheels, and bomb targets. These are the bomb flowers; this is the bomb garden.

Seckon is all too familiar with Cambodia's stereotypes of strife and genocide for the rest of the world, a fact that he both plays into and rejects. In an interview with the curator Tara Shaw-Jackson, he states, "Cambodian history is not only about Pol Pot and today people are getting on with life, although of course Cambodian society has been changed forever, and people's health is affected, and their relationships." Telling traumatic histories, his work is also disconcertingly decorative. There is a reason to his logic: "To always talk about the difficult details of life and history hurts and makes people upset, so, my work is full of flowers too! So yes, you might think you see a bomb in my painting, but it is a bomb garden."[56] Every day in the halls of Tuol Sleng, visitors place white flowers on the metal-framed beds used for torture. Over time the beds have rusted to the color of dried blood. The white blossoms are prayers; they assuage the ghosts roaming the halls—grace and beauty amid horror. After a lifetime of grief what is left to do but to smell the flowers, to cry and laugh? Bombs and rock-and-roll.

As strategy and subterfuge, Seckon's ornate, gorgeous compositions reveal that images and text can be deceptive. His work is gorgeous, overladen in a faux-naïve way. Humor and horror coexist; wit can be a coping strategy. Difficult times call for absurdity. Despite all of the horror evoked by his paintings, they are above all, beautiful. Seckon tells harsh, painful stories about the past, but in a beatific, beautiful Buddhist way. So much beauty and so much devastation. The flowers serve as camouflage.

Using a similar strategy of camouflage, the Seoul-based artist Lee Young-baek's (b. Gimpo, 1966) large-scale video installation *Angel Soldier* fills the viewer's field of vision with a wall of bright flowers, thousands of fake flowers. Look carefully and you will see soldiers stealthily, almost imperceptibly, moving through the flowers; they wear military uniforms camouflaged with flowers. This jarring video subverts the conventions of camouflage with flower power, the antiwar symbol in the United States associated during the American War in Việt Nam with hippies and antiestablishment movements. This playful and provocative work captures the residual, anxiety-laden affects of Korea's military legacy. The plastic flowers and the soldiers in Lee's video and the "bomb flowers" in Seckon's painting point to the flowery rhetoric that disguises military aggression. Things are hidden in plain sight. In the works of both artists, perceptual shifts within a single image, suggesting how worlding, un-worlding and re-worlding happens on the same plane.

I now focus the discussion from metaphorical to literal planes. The aircraft in "Golden Flower Skirt" are nowhere in sight, then everywhere. This ambiguous space reveals the shock of recognition: what first appears to be an idyllic landscape of homes and greenery turns into a map of wreckage. This painting evokes the grainy 1970s documentary footage of airplanes bombing Southeast Asia. First we see foliage and thatched roofs, a village from a distance. Then we see flashes of white—beautiful bombs bursting in air—then orange and red: fire and blood everywhere amid the green. The mundane surface of everyday life conceals terror. In Cambodia, like many parts of the world touched by strife, historical trauma lies just beneath the surface, obscured. This seeming subterfuge is a strategy of survival. Beauty and devastation.

The devastation continues. Yet the modernist grid remains in "Flicking Skirt (Somphut Bohbaoeuy)" (plate 8). The grid may symbolize an attempt at normalcy, at retaining a sense of order despite the overwhelming ruin. Here the ashen squares have turned into graves, bomb craters consisting of flowery pattern. Still flowers grow. Through these grids, Pamela Corey sees Seckon's practice embracing both earthly and spiritual realms: "Aside from the meditative process of artistic labor, this notion of psychological transcendence is visually enacted through a recurring perspectival vantage point in his work, such as in the form of a bird's eye view in his mixed-media painting, with the artistic gaze cast from above upon planes flying in formation or parachutes descending upon a landscape."[57] The warplanes, the hell birds, have turned into thin birds or spirits, mouths agape, rising from the craters. Birds are among the few things able to escape from the carnage, as are the child protected by deities in the center of the frame and the mother holding her son in fear. Seckon tells me the story of how, as a one-year-old child, he miraculously survived a bombing unprotected while his mother and brother were stuck inside a bunker, unable to reach him.[58]

At the top center of "Flicking Skirt" there is a monochromatic stenciled outline of what looks like the iconic American eagle as it appears on official crests and currency, its wings and legs, well, spread eagle. At the bottom of the painting appears a *naga*, a mythical snake from whom Cambodians trace their lineage. The positioning of the eagle and the snake reveals something about the two countries' relative positioning within the world, then and now: the United States, although struggling, is still the world's top superpower, while Cambodia often appears near the bottom of world rankings. For instance, in 2010 the World Economic Forum ranked Cambodia as the worst performer in terms of business climate of the Association of Southeast Asian Nation (ASEAN) member nations.[59] The global imaginary still sees Cambodia as a poor little country, not the developing economic tiger it strives to be.

According to folklore, the Nāga King's daughter married an Indian Brahman named Kaundinya. Their union produced the Cambodian people. There are also nāgas within Buddhist imagery; the best-known nāga is Mucalinda, which is often shown protecting a meditating Buddha. Nāga imagery is everywhere in Cambodia, adorning the Royal Palace, bridges, staircases, and pagodas. Phnom Penh's glitziest casino is called NagaWorld, of course.

There are many world legends regarding eagles and snakes, including in Babylonian, Aztec, Hindu, and Albanian mythology. In the Sanskrit epic Mahābhārata, sister of the Hindu epic Rāmāyaṇa (both are often quoted in Cambodian art, particularly the latter), the giant eagle king Garuda and the nāga were born cousins. To cut the story short (the Mahābhārata is four times the length of the Rāmāyaṇa and ten times the length of Homer's *Odyssey* and *Iliad* combined), Garuda and the nāga become mortal enemies. Seckon makes a pointed comment about power and the tense history between Cambodia and the United States. Although the United States normalized relations with Cambodia and lifted its trade embargo in 1992, the past still casts a long shadow, just as the shadow of the birds and the warplanes hover in Seckon's work. What happens before, after, in between? Time is suspended. Traumatic temporality is a suspension of time and place. Pain is an eternity. Painful memories become the present. We are stuck. Seckon describes this sense of "stuckness" in "Stuck-in-the-Mud Skirt (Somphut Gop Phuot)," a painting about "the Khmer Rouge time." A frontal grid of human

169

bodies, some wrapped in *krama*—a traditional Cambodian scarf—their faces echoing the infamous portraits of Tuol Sleng. They are laid head to toe, as the doomed prisoners were. Some figures are entirely white, head to toe; they are ghosts. Others have white bodies with faces; they are becoming ghosts, the blood drained from their bodies. Again flowers bloom like blood wounds. They are mummies, zombies. "They [are] still alive, but ... like *stuck*," Seckon elaborates.[60] "They [are] alive and dead. The living dead."[61] This is the most painful yet most stereotypical image from the series.

This is the expected requisite image of terror for an international audience from a Cambodian artist. Will Seckon be *stuck*, or "typecast," as a Cambodian artist, eternally expected to spin tales of woe for a wide-eyed audience? He stitches the delicate line between (self-pitying) traumatic identity politics and formal play—beauty for beauty's sake. That is what makes his work refreshing, although it is odd to call it that. If you will, there is a sense of honesty and straightforwardness to his practice. It is not the standard chic, distanced irony of so many young and established artists.

Seckon also deals with spirituality in his art, unlike many contemporary artists who focus on secular themes. Seckon speaks about meditation and healing through his art practice. Look at "Stuck-in-the-Mud Skirt" again. Corey notes that the "grimly iconic" photo portraits of Tuol Sleng prisoners also feature faint smiles. Their grid-like placement recalls Vann Nath's paintings of the same population sleeping head to toe on the floor of the former high school. Yet this may also be an image of transcendence and hope that the "souls can be at peace and soar above the ground, floating away to a better places."[62] Corey calls Seckon's oeuvre, focused on personal and social transformation, a "meditative process of artistic labor."[63]

Take it all in: it is about acceptance, about getting on with it. The sinking in breath: feel its weight in your body. The out breath: let it go—levity. Stitching and painting are meditative processes, Seckon says. He does not just dwell nostalgically on golden eras, traumatic history, or the ambivalent present and future. His work reflects focused concentration in building up an image that resembles sitting meditation: applying layers of paint brushstroke by brushstroke, the repetitive motion of pushing a needle through fabric.

The cycle is the Wheel of Life, the cycles of samsara. Reincarnation. Move through the hell realms, through the realm of hungry ghosts, to reach enlightenment—nothingness. Outline the past, future, and present with paint and thread. Seckon counterbalances his harrowing narrative with a sense of the magnificence of the everyday. "Cambodian history," let him remind us again, "is not only about Pol Pot." Cambodia is *not* genocide. Việt

Nam is not a war. He is no melancholic. "Today people are getting on with life," Seckon told me in his studio.

It is telling that Seckon decided to make his first "autobiographical" body of work for his first significant international solo exhibition. His earlier work dealt with environmental issues using mythic creatures. These projects include the fabrication of a 740-foot-long, site-specific nāga installation from recycled plastic on the Siem Reap River for World Water Day in 2008. As an artist in residence at the Fukuoka Asian Art Museum in 2009, he constructed a *Makara* (a mythical Khmer dragon) made of plastic and fabric. The large Makara was then upheld by 110 dancers in a winding performance piece for the Fourth Fukuoka Triennale. These two large-scale projects provided a crowd-pleasing spectacle of a different sort. But would giant lizards on parade work for the jaded London art world—the much-touted white-hot epicenter of urban hipness and home to the now legendary Young British Artists (YBAs), whose works command millions at auction? Seckon bet against that. He offered instead a humble and humbling exhibition.

Seckon's aerial vision of contemporary Cambodia, "Salty Flower Skirt (Somphut Picar Ompul)" (plate 9), looks like a postapocalyptic landscape. A river runs through it. More specifically, Tonlé Sap (ទន្លេសាប, or the Sap River) meanders through the composition and the country, from north to south. At the bottom of the painting, one can see homes floating in a giant lake, the river connected to it. A combined lake and river system, it is the largest lake in Southeast Asia and is of great importance to the Khmer psyche and livelihood. The nation's largest national holiday is the annual Water Festival in November, celebrating the reversal of Tonlé Sap's currents back to the Mekong. Millions flock from the provinces to party in Phnom Penh. Some 75 percent of Cambodia's freshwater catch, supporting three million people, comes from the lake. Cham, Cambodians, and Vietnamese make their homes in the lake, a floating world.[64]

Other patches in the painting reveal different sites. The symbols from the other paintings reappear: the wound flowers, the flower bombs, the camouflage body bags/bombs/penises. The entire series *is* the Wheel of Life; it chronicles the cycle of existence—life, death, rebirth. The shadows of airplanes still hover. But instead of warplanes, perhaps they are the new commercial Cambodia Angkor Air fleet (the national airline), 49 percent owned by the Vietnamese government. Look, here is Angkor Wat in miniature, and there—plots of graves (skulls and skulls), zombies in karma. And there, still, landmines and bomb craters. One cannot escape the minefield of the past. Stubs of trees: deforestation. A single spade tree rises from the hacked trees.

Personal and Public Archives

It echoes the spade trees of the past, the beautiful modern garden. Cracked earth. *Samrab chul* (For Sale) read two signs on two fenced plots of land in Khmer and English. Land is being indiscriminately sold off to the highest bidder. In the lower portion of the composition, one can see the sleek and shiny Canadia Bank building, a crane next to it—symbols of development.

Direct foreign investment has poured in to the tune of billions of dollars over the past decade.[65] Hundreds of millions are being poured annually into infrastructure development by foreign powers, including China, Australia, South Korea, and Germany. After ten years of rapid growth—about 10 percent each year—the economy slumped, growing only about 2 percent in 2009. This has rippled down to all sectors of society, adversely affecting big and small businesses, as well as workaday *tuk tuk* (taxi) drivers,[66] observes the World Bank analyst Stéphane Guimbert.[67] From 2010 to 2018, the economy recovered, "spurred by the robust performance of the tourism, construction and garment sectors," according to the National Bank of Cambodia (NBC). In 2018, the NBC was forecasting a 6.9 percent growth, a rate that is echoed by other international bodies. The International Monetary Fund (IMF) predicted Cambodia's 2018 growth at 6.8 percent; the World Bank, at 6.9 percent; and the Asian Development Bank, at 7.1 percent. Since the 2020 pandemic, the IMF predicts Cambodia's growth to be negative at −1.7 percent; should a vaccine be produced in the latter half of 2020, Cambodian growth is anticipated to be 6.1 percent, with the overall global economy expected to grow at 5.8 percent.[68]

The NBC report notes that "garment exports, meanwhile, will be supported by access to preferential treatment from the European Union (EU) and the US, as well as an increase in exports to Japan and Canada, which will help us reduce our reliance on just a few markets."[69]

The growth of the garment industry with diversified international exports also has a downside, as outlined earlier in this chapter: the Business and Human Rights Resource Centre called out European, North American, and Asian companies for human rights abuses at garment factory, including Uniqlo (Japan), H&M (Sweden), Marks & Spencer (UK), Calzedonia (Italy), and Inditex (the Spanish parent company of Zara, Massimo Dutti, Pull & Bear, etc.), among others.[70]

More than two decades ago, 60 percent of the Khmer population lived below the poverty line.[71] In 2018, the United Nations Development Program (UNDP) noted that 10 percent of the population live below the national poverty line.[72] According to the World Bank, although Cambodia is now classified as a middle-income country, it is still underdeveloped: 4.5 million of its 15.6 million (2015 census) people currently live near the poverty line.[73] The UNDP warns that positive baseline statistics can be misleading because they do not account for socioeconomic complexities. As of 2015, according to the World Bank, 70 percent of Cambodia's population (12.3 million people) did not have access to a piped water supply, and 58 percent (9.3 million people) did not have access to improved sanitation.[74] Populations are still vulnerable: "Over 50 percent of the population, although not poor, are highly vulnerable to poverty, and . . . an income shock of just 20 percent would more than double the headcount rate. In today's uncertain and highly interconnected and interdependent world, a severe environmental event or a global recession could wipe out decades of poverty reduction."[75] The Asian Development Bank echoes this sentiment, stating that in 2018 "more than 70 percent of Cambodians still live on less than $3 a day, which means that many of them remain vulnerable to falling back into poverty."[76] Maybe Hun Sen is right. Maybe the conditions are ripe for another civil war. The gaps between the haves and the have-nots widen.

In the following segment I discuss the Vietnamese American experimental video artist Hồng-Ân Trương, who also deals with still-present pasts through patchwork techniques. Trương uses archival images to challenge constructions of national and individual identity and colonial and postcolonial subjectivity.

Silence and Void, or Double Trouble
HỒNG-ÂN TRƯƠNG'S VISUAL ARCHIVES

The total result looked for by colonial domination was indeed to convince the natives that colonialism came to lighten their darkness. —Frantz Fanon, *The Wretch of the Earth*

As a viewer, I'm constantly looking for my family. For me, the process of going through the archives, there's always the process of looking for family members and not seeing oneself there. —Hồng-Ân Trương, interview, November 10, 2010

Like Leang Seckon's work, Hồng-Ân Trương's art stitches the torn seams between memory and loss, desire and void.[77] She, too, explores modernity's representations and the archive, grappling with modernity's representational shifts in space and time. Mariam Lam, Isabelle Thuy Pelaud, Lan Duong, and Kathy L. Nguyễn, the editors of *Troubling Borders: Southeast Asian Women in the Diaspora*, write that Trương's work conveys a "compelling narrative not only about the archive and the stories that it holds but also of artifacts and the stories underlying them."[78] Trương unfixes what remains: stories, archives, and artifacts.

National and personal memory, historical trauma, and colonial desires are undone, briefly pulled together, but the absences stretch open, immense. In Trương's works, the past is ever-present in archival black and white, darkness and light. So are the historical periods of Việt Nam, demarcated by the presence of Others: French colonialism, the American war; crisp white linen suits, somber Catholic tunics framed by white hands; white artillery sparks in a black sky. The legacy of Enlightenment and Cold War discourses for "dark-skinned" people remains spectral, stereoscopic: postcard Paris, camouflage, and *colons* (colonial settlers). Dark jungles and wide white boulevards, black robes and white heat. Lam and her colleagues observe that Trương's oeuvre draws on "the fragmented memories that constitute the refugee imagination."[79] Trương is the recipient of a 2019 Guggenheim award; press around her work likewise highlights her politicized focus on "immigrant, refugee and decolonial subjectivities."[80] Her work examines structures of power in the (raced, classed, gendered) production of labor, memory, and knowledge across national regimes.[81]

Within the larger context of diasporic cultural production, I discuss Trương's solo exhibition at Duke University in 2010, *The Past Is a Distant Colony*, which features the video installation object, or video "sculpture," "Furniture to Aid in the Viewing of the Lover" (2009), and her video trilogy *Adaptation Fever* (2006–7), which comprises "The Past Is a Distant Colony," "It's True Because It's Absurd," and "Explosions in the Sky (Điên Biên Phu 1954)." I focus on the trilogy, which Mimi Thi Nguyễn characterizes as a "refugee return," and extend it as a return engagement, with emphasis on the militarized connotations of the term *engagement* that I have outlined.[82]

For diasporic subjects, the gaps between official history and individual memory are immense. Personal narratives are often rendered invisible within public discourse, a mute void. Our families, our own bodies are rendered both invisible and hypervisible as stereotypical boat refugees, gangsters, model minorities within Western mass media. The so-called 1.5 generation of refugees and returnees are caught between history and memory and uneven modernities. But what constitutes history and memory, home and exile? The eternal process of looking and not seeing oneself reflected, refracted constitutes loss, liminality. Trương's ongoing search to find traces of her family and herself within historical archives possibly points to melancholic mourning. Like Freud's melancholic subject, she endlessly grieves her loss, revisiting the site of absence. The postcolonial scholars David L. Eng and David Kazanjian reconsider the melancholic's position and reformulate loss from fixed pathology to paths of engagement, which I build on in chapter 1. The writer and performance artist lê thị diem thúy also searched for hints of recognition and familiarity in old postcards of Vietnamese colonial subjects found in Parisian flea markets. These images of strangers reminded her of her family, of herself. Instead of mourning the archive, lê proclaims, "I thought of these images as my inheritance."[83] These artists' liminal positions—as diasporic subjects living and working in between physical and psychic spaces and times—offers them a unique critical vantage point. In mining visual archives of black-and-white colonial postcards and grainy celluloid footage, nostalgic and horrific, Trương suggests that things are not so, well, black and white.

Following current reformulations of diaspora that address many migrations rather than one-way conceptions of "home/exile," Trương's palimpsest work recognizes that identity is not binaristic, highlighted by the "doubled" vision created by the split-screen repetitions in some of her videos. Scholars such as Lisa Lowe, Gayatri Gopinath, Rey Chow, Kobena Mercer, Martin Manalansan, and Paul Gilroy have shifted the discourse on diaspora away from essentializing binaries to one that addresses repeated geographic crossings. This approach reflects an unexpected and vigorous multiplicity of movements, influences, and identifications. Experimental video artists, including Peter Fung, Patty Chang, Ming-Yuen S. Ma, Paul Wong, Erica Cho, and Nguyễn Tân Hoàng, have used various strategies in their artwork to address the tensions of complex cultural negotiations and histories.[84] Having come of age in the shadow of 1990s multiculturalism, Trương creates work that destabilizes fixed notions of nationhood and identitarian politics. The ghost of multiculturalism darkens "white cube" spaces in the form of exhibitions featuring carefully selected cultural representatives. While Trương is occasionally (institutionally) championed as an artist of Vietnamese descent, her work is *not* about claiming a singular personal or national narrative. It is about the construction, and the blind spots, of those narratives. She examines how subjects are varyingly constructed and interpellated through religious and state institutions. Referring to *Adaptation Fever*, Trương states, "I was looking at Catholicism in terms of it being a very obvious and powerful process of colonization, and an irreversible part of the war. At what point does colonization become not objectifying? I was thinking about it in the context of politics and the wars, and Catholics who stayed in the North and what their sympathies are because we assume that all Catholics left and moved to the South. I wanted to break down what we think about Vietnamese politics and identity."[85] That final sentence suggests that Vietnamese subjectivities are complicated, shaped by religion, war, and displacement. Many migrations inform *Adaptation Fever*: colonial movements of laborers, clergy and colons; the 1954 internal exodus of Vietnamese (largely from North to South Việt Nam) after France's defeat and withdrawal from its former colonies; and more recent resettlements both internally and overseas.

Currently, there are approximately three million overseas Vietnamese who fall into four groups, culturally and historically. The first group left Việt Nam before 1975 and settled in neighboring countries such as Laos, Cambodia, and China or, because of colonial legacies, in France. The second, and largest, left Việt Nam after 1975 as refugees. According to the United Nations Population Division's mid-2015 estimates, the United States has the most Vietnamese immigrants (1.3 million), followed by Australia (227,000), Canada (183,000), and France (126,000).[86] Of these groups there are two "waves" of immigrants. The first wave relocated after the fall/liberation of Sài Gòn on April 30, 1975; the second wave emigrated as political refugees after 1977.[87] Trương's family belongs to this second wave, as does mine.

Truong differs from the diasporic artists I discussed in the chapter 2, who have challenged Việt Nam's metonymic function within the Western imagination—noteworthy only as a site of US military intervention.[88] Rather than focusing on the long shadow of the audiovisual carnage of the Việt Nam–American War and its current echoes, Trương's elegantly elegiac, disquieting gaze instead focuses steadily on the "scopic regime" of French Indochina.[89] The countermemories of the colonial era are disquietingly dis-remembered and dismembered, evoking other visual histories of decolonization and struggle, such as *The Battle of Algiers* (Gillo Pontecorvo, dir., 1965). This "regime" of colonial narratives is cast in tragic relief against the carpet-bombed destiny awaiting Việt Nam.

The term *Indochine* triggers Orientalist visions of disappearing verdant (neo)colonial splendor—the good life on plantations and villas across Việt Nam, Laos, Cambodia—in the imagination of authors, auteurs, gourmands, and globetrotters. This "Pearl of the Orient" past is also evoked in chic dining establishments (French bread and wine, Vietnamese crepes, *nước mắm*) across several continents for today's cosmopolitan consumers. Global franchises such as Louis Vuitton; Au Bon Pain (founded and headquartered in Boston); and fashion mega-houses such as Chanel, Yves Saint Laurent, Dior, Lacroix, and Gaultier attest to the potency of the allure of French civility, a civilizing capacity gracious and melancholic as it thrives amid its own decay in distant jungles and Casbah labyrinths.

In their essay "Nostalgia without Pain," Laura B. Kennedy and Mary Rose Williams look at the packaging of tourism toward First World (Western) foreigners in Việt Nam. They posit that, although all tourist development must be state-sanctioned, the state has largely ceded the process of image making to international developers who are hawking visions of premodern, Edenic tours of rural areas and invoking a nostalgic French colonial past updated for postmodern tastes at luxury hotels in urban areas in which locals are submissive servants. In another variant, the traumatic sites of the Việt Nam–American War catering to foreigners "trivializes" those sites by making the painful past manageable, digestible, consumable. While nostalgic Indochina pleases the culinary and cinematic palate, Trương's appropriated, disjointed documentary footage (sometimes literally showing disjointed humans) questions this force-fed diet, this insatiable cannibalistic hunger.

"The Past Is a Distant Colony" is formally striking in its symmetry: uncanny archival images of French-occupied Việt Nam play across from each other, mirroring each other, framed by black borders (plate 10). Dealing with the formation of colonial subjects and their ambivalent subjectivity, the video features panning shots of benediction, mass, and ecstatic gestures and smiling faces at what seem to be political rallies or celebrations. A few images repeat: two boys barely beyond babyhood awkwardly learn to cross themselves—one is unsure and glances in slow motion at the confident movements of his companion; a woman grieving, looking over her shoulder with an indeterminate expression hovering indefinitely between surprise and fear, a white-clad torso behind her; a rakish, elegantly suited Vietnamese man—perhaps the anticolonial leader and former Vietnamese Prime Minister Phạm Văn Đồng in his youthful prime—striding a cobbled, columned courtyard. As the video unspools, the scenes move from the colonial periphery to the metropolitan, radiating center—kaleidoscopic shots of a teeming fin-de-siècle Paris: boulevards, the Arc de Triomphe, and Walter Benjamin's arcades are interrupted, only briefly, with a burning Vietnamese village, French lessons scrawled with white chalk on a blackboard (which brings to mind Theresa Hak Kyung Cha's disjunctured dictation lessons in *Dictée*),[90] an Egyptian-themed musical spectacular, a graceful corpse lying in long grass, a glamorous close-up of the chanteuse Josephine Baker (La Baker), decapitated Asian heads in baskets. This *is* the "frenzy of the visible"—modernity's emphasis on visuality and conquest above all else ("to see is to conquer").[91]

Trương mines the debris of Indochinese popular culture (postcards, lavish film productions, documentary footage), just as the media artists Bruce Yonemoto and Patty Chang use the rubbish of American popular culture. Yonemoto appropriates the vernacular of mainstream movies and television (1950s Americana, 1980s soap operas). Chang upends cultural and gender stereotypes through humor and parodic performance, inhabiting pop icons that range from Bruce Lee and Anna Mae Wong to Chinese acrobats. All three, as (art) schooled postmodernists, use irony to various ends in their work. Trương's ironic stance seethes below the surface. Chang's and Yonemoto's often playful work is by turns witty, wry, elegant, and bombastic. However, Trương relies on serious, subtle understatement rather than mischievous overstatement to make her point. For Chang and Yonemoto, Benjamin's angel of history is a drag diva; for Trương, he is a melancholic (perhaps with a dry, dark sense of humor), endlessly examining history's wreckage, looking for loved ones, for oneself. The excesses of empire are revealed: things fall apart; *the center cannot hold*.[92] And so every image splinters from itself, peels apart precisely at the center, pulling away into indeterminately true mirroring doubles of itself. Even as the center fails, the object demonstrates its infinite reproducibility. But what do we do with endless "truths" beating like wings of the dark angel?

The "true" visual center of "The Past Is a Distant Colony"—"a thin demilitarized zone between opposing images," as Việt Thanh Nguyễn describes it—is void.[93] Moving images mirror each other on the periphery—East and West; North and South Việt Nam. Desire and void, darkness and light. The legacy of the scopic regime of Enlightenment rationality, a singular Cartesian worldview, with its overarching monofocal vision of civilization's grand vistas, is disrupted, doubly troubled.[94]

The verbal soundtrack for these disconcerting images consists of two women speaking intermittently in Vietnamese and in French, with the only subtitles briefly stating, "A nun talks about her suffering" and "A woman talks about her childhood in French Viet Nam (*Indochina*)." They are not even subtitles but spare indexes. Between the brief monologues is silence and void. The refusal to translate is important. Trinh T. Minh-ha has also dealt with the politics of translation, gender, representation, and the nation-state in experimental films such as *Surname Viet, Given Name Nam* and theoretical texts including *When the Moon Waxes Red*. The voices of Trinh's women (dis)embody multiplicity, remaining unplaceable, implacable: characters and voices shift on-screen. Trinh's commentary about metanarratives, Derridean logos, and the failures of language and representation are dealt with in a more intimate and direct manner in Trương's video. As I discussed in chapter 2, logos and the unrepresentable are highlighted through silences in Panh's and Siv's films. For Trương, instead of voices unheard, faces are unseen, off-screen.

Misrecognition and mistranslation are central in Trương's work. The two female protagonists in "The Past Is a Distant Colony" are disembodied voices; they never appear on-screen, as they do in Trinh's work. In over-lapping narratives, the Vietnamese Catholic nun speaks in a northern ac-cent about the fear of religious persecution, spiritual desire, and religious ecstasy, while the French woman speaks about sexual desire and ecstasy: "Since I was a young girl I knew I wanted to help those in pain. . . . I was a sad girl who always wanted something. . . . I kissed the statue of the Virgin Mary in Sài Gòn. . . . What do I want? The Virgin Mary is what I need. . . . He stripped me naked, this is what I wanted."[95] Corporeality and spirituality, mind and body, Cartesian duality. Several scenes feature the 1954 exodus of Northern Vietnamese on barges to the South in the hope of escaping re-ligious persecution. Shots of the wide sea, clouds, and rafts visually echo the later exodus of boat people in the aftermath of the Việt Nam War. The French voiceover states, "We were lying in bed smoking cigarettes. We were caressing each other. The sea was motionless and quiet. The smoke was bil-lowing ahead like small clouds. . . . We parted in silence." The irony is appar-ent only to those who understand French. The intentional lack of subtitles underscores the gulfs between lovers and languages, as well as audiences. Later, the same French female voice states, "I wanted to disappear in his gaze until I disappeared myself." Desire and void. What possesses this woman to enunciate with so much ennui the careless demand implicit in colonialism's totalizing gaze?

The female voices reflect a double consciousness—a stereoscopic, stereo-phonic, perhaps schizophrenic subject.[96] The final sequence spoken in Viet-namese and subtitled faithfully in English reads, "What we are constantly moving toward / but never quite reaching / is some sense of union with the ultimate being, / a constant revelation. / *Like looking in the mirror at some-one who is me / who is not me*" (emphasis added). This doubling, mirroring speaks of how colonial (and religious) subjects are formed, as well as the pro-cess of disidentification. The postcolonial theorist Frantz Fanon has written about how the colonized mirror the actions and agendas of their colonizers. Yet the mimicry is imperfect; the mirror's reflection, refracted, distorted. In the mirror's gaze, there is misrecognition . . . *the process of looking . . . but never seeing oneself there.* For the psychoanalytic theorist Jacques Lacan, the mirror stage is a crucial stage in establishing the formation of the ego, of distinguishing the imaginary from the real.[97] But what is real and what is fantasy in the colonial imagination?

Michel Foucault notes that the mirror is a symbolic space of absence and presence, both a heterotopic (real) and utopic (imagined) space. It is a liminal position in which one's image is negotiated, negated, and constructed. Describing his vantage point, Foucault writes, "I see myself there where I am not. . . . I am over there, there where I am not, a sort of shadow that gives my own visibility to myself, that enables me to see myself there where I am absent."[98] This space is both a reflection of reality and a site of fantasy and projection. Perhaps it is finally a way of seeing oneself, a process of self-recognition. One is both object and subject of the gaze: *like looking in the mirror at someone who is me / who is not me.*

In Vietnamese government policy, as well as cultural representations (Western *and* Eastern film, literature, visual art), the Vietnamese female body and psyche become the contested sites of ideological tensions. The postcolonial critic Panivong Norindr notes that the legacy of French colonial conceptions of Indochina, particularly Việt Nam as an "exotic and erotic" entity, still lingers.[99] Mainstream cultural productions featuring American involvement in Việt Nam such as *The Quiet American, Apocalypse Now, Miss Saigon,* and *Heaven and Earth* allegorize Việt Nam as a female protagonist in need of salvation or as an unyielding, mysterious, feminized landscape to be dominated.[100] In Trương's work, Vietnamese womanhood is neither exotic nor erotic. The gaze is reversed, reflected. Trương's women are not mute witnesses, victims of history, or unwitting subjects. They have agency, however circumscribed.

"It's True because It's Absurd" also features a female voice recounting a personal narrative: a retelling of a true story Trương's mother told her about witnessing a child playing with a gun shoot his mother accidentally: "I was standing there holding your hand. She was standing next to me holding a baby and the baby fell." The background sound drones; in the distance, soldiers can be heard. The processed voice speaks in a measured cadence, belying the measured distance of recollection and its unreliability. The voice sounds like a ghost in the machine.

"It's True because It's Absurd" opens and closes with a black-and-white shot of a dirt road between rice fields—soldiers hidden in the roadside foliage suddenly appear in a long column (plate 11); the footage rewinds and they are again invisible in their cycle of camouflage. In-between this looped footage the viewer sees planes dropping rations; close-up footage of urban streets during wartime—debris and dirt, children staring vacantly with their packed possessions, their home vacated; a young man lying bloodied on the street, still alive, with a woman crouched next to him; smiling children playing with a gun; two identically dressed women in front of a political sign. One cannot tell exactly what year, what decade this is, only that it is wartime. Instead of literally mirroring and doubling images, the images are uncanny, full of doubles: two parallel rows of soldiers, visible then invisible; two children with their tongues sticking out playing stick-up; two women in white hats and outfits, their gaze blocked by sunglasses (plate 12). "Do you remember?" the disintegrating voice asks again and again. This is the way memory works: it loops back on itself; mental images replay, rewind, and become distorted. She says, "I remember it later, afterward." Trương's mother is perhaps the sole bearer of these memories, not the artist, not the woman who got shot by her child. All of the details have been forgotten; the documentary footage sutured together forms another recollection, both imagined and real. The initial site of shock and trauma is later reconstituted in memory, reconstructed verbally and visually. The forgotten past suddenly appears, like the anonymous soldiers once hidden in the spare cover along the straight road leading through the rice fields, *a hiding place we did not even know could exist until the hidden reveals itself.*

In Trương's work, images shift, like the way personal and political memories reshape—abstract forms become recognizable shapes; the hidden reveals itself. Darkness and light. In "Explosions in the Sky (Diên Biên Phu 1954)" (plate 13), a black screen suddenly reveals white explosions, a French cannon positioned in the forest, shooting heavenward. The white blasts become strobe-like as the tempo of the soundtrack picks up, a Vietnamese cover of Simon and Garfunkel's 1966 smash "The Sound of Silence." The familiar, haunting melody and lyrics become unnerving: "Hello darkness, my old friend." Written as a song about youthful alienation, it was subsequently claimed by an American generation as an anti–Việt Nam War anthem, although that was not the songwriter Paul Simon's original aim.[101] For this flower power generation's Vietnamese counterparts, the song embodies the ambivalent legacy of the American War in Việt Nam—the smoky mental image of dimly lit Sài Gòn bars blasting American songs; American and Vietnamese soldiers memorialized by Hollywood war epics.

The refrain echoes, "And the vision that was planted in my brain / still remains." Trương's use of popular culture—particularly music—has a more somber cadence and affect than Nguyễn Tân Hoàng's campy/poignant use of found footage and war-era songs sung by an exiled Khánh Ly or French love

songs covered by Thanh Lan in videos such as *PIRATED!* and *Forever Linda!*
The Vietnamese lyrics anonymously sung in "Explosions in the Sky" are not
a direct translation of the original "The Sound of Silence": "Tung người đi
qua bóng tối đến / cùng cầm tay đi với nhau" (Figures walk through the
shadows of night / holding each other's hands). I imagine South Vietnamese
soldiers—perhaps my then fresh-faced uncles, now permanently careworn
by abuse in the reeducation camps—half-lit by fire, strumming this song in
Vietnamese, their voices echoing in the dark. The half-life of longing and
loss. "Hello darkness." Their voices make me homesick, but I do not know
where home is. Perhaps homesickness is, as Trương notes, "the process of
looking for family members and not seeing oneself there."[102]

The soldiers' distant voices echo in the present, softly reverberating in
the small living rooms (altars of memory and incense) in Little Saigons all
over the world. Their voices echo outward, forward to the grainy distant
past, flashes of brilliance.[103] Then void. But things have not disappeared entirely. Mimi Thi Nguyễn notes that the term *cover* means "to repeat," as well
as "to obscure." Constant (rhetorical) repetition suggests that war is not a
singularity. Empire's wars are iterative, enduring: "What we might understand as formal and social contracts to repeat and return to the event or
feeling."[104] These "formal and social contracts" bind us to yet another return
engagement—social, intimate, militarized. Like moths, we are blinded. Brilliance, then void.

The past, indeed, is a distant colony. The French lost the 1954 Battle of
Diên Biên Phu to the Việt Minh, foretelling the demise of its colonial empire and the bifurcation of Việt Nam into North and South.[105] The dividing
line of state history and individual memory is blurred in Trương's work.
The ever-present past is represented not by a barricade of images but by
an abstract barrage of black and white—flickering ghosts. Discussing "Explosions in the Sky (Diên Biên Phu 1954)," Mimi Thi Nguyễn observes that
Trương calls for multiple returns, seeing erasures across continents and
disciplines (like Lowe); hearing the past in the present—uncanny echoes.
Nguyễn states, "We find that these sounds of silence, these flashes of danger,
are still with us, and that we who are indebted are in a cover, a repetition, in
new wars."[106] Yet each iteration, each new war coverage, does not mean the
same old story. Each repetition redraws the line demarcating whom we have
compassion for. This "ethics of remembering," writes Việt Thanh Nguyễn,
"expands the definition of who it is on one's side to include ever more others,
thereby erasing the distinction between the near and the dear and the far
and the feared."[107] Trương mars this distinction between the near and far,

our colonial and contemporary reverberations, sung side by side. These are our continued intimacies crossing continents, after Lowe, remapping structural sorrows and solidarities. Hailed through spectral voices and rhythmic blasts, Mimi Thi Nguyễn states, "We may join an audience of those who have heard this song of freedom and empire before, and therein lie other passages to an unknowable future."[108] Like all return engagements, with each new iteration and historical echo, with each cover, with each intimate and distant space therein, may we take cover—may we seek and give shelter.

Again we are looking at the night sky. Voices echo; desire and void. The artillery fire—darkness and light—rends gaping holes in sky; it slowly burns constellations in the mind's eye. We suture what remains, the gaps immense.

Trương and Seckon deal with the disjunctures of modernity and postcolonial subjecthood through their use of disjointed narrative and images. They both comment on the costs and displacements of modernity—what Arjun Appadurai has termed "disjunct registers of affiliation."[109] With fragments, Trương and Seckon suture different affective archives while negotiating the art world's contradictory demands of deterritorialized transnational outlooks and situated subjectivities. Space and time are collapsed in their work to different ends. Seckon's pastiche images point at the splintered nature of memory, whereas Trương's fragmentations speak about the gaps in official history. The postcolonial theorist Timothy Mitchell observes, "The experience of modernity is constructed as a relationship between time and space."[110] He notes that a byproduct of modernity is the spatialization of time. Although modernity is seen in historical time as a "stage," a point of arrival within linear narratives of progress and development, it is actually a constant deferral, a staging of differences. Mitchell notes that it is "the very displacement of the West that enables modernity to be staged as 'The West.'"[111] Modernity, synonymous with Western Manifest Destiny, manifests itself in other locales as both different and similar. The West is displaced by the rest of the modernizing world but in its very displacement it allows the image, "the West," to propagate endlessly. Corporations such as Gap, Nike, and Coca-Cola, largely associated with the West, have largely shifted their operations to the global South. Offshore production maximizes profits by taking advantage of cheaper workforces. The displacement of the manufacturing process enables the modernization that comes with the relocation of these plants to developing countries to be staged as "the West." In short, the "displacement" of corporate giants associated with the West to other regions allows for its proliferation. Signs of the (post)modern appear as cholesterol-laden fast-food restaurants and other chain retailers in

Southeast Asia. Kentucky Fried Chicken, a dietary staple of the blue-collar set in the United States, gets an upgrade in Cambodia and Việt Nam. Cool cosmopolitan teen and white-collar adult hangouts, fast-food outlets are chic signs of development and an emergent middle class. Along with Adidas, Mango, Louis Vuitton, and other ubiquitous name-brand storefronts, the West's chain stores and attendant billboards are one of the visual indicators of that country's "arrival."

What we think of as linear unidimensional time becomes intertwined with our experience of space. As Benedict Anderson suggests with "imagined communities," members of a given culture are connected through a shared temporal narrative as well as affinity for a geographic space ("homeland").[112] Time and space (and community) cannot be separated. This builds on Benjamin's and Henri Bergson's earlier insights on "homogenous empty time," time measured by the voids demarcated by the ticking clock, the grids of the calendar, and the timetable.[113] It is generic time, the daily humdrum. It is a psychic grid, a net of synchronized time ensnaring the globe. This sense of time makes strangers feel conjoined in space and time, giving them a sense of simultaneity: they may not be aware of one another's existence, but they inhabit the same time in the same geographic spaces. Trương's teeming fin-de-siècle masses going to and fro may represent this "homogenous empty time," or her Vietnamese subjects repeating the same gestures again and again may: the two Catholic boys crossing themselves, the suited man striding the courtyard, the soldiers doing military rehearsals. The routines of modernity are regulated through the clock, the calendar, the alphabet, and the gridded boulevards. Space and time become coterminous agents of biopower. There is no way off the grid. The recurring grids in Seckon's paintings also evoke the discipline that has been ingested, inculcated into the everyday. All the streets of Phnom Penh are gridded, thanks to the foresight of its French colonial city planners. In his paintings, the gridded fields and gardens become a lattice of destruction. It is the dead-end logic of modernity. The insidious logic of homogeneous empty time writ large on a heterogeneous world demands violence as it aims to regulate and civilize. This empty time may also evoke the sense of "stuckness" Seckon describes before, during, and after wartime. This sense of time and space simultaneously connects and alienates its subjects.

In *Translating Time*, Bliss Cua Lim discusses Bergson's views on homogeneous time, as well as the postcolonial critique of ideas of progress and linear time. She observes that seemingly neutral modern global time—undergirded by imperialistic notions of teleological advancement and expansion—relegates "peripheral" geographies and subjects to occupying a "past" time and space within the present moment. This is the comparative rhetoric of "developed" and "developing" countries. In short, universalizing homogeneous time deals with heterogeneous localized views of time by deeming it obsolete, backward. Difference is domesticated through clock time and time zones. Lim would advocate for Trương's approach to cinema: the filmmaker reveals myriad temporalities that are coeval with, but chafe against, homogeneous time. The time-space of memory and trauma is contained within modern global time—perhaps it is exacerbated by it— but traumatic memory is a distinct temporal consciousness. Although traumatic memory is carried or relived and revisited in the present, it is often seen as a relic of the past. Trương reverses this equation: modern global homogeneous time initiated by colonial conquest is represented by archival footage—images of the past. These are "scenes of imperial remains," as Mimi Thi Nguyễn describes Trương's video.[114] The past is a distant colony. The past is a distant colonizer. Traumatic memory seethes into the present. It *is* the present.

In Trương's videos, the present is marked by absence. The global present is a particular form of time consciousness that Seckon and Trương question. Heterogeneous times and places consist of the temporal consciousness expressed by their fragmentary approaches. Nguyễn observes that Trương's work "disrupts our consumption of time, conceived multiply as periodicity, as history, as process, and as repetition."[115] Trương and Seckon proffer perspectives from multiple vantage points, not from a single location. Their subject positions are also multiply situated.

The modern is experienced as contemporaneous existence. Although Seckon's "Salty Flower Skirt" is a present-day mapping of Cambodia, the traumas of history and development are indelibly inscribed on its landscape. Past, present, and future merge. I observed earlier that the piece represents a more cyclical, Buddhist view of time and space, the Wheel of Life; birth, death, and rebirth cannot be separated. For Trương, the empire's center and its peripheries cannot be separated. Although they occupy separate spaces, they are connected psychically through military presence and regulations. Another connection is implicitly drawn between the violence of the colonial past and current regimes. She also presents the viewer with an endless ring. Both artists defy conventions of linear time and narrative, proffering instead circles of association.

The difference among the premodern, the modern, and postmodernity lie in their different approaches to representation. The modern is a rupture from the premodern; in a similar manner, the postmodern is demarcated by its predecessor. In subsequent stages, we are increasingly removed from the "real" and originary. As postmoderns, we live in a universe of signification, of eternal deferral. In a similar way, the West and its project of modernity is defined by its relation to the non-West. Yet the direction of source to copy moves in the opposite direction. The West is the progenitor of modernity. Its peripheries are duplicates with a difference. Thinkers who advocate for models of exchange and overlap, such as Appadurai, question such West-and-the-rest binaries. The assumption that modernity is a Western model depends on the differences manifest in other locales, its discrepant histories and "discrepant modernities." Again, modernity is not a historical stage but, rather, a staging.[116] It is a staging of narratives of power and domination, of development and destruction. In different countries, the staging varies. Modernity is representation, an endless replica of itself, imperfect. Seckon shows us that during Cambodia's "golden age," the staging of the country's modernity took on a particular valence in the wake of independence: rock-and-roll, sharp-edged modernist public structures, and mod dress. It was Jacqueline Kennedy "fulfilling a lifelong dream of visiting Angkor Wat," as a framed photograph at Le Royale Hotel in Phnom Penh declares proudly. Her arrival embodied the hope that Cambodia had arrived on the world stage. This staging was a vision of the brave new world. It was Cambodia crafting a sleekly modern image of itself. Now, three decades later, it is doing the same, picking up where history once paused and returned to the year zero. Trương demonstrates that the groundwork for modernity was quite different in Việt Nam, although the two countries answered to the same colonial master. She maintains that the brutal staging of Vietnamese modernity is revisited, reimaged. Việt Nam's vicious colonial past is restaged as romantic period films—modern love unto death.

Of course, these stagings of modernity require an audience, spectators. It is double vision: the global audience and the (post)colonial melancholic subject. It is bifurcated vision: the past shapes the future; the image of the future is crafted as the antithesis of the past. The present is a blind spot, an open question. The oppressively elaborate colonial mansions, its pomp and circumstance of Corinthian columns, is displaced by the clean, spare outlines of modernism's angles. The psyche is split, doubled, a doubled consciousness. Trương's mirroring points at this doubling. Mitchell notes that there is a "double difference" in modernity's project: the first sites are "the displacements opened up by the different space" of the non-West. The doubled difference is "the ways in which this space is made to appear different."[117] "Western" modernity demands multiple displacements, both physical and psychic. Modernity in developing countries depends on this divergence and dislocation. It is a "different" modernity from the West, but the ways in which this difference is legible hinge on the representation of a modern West. It is a double difference and a double bind. Trương's and Seckon's works are restagings, as well. They retell the invisible stories of what happened, or what might have happened. Their projects depend on the almighty West as instigator for the bifurcated narratives to play out. The West becomes another Other—a mirror or a mirror image.

The Night Sky (Conclusion)

Trương's and Seckon's work foregrounds the displacement of the West and its imperfect double. Like Sandrine Llouquet and Tiffany Chung (see chapter 2), they defamiliarize familiar narratives and aesthetics, making them uncanny through (re)appropriation. Here the "authentic" copy is the artist's strategic performance of trauma. These knowing performances of trauma (modern, colonial, and personal) form a mirror archive, reflecting and refracting Western hegemony. Though the lines between inside and outside are blurred, the archive must eventually be located in the public realm. Derrida observes that an archive's existence depends on its "consignation in an external place which assures the possibility of memorization, of *repetition*, of reproduction, or of reimpression."[118] Art is an archive, and artists are public intellectuals. Artists embody authority concealed and revealed. Trương's archive reproduces reproductions, an endless repetition. She looks at archival footage again and again, hoping to see a glimmer of recognition that cannot be found; an endless grief for the lost object, her family.[119] Although I proclaimed earlier that Seckon was no melancholic, since he urged us to "get on with life," perhaps he himself is in denial. His repetitive gestures of sewing, patching, and revisiting the past show that the mourning process is not quite finished yet. If the baleful contemporary landscape of "Salty Skirt" is any indication, the country has not successfully mourned or healed from its wounds, either. But to view their archives through the lens of the pleasure principle, a perspective that "affirms the past, present, and future," opens up new possibilities for engagement. The archive does not have to be "stuck" (to use Seckon's term) in meaningless repetition and reproduction. The nature of archives has radically shifted since the *archons*. Art is a malleable archive.

Again we are left with holes in Trương's night sky and blooming wounds on Seckon's canvases. Through this chapter, I have highlighted strategies these two emerging artists use to speak of the voids in memory and history, the gaps between individual identity and nationhood. Their very different approaches to fragments and fragmentation address the spatial and temporal contradictions of modernizing projects. Although Trương and Seckon constantly return to sites of trauma, they are not melancholics. Their return to personal and historical archives indicates archive fever. It is both symptom and desire. It is both the death drive and the pleasure principle. It is love unto death; the frenzy of the visible. It is a fever pitch. In the mind's eye, still, the planes hover, and the bombs burst. Everywhere these blooms bleed.

Town and Country

Sopheap Pich's and Phan Quang's
Urban-Rural Developments

THIS FINAL CHAPTER DEALS WITH urban-rural development for economic return in Cambodia and Việt Nam through the work of the Phnom Penh–
based sculptor Sopheap Pich and the Sài Gòn–based conceptual artist
Phan Quang. I assert that Pich's and Phan's translation of these issues
for an international audience are (self-)exploitative gestures, reiterating traumatized narratives of wartime displacement and rapid development. As "return engagements," on which I elaborate later, these
artistic revisitations anticipate economic returns. In using the term
exploit, I suggest that their strategic positioning is a resourceful
extraction of natural resources: nature (as art subject and art material) and their own naturalized self-narratives.

Etymologically, the word *exploit*, first used in Middle English (twelfth–fifteenth century), derives from the Old French
esploit (*n.*, late fourteenth century), based on the Latin *explicare*, meaning "unfold, unroll," according to the *Oxford
English Dictionary* (OED). The Latin *explicare* is connected
to the term *explicate* "to explain." Hence, action, deeds
(exploits), and language (explicate) are tied. Related to
both exploit and *explicare*, the Latin *explicitum* means
"a thing settled, ended, or displayed" (OED). Here the
relationship of contracts ("a thing settled"), social
death ("a thing ended"), and display is evident. To
be a museum artifact is to be ossified. The objectified person and culture are laid bare: *explicitum* "explicit for all to see" (e.g., ethnological

displays of "savage cultures," such as Bontoc Igorot tribespeople at World's Fairs shown in explicit contrast to "advancing" cultures). Thus, unfolding narrative explanations (such as Phan's and Pich's mining, and miming, their histories) are intrinsically linked to conditions of exploitation. To exploit onself is to explain, to display, show oneself—under contract, with institutional conditions ("a thing settled"). Implicit understandings are externalized, made explicit. (I discuss the relationship to inside and outside, voice and visuality later.)

Exploitation can be "transactional or structural," as the philosophers Matt Zwolinski and Alan Wertheimer point out. In the former, exploitative transactions exist between two or more individuals (e.g., low-paying sweatshops discussed in chapter 3). In the latter, exploitation—via a Marxist lens—is structural, "a property of institutions or systems in which the 'rules of the game' unfairly benefit one group of people to the detriment of another" (e.g., apartheid, colonialism, patriarchy).[1] Zwolinski and Wertheimer also aver that exploitation can be "harmful or mutually beneficial." They ask rhetorically, "On what grounds might we justify interfering with consensual and mutually advantageous exploitative transactions?"[2] For artists such as Phan and Pich, exploitation is at once transactional and structural, mutually benefiting both the individual artists and the institutions that display their work.

These "return engagements" are individual (transactional) and institutional (structural). To exploit is one facet that the term *return engagements* encompasses—repeated social, military, and economic turns and upturnings. It is not singular but iterative, with the potential for powerful shifts. In my introductory discussion, I outline the entwined concepts of revolution (from the French root *revolver*, "to roll"), evolution (Latin, *evolver*, "to unroll"), and return (Spanish, *volver*, "come back, to become"). As Raymond Williams points out, the Latin root of *evolution*, *evolver*, refers to the unrolling of a text or scroll—the " 'unrolling' of something that already exists"—at once the reinstantiation of an existing narrative tropes, but also its undoing, a revolt. To exploit (Latin, *explicare*, "to unfold, unroll") is part of becoming undone *and* reconstituted, enfolded. By being put on display, explicitly undone, one is consumed, remade by the institution.

In the turning (or rolling) of fortune's wheel, revolutionary (*revolver*, to roll) processes unfold (*explicare*, unroll) as socioeconomic positions are upturned (the top of society is now at the bottom, and vice versa) again and again—part of a cycle. To unfold (*explicare*), to be singly exploited (undone, unfurled), is not opposed to rolling (*revolutare*)—to be enrolled, enlisted in service of communal politics.

The term *revolution* invokes battle and profit, sharing key aspects of the word *exploitation*. According to the OED's definition of *exploit*, its "early notion of 'success, progress' gave rise to the sense 'attempt to capture', 'military expedition', hence the current sense of the noun."

The term *return engagements* also connotes wartime interactions (as in military and social engagements). I want to underscore the militarized aspects of these returns—physical, psychic—as both loss and gain. As I have argued throughout this book, artists from the periphery are both embattled by and profit from their evocations of exploitation, during times of rabid destruction and postwar rapid development. Battle lines are also drawn between the urban and the rural; space and time; nature and the nature of humanity. I delineate, and intentionally reshape, these demarcations later.

Nature and Naturalized Discourse

Orientalizing discourse links the body of the native with her or his habitat—at once sublime and savage. Nature is equated with the native. In the same manner that nature (unruly, unbidden) is to be dominated, one's nature (uncontainable, uncategorizable) is likewise to be subjugated. Thus, a distinction between outside (nature) and inside (human nature) is constructed. By extension the savage/nature/Other is outside the parameters of the civil and civil society. The phrase "barbarians at the gate" suggests that uncontainable, unknowable bodies threaten to destroy cultural integrity. Thus, institutional and cultural identities must be known and named (insider/outsider). Against Walt Whitman's universalist, "Very well then I contradict myself, / (I am large, I contain multitudes)," Southeast Asian artists cannot contradict themselves, cannot have multiple subjectivities (e.g., local, diasporic, transnational).

Both Phan and Pich traffic in urban-rural tropes: idyllic countryside themes; citywide threats. For example, Pich's work addresses the twin traumas of Khmer history and development, particularly displacement from Boeung Kak, a lakeside community now filled in with sand. Likewise, Phan's "translations" of rural Vietnamese subjectivity for a global audience reaffirms spatiotemporal dyads of lazy rural backwardness versus frenzied urban advancement and alienation.

Through Cartesian duality (mind-body split) we have become disconnected from both nature and our own nature. We see our individual bodies and the body politic as ruptured. In the chapter "Art and Nature," Herbert Marcuse proposes that nature is key to bridging the personal and the political.

This remaking and reconnecting of ourselves and our environs—nature and humanity—is crucial. For Marcuse, return is vital.

I suggest that Phan and Pich ambivalently chart "return engagements" of their own accord, beyond nature and human; native and foreigner; exploiter and benefactor. It is not a singular, divisive mapping but myriad crisscrossings of identities and topographies: the repeated routes through the countryside and the city, in one's mind and heart. To be reengaged means constantly reconsidering what has been naturalized as limits.

In *Saigon's Edge*, the anthropologist Erik Harms studies how Vietnamese citizens navigate liminal rural-urban zones by adopting fluctuating orientations beyond Cartesian dualities. He asserts that the "poetics of lived space constantly thwart simplified notions of reciprocity and linear change. In actual practice, according to Gaston Bachelard, "The dialectics of inside and outside multiply with countless diversified nuances."[3] Do I contradict myself? Indeed, I contain multitudes. Yet multiplicity is a threat to institutions, as I have argued. To be legible, there can be only one way that one's cultural narrative unfolds (*explicare*). One's relationship to—and representations of—trauma cannot be obscured. Exploitation must be made explicit.

Harms asserts that acts of (re)producing these categories (rural-urban, inside-outside, disaster-redevelopment) point to other possibilities: "Producing these discrete spaces also creates the potential for a level of transcendence, a powerful space that straddles both realms. The ability to *oscillate* between different spatiotemporal modes of social relations represents a form of power that is both symbolic and material at once."[4] Building on Harms's concept of spatiotemporal oscillation, I maintain that artists shift through multiple modalities as they negotiate the various worlds they inhabit. Harms writes, "The power of special temporal oscillation depends not so much on expressing a distinctly rural or urban time orientation but on the ability to move, according to contingency or circumstances, between states."[5] The emphasis on agential, context-driven affiliation is key. In thinking beyond urban-versus-rural space-time schemes, and in straddling both, Pich and Phan also move beyond local/national/regional/transnational categorizations and occupy the frame accordingly, fulfilling personal (inner, transactional) and professional (outer, structural) demands.

Here I loop back to the earlier, positive valences of *exploit*, which means "to fulfill" (*v.*, ca. 1400, Old French) and "a productive working" (*n.*, 1803, English). I yoke this with its latter negative sense of to "use selfishly" (*v.*, 1838, French) (*OED*).[6] Tethering these dual connotations, I frame artistic "self-exploitation" as both positive and negative, harmful and beneficial, nonproductive and "a productive working"—a working on and through. I also parse the relations between to use one's self and to "use selfishly." To self-exploit is to do both: aspects of the self are proffered for use value and to be of use. The word *use* connotes "used" (despoiled, taken advantage of, an aspect of the term *exploit*) and "used to" (accustomed, naturalized). In putting forward negative and positive aspects of *exploit* and underscoring the term *use*, I highlight the conditions that "peripheral" artists get used to—self-exploitative terrain that gets normalized.

Following this oscillating split, two tracks emerge: (1) artist-in-nature; and (2) nature of the artist. In a metonymic and melancholic relation, the artist's nature (as traumatized vessel) is somehow resolved by the artist's reconnecting to nature, the very site of trauma. During the wars in Southeast Asia, jungles were bombed, defoliated; after war, rural displacement runs rampant. By briefly revisiting Đình Q. Lê's earlier work on Agent Orange, I highlight problems affecting rural life, as well as the politics of representation. All three artists (Pich, Phan, and Lê) make work tied to geographic locale, a strategic move that has benefits and drawbacks.

Pich's and Phan's "return" to the problematized pastoral echoes Leang Seckon's and Hồng-Ân Trương's revisiting of traumatic pasts (personal, colonial, and postcolonial) in their artwork, outlined in chapter 3. Like Seckon and Trương, Pich and Phan hold a reflective mirror to international wants and local desires: doubling, redoubling, *and* subverting expectations. At the same time, this refracted mirror—of urban and rural divides—are images at once familiar and foreign, splintered and whole. Locals and international nongovernmental organizations (NGOs) evoke regional representations of poverty/progress again and again.

On Timelines

I focus on 2008–10, pivotal years in Pich's and Phan's careers in which they had important shows that brought them international attention. This period is also marked by the global financial crisis of 2008, centered on Euro-American banking systems, and the Asian markets' relative fiscal stability and subsequent growth (see the introduction). Finally, this initial time frame leads to what Pamela Corey historicizes as the rise of Khmer contemporary art on the international art scene in 2011–13. I would open this frame to include Vietnamese contemporary art, as well as an attentiveness to artists in the Southeast Asia region.

As a case in point, the growing attention to Southeast Asian artists is evidenced by the atypical critical mass included in the 2012 Documenta (13) exhibition, one of the three most visible group shows on the global art circuit. Olga Viso, executive director of the Walker Art Center in Minneapolis, noted that, in addition to the usual international art stars, Documenta (13) included "a number of artists from . . . countries in Asia not typically represented, including Thailand, Vietnam, and Indonesia."[7] In the 2012 iteration of the quinquennial exhibition, based in Kassel, Germany, American military interventions in Cambodia and Việt Nam, their echoes in the Middle East, and "other 20th-century conflicts" were a "recurring leitmotif," observes the *New York Times* art critic Roberta Smith. She suggests that the "emphasis on the trauma of war is consistent with" the artistic director Carolina Christov-Bakargiev's view of Documenta "as a show born of trauma, [as she] expressed in an essay in one of the show's three catalogs."[8] Fittingly, artists representing Cambodia and Việt Nam—among them Sopheap Pich, Vandy Rattana, Đinh Q. Lê, and Vũ Giáng Hương—addressed the visages and vestiges of war. In a feedback loop, Smith notes that Documenta's founding was also rooted in war: "It grew, after all, out of the ruins of World War II—Kassel was heavily bombed by the Allies—and was an attempt to bring Germany up to speed with modern art, both banishing and repressing the cultural darkness of Nazism."[9] Thus, the returns of war through cultural production and institutions is an engine for diplomacy, as well as socioeconomic advancement. Throughout the book, and this chapter, I make the case that cultural and economic development are intrinsically linked through national and individual self-exploitation, which are at once harmful and beneficial.

Sopheap Pich   PRESENTS AND POISONS

Years after Sopheap Pich first moved back to Phnom Penh in 2002, he still embodied the stereotype of a "struggling artist," sleeping on a cot in a cramped room built inside his studio space in the low-rent Boeung Kak area. Pich was born in 1971 in rural Koh Kralaw, Battambang Province, in northwestern Cambodia about a five-hour drive from Phnom Penh. During the Khmer Rouge period, his family was displaced, shuttling among various towns and villages in the province. They ended up in a refugee camp in Thailand. In 1984, Pich's family settled in Massachusetts, where a significant number of Cambodian refugees landed. These traumatic journeys are the subject of a body of work I discuss in the first half of this chapter. Pich attended the University of Massachusetts, Amherst, changing from pre-med to painting, against his father's wishes. Nonetheless, Pich's early medical training—and trained clinical observant eye—has proved useful in his art practice: human and plant systems, biology and botany, and biopolitics are recurring motifs. Pich eventually earned a master's in fine arts from the School of the Art Institute of Chicago in 2002, then returned to Cambodia the same year. The son at first seemed to embody his father's grim predictions; he slept on the ground in his former apartment. For years, he employed two craftsmen, Tomai and Sophai, to help make his labor-intensive sculptures. During my last visit to his studio in January 2018, Pich had a large live-work compound an hour's drive south of Phnom Penh that employed more than seven men.

I highlight Pich's international breakthrough shows in 2009–10 as a moment in which growing international interest in Cambodian contemporary art dovetailed with the artist's rise. In the decade since Pich's pivotal solo exhibition, *The Pulse Within*, was installed at the Tyler Rollins Fine Art gallery in New York in 2009, he has had five solo shows at the gallery: *Morning Glory* (2012), *Reliefs* (2013), *Structures* (2015), *Rang Phnom Flower* (2016), and *Expanses* (2018). Tyler Rollins is Pich's main gallerist; the works in these exhibitions led to shows at the world's leading art venues, including the Solomon R. Guggenheim Museum, the M+ Museum for Visual Culture in Hong Kong, the 2017 Venice Biennale, the Singapore Art Museum, and Documenta (13). The Metropolitan Museum of Art (New York) and Centre Georges Pompidou (Paris)—both bastions of high Western art—have acquired his work through Rollins. The exhibitions at the Met and the Guggenheim were connected to the Season of Cambodia Living Arts Festival in New York, which Corey writes about in detail.[10] Season of Cambodia was initiated in 2012 by the nonprofit arts organization Cambodia Living Arts of Phnom Penh; its mission was to "illuminate and to advance Cambodian arts and culture, driving international support and attention to the creativity and diversity of cultural expressions in Cambodia today."[11] In short, Season of Cambodia aimed to bring artists from the "periphery" to the centers of cultural production, metaphorically and literally, through programming at world-class venues in New York City in 2012 and in Paris in 2018.[12]

The formal and conceptual hallmarks of Pich's oeuvre found some of their earliest sustained expressions in *The Pulse Within*, his first significant Western exhibition after some shows in Southeast Asia and Asia. *Morning Glory*, *Rang Phnom Flower*, and *Expanses*, for example, all featured organic forms (flowers, seeds), which Pich rendered at immense size in rattan and bamboo—outsize symbols of Cambodia. *Rang Phnom Flower* conjures the flowering tree where the Buddha was born; hence, it is planted in many

Khmer temples, including those near Pich's studio.[13] Spirituality, sensuous forms, and loss are recurring themes in Pich's practice, as I discuss later.

It took Pich a while to find his way, to find his artistic voice. But now his individual artistic voice is also the cultural voice of a nation: Rollins frames him as "Cambodia's most internationally prominent contemporary artist."[14] Trained as a painter, he had several solo painting exhibitions in Phnom Penh when he first arrived. But he felt limited by painting—that the local community could not relate to it; that he was too preoccupied, as he told me, "with making an image on a limited space."[15] Then he made his first sculpture, using rattan, bamboo, and metal wire, for a group exhibition at the Centre Culturel Français in Phnom Penh in 2004.

Cycle (plate 14) was the second sculpture created after Pich's initial breakthrough in 2004: a pair of grated rattan lungs. He created this pivotal work in several iterations, including as a monumental outdoor sculptural installation in cast metal at the new King Abdullah University in Saudi Arabia. Continuing Pich's investigation of internal organs, *Cycle* is essentially two stomachs, connected. When one encounters the piece in a gallery space, one experiences it as form and line, both open and enclosed, shadow and light. Its sheer formal qualities impress the viewer first, then the conceptual references step in. Pich's work stands in stark contrast to other conceptual work that does not privilege aesthetics, a sort of anti-aesthetic aesthetic. The stomach is a merely a launching point. In his artist statement about the piece, Pich writes, "A major issue in Cambodia, as I knew it, has always been the stomach. It was either that everyone's concern was to fill it or to cure its diseases. *Cycle* took the shape of a stomach as a starting point to symbolize society in general. It suggested ideas of strong family ties or a society held together by simple means. It was also about fragility, controlled chaos, movement, and the ambiguity of the interior and the exterior. So there were questions about identity: *am I inside? or outside?*"[16] Pich's open-weave work is open to multiple interpretations. His statement emphasizes his formal preoccupations: chaos, movement, fragility. In a way, it is art for art's sake, the antithesis of work dealing with identity or idea-driven work. Most of his early sculptures are driven by form. But as the title of his show suggests, Pich is still preoccupied with inside and outside, what lies beneath the surface. His rhetorical questions "Am I inside? Or outside?" point at his liminal subject position in Cambodia and abroad. He is both an insider and an outsider.

As I argue in chapter 1, the diasporic artist's subject position is used strategically. Pich, as an example, is an "insider" for the globe-trotting curators and collectors looking for "local" flavor. Here I apply Erik Harms's thinking on liminality and code switching, outlined earlier. Pich intentionally engages "spatial temporal oscillation" between urban and rural mindsets, between inside and outside. The statement's introduction of the "major issue" in Cambodia as being the stomach marks his status as a cultural insider, a genuine Cambodian with knowledge about the country's mores and obsessions. "A society held together by simple means" implies connections to agrarian ideals. This body of work evoking modest organic forms and ways of life stands in contrast with his work on urban structures and development, discussed later in this chapter. Thus, Pich situates himself between urban and rural spaces, betwixt Cambodia and the world. As an artist from abroad with education, flexible citizenship, and language skills, Pich has cultural capital that sets him "outside" the norm, above and beyond the pack. He knows how to translate this insider knowledge to the outside world. This tactical oscillation propels him to the uppermost limits of the art world. Yet he can be doubly marginalized, as well, "trapped" by his chosen home and his history.

Pich's explanation of *Cycle* differs from the critic and curator Brian Curtin's interpretation of the artist's pieces in a review in *Frieze Magazine*. Curtin reads the artist's work as simple signifiers for issues plaguing Cambodia: "Each piece functions symbolically: the stomach for hunger; the dogs the ubiquitous sign for scavengers in South East Asia."[17] Curtin projects stereotypes of Southeast Asian hunger and famine, poverty and despair onto Pich's work. Cambodia is not a growling stomach, a pitiable developing country, a developing ulcer. The latticework grid dogs are a recurring presence in Pich's oeuvre. They are not scavengers; they embody loyalty, luck, and fidelity. "*Cycle* has . . . kind of suggestive tendencies," Pich says, concurring that the work may evoke cultural specificities. Yet he also disagrees: "But it remains a sculpture; *it doesn't try to tell a story*."[18] Historically, painting often proffered narrative, representing the world. It was not until the "revolution" of abstract expressionism that painting broke free from its bonds of narrative.

Pich's work strides the line between abstraction and representation, between minimalism—as Curtin suggests—and the politics of identity. It is this in-between space that leads to uneasy, overdetermined interpretations. Pich's refusal to tell a story perhaps has exactly to do with his insider-outsider status. He wanted not to trot out his traumas but to deal with the current sociopolitical condition of Cambodia in an abstract, evocative manner. But Curtin's growling stomach is very different from Pich's symbol of society. Pich may be articulating the differences between media—between his original discipline of painting and his later adopted medium, sculpture.

For Pich, sculpture is largely a formal exploration that does not tell a story. Stuck between inside and outside, he must be a cultural interpreter, but he is dictating the terms of engagement, controlling the storyline.

The Pulse Within and Outside: Local and Global Housing Crises

After being included in the 2009 Asia Pacific Triennial, one of his first significant international shows, Pich moved to an apartment near the dignified peaked-roof outline of the National Museum. A sign of his success, Pich also rented another "studio": a relatively unfurnished, airy three-story house one door down that he used to store and display his large-scale sculptural work. All three studios perch on the edge of the green-tinged lake. During my first visit to Pich's then new studio space in September 2010, he and I took a break on the second-story balcony, which has clear views across the 222-acre (90-hectare) lake to the other side of town. He pointed out recent construction, including the sci-fi-looking pyramid-within-a-cutout-square structure that houses the Ministry of Defense. Closer were dilapidated wooden shacks. Joking about his days of sleeping virtually on the floor, we said, "The view's nicer up here."

"It's pretty here," Pich agreed. Surveying the lake's confetti of unidentifiable rubbish, plastic bottles bobbing like miniature buoys and silvery snack bags glimmering like dead carp, he sighed. "But don't look too close." In 2019, the scenic, polluted lake—once the largest freshwater lake in Phnom Penh—was entirely gone, like a mirage. Pich's *The Pulse Within* exhibition specifically dealt with the controversial development of Boeung Kak (Kak Lake) and the price of Cambodia's growth in general. As the title of the exhibition implies, things are very different beneath the surface.

After the defeat of the Khmer Rouge, many people returned to Phnom Penh in the 1980s to start again after years of uncertainty. Squatters and refugees settled in Boeung Kak, an unwanted area, subsisting off the lake and erecting shacks on stilts—brown water fowl balancing their bodies on spindly legs.[19] Ironically, as developing countries such as Cambodia increase their gross domestic product (GDP), the poor become further marginalized. When Pich had his studio on the lake, many of his neighbor's homes hovered over the water, built on planks. Most of the settlers have rights to their land under Cambodia's 2001 Land Law. According to the Bank Information Center, a watchdog group, the titling team from the World Bank–financed Land Management and Administration Project adjudicated and denied the area's residents title en masse in 2007, in defiance of this law. The announcement came on February 6, 2007, that the municipality of Phnom Penh had granted a ninety-nine-year lease to Shukaku Inc., a local private developer, to develop 329 acres (133 hectares) of the Boeung Kak area, including the lake itself. Kep Chuktema, then Phnom Penh's governor, signed the lease "at a throwaway price of $79 million without any prior public consultation," according to the *Phnom Penh Post*.[20] Shukaku is run by Lao Meng Khin, a senator and "major donor" to the ruling Cambodia People's Party. He is also director of the logging company Pheapimex.[21] The filling of the lake began in August 2008; the developers contacted some of the more than four thousand families (comprising twenty thousand people) living around the area and not others.

Even though the World Bank was called to intervene in Boeung Kak, it is implicated.[22] In September 2009, the NGO Centre on Housing Rights and Evictions and Cambodian housing rights groups filed a formal complaint against the World Bank, which had funded the land titling project that was supposed to make Boeung Kak residents' status official and protect them from land grabbing. The complaint alleges that the World Bank "breached its own operational policies" by not adequately monitoring the Land Management and Administration Project.[23] Indeed, the World Bank's stated mission is to "fight poverty with passion," not exacerbate it.[24] That same month, the Cambodian government announced it would not cooperate with the program due to the bank's slow pace for the titling project and a disagreement over social safeguards—the Policy on Involuntary Resettlement instituted by the bank.[25] As a consequence, the World Bank indefinitely suspended its loans to Cambodia.

The World Bank undertook an investigation of the project in November 2010 in response to the complaint. Its report indicated that developers had harassed families to leave, offering no more than $8,000 to families who agreed to relocate within a given time frame. The former resident Heng Mom stated that the compensation was not "nearly enough to buy something new—not around here."[26] Filling the lake with sand caused structural damage and flooding to the surrounding homes, adding further stress on residents who might have preferred to stay.

In October 2010, Leang Seckon (Pich's studio neighbor) moved all of his artwork from his working studio/family home in Boeung Kak to his house in the center of the city. "Anything could happen at any time," a mutual friend explained. "[Leang] is very concerned. Some people have lost everything."[27] Another artist I know returned after her family took compensation and departed. "Some closer to the development on the other side of the lake were contacted," she recalled. "My family moved, but I come back." She is using her former family home as combined living space and studio. "You can see the change. Every day more and more families move out because they are scared."[28] The local newspaper *Khmer Machas Srok* summarized, "Some citizens did not want to suffer violence from the authorities and decided to leave with tears."[29] More than a thousand undercompensated families moved without being notified of their rights.

Khmer Machas Srok noted on March 18, 2010, that two foreign companies that had partnered with Shukaku on the project officially withdrew. The paper quoted a senior economist who said that the companies feared for their reputations worldwide because of the poor treatment of residents. The Cambodian government effectively reversed its 2001 Land Law by issuing a subdecree to convert the Boeung Kak area from state public land to state private land in August 2010. To appease critics, the municipality of Phnom Penh announced a proposal for the displaced.[30] Thus, the project and the developers attached to it are not solely or originally responsible for the displacement.

Banks and Embankments: Global Fiscal Crisis | Land Grabbing

Boeung Kak is a case study for the larger "strategic cartographies" spurred by the 2008 global fiscal crisis I discuss in the introduction. It may be useful to apply Ken MacLean's insights on citizens and governments maneuvering mutual distrust through "strategic action and tactical maneuvering."[31] The major players in Boeung Kak—the government, Khmer residents, and outside institutions such as the World Bank—all exist within a political economic environment of what McLean calls "partial legibility."[32] On one hand, each constituent's actions and aims are relatively clear (e.g., residents' housing rights, government development, the World Bank's and other NGOs' emphasis on "transparency"). Yet these seemingly clear aims are obscured by larger transnational agendas and stressors, such as global economic downturns.

For fiscal stability and support, Southeast Asian countries are increasingly facing east rather than traditionally farther west. In 2008, as Euro-American banks and housing markets were reeling from collapse, East Asia and Southeast Asia strengthened their inter-regional fiscal infrastructure. Cambodia is unconcerned about the end of World Bank support. China is investing billions, in addition to the millions from longtime aid donors. An official spokesperson stated that Cambodia "no longer appreciate[s]" World Bank loans.[33] In a self-critical review, the World Bank admitted that it had "failed to protect the lakeside residents, and had broken many of its own regulations which were supposed to prevent forced evictions," according to a *BBC News* report.[34] Although composed of 188 countries, the World Bank, headquartered in Washington, DC, has been criticized for privileging the global North's economic interests through unequal voting power. Its agenda—neoliberal free-market reform—is pushed via development loans to the global South. A report by the US Senate Committee on Foreign Relations critiqued the World Bank and its sister international fiscal institutions (such as the International Monetary Fund, also founded at the Bretton Woods Conference in 1944) for focusing too much "on issuing loans rather than on achieving concrete development results within a finite period of time."[35] This is an example of MacLean's top-down "papereality" enacted by institutions and governments: idealized goals, agendas—and attendant paperwork—which may not match real-world needs. These establishments champion abstract neoliberal policy frameworks, inadvertently increasing localized bureaucracy without effectively realizing constituent long-term needs. As a case in point, the World Bank–funded land titling project that was to empower Boeung Kak residents, as well as hundreds of thousands of others, proceeded at what *BBC News Phnom Penh* called "a snail's pace before being finally being cancelled by the [Khmer] government [in 2009]."[36] Thus shape-shifting cultures of "partial legibility" allow for the Cambodian government and its citizens (occasionally in opposition, as I have traced) to more flexibly respond to sudden and long-term socioeconomic pressures from without and outside. These tactical responses yield partial goals and mixed outcomes, both valiant and violent.

The Boeung Kak debacle is an inverse of the 2008 subprime housing market crash in the United States, in which foreign investors were blamed for destabilizing domestic US banks. In this case, intra-Asian investment buffers Cambodia from the full effects of the 2008 crisis. After shaky "fits and starts" over the years, Shukaku's lake redevelopment was "revived" in 2016 by new Chinese backers.[37] This a growing trend as Chinese investors develop the Mekong Delta region as part of a long-term strategy to build a new Silk Road. In the works is a new, $80 billion capital project north of Phnom Penh, called Samdech Techo Dragon City, after the official title and zodiac sign of Prime Minister Hun Sen, an avid China supporter.[38]

As I have stressed throughout this book, development is also a traumatic process. In all, about 4,250 families (or twenty thousand residents) had been forcibly evicted or evacuated by 2017 to create what Shukaku has dubbed Phnom Penh City Center: The Pearl of Cambodia.[39] What was once waterfront is now a construction site. The outlines of condos, office buildings, and shops are visible on the horizon: a new economic zone and an old ideological battle zone. Environmentalists and others decry that the lack of lakes decreases biodiversity, eradicates sustainable livelihood (farming, fishing), and increases city flooding during the wet season. Boeung Tumpun (Tumpun Lake), Phnom Penh's only remaining lakeside community, faces the same fate as Boeung Kak, as it, too, is being filled with sand.[40]

Some former Boeung Kak residents are still fighting to retain their rights. Twenty-two families protesting their evictions from Boeung Kak finally agreed to land titles on December 26, 2017. Ten families are still holding out, more than a decade after the area was first sold and filled in with sand. The families from Village 1 who accepted the city's offers each received plots of land measuring 13 × 54 feet (4 × 16 meters) in Village 22, on the other side of the former lake. "We have been negotiating since 2007," the community leader Chan Puthisak said in a public statement. "If we had not struggled, we would not have gotten it. This is the result of a lot of struggle and a lot of sacrifice. This is the achievement of our hard work."[41]

Although Boeung Kak has disappeared, the battle over it remains a vexed symbol. Tepp Vanny, well-known land eviction and human rights activist, was imprisoned for more than two years for her peaceful activism.[42] The Cambodian League for the Promotion and Defense of Human Rights (LICADHO) reports: "At a protest in Phnom Penh on 13 March 2013—over the jailing of another activist—parapolice beat and injured several members of the Boeung Kak Lake community. Nonetheless, Tep Vanny was convicted by Phnom Penh Municipal Court on 23 February 2017 for 'intentional violence with aggravating circumstances,' despite a lack of credible evidence."[43] Amid controversy, the Supreme Court upheld Vanny's conviction on February 7, 2017.[44] Her supporters held a religious vigil in Boeung Kak on August 15, 2018, to mark the two-year anniversary of her incarceration. Perhaps as a response to ongoing public outcry, Vanny was released from prison after being pardoned on August 24, 2018.[45] On the same date, however, she and five other fellow Boeung Kak activists—Nget Khun, Cheang Leap, Kong Chantha, Tol Sreypov, and Heng Mom—each received a six-month suspended sentence for making a "death threat" against a former community member, Ly Mom, when she accepted a land title.[46] Mom filed her complaint in 2012 but dropped it in 2016; however, the case was revived later that year. According to the BTI 2018 Cambodia Country Report, by the German civil society Bertelsmann Stiftung, these juridical obstacles may be one of the Hun Sen regime's means of deterring activists: "[The] threats and intimidation [through] legal persecution—based on fabricated allegations and show trials—have become the main tool against the opposition and independent civil society organizations for years."[47]

Others who are experiencing displacement are invisible to me and to the international audience that has been drawn to Boeung Kak. Domestically, apart from localized incidents, land grabbing has not yet garnered national attention: "Despite its systematic character and negative impact on the livelihood of more than 800,000 Cambodians, land-grabbing has remained as locally isolated cases that have not generated nationwide unrest yet."[48] Land grabbing, nonetheless, is a serious issue throughout Cambodia. In 2009, Human Rights Watch reported that the country's "epidemic" of coerced displacement of the urban poor and the confiscation of villagers' farmland had "reached crisis proportions. . . . Military units were often deployed to carry out forced and violent evictions of villagers whose ownership claims to the land had never been properly or fairly dealt with by a court." In Phnom Penh, 10 percent of the city's approximately 1.3 million residents—about 133,000 people—have been displaced since 1990. As noted, country denizens are vulnerable, as well: "Rural landlessness has skyrocketed from around 13 percent in 1997 to as high as 25 percent in 2007."[49] The trend continues. "Distribution conflicts are likely to increase if plundering of natural resources for one-time, non-recurring gains continues," warns BTI. In the decade since Boeung Kak was bought and being redeveloped (2007–17), Cambodia transformed from a subsistence economy into consumer-driven one. Thus, the vanished lakeside farmers and fishers replaced by as-yet-unoccupied shopping malls and high-rises are apt symbols of socioeconomic change and damage.

As the Cambodian economy and infrastructure development rose, individual debt metastasized. In 2007, total household debt was $200 million, compared with $2.9 billion in April 2018. The Cambodian economy was projected to grow at 7.2 percent in 2018–19. Concurrently, Phnom Penh was undergoing what Bloomberg News calls "one of the world's fastest property booms," fueled largely by Chinese investors and buyers.[50] The high-end condo high-rises remain largely empty in the capital's center, as domestic city dwellers—whose annual income averages $11,000—are outpriced.[51]

In addition to land grabbing, an increasing reliance on high-interest loans is causing displacement. Although equitable land titles were one of the main objectives for the evicted Boeung Kak residents, this does not make them immune from further displacement. Land titles, often used to as loan collateral, makes borrowers "compelled to repay the loans by selling land," states Oxfam Country Director Solinn Lim.[52] As a result, according to an *Asia Times* article, the landless are forced into "debt bondage" (transferring their debts to factories and working wageless until the debt is repaid) or into migrating for labor.[53] For instance, about 1.5 million Cambodians were working in neighboring Thailand in 2019, with a third of the migrants working illegally or trafficked.[54] In short, microloans exacerbate poverty; they do not help mitigate it.

Although the gleaming high-rises in Phnom Penh beckon at an industrious, commodity-filled future, the present shift from a subsistence economy to a consumer-driven one is still in progress. Currently, 60 percent of Cambodians earn their livelihood from agricultural production.[55] To put this in context, 35 percent of Cambodians are still living in poverty; the majority are part of the rural populace, according to the 2018 global Multidimensional Poverty Index (MPI), jointly released by the United Nations Development Program (UNDP) and the Oxford Poverty and Human Development Initiative (OPHI).[56] Of this number, "40 percent of the rural population is living in multidimensional poverty, compared to 7 percent in urban settings," stated UNDP Country Director Nick Beresford.[57] Due to the rural-urban poverty divide, recent studies show, approximately 1,085,000 rural households were indebted (versus the 31,000 households in Phnom Penh and 137,000 households in other urban centers). Furthermore, interest rates were usually higher in the countryside.

Together, high-interest microloans and land grabbing form cycles of alienation and disempowerment for Cambodia's disadvantaged. The BTI argues that, although the Hun Sen government has tried to win over the general public "with numerous policies such as yearly minimum wage increases in the apparel industry [as discussed in Leang Seckon's work] and the alleged distribution [announced in February 2016] of almost one million hectares [2.5 million acres] to poor, landless people, the regime struggles to regain popularity among the citizens."[58] So far there has not been any known (re)distribution of land, aside from the highly documented—and disputed—Boeung Kak case. These overlapping, ongoing issues of wages, loans, and land rights are about setting viable, livable bounds. At its heart, land grabbing—and global capital—is about not having limits.

Pich's work from *The Pulse Within* addresses land grabbing and related development issues. His sculpture *Raft* (plate 15), a grid of bamboo and rattan strips, speaks of Boeung Kak's lake-filling project. Evoking the homes on stilts of the lake, the piece is a rectangular building perched on two elongated cylinders—a pontoon-like structure. The edifice recalls the new constructions going up throughout Phnom Penh, the impossible stacks of boxes perched precariously on top of motorbikes zooming through town to deliver their cargo, as well as carts filled to the brim with items for recycling. Speaking of these carts, Pich writes, "On the Thai-Cambodian border, carts and tricycles filled with all kinds of scrap materials are pushed and pulled by handicapped people every day to sell to Thai factories."[59] Many living on the border make their livelihood by recycling debris of the past: "And when I see the workers building the buildings, it is as though I'm looking at the same people who scavenge for metals."[60] The refuse of the past is being refashioned. Blood, sweat, and steel. It is a Trojan horse. One can see this "raft" and its high-rise cargo on the river—a foreboding vision of development. The "shiny" buildings, the golden miles, are all being transported on this raft across the lake, across the rivers that bisect Phnom Penh, across the River Styx.

The cubicle of the crisscrossing structure also brings to mind small tombs. The stark formality of the square boxes evokes the Turner Prize–winning British sculptor Rachel Whiteread's inverted casts of interiors. Her piece *Ghost*, which first garnered critical attention in the 1990s, is the cast of the entire living room of a Victorian house. The off-white form looks like a mausoleum. The "negative" space, the void between walls and floors, is filled; emptiness becomes solid, absence becomes presence. In the opposite manner, Pich's forms are not solid at all. They are open, lines made of organic materials. The bamboo and rattan form a lattice, a skeletal structure, an X-ray, a blueprint line drawing in three dimensions. The cylindrical vessels that support the mausoleum-like "building" also look like missiles or bombs, bringing to mind the horrific past. In this piece the past and present converge. As I look at the piece and muse about the title, I think of my own history, escaping Southeast Asia on a raft, ending up in a refugee camp in Thailand, presaging Pich's arrival by three years. The past repeats itself. Today's forced evictions echo the displacement of thousands by the Khmer Rouge. *Raft* is a monument and a memorial to development and destruction. In the shadow of the former Boeung Kak emerges a modern city, another oasis, another hallucination. The lakeside studios of Pich and Seckon have also been demolished. Only the debris remains.

Junk Nutrients (plate 16) is an abstract intestine spilling out strands of garbage, including blue piping, caps, rope, plastic bottles, mesh, tubing, and so on. It also resembles a decapitated mythical nāga. Its blood spills out, solidifying as streamers of refuse. In Southeast Asia, snake blood and snake wine are reputed to have a wide range of medicinal as well as sexual benefits. But this nāga's blood is not like Zeus's blood in which offspring spring forth. The piece also looks like the aftermath of a divination using the entrails of some rough beast. Entrail divination has been used in many cultures throughout time, ranging from sacrificial animals to human viscera.

While these pieces are still structured of bamboo and rattan, gone are the open grids of Pich's earlier work. The winding tube that resembles an intestine is covered in large, alternating stripes of burlap, used by farmers, framed by strips of bamboo. In an uncovered section without the dyed crimson burlap one can see within. The intestine is also filled with trash. The nāga, like the settlers of Boeung Kak, has been surviving off the lake.

Because it was filled with sand, the lake no longer contains reeds and vegetation; it subsists on a diet of junk food. This work marks a formal departure for Pich. His other sculptural work is quite Spartan: just bamboo, rattan, and metal wire. He describes the advancement of his artistic vision this way: "New questions began to appear, and so new steps or experiments were taken: I began to use other materials—burlaps, farm tools, wood, plastic, paints, etc. There was a need to put a more distinct 'subject matter' in the objects."[61] Where does this need to have more distinctive subject matter come from?

Materials and Materialism

Pich's sculptures cast a net of shadows on the wall; the lines go on seemingly endlessly, implying diverging narratives, pathways. The bamboo, rattan, and metal wire is the "common language" of household objects in Cambodia: from these basic units, baskets, furniture, brooms, and other daily utilitarian items are constructed. Everywhere one can see bamboo and rattan stitched together with metal wire: in the markets of Phnom Penh, in Pich's rural rice-farming community of Koh Kralaw. These materials speak of embodied memory, of the comfort of home. Now these simple materials, materials Pich played with as a child in the countryside, are the main vocabulary of his practice.

Pich employs these "local" materials in an updated manner for his contemporary art practice. Đinh Q. Lê, another diasporic artist who has lived in Southeast Asia for a long time, has also risen to prominence on the international art stage for using updating "native" media. For the works that he calls "photo-weavings," Lê uses a "traditional" grass-mat weaving technique he learned from his aunt. His practice encompasses other media—most recently, video installation—but he first built his career on these weavings; in fact, he told me that he worried about being "typecast" because of them.[62] Just as Pich is synonymous with contemporary Cambodian art, Lê is synonymous with contemporary Vietnamese art. I might speculate that the visibility both enjoy has led to this choice of "essentializing" media with a twist. Their works beg the question: Is the medium the message? What is it saying?

In a competitive art market, formal innovations such as the consistent use of bamboo, rattan, and metal or weaving helps make an artist's output memorable to the larger public. When that artist is associated with a developing country, the formal and conceptual links are further cemented. Pich's use of, and "return" to, the materials of his motherland, of his childhood, is compelling. The medium (re)connects the returnee artist to his roots. Pich's frustration that contemporary painting is a medium that laypeople in Cambodia could not relate to is valid. Painting has a different philosophical history; it has different cultural, political, and art-history references. Art is political. It reflects a given sociocultural vantage point, no matter how apolitical it claims to be. The medium is the message. So Pich's return to these humble materials has political and aesthetic dimensions. Lê's appropriation and innovation of a weaving technique used by Vietnamese villagers is a smart move: it combines tradition and modernity.

Southeast Asian artists, both local and diasporic, are representatives of their countries, a burden other artists invariably carry. They have flexible citizenship as globe-trotting art stars, but they are not truly cosmopolitan in the art world. Their work is often reduced to a local context. Curtin's proclaims, "Expectations of Sopheap Pich's first solo show in Bangkok [2008] were high. . . . Of course the interest in the artist probably extends more generally to the burgeoning Cambodian art scene."[63] This statement partly reveals that the artist and his country of origin are being conflated. Pich is an ambassador for Cambodian contemporary art, which carries a privilege and a burden. *Frieze* magazine, based in London, is a high-gloss, high-power magazine firmly rooted in the center (psychically, if not physically) of the still Eurocentric art world, with short spotlight articles about its periphery. It claims to be the "leading" rag about contemporary art and culture. If Pich were showing the same work as a resident of, say, Lowell, Massachusetts, he would not get the same level of international or even national attention. Pich would be a representative of the Cambodian American community, a small minority within a large nation, not the artistic heir of an entire country.

Curtin's review further observes that Pich's work "evokes *local* contexts through [his] materials and ostensible concerns but could never . . . be reducible to local contexts because of [his] methods."[64] The discussion of formal technique reveals the artist's (or the reviewer's) ambivalence. Pich's method is similar to the method of certain chain restaurants in Cambodia and Việt Nam: provide "local" flavor with a modern twist and upscale

Town and Country

wrapping. But it is more complex; it is not such a simple formula. Pich addresses both local and international audiences in his work, audiences with expectations of what art should be. Pich's methodology is more open-ended than simply referencing local context, evoking local flavor. Elaborating on Pich's chosen medium, Curtin states, "At the level of form, rattan as a signifier of vernacular or indigenous craft is very much resisted and the near minimalism fits expectations of contemporary art very well."[65] I disagree with this assessment, which pitches "craft" against high art. Minimalism was marketed in its heyday as the ultimate "apolitical" art movement. In the article, the universalist expectations of minimalism are contrasted with the local, politicized specificity of indigenous craft. Although Pich does not create "precious" objects—cute oversize rattan baskets per se—his potency as an artist lies in straddling craft and high art. Craftsmen create his work using the same techniques used to make rattan tables and chairs. Pich resists simple references. His intervention is largely a formal one: taking the "vernacular" of rattan and transforming it. While his work is formally stunning and can be appreciated for its geometry and undulating lines, his conceptual engagement does not follow minimalism's philosophical lineage.

Identity can be a trap. Where is the trapdoor to escape? Curtin concludes his review of Pich's work by writing, "To the extent that Cambodia provides his inspiration one can only hope he never becomes trapped by the country he is working out of."[66] No one would write such a thing about Jasper Johns's seminal interpretations of the American flag. Johns's caustic takes on midcentury America did not limit his career. It is like writing that Andy Warhol was "trapped" by America and its celebrity culture—that he was a one-trick pony. Cambodia's vast landscape and vast issues are viewed by Curtin as too small a terrain. But maybe he has a point: Pich's formula is too simple. Pich can be "trapped" by the country he is working out of, especially if he wants to be an international artist whose artistic terrain is not limited by identity. But the country and the located topics that are trapping him also give him legibility. This is a double-edged sword. Like his Vietnamese American counterparts, Pich is called to represent his homeland but must find a way to maneuver the constraints of identity politics. As Curtin points out, Pich may fall prey to making work peddling in easy symbolism for local issues; he warns, "An engagement on this level would quickly run dry."[67] The reviewer's and the artist's uneasy relationships to Cambodia and contemporary art are revealed. For Pich, the uneasiness comes from simple categories others place on him—craft versus high art, local versus global. In

Curtin's view, local and "international" vantage points are at odds. This kind of thinking is a trap.

This "trap" does not belong just to expatriate reviewers. Cambodia also calls on Pich to be its standard-bearer, its cultural ambassador. Cambodia's Cultural Profile (2014), which the Ministry of Fine Arts developed with assistance from the Rockefeller Foundation, featured Pich along with two other artists, Chath Piersath and Marine Ky, as being exemplary returnees, bearers of the cultural torch. The profile serves as an electronic resource for "cultural professionals and the general public," a sort of diplomatic internet gateway.[68] Pich does not care much about the hype.

Pich tries to get to the heart of the matter in his explorations of land grabbing. As its name suggests, *Caged Heart* (plate 17) is a heart-shaped form enclosed in a low, gridded circular cage. The heart itself echoes the construction of *Junk Nutrients*: parts of it are wrapped in burgundy burlap, with strips of bamboo providing structure. One can see inside the empty heart. Inside the cage are metal hand tools used by menial laborers. The art historian Boreth Ly observes about this piece, "The metaphorical and linguistic reference to a good versus a bad heart (as a way to characterize a person's ethical and moral standing in society) is a common assessment in Cambodian culture."[69] The fact that the heart is caged implies that it is not a boundless, compassionate heart. It could be the greedy heart of a government bureaucrat or an insatiable developer. Yet circumstance also constrains this "bad" heart. Its owner cannot escape the golden cage he has erected. It is indeed an empty heart. The journalist Ron Gluckman writes, "Coupled with the absence of tenant security, rapidly increasing land values have led to rampant land grabbing by powerful and wealthy elites, to the severe detriment of local communities."[70] The powerful and wealthy elites do not care for the workers, the farmers, or the villagers; they are not concerned about the well-being of their fellow countrymen. They are bleeding them dry. Their greed grows; it cannot be contained. The increasing land values or the rising greed and resultant mounting poverty can be symbolized by the heart, which looks like it is swelling, growing beyond the limits of the cage. Perhaps the cage is not a cage. Perhaps the cage is a symbol of order and constraint, of moral limits.

Or it could be that the owner of this benevolent, loving heart is "trapped" by his country. The heart could belong to one of the construction workers building the tall buildings, or to a farmer or a landless villager. He is constrained by his situation, caged. The heart could belong to one of the former residents of Boeung Kak. Ironically, Cambodia's growth would seem to guarantee a raised standard of living for its constituents, but, unfortunately, the opposite seems to be true for those who are already disadvantaged. Gluckman bemoans this pattern, noting that "frequently the projects driving this displacement are beset with corruption and unjust practices, perpetuating a development model that favors powerful interests at the expense of deeper poverty and increased hardship for the most vulnerable."[71] The cycle continues.

Similar to the way that Pich's sculptural stomach symbolizes a society, this tattered heart is the symbol of a country with so many contradictions: generosity and greed, corruption and kindness, beauty and devastation. The gridded fence recalls the scaffolding erected around construction sites. Cambodia *is* a construction site, a work in progress, for better or for worse, for good or for bad. It is being built up and torn asunder at the same time. Its heart is torn.

For a brief period from 2013 to 2015, Pich was torn. He resisted telling stories. Instead, he showcased work that was largely formal and abstract: rattan grids forming uniform open squares. During his artist residency at the Bay Area's Headlands Center for the Arts in 2016, I conducted a studio visit as Pich made medium-size abstract paintings. Dipping rattan and bamboo sticks in natural pigments (red iron oxide) and gum arabic formed repeated impressions on watercolor paper of undulating grids of vertical lines—visualizations of a sonic Rorschach landscape. While "dealing with abstraction directly," as Pich calls the sculptural open-grid paintings and works on paper, the materials and pigment also intentionally evoke Cambodia while gesturing at discrepant modernist timelines. Pich writes in his Headlands artist's statement (another iteration appears on his website), "When writing about my work, people have often evoked the Khmer Rouge while describing my sculptures, a reference I find too limiting. While certain works have relation to that time of my life, I think of the objects I make as possessing potential for energy and a sense of discovery." He recognizes that his work is framed by a traumatized topography (he is also complicit in this framing) but also seeks to highlight unexpected wonder and vitality within that limited landscape (hence, the organic forms). Pich concludes, "I believe that the expression of labor and time through my art will lead to some kind of freedom."[72] Within a Buddhist cosmology, the limits of the body and mind can be transcended through enlightenment—a freedom from the cycles of samsara. During our visit, Pich described the process of making his works on paper meditative, transcending the moribund bonds of identity. Unlike the large sculptural works, which require a team, the works on paper can be created by Pich alone. Thus, the physical is connected to the spiritual. The works bear the marks of devoted "labor and time." Like meditative practice, the return to the breath, the ritual of coming back again and again to the same gestures leads to "some kind of freedom."

From all of these shows, which oscillate between abstraction and representation, two simultaneous tracks appear, as outlined earlier: the artist in nature and the nature of the artist. While seemingly opposed, the dyads under this larger umbrella form a dialectic between physical and metaphysical, rural and urban, abstraction and representation, external and internal, traumatic memory and modernity, present and poison.

For example, the *Expanses* show in 2018 (plate 18) featured both the tightly controlled abstract "urban" compositions (echoing industrial, man-made forms) and undulating representational "rural" sculptures (natural seed and plant shapes, flowers). The highlight of *Expanses* is a seed pod from the Ordeal tree (*Erythrophleum guineense*). On a formal register, the natural materials (rattan and bamboo) Pich uses to render the mammoth seed pod connote the first track, the artist in nature—a seemingly apolitical gesture. "Rendered in an enormously oversized scale . . . [the organic forms] dwarf the viewer, confronting him with the mesmerizing beauty and overwhelming power of nature," writes Rollins of the related plant-based works.[73] As one delves deeper into the history of the Ordeal tree seed, and other plants (morning glory, rang phnom flower) that Pich makes into memorializing monuments, the second symbolic track emerges—the nature of the artist and, by extension, his society. A press release describes the seed pod as both a healing gift and toxin: "Powder made from its bark can be used as medicine but is poisonous in high doses. In the past it was used as part of a 'trial by ordeal' in which the accused was given a potion made by soaking the bark in water; if he died after drinking it, he was considered guilty, but if he survived, he was acquitted."[74] The viewer may see this "trial by ordeal" as a veiled reference to the Khmer Rouge tribunals (discussed in chapter 1), which were concluding in 2017–18—and continually on the news and on the artist's mind when I visited his studio as he was finishing this work.

In the *Morning Glory* show (2016), the fine balance between gift and threat was also an underlying theme. The morning glory plant is an invasive species, choking off Mekong Delta waterways; some species' seeds have toxic lysergic alkaloids (LSA, also called ergot alkaloids).[75] High levels of ergot alkaloids are lethal to cats, dogs, horses, and humans. In addition, in humans they can cause vomiting and even psychosis.[76] Like the Ordeal tree's dual uses as tonic and toxin, morning glory seeds can speed healing: they are used to treat migraines, heavy bleeding, and Parkinson's disease. Within spiritual and recreational contexts, morning glory seeds can induce hallucinatory, psychotropic visions (LSA is chemically related to LSD).[77] Yet the water morning glory plant (*Ipomoea aquatica*, or "swamp spinach") is also a popular staple of Southeast Asian kitchens. It grows easily, and "Pich recalls it as a vital source of sustenance during the near-famine conditions of the Khmer Rouge period (1975–79). . . . [A]s such it has a powerful emotional force that evokes issues of survival, family, and basic human togetherness," Rollins writes.[78] Hence, the tropes of the sublime, the artist in nature ("mesmerizing beauty and overwhelming power of nature"), are conflated with the suffering artist's nature (a melancholic "powerful emotional force").

Pich's representational and abstract works proffer presents and poisons. Both the abstract grids and the Ordeal tree's oversize seed pods can be seen as open-ended containers, packages, holding hidden messages—strategies for survival. Thus, the present and the poison. The trial by ordeal may also refer to the long, difficult return journeys the artist has made, from refugee to expatriate, from the country to the city and back again and again, in becoming Cambodia's most renowned contemporary artist.

Rice Country   PHAN QUANG'S ART OF PLACE

Many Vietnamese regularly make the pilgrimage from city to country for visits home (*thăm quê*), then return to the city to work. According to the last official census, in 2009 (the next census would be conducted starting in April 2019), an overwhelming 70.4 percent of Việt Nam's approximately 85.8 million inhabitants live in rural areas. In 2018, according to World Bank estimates, rural residents made up 65 percent of the 96.49 million Vietnamese.[79] The remaining 35 percent were urban dwellers. As rural-urban migration increases, the distinctions between town and country blur.[80] Tellingly, anthropologists such as Philip Taylor have referred to Việt Nam as a "migration nation."[81] Despite the large number of rural residents, the US Central Intelligence Agency notes, the agricultural sector's economic output has been steadily shrinking, from 25 percent in 2000 to 21 percent in 2009. In 2018, agriculture made up 20 percent of the country's GDP. This decline is expected to continue at a steady 0.5 percent per year.

Industrial production now constitutes more than 40 percent of the country's GDP, effectively displacing agriculture's dominance. Of the $217 billion in total 2017–18 exports, seven of its top ten products were manufactured. They were (1) electrical equipment (e.g., phones, cables); (2) footwear; (3) electronics (e.g., circuit boards); (4) clothing; (5) furniture; (6) coffee; (7) fish; (8) crude petroleum; (9) leather; and (10) fruit, vegetables, and nuts.[82] Despite its small landmass, Việt Nam is among the world's top exporter of agricultural and man-made products, including cashews (number 1), coffee (number 2), footwear (number 4), and furniture (number 8).

As yet another example of strategic cartographies, Việt Nam is looking both east and west as it grows economically. Currently, its top export and import partners are predominantly Asian countries. Việt Nam's top-five export partners, in order, are China, the United States, Japan, Korea, and Germany. Its top import partners are China (25.8 percent), South Korea (20.5 percent), Japan (7.8 percent), and Thailand (4.9 percent). Although China is Việt Nam's top trading partner (import and export), it may also be a main threat, notes the Pan-Asian investment firm Dezan Shira and Associates: "With its rising costs, China is no longer the go-to destination for many businesses, and Vietnam has arisen as a serious competitor. . . . Recent trends show that the number of orders shifting from China to Vietnam has seen a significant increase. In the past few years, a growing number of businesses have relocated their operations from China to Vietnam in an attempt to escape rising costs and an increasingly complex regulatory environment."[83] As China is increasingly outpriced, Việt Nam is emerging as a regional contender because of its "inexpensive, young, and, increasingly, highly skilled" labor. Cambodia is also losing some footing within this crowded market, as discussed earlier. The economic analyst Kyssha Mah writes, "Currently, labor costs in Vietnam are 50 percent of those in China and around 40 percent of those reported in Thailand and the Philippines."[84] The balance between business and ethics—keeping costs globally competitive while assuring fair living and working conditions—is tough.

As the Asia Pacific region gains global fiscal ascendancy, Western countries are looking for both producers and consumers. "Located in a *strategic position* for foreign companies with operations throughout Southeast Asia, Vietnam is an ideal export hub to reach other ASEAN [Association of Southeast Asian Nations] markets," touts Dezan Shira and Associates, whose tagline is "Your Partner for Growth in Asia."[85]

As the China-US trade war continues and China is no longer a cheap manufacturing hub, other Western countries are seeking alternative Asian hubs. "China's Pearl River Delta, long known as one of the key factory centers for the world's manufacturers (particularly those from Hong Kong) has now become too costly for many companies to stay in the region," writes Mah.[86]

Town and Country

Việt Nam is positioning itself as a skilled hub between East and West, as a gateway to Southeast Asia. The historic EU-Vietnam Free Trade Agreement (EVFTA), which establishes special bilateral trade conditions (low taxes, investment incentives, and so on), took effect August 1, 2020. The European Commission has described the EVFTA is as "the most ambitious deal of its type ever concluded between the EU and a developing country." Currently, Singapore is the EU's biggest trading partner in ASEAN, with Việt Nam coming in second. Within this competitive market, there are already concerns over workers' rights and salaries, as voiced by the international nonprofit forum Unrepresented Nations and People Organization (UNPO): "The most vulnerable sectors of Vietnamese society might suffer from the competition with EU-produced goods: while Vietnamese workers are not allowed to form independent unions under national law, economic competitiveness is very likely to lead to the deterioration of working conditions and the decline of salaries."[87] Economic benefit may override neoliberal rhetoric about fair practices; the organization cautions that EU "cooperation with Vietnam should be evaluated in the light of other criteria than economic benefits." The UNPO notes that such positionings may come at the continued cost of human rights: "In particular, Vietnam's human rights record remains extremely dire in every domain: the monopoly of the Communist Party over politics threatens basic freedoms such as that of speech, press or religion; human right defenders, bloggers and journalists face physical assaults, harassment, threats; minorities such as the Khmer-Krom suffer repression and marginalisation."[88] The UNPO puts the blame largely on human rights violations without addressing larger structural, strategic triangulations. Regardless of whether the EU exerts its pull on humane practices, turns a blind eye, or actually exacerbates conditions, it will still continue its quest for maximal returns. The rhetoric of fair wages and best practices contradict economic superpowers' bids for ever-cheaper and -faster production hubs. As Việt Nam's development accelerates, detractors warn, quality of life deteriorates for both urban and rural denizens. The artist Phan Quang reveals that Vietnamese citizens are stuck in the crosshairs, in between, stuck in the mud.

For his solo show at Galerie Quynh in October 2010, Phan dealt with Việt Nam's urban-rural divides and accelerated socioeconomic transitions. Through site-specific installations, large framed color photographs, and a video project he commented on rural subjectivity. The exhibition was the launching point of his international fine art career. So far, the works in this first show have also been exhibited the most widely.

Subsequently, Phan has shown in group exhibitions at the Institute Français du Cambodge (*Photo Phnom Penh* [2011]); the Kadist Art Foundation, San Francisco (*Poetic Politic* [2012]); the Kumho Museum of Art, Seoul (*Cross + Scape: ASEAN-Korea Contemporary Media Art Exhibition* [2011]); *The Fifth Fukuoka Asian Art Triennale*, Fukuoka, Japan (2014); the Bangkok Art and Culture Center (*Triennale Photo Bangkok* [2015]); and the Mistake Room, Los Angeles (*Where the Sea Remembers* [2019], see chapter 2), among other venues. I was able to conduct several studio visits and interviews with Phan as his career developed, in Sài Gòn in 2010; Phnom Penh, 2011; San Francisco and Los Angeles, 2012; Phnom Penh, 2016; and Sài Gòn again, 2017 and 2019.

Born in the farming community of Bình Định, Phan currently lives and works in Sài Gòn. He is the embodiment of the blurred boundaries between the city and the countryside. Within and outside the country, the city and the countryside become archetypes, bearers of modernity and tradition. The countryside takes on a mythic presence. In past propaganda, agrarian life embodies communist ideals of labor, equality, and productivity. In current socialist-capitalist advertisements for tourism, shots of abundant rice fields signify Việt Nam's "hidden charm"—a lushly exotic country.[89] Phan states, "I was born in the countryside; farmer's blood runs in me, but the city is where I choose to live. I know many people who reach a certain social position and then try to deny their origins. I think that's a tragedy. Our whole life is a series of actions based on continuous effort to reach a certain result, to become a certain someone or to reach a certain purpose. You could say that the effort is to outgrow ourselves, to eliminate 'backward' influences in order to move forward. But afterwards, are we happier and more peaceful?"[90] The effort to "outgrow ourselves" may also refer to Việt Nam's attempt to "move forward," to develop. Instead of praising the logic of progress, his statement critiques the individual's and, by extension, society's effort to eliminate "backward influences." Political and cultural context determines what is considered backward. He challenges the assumptions of modernity. Việt Nam's long-awaited membership in the World Trade Organization cemented its "arrival" within the global economy. Its đổi mới economic liberalization policy of 1986 ushered in a new era of market development, as well as inequities and labor exploitations. Within the rhetoric of global development, Việt Nam is quickly moving forward, without a glance back at its recent past of poverty and dirt. If the city is the future, the countryside is the past.

Quê refers to one's birthplace; *quê hương* refers to one's homeland. *Quê* is also slang for tacky, backward, or "country." Phan elaborates, "In reality, in the soul of each Vietnamese, from the government to the people, in culture as well as politics, all regard farmers as second-class citizens, second place."[91] Farmers are simultaneously exalted and demeaned, regarded as both the country's backbone and its burden.

Umbilical Umbrella

Phan's site-specific durational installation *The Umbrella* (plate 19) included a giant umbrella set in a large rice paddy for about three months—seventy-nine days, to be exact. He recorded the growth of the field and the disintegrating umbrella at a distance, from a single visual vantage point, through various media (video, photography, and a text-based log or "diary"). The umbrella is mustard-colored and crimson-lined. It evokes the colors of the Vietnamese flag and the umbrellas that imperial noblemen used for shade. It can be seen as a symbol for long-standing power and the government. Phan notes that, at first, the rice grew quickly under the umbrella's shade. However, after the initial growth spurt, the shaded rice's growth became stunted due to lack of photosynthesis. The rice growing without protection from the sun thrived. Phan told me during the studio visit in 2010, "The umbrella represents an exalted, elevated part of society, while the rice represents what lies beneath, what remains underfoot, yet comprises the majority of society." In short, the umbrella may symbolize the highest echelons of society (perhaps its rulers and urban elite) while the rice stands for "the other half"— or, rather, the 70 percent of the population that continues to farm.[92] Roger Nelson, curator and historian of Southeast Asian contemporary art, wrote about the project, "It was an act of utter futility and also of great purpose; an indictment of a human system and a celebration of a natural order."[93]

Depending on the viewer, one may see a critique of state policies, institutionalized hierarchies, corruption, or social and economic divides within Việt Nam. In *The Umbrella* (plate 20), the farmer's absence creates the gaps in images and text. These gaps may also speak of greater fissures. A large photographic diptych documents the project, which took place from February 2, 2010, to April 21, 2010, in Bảo Lộc. The first large photograph (plate 19) consists of a grid of smaller photographs of the umbrella and rice fields spanning approximately three months. These photographs are the postmodern equivalent of Claude Monet's famous Impressionist haystacks captured in shifting light and weather conditions. Monet produced about thirty paintings near his home in Giverny between summer 1890 and winter 1891.[94] Both projects, situated in the Orient and the Occident, respectively, more than a century apart, document nature's sublime, mercurial beauty. Phan's straightforward framing evokes Bernd and Hilla Becher's "objective" photographic images of Western industrial buildings. Yet Phan's project insists on a more critical, politically charged reading.

The second large photograph of the diptych is the daily log that Phan's artistic assistant, a farmer, inscribed in blue ink in a formatted brown paper ledger (plates 21 and 22). The notes are mostly minimal: "Another hot day. I'm very tired today"; "Today my friend is visiting, have to get him drunk"; and so on. For the viewer who cannot read Vietnamese, the untranslated scribbles become a formal composition. The diary again highlights Derridean logos and the gaps and impossibility of representation.

Also using diary entries, Byron Kim's long-term *Sunday Painting* series, referencing Monet, uses images of nature—a color field sky. Kim reinterprets the Daoist Chuang Tze's writings on the infinite and the seemingly insignificant: he pairs the magnificence of the sky with the mundane details of Kim's life.[95] Phan's work draws a similar analogy: it contrasts the immeasurable power of the state with the impotence of its people. In a different reading, the umbrella eventually falters, disintegrates, while the rice endures and thrives without protection. The image grids that constitute "A Farmer's Diary" echo the grids of fields and flowers in Seckon's work. Both artists comment on the state and its shifting states of mind.

A component of "The Umbrella" is a four-minute time-lapse video, rapidly edited to show changes in season—rice growing and dying. The camera remains static as the clouds move and the umbrella sways in the wind. This idyllic imagery has an up-tempo pop soundtrack: it seems like everything moves to the synthesizer beat, particularly the shifts from one frame to the next. The resulting dissonant video reminds me of Asian karaoke videos in which the images do not always sync with the pop songs. Yet everywhere in the countryside in Việt Nam, Thailand, and Cambodia one can hear the latest K-pop hit, Britney Spears bump-and-grind, or Euro-trash synth echoing from cell phones and boom boxes, from pools and pool halls.

Phan states, "I want to describe a farmer's life cycle, whose birth and death doesn't have much effect on modern life."[96] Even though they are considered an insignificant demographic, Vietnamese farmers have profoundly affected Việt Nam as a modernizing state. The decollectivization of the agricultural sector was an integral component of Việt Nam's transition to a market economy.[97] From 1990 to 2005, Việt Nam's food production nearly doubled. The country shifted from importing food to being the world's largest exporter of pepper and the world's second-largest exporter of rice and coffee. This agricultural productivity helped fuel the rest of the country's developing economy.[98] While this economic turnaround created an emergent middle class, the gaps between the rich and the poor continue to widen within Việt Nam, as well as outside the country.

A case in point is China, which now has the world's largest urban population: 57.9 percent of its total population of 1.41 billion, according to United Nations estimates in 2019. Despite a booming middle class, China's urban-rural income gap has been increasing since the country liberalized its economic policies in 1978.[99] From 2000 to 2010, migrant populations living in urban areas increased by 80 percent.[100] According to the *Los Angeles Times*, China now ranks as the world's second-largest economy. While China is the world's third-largest consumer of luxury goods, 372.8 million people live below the international poverty line of $5.50 per day—or approximately $2,000 a year—according to 2019 World Bank estimates.[101] Urban-rural migration has actually reversed in that 200 million rural Chinese laborers who relocated to cities to find work in 2010 have begun to move back to their villages due to lack of employment in the cities.[102] As of 2018, more than seven million have returned to rural areas to "start their own businesses," according to the Chinese Ministry of Human Resources and Social Security.[103] Poverty rates are three-and-a-half times as high in rural areas as in urban areas (8.1 rural versus 2.3 urban, with 5.2 as the median, according to the UNDP).[104] The Ministry of Agriculture official Song Hongyuan stated, "I am afraid the [urban-rural] income gap will continue to expand as the country focuses its efforts on urban sprawl, rather than rural development."[105] A 2018 rural policy reform aims for rural rejuvenation by 2020 and agricultural modernization by 2035. The news agency Reuters notes that "China has the largest agriculture sector in the world and hundreds of millions of people work as farmers but productivity is low."[106] As Việt Nam's urban areas spread out, will its future mirror China's present inequities?[107]

About Face Value: Conceptions of Self and Rural-Urban Belonging

A related large-scale photographic series features people from the countryside: some are nude, some are covered in mud; some men wear only safety helmets and trousers, some women wear white frocks. The scene is corporeal yet also clinical. Trash and rice bags become body bags. Faces, eyes, and farming equipment are pointed heavenward, as if seeking salvation or redemption. These various images are all haunting, staged portraits following in the photo conceptualist tradition of Zhang Huan (b. Anyang, China, 1965), Jeff Wall (b. Vancouver, Canada, 1969), Pipo Nguyễn-Duy (b. Huế, 1962), and Gregory Crewdson (b. Brooklyn, New York, 1962). These artists, like Phan, employ an aesthetics of uncanny disquietude. In one striking composition, huddled farmers caked in mud confront the viewer. One's field of vision is sludge-colored. I am reminded of Pompeii, its citizens frozen in time, covered in ashes. Or the underworld of life-size Chinese terra-cotta warriors, staring blankly ahead through space and time, mute witnesses. Phan's country denizens become sculptures of mud, effigies. He writes, "Mud is only a temporary cover, it doesn't last forever. The farmers, regardless of who they are, can't hide their original nature, where they came from. . . . When I am able to be truly myself, I still want to speak with the accent of where I was born."[108] This view of origins is a nostalgic, romantic one, yet it resonates with many Vietnamese. One's hometown shapes one's values and one's worldview.

Phan speaks of the psychic changes of shifting from being a rural to an urban subject. As the American saying goes, "You can take the boy out of the country, but you can't take the country out of the boy." In a different vein, in Vietnamese, *nhà* means house, residence (or even spouse) and *quê* means country. Together, however, *nhà quê* denotes country people or, pejoratively, country bumpkin or yokel. Yet reversing the words as *quê nhà* denotes home, homeland, hometown, or "back home," suggesting close ties to the land and one's hometown, no matter how far away one is. Finally, *quê hương* is defined as country, nation-state, home, or motherland, connoting the close links among conceptions of belonging, rurality, and the nation. Before rapid urbanization, Việt Nam was a nation of farmers and fishers, beholden to the land and the sea.[109]

Infrastructure development is changing the nature of rural life and how one see's one's nature (as *quê*, "backward," or *hiện đại*, "modern, up-to-date"). The Vietnamese government has bought large swaths of countryside and given farmers a subsidy for their property. Other areas once considered countryside are becoming increasingly urbanized as the urban centers sprawl outward. Hà Nội is rapidly expanding outward; some claim that it will become one of the largest capital cities in the world. Sài Gòn is following suit. Construction can also be seen in resort towns such as Đà Nẵng and Vũng Tàu. The face of Việt Nam is changing almost beyond recognition.

In *Saigon's Edges*, which analyzes such urbanized rural liminal zones, Harms argues against easy distinctions between rural and urban as well as discrete categories of space and time. He observes, "As idealized asymptotes, the inside is understood as having a certain urban time orientation regimented by the clock and the outside as having a certain rural time orientation regimented by cycles of agricultural production."[110] In describing

Town and Country

mud as a "temporary cover" and code switching—("When I am able to be truly myself, I still want to speak with the accent of where I was born"— Phan suggests that he, too, is not tethered to these twin poles of rural and urban identity (urban/clock/inside versus rural/agricultural cycles/outside). Harms observes that "successful people are able to settle both time orientations." Phan uses both frames to his advantage in his work. As Galerie Quynh notes, Phan's oeuvre attempts "to reconcile urban and rural divides." He thus becomes the "embodiment of the blurred boundaries between the city and the countryside."[111] Here we can also apply the oscillating two tracks I discussed with Pich's work: artist in nature and the nature of the artist. Through Phan's images and affiliations as a rural outsider ("The farmers, regardless of who they are, can't hide their original nature"), he becomes the countryside's representative for an urban audience. Hence, he successfully (self-)exploits his outsider status (through images of agricultural cycles) to become an urbane art world insider.

I argue against the (self-)framing that Phan productively "reconciles" both rural and urban time orientations whereas his subjects do not. Harms notes that the "power of spatial temporal oscillation depends not so much on expressing a distinctly rural or urban time orientation but on the ability to move, according to contingency or circumstances, between states."[112] Phan specifically positions himself between these two states but frames his subjects as being outside. His earlier statement that his work on "a farmer's life cycle . . . whose birth and death doesn't have much effect on modern life" underscores this idea. Implicitly, Phan frames himself as empowered but his subjects as not having the power of spatiotemporal oscillation. Nhà quê, hillbillies, do not have the wherewithal to shift psychologically between rural and urban orientations. Their lives are an endless loop of agricultural rotations.

Phan deals with cycles of life: agricultural production and human reproduction. Throughout his work, different forms of labor inadvertently overlap: rural and industrialized labor; the labor of birth. In addition, his labor extracts surplus value from these images of faces, bodies performing for his camera. Encompassing maternal labor and manual labor, a surreal photographic image entitled Dream (plate 23) reveals an interior with a row of pregnant women standing in a line. Their formation suggests a factory assembly line. As discussed, Việt Nam prides itself on its skilled feminized, "obedient" workforce. The lineup also suggests the uniform state policies enacted on families and the policing of sexualities. For example, the official policy of một hoặc hai con—a family-size goal of one or two children—implemented in the 1960s is still in effect.

Phan alludes to domestic and international pressures through the women's white outfits, a color of medical cleanliness, factory efficiency, and purity, and of mourning. The women wear white smocks over their colorful outfits; each smock has a circular cutout at the stomach area. The cut of the smocks evokes lab coats or hospital garments. The vaguely clinical quality of these outfits bring to mind a host of associations: scientific experiments gone awry; a fertility clinic; or even the popular children's characters Teletubbies, colorful interplanetary creatures that also have protruding bellies. Underneath these smocks the women wear colorfully patterned outfits that are commonly seen in Việt Nam. Phan notes, "These mothers all hope for the best for their unborn children, like my mother, my wife and all of the other women from generation to generation. I cut the shape of a TV in front of their stomachs; I want to say that these hopes of theirs are also hopes that dwell deep inside of each individual's soul."[113] The "TV"-shaped cutouts may refer to mass-media discourse within and outside the country. Within the heteronormative purview of the image, one thinks of what is outside the television and photographic frame. For example, Việt Nam's labor abuses have been overshadowed by celebratory international press since its ban on gay marriages was lifted in 2015. "Although same-sex marriage is permitted in Vietnam," *Time* magazine notes, "lawmakers have not granted full recognition to the unions, which do not provide legal protections for spouses."[114] Within neoliberal doctrine, the biopolitical rhetoric of free-market reform is also tied to patronizing discourses on gender and sexuality. These women (without their husbands) become the hypervisible faces and bodies of a (re)productive forward-looking Việt Nam.

Here the term *face value* takes its dual valences as (1) the value or price shown (e.g., on a bill, stamp, coin); and (2) the apparent worth or implication of something ("her lie was unconvincing, but he took it at face value") (OED). The women's expressions reveal both hope and anxiety. The disquieting hospital interior and the women's deadpan upward gazes conjure an ominous mood. They are facing the future, hopeful and bleak.

In Vietnamese, the value of face has different meanings. Translated literally, *mặt tiền* is "face money" (*mặt* is "face" and *tiền* is "money"). *Mặt tiền* refers to the front or façade of a residence or business, as many businesses are operated on the ground floor or at the front of a building. For instance, many homes have small shops in front, with living quarters in the back and on the upper floors. *Mặt* can also be tied to the land: *mặt đất* (earth, Mother Earth, grass, ground; lit., "face earth") and *mặt đường* (pavement, road, street; lit., "face road"). Thus, face belongs not only to humans or mammals.

Town and Country

It is also tied to both land and money. As an example, under Vietnamese law "land is a national good," notes the Vietnamese lifestyle information company City Pass, "so you can only own the structure built on a property, not the land that it is on."[115]

The concept of face is also associated with nonmaterial, nonphysical aspects (beyond land, money), yet it is still linked to value or status. Contrary to Western conceptions of "face" as being individually autonomous, the linguist Phạm Thị Hồng Nhung notes that Vietnamese concepts of saving or losing "face" (*mất mặt*) fluctuate according to collective conditions, as well as individual agency. Losing face is not only about effacement, diminishing oneself—a reduction of individual status (as in Western frameworks). It is also a question of communal good—akin to the ways that land is "a national good." "Vietnamese do not feel that their face is threatened or lost when their autonomy is not respected," Phạm writes in the conclusion to his ethnographic study. "Face in Vietnamese is both an individual and collective possession and a subjective value, conditionally dependent on social evaluation."[116] I connect this concept of being "conditionally dependent" to Harms's assertion that self-worth for liminal Vietnamese citizens lies in "the ability to move, according to contingency or circumstances, between states."[117] In facing and embracing the dyadic temporal spatial orientations of the country and city, one does not lose face or risk being embarrassed by being seen as *nhà quê* (a backward bumpkin). It becomes a source of strategic pride and profit.

In revealing the faces of the countryside—and becoming the artistic face that can straddle rural and urban fissures—Phan's work increases in face value. Yet taken "at face value," the artist's interview statements devalue his subjects' worth, suggesting they are outside "modern life"; that their lifecycles are of peripheral import to the city's centers of power. Yet these women and men negotiate interior cycles with exterior cycles proactively, beyond being mere pawns of change, or artistic props—country bumpkin backdrops. The artist traffics in long-standing tropes: the female body as a site of labor, fertility (like the pregnant rice fields), and social projections (e.g., TV screen cutouts); the disenfranchised, displaced farmer (stripped of possessions or beholden to them). To "reconcile urban and rural divides"—per Galerie Quynh's phrasing—also means to reside with these differences, side by side, as the pregnant figures stand, literal embodiments of the motherland. Thus, a residence (*nhà*) and the country (*quê*) become at once home (*quê nhà*) and unhomely, alien, uncanny (*unheimlich*), familiar and unfamiliar.

In a way, Phan's homely images are self-portraits of the artist and of Việt Nam, taken from the liminal vantage point of an insider and outsider. He uses both "inside" (urban) and "outside" (rural) temporal modes. Since Phan claims the countryside as his own, there is an intimacy and immediacy in the compositions. Nonetheless, Phan's critical eye does not celebrate and embrace everything that is "rural." For the artist, rural and urban spaces are undergoing tremendous physical, psychic, and political changes.

In the Vietnamese popular imagination, the city stands for modernity and the countryside represents tradition.[118] Shuttling between the two, Vietnamese are stuck in limbo. Yet it is the very act of leaving, if only in mind—and returning to *quê nhà* (one's hometown), however far away, if only in spirit—that empowers us. It is this very "spatial temporal oscillation," as Harms terms it, that gives those negotiating the city and the country their power. How does one spend one's life trying to find one's way home? *Một cõi đi về*. In transit and in transition between the city and the countryside, things get lost and lost in translation.

Loss and Gains: Space/Limit and Re/Cover

Phan has continued his multimedia explorations, focused on surreal stagings—often using large metaphorical props—of ethnographic portraits of Vietnamese subjects caught in limbo. Phan has had two solo shows since his 2010 debut: *Space/Limit* (2013) and *Re/Cover* (2015). *Space/Limit*, at Sàn Art in Hồ Chí Minh City, consisted of large photographs of citizens in the city and countryside inside large bamboo cages (plate 24). From the patio of the space to the gallery, Phan created a giant cage that the viewer had to traverse, in effect performing what the photographs convey. Similar to Pich's rattan and bamboo cages (e.g., *Caged Heart*), Phan's cage wrestles with the idea of social and government constraints. Ironically, or perhaps tellingly, seven out of nine of the photographs in the *Space/Limit* series were censored by the Vietnamese government; only two images, which did not show citizens enclosed in cages, were displayed. A review in the publication *Art Radar* noted, "The artist juxtaposes this rustic container with imagery of modern living. . . . Quang's work [asks], How can an individual maintain integrity within a community while seeking innovation beyond what is already practiced or believed?" I disagree with this suggested binary between collective constraints and individual freedom, between losing and saving face, between rural "rustic" tradition and innovative modernity.

Instead, the relationship between human and animal is the key to unlocking part of the work's meaning. As Zoe Butt, former executive director of Sàn Art, noted, "Such cages are common on the street corners of [Việt Nam] housing roosters used not only for eating, but also for the gambling sport of cockfighting."[119] In the show, instead of roosters, humans inhabit the cages. The rooster has different meanings. Mythological roosters appear on Vietnamese Đông Sơn Bronze Age drums as symbols of agriculture; today they are seen as sacred animals. Previously sacrificed during Lunar New Year, roosters are symbols of health and prosperity.[120] In the context of the American–Việt Nam War, "rooster" was a nickname for M60 gunners because the muzzle flash resembled a rooster's tale. Some US veteran groups suggest that local Vietnamese called the soldiers of the US 101st Airborne Division "roosters" or "chicken men" after the "Screaming Eagle" patches on their uniforms.[121] Phan's missing roosters may encompass all of these meanings and gesture to loss in general. In placing his rural and urban subjects inside these ubiquitous containers, Phan implies that ideological casings—whether communism, capitalism, or a hybrid (socialist capitalism)—renders its captive audience like caged game fowl: at once game and gambit.

Continuing the exploration of returns and loss, *Re/Cover*, at the Blanc Art Gallery in Sài Gòn, featured photographs of Hà Nội widows of Japanese soldiers (and occasionally their adult children) sitting in their homes under giant white shrouds. The mysterious clouds of chiffon simultaneously highlight and obliterate what is underneath. Butt notes that the "idea of history being absent, annihilated or controlled speaks to [Phan's] photographic work."[122] Control, constraint, and invisibility are recurring motifs in his photographs. Echoing Butt, Roger Nelson observes, "That [the widows'] story remains largely unknown and untold is part of a larger phenomenon of secrecy and silence that has been pervasive for the artist's whole life, and for longer."[123] Japanese soldiers were stationed in Việt Nam during World War II, from 1940 until Japan's defeat and withdrawal in 1945. Some soldiers stayed longer, until 1955, when their government demanded that they return. The resulting mixed Vietnamese-Japanese families who stayed in Việt Nam do not fit within dominant Vietnamese historical narratives and are thus unacknowledged, unspoken. Their histories hanging heavy like the shrouds in the photographs. Through an intimate and intensive research process, Phan interviewed women who had had children with Japanese soldiers from 1940 to 1955. The white cloth covering the subjects evokes domesticity and death: traditional Japanese wedding veils, common mosquito nets, and Vietnamese funeral shrouds.

The *Re/Cover* series embodies some of the difficulties of return engagements—revisiting the intimate, intricate, militarized past within the present. In the series, scenes of domestic bliss are (re)staged as sites of trauma. Wedding engagements (wedding veil) becomes conflated with the toll of military engagements (funeral shroud). The title of the series, *Re/Cover*, is apt, as the artist indeed sets out to "recover" these forgotten stories of romance and war. The art critic Ben Valentine's review in *Hyperallergic* suggests that Phan's "*Re/Cover* is a mirror for us to look back at history, to reflect on all of its complexities and the very human stories at its center."[124] When looking at this "mirror," though, the "very human stories" are still mute, largely untold, as the artist chooses not to convey individual details. The secrets stay with the artist and his subjects. Once again, Vietnamese women are represented as long-suffering, mute. *Re/Cover* may have an unintended connotation: Phan's subjects are covered again under history's weight, buried by the artist's heavy hand. Like the white scrim, "screen memories" can be projected onto these images. As Marita Sturken reminds us of Freudian screens, pathic projections obscure what is truly underneath the covers, behind the scenes. We cannot truly "look back at history" through the mirror of art and artifice without addressing its reconstructions and refractions.

In *Re/Cover No. 5* (plate 25), a Vietnamese widow holds a death portrait of her late Japanese husband; behind her is an ancestral altar where another portrait of a loved one rests. The long, horizontal, rectangular frame of her husband's portrait is echoed twice more, in the oblong mirror and the quadrangular television set, its screen a black void. The three surfaces make up a triumvirate and unwhole trinity—the Father, Son, and the Holy Ghost in one image. Each of the rectangular mirrored surfaces—television, mirror, photograph—reflects our desires unto death, presences of absence: mirrors upon mirrors. Perhaps on their shiny surfaces, as divination, we can "look back at history" to look forward, to "reflect on all of its complexities." As the melancholic mothers and grown children in the *Re/Cover* series suggest, forever grasping partial glimpses, the Lacanian mirror stage is beyond our full vision, histories forever unknowable and untenable, *objet petit a*. In looking at these opaque, veiled mirrors, the return gaze is a blank stare.

As a way to develop, Việt Nam attempts to lose its associations in the global imaginary with strife and suffering. Travel images advertising a lush paradise getaway have replaced journalistic photographs of decimated jungles during wartime. The same foliage is rebranded. The next section discusses Đinh Q. Lê's artwork on the persistent legacies of Agent Orange, the infamous chemical defoliant. The artist deals with trauma and tourism in Việt Nam and the shifting depictions of both.

Town and Country

Art, Dioxin, and Development
ĐỈNH Q. LÊ'S *DAMAGED GENE* REVISITED

His eyes are staring, his mouth is open, his wings are spread. This is how one pictures the angel of history. His face is turned toward the past. —Walter Benjamin, *Theses on the Philosophy of History*

An eight-year-old Vietnamese boy's face appears pockmarked in the grainy black-and-white photograph. This is my angel of history.[125] Look closer. According to the caption, his skin is shredded by shrapnel. His mouth is half-open, perhaps in shock or sorrow; his eyes are a blank stare. A row of large glass jars house dead, deformed babies, conjoined, monstrous—victims of Agent Orange. On a nearby wall hang photographs of the toxin's living byproducts: villagers and urbanites disabled, disjointed, animal-like. The horrific collateral damage of war seethes from the displays of the War Remnants Museum in Sài Gòn: breathing figures variously half-burned, mutilated by shrapnel, deformed by dioxin.[126] This is the aftermath of the American War. Beyond the tree-lined streets of the memorializing space formerly called the War Atrocities Museum, this traumatic history seems to be forgotten. The endless motorcycles, gleaming storefronts, and high-rises beat the staccato rhythm of a modern metropolis. The horror and devastation of a country ravaged by warfare is invisible, obscured by seductive billboards, malls, street vendors selling rainbow-hued plastic-wrapped goods, dreams of magnificent miles. Yet the American War's legacies remain hidden underfoot, beneath the concrete jungle's well-heeled pavement, seeped in soil, streams, and blood.

Congenital disabilities such as cerebral palsy, spina bifida, and cleft palate; neurological conditions; cancer; diabetes, and other medical conditions are the alleged result of direct dioxin contact, as well as indirect contact, such as consuming food grown in contaminated areas. "Dioxin stays in the soil and in the sediment at the bottom of lakes and rivers for generations. It can enter the food supply through the fat of fish and other animals," states an Associated Press article from 2018.[127] Contaminated soil can also spread into nearby drainage ditches, lakes, and ponds, increasing the total amount of sediment and soil that needs to be treated.[128] More than half a century later, both Việt Nam and the United States are still grappling with dioxin's effects.

For a decade (1961–71), US warplanes sprayed twelve million gallons of Agent Orange to clear the lush tropical vegetation of South Việt Nam for easier airstrikes, as well as to deny Việt Cộng cover and food crops. A total of twenty-one million gallons of defoliants were used.[129] More conservative estimates put that volume at eighteen million gallons.[130] At that time, the US government claimed the toxic herbicides it had spread were harmless to humans. The defoliant dioxin most commonly used was called Agent Orange, for its orange-striped containers.[131] The anthropologist Tine Gammeltoft observes: "The precise impact of Agent Orange on human health remains contested, but mounting evidence suggests significant associations between dioxin exposure and increased risk of cancers, endocrine disruption, neurological damage, and reproductive health problems such as miscarriages and birth defects."[132]

Several generations later, Vietnam has anomalously high rates of birth defects and cancer.[133] As US-Việt Nam trade and diplomatic relations rekindle, the United States is willing partially to address the past, with an eye on the future. The first large-scale efforts at environmental Agent Orange cleanup began in 2010, at the behest of the Vietnamese government. A full cleanup could cost billions. A year before President Barack Obama's historic visit to Việt Nam in May 2016—perhaps promising cozier (trade) relations between two former enemies—the US Agency for International Development (USAID) announced the "successful treatment of approximately 36.48 acres (45,000 cubic meters) of dioxin-contaminated material" at Đà Nẵng International Airport. The airport is a dioxin hot spot—one of two dozen locations previously used to store the toxins. Perhaps tourists and others who fly directly from Moscow, among other locales, to revel at Đà Nẵng's five-star beach resorts and nearby UNESCO World Heritage sites, such as Huế Imperial City and Old Town Hội An, do not know this. By November 2018, the five-year, $110 million cleanup project had been completed at the Đà Nẵng airport and surrounding areas, totaling 74 acres.

At the Đà Nẵng cleanup ceremony, Vice Defense Minister Nguyễn Chí Vịnh stated, "It is proof that we are opening a future of good cooperation between the governments of Việt Nam and the United States." Echoing this sentiment, US Ambassador Daniel Kritenbrink announced, "This project truly is a hallmark of our countries' shared vision to be honest about the past, deal responsibly with remaining legacy issues and turn a point of contention into one of collaboration."[134] The contested, controversy-laden past is now a rebuilding and rebranding effort. The largest cleanup effort, estimated at $340 million, started in early 2020 at Biên Hòa Air Base, about 16 miles (25 kilometers) north of Sài Gòn. It will take a decade to complete. A study of the base conducted in 2011 by a private consulting firm noted that the area of direct dioxin contact might have spread through leaks, contaminating soil and nearby waterways.[135] The resort advertising banners and US veteran

227

reunion tours at Biên Hòa Air Base do not mention contaminated deltas or the disabled and incapacitated mothers, fathers, children, and grandchildren—Vietnamese and American—living in the long shadow of dioxin.

Strategic cartographies are used by these nations to transform contested geopolitical battles over land (and sea) into mutually advantageous prospects. Ambassador Kritenbrink said that working on past issues "builds *strategic* trust and enables us to further strengthen our forward-looking partnership that advances shared interests and strong people-to-people ties."[136] In keeping with my discussion on self-exploitation as both beneficial and detrimental, both countries must admit their losses ("be honest about the past, deal responsibly . . . with legacy issues") in order to advance. Both literally and metaphorically, the toxic foundations of lingering pasts must be purified to reap future rewards.

Following my notes on the gift as both giving and taking, present and poison, the United States' "gift of freedom" (as Mimi Thi Nguyễn calls it) bestowed on militarized Southeast Asia (Cambodia, Việt Nam, Laos) and its refugees in the 1970s return as the rhetoric of collaboration and commerce. The high cost of toxin (in lives and cleanup dollars) is to be a fertile foundation for investment. The meanings of freedom oscillate between democratic freedom (versus communism) and the neoliberal freedom of free markets.

Strategic cartographies also entail shifting toward advantageous geopolitical affiliations and alignments: staking out turf. For instance, Kritenbrink's use of the term *strategic trust* may point to larger geopolitical positioning in terms of global allies and foes. Phil Stewart of Reuters suggests that the "warming relations" between Việt Nam and the United States is actually triangulated via China: "[Current] ties between the United States and Vietnam are less seen through the prism of the conflict [of the Việt Nam War than] through shared concerns over China. Vietnam has emerged as the most vocal opponent of China's territorial claims in the South China Sea and has been buying U.S. military hardware, including an armed, Hamilton-class Coast Guard cutter. The United States, in turn, accuses China of militarizing the *strategic* waterway, through which more than $3 trillion in cargo passes every year, and sees Vietnam as a crucial ally in drawing regional opposition to Beijing's behavior."[137] One of the driving forces for the American wars in Southeast Asia was the that Việt Nam was seen as China's "friend" (or, at least, as vulnerable China's to influence) and hence was a key territory in the United States' anticommunist "domino theory" of containment, which was in operation from the late 1940s through the 1980s. Then, as now, Việt Nam was positioned as a crucial regional player within these oscillating strategic cartographies. Whether Việt Nam is "friend" or "foe," these ambivalent alignments forgo and forget its longer timelines of nationalist, anti-imperialist resistance against occupation: Chinese (111 BC–938 AD), French (1887–1957), and American (1964–75). The past is tactically addressed and used to build a "strategic trust." Reuters reported that "U.S. officials including [US Secretary of Defense Jim] Mattis—who is on his second trip to Vietnam just this year [2018]—hope that addressing America's wartime legacies like Agent Orange can become a vehicle for further strengthening ties."[138] In returning to wartime legacies, both the United States and Việt Nam hope to reposition themselves against a perceived common threat: China as both a military and an economic hazard. In these circuits of exchanges, selective memory is both militarized and monetized. Traumatic returns alchemically transform into fiscal returns. The combative past becomes a reconciliatory present, a "collaboration." Geopolitical futures and fortunes are at stake. Thus, the gift is both present and toxin.

Agent Orange Continued

Despite finally attempting to address "wartime legacies," the US government continues to downplay or dismiss Việt Nam's continuing dioxin-related health issues, as well as the issues that its own veterans experience.[139] The Vietnamese government states that up to four million people were exposed to the herbicide.[140] Official figures state that biological warfare caused 150,000 cases of birth defects and up to three million cases of other related illnesses.[141] Washington disavows links between the chemical and illness, accusing Hà Nội of inflating statistics.[142] In 2018, the Associated Press reported that Washington still denies full responsibility for the damage done: "The U.S. government says the actual number of people affected is much lower and that Vietnamese are too quick to blame Agent Orange for birth defects that can be caused by malnutrition or other factors."[143] Under condition of anonymity, a USAID official stated, "The impact on the community is very difficult to measure. Dioxin has impacts (on health) at very low concentrations and they're not real consistent."[144] What is clear is that, according to the US Congressional Research Service, a soil sample from Biên Hòa, the largest future dioxin cleanup site, had a "toxic equivalency" more than one thousand times the international limit.[145] Seven US chemical companies have settled with about 291,000 US veterans for $180 million ($240 million with interest). The Second Circuit Courts ruled in 1980 that chemical companies are not liable for damage from biological warfare in Việt Nam because they are government contractors.[146]

Town and Country

Apart from the horrific display at the Sài Gòn War Remnants Museum, the Vietnamese government largely has not pressed the issue of biological warfare.[147] Diane Niblack Fox attributes this to two factors: the government already promised not to bring up Agent Orange as a precondition for normalized US trade relations, and international attention to the toxin could adversely affect Việt Nam's agricultural and seafood markets.[148]

According to Việt Nam's Ministry of Agriculture and Rural Development, agricultural exports had reached $15 billion as of June 2016.[149] This figure grew to $36.5 billion in 2017 and to $40.5 billion in 2018 and was growing by 2 percent in 2019.[150] A report commissioned by the EU anticipates growth in the agriculture sector of an additional $1 billion by 2020.[151] Việt Nam is also the world's largest exporter of cashew nuts and the second-largest exporter of rice (after Thailand) and of coffee (after Brazil). Agricultural exports account for nearly a third (27.2 percent) of Việt Nam's GDP.[152] Images of exotic fruit and Edenic foliage draw in nearly eight million international tourists yearly, according to the Việt Nam Ministry of Culture, Sport and Tourism. Yet Agent Orange's purpose was to denude this.

In 2004, the NGO Vietnam Association for Victims of Agent Orange/Dioxin filed a class-action lawsuit in US courts against thirty-seven chemical companies that produced Agent Orange, including Dow, Monsanto, and Diamond Shamrock. The lawsuit failed. A federal appeal in 2008 also proved unsuccessful. The court denied direct links between herbicide use and Vietnamese illnesses, upholding previous US court rulings. This is a Catch-22 situation: chemical companies are not accountable as middlemen; the US government claims sovereign immunity (governments cannot be sued).[153] Jonathan Moore, an attorney for the Vietnamese plaintiffs, said that the decisions were the end.[154] As the United States grapples with an economic slump and wars abroad, it is not likely that the high cost of Agent Orange reparations will be a priority.

The US government consistently maintains that no scientific evidence connects Agent Orange and dioxin to negative health effects in Việt Nam.[155] While it paid $16.2 billion in damages in 2010 to more than a million American veterans of the Việt Nam War,[156] and the Agent Orange Act of 1991 benefits service veterans and their offspring suffering from a list of officially approved ailments, it disavows any direct connections between this compensation and dioxin/Agent Orange contact. Since *Nehmer v. Department of Veteran Affairs (VA)* (1991), a class-action lawsuit on behalf of all American Việt Nam War veterans, a decree has been issued stipulating that the VA must rehear cases if ailments are added to the official list. In addition, from

1991 to 2018, $5 billion has paid in retroactive decisions, so the government is reluctant to add new diseases to the list.[157]

The US government pays no compensation to affected Vietnamese. Congress allocated $7 million for a disability and health program in Việt Nam in 2016, but the program made no connections to Agent Orange, thus excising any connection between chemical defoliants and genetic defects.

The Afterlives of Trauma

How does Việt Nam deal with its horrendous history as it embraces its new role within the global economy? The rhetorical and representational contradictions of the country's horrific past and modernizing present forms the core of Sài Gòn–based artist Đinh Q. Lê's oeuvre. Lê first conceived of *Damaged Gene* in 1989 as a site-specific art project in Sài Gòn. Chanika Svetvilas's essay "The Art of War" features Lê's description of the project: "I rented a kiosk in the open market and sold handmade clothing for conjoined twins. . . . I also sold Siamese twin figurines and T-shirts printed with statistics about the use of Agent Orange and the damaging genetic effect it has had in Vietnam." The figurines, T-shirts, and hand-made clothing were not meant for a Vietnamese audience. The statistics are printed in English, aimed at expatriates and tourists. For locals, the art objects questioning high-versus-low divides are merely an oddity during a time when art is expected to be displayed in a gallery, not at a market kiosk. Such a display was transgressive, as Lê explains: "The project is a big departure for me. . . . Culturally I was bringing a taboo subject and putting it right in the middle of the market for one month. It was the scariest opening I have ever held."[158] I am not sure how taboo the subject is in Việt Nam. The art project did not differ ideologically from the messages about Agent Orange at the state-run War Remnants Museum. The project echoes the party line, even if it is presented differently (although no less creatively than the jars of deformed Agent Orange fetuses).

Lê may have been nervous, but the claim of danger increases the project's value among international art audiences. *Damaged Gene* has been exhibited subsequently in museums and cultural institutions worldwide. The small resin Siamese twin figurines, orange-hued modified plastic dolls with two heads, and pacifiers and knit sweaters made for twins conjoined at the chest are beautifully displayed in multiples, simultaneously evoking limited-edition art objects and tchotchkes for sale at a gift shop or vendor's table.[159] In the (postmodern) age of mass reproduction, the distinction between "high" and "low" increasingly blurs. In this project, art becomes commodity, and vice versa (with a nod to Marcel Duchamp, Andy Warhol, Jeff Koons, Takashi Murakami, and Walter Benjamin). Birth defects become bankable, even bourgeois objets d'art.

Lê's *Damaged Gene* project was launched a few years after đổi mới, a comment on the challenges of both trade and trauma. It deals with the complexities and contradictions of Việt Nam's historical atrocities and contemporary market economy, as well as trauma tourism. Today, Việt Nam's tourism industry markets the country's tropical beauty, as well as its French colonial architecture and neocolonial charms. Echoing French colonial discourse, Việt Nam is a jewel of Asia, a pearl of the Orient. "Trauma tourists" flock to sites such as the War Remnants Museum; the Demilitarized Zone between North and South Việt Nam; and the Củ Chi tunnels near Sài Gòn, a seventy-five-mile labyrinth of tunnels that South Vietnamese soldiers used in guerrilla warfare. Laura Kennedy and Mary Rose Williams note that the traumatic sites catering to foreigners "trivialize" the war, making the painful past manageable, digestible, consumable.[160] They write, "Turning the war into a tourist attraction means retelling, for profit, the story of Việt Nam's victory. Since the profit must come from those who lost the war, aspects of the story must be muted and key roles recast to make the story more palatable."[161] The palette used to repaint traumatic scenes is severely limited, circumscribed. American losses are downplayed; centuries of anti-imperial sentiment, muted.

To echo the historian Hồ Tài Huệ-Tâm's question, "Who owns the past?"—the intersections between history and memory and the politics of remembrance can be a minefield (in some instances both literal and metaphorical).[162] She notes that in socialist systems, public activities closely reference official cultural policies. Lê's public "intervention" more than a decade ago, in the first incarnation of *Damaged Gene*—the rented kiosk in an open Vietnamese market—challenged official policies in both Việt Nam and the United States. It critiqued the handling of Agent Orange as an issue and the attendant politics of the market and memorialization. His intervention and challenge revisited, in another context and country, remains that were urgent and timely. Again, this is a time of war, a time of market crisis. In dealing with the market, reparations, and memorialization, Lê questions the ownership of discourse on public policies and private pain. This question of ownership speaks of agency and commodity, art and commerce, authenticity and commemoration.

The afterlife of trauma is indelible, spectral. From the halls of the War Remnants Museum, the eight-year-old Vietnamese boy stares still—my angel of history, mouth agape in shock and sorrow—into the past, the present, the unfathomable future.

Collateral Damage

collateral damage (*noun*): injury inflicted on something other than an intended target; *specifically*: civilian casualties of a military operation. —*Merriam-Webster Dictionary*

Within military parlance, collateral damage is the unintended consequence of war: laypeople lying dead. Untargeted, they become unintentional victims. To use "collateral damage" as a metaphorical framework, the artists in this book engage in a collateral damage mode when dealing with traumatic subject matter. They are both the unintended targets of shock *and* the ones who are targeting their marks. Woeful tales—snippets *and* snipers (shooting for art stardom). The artists' target audience(s) are both the anticipated and the unanticipated recipients of these narratives of strife. These artists are at once object and subject of the violent mark. The wound—the *punctum*; that which pricks (à la Barthes)—is unnamable, unintended. Yet this damage fills the whole frame. The wounds of history, of modernity—its marks must be remarked on, collated for the art collector. Collateral is a deposit, a guarantee: property as security in loan. In this loan of worldviews, intellectual property is forwarded as vouchsafe—cautionary tales to ensure (by contrast) our First World safety, security, and comfort. Simultaneously, these artists present themselves as unwittingly targeted (damaged by a localized past, by Third World development) and willfully targeting (translators for an international stage).

The three artists discussed in this chapter—Sopheap Pich, Phan Quang, and Đinh Q. Lê—all deal with traumatic changes within specific geographic locales, whether the city or the countryside. They have developed various strategies for presenting topical political subjects, ranging from formal investigations of line and shape (Pich) to surreal image juxtapositions (Phan) and kitsch (Lê). All three have leveraged the politics of place and identity to attract varying levels of attention in the art world.

I maintain that Phan's and Pich's works dealing with exploitation and development are self-exploitative maneuvers. Their privileged insight as cultural insiders allows them to create work that has a distinctly unique perspective. I doubt that a Caucasian Australian colleague could make work about Boeung Kak development or Khmer Rouge trauma in as heart-rending a manner as Pich can. Perhaps this is my bias about authorship and auteurship. The audience wants insider knowledge. As a city slicker, I cannot claim the same level of intimacy with the countryside that Phan can. I cannot package this knowledge into a solo show. Phan presents himself as a country boy made good. He is the living embodiment of the vast changes within Việt Nam. One can argue that all cultural producers use their own biographies and obsessions to fuel their work. Although fictional, every work is autobiographical in that it reveals its creator's passion. In short, every artist exploits herself or himself. Of course, work that is deeply personal is highly resonant. As a college art instructor once proclaimed, "The more intimate and personal it is, the more 'universal' it is." I do not agree with this statement and the claim to universality, but it captures a grain of truth. The personal is what one knows best. Autobiography is self-exploitation, although it is not seen that way. It is viewed as intimate knowledge. Pich and Phan not only offer up this knowledge in their works; they sell their status as "authentic" specimens. Nora Taylor notes, "Only personal testimony and biographical records can act as validation of the past. For all of the aesthetic associations between war and nationalism that have been played out in contemporary art, the game of identity politics is effectively reduced to individual stories."[163] For some collectors, only an authentic country dweller can make convincing work about the countryside. Only an authentic survivor can make work about survival, unless, of course, the work is fictional or ironic. But Pich and Phan do not make fictional or ironic work. What they offer is a vision of difference. The international community does not see their works as separate from their personal biographies.

Instead of resisting this perspective, Southeast Asian artists wisely play to strategic cartographies. They do not make overly emotional work. Their work is not ethnographic or journalistic. It does not scream, "Woe is me and my malnourished developing country!" Like the developers turning over bits of land for profit, Phan and Pich turn over bits of their geographic and psychic turf for gain. As Cambodia's secretary of state noted in 2009, it is a game—and a race—of "economic growth and social progress."[164]

The most seasoned and possibly the savviest artist of this Southeast Asian triumvirate, Lê eschews any autobiographical details for work that is pointedly political. He also uses his subject position to establish himself as Việt Nam's premiere artist but engages in a different kind of exploitation. In the *Damaged Gene* series, Lê uses humor, "cuteness," and kitsch as a strategy for dealing with the ugly realities of dioxins and birth defects. On one hand, his figurines and knitted twinsets for Siamese twins are highly collectable and unthreatening. On the other hand, the continuing problems that his works signify point at dreadful realities. Increasingly, sites of trauma tourism such as the Củ Chi tunnels resemble amusement parks, complete with animatronic figures. Even the War Remnants Museum and Tuol Sleng have gift shops.

Lê makes past horror palatable, collectable for a mass audience. In contrast, consider the War Remnants Museum's handling of Agent Orange: pickled fetuses and grotesque photographs. Not a pretty sight. And not collectible. Where to display it that would not ruin one's lunch?[165] So is Lê using these horrors for personal gain? Well, yes and no. Lê once stated that artists are public intellectuals, and perhaps he is using the white cube (gallery or museum space) as an educational forum to enlighten foreign tourists about biological warfare and its lingering effects. The artist is also a political activist and educator. Presenting a deadly serious topic in a humorous form asks consumers to take Lê seriously as a high-minded conceptual artist. Further consideration shows that Lê's work is insidious. It is not only about Agent Orange and trauma tourism. It is also about the art world. He challenges old paradigms: high and low, terror and cuteness, mass-produced tchotchke and limited-edition fine art object. He may also be insinuating that the collector, gallerygoer, and art institution engage in trauma tourism (perhaps of the armchair variety), forever on the thrill-seeking hunt for the grotesque, seeking objects to display in their cabinets of monstrosities. He seems to say, "You want traumatic stories? I'll give them to you endlessly. Here they are in their most gaudy, degraded form." Sanctified subject matter (deformed babies! the horrors of war!) becomes profane knickknacks. Presaging Murakami, Lê imbibes the culture of trauma and consumer culture and heaves it back at the viewer.

Again, "local" artists serve as translators for a global art world about "local" issues that the rest of the world forgot about or did not know even existed. They will forever be known only as "that" Cambodian or Vietnamese artist, albeit the best-known one. Whether on the assembly line or in the gallery, markets are cutthroat, and its producers willingly come, day in and day out, to be exploited.

Conclusion

Traumatic events cause a radical breach in "normal" life, drastically undermining psychological, social, and physical stability.[166] The economic growth of Cambodia and Việt Nam has resulted in a dramatically shifting sociopolitical, economic, and cultural climate. The trauma theorist Ann Kaplan notes that modernization is a traumatic process. In this chapter I have discussed the difficult changes and displacements that are part and parcel of modernity. The works of Sopheap Pich and Phan Quang clearly reveal that seismic shifts in urban and rural landscapes and psyches are anything but jarring. Pich, Phan, and Đinh Q. Lê make the case that the traumas of history are not separate from contemporary life. The World Bank notes that rapid economic growth in Cambodia has resulted not only in decreases in poverty rates but also in increases in inequality. Despite Việt Nam's and Cambodia's congratulatory narratives of achieved "progress," "speedy growth," and glamorous visions of retail splendor and creature comforts, vast inequities make these changes possible. It is not enough to acknowledge these gulfs or even make artwork about it. Creative work is a way of processing these occurrences; it is a public exchange, but in the end it will not affect public policy. These traumas become aestheticized, anesthetized. These incomprehensible stressors become contained as art objects. The excruciating transitions become dulled. To echo Patricia Yaeger, is creative work, alongside critical discourse, another form of ineffectual navel gazing? We are merely consuming trauma. Artists are cannibalizing trauma for their benefit. They may knowingly or unwittingly offer themselves and their experiences up for ingestion—cultural cannibalism. Discriminating connoisseurs tire of consuming the same, standard fare and sometimes crave "exotic" flavor.

"Progress" has its upsides, including higher standards of living and name-brand shopping for those who can afford it. Modernity is marvelous.[167] But modernity and postmodernity are complicated. It is hard to comprehend the changes happening in Cambodia and Việt Nam. Because they are allies and competitors, it is even more difficult to draw out similarities and differences between the two nation-states, including their speedy growth and social progress.

Although the clock of progress operates on homogenous time, many have challenged its assumptions. Michel-Rolph Trouillot has problematized the view of modernity as a "North Atlantic universal."[168] Heterogeneous times and timelines exist for heterogeneous geographies. The cultural theorist Andreas Huyssen writes, "Alternative modernities with their deep histories and local contingencies now seem to offer a better approach than the imposed notion, say, of postmodernism in Asia or in Latin America."[169] The critical embrace of alternative modernities acknowledges the complicated histories of specific locales. Modernity happens not overnight but in fits and spurts, through several periods. Over the long history of colonial encounters, postcolonial nationalist fervor, and the current influx of mass media, nations develop unique identities.[170] But the implicit question of the term *alternate* or *alternative* modernity is: It is alternate to what? The term re-inscribes center-periphery and mainstream-alternate paradigms. Alternate modernity implies it is an alternative to the "North Atlantic universal" of teleological advancement. We should have alternative models, but not ones that perpetuate this core difference.

I prefer Lisa Rofel's conception of discrepant modernities to alternate modernities. "I mean a world of forced and violent interactions," she writes to explain the concept, "in which emerges an imaginary space that produces deferred relationships to modernity."[171] With Benedict Anderson's and Arjun Appadurai's imagined communities of affective identifications in mind, this imaginary space is the psychic space in which the brutal interactions are processed. Modernity itself is an act of imagination, a projection of fantasy that transforms reality through the implementation of ideology. This space may also be the spaces that artists such as Pich, Phan, and Lê create to grap-ple with the violent interactions they witness and attempt to bear witness to.

Rofel notes that modernity is a political enterprise, not an abstract, ob-tuse configuration over which critics and academics muddle (though we do anyhow). She writes, "Modernity is something people struggle over because it has life-affirming as well as life-threatening effects. This struggle is what people share, like the floor of a boxing match (including fixed bets and out-comes), rather than a universal form with its local particulars."[172] Modernity is not simply good or bad, a solution or a problem. It morphs and changes; it is a shared struggle dependent on its actors. Like Shiva, it is both destroyer and creator. Boeung Kak and areas like it will inevitably be destroyed for a new vision to be created. The framework of discrepant modernities takes into account the incongruent, divergent developments that occur over a long period.

The term *strategic cartographies* deploys geographic identities and (dis)identifications in a tactical manner. It is a considered mapping of psychic and physical terrain, connections, disconnections, and affiliations. These subject positions based on national, regional, and transnational coordinates are an ambivalent terrain, both useful and fraught ground for creative and critical inquiries. This project critically interrogates but does not abandon national and regional framings. I join many other artists and academics in ambivalently embracing and interrogating the categories and cartogra-phies that determine "Southeast Asia" as a field. In doing so, we deliberately chart discrepant routes. Dipesh Chakrabarty notes, "European thought is at once both indispensable and inadequate in helping us to think through the experiences of political modernity in non-Western nations, and provincializing Europe becomes the task of exploring how this thought . . . may be renewed from and for the margins."[173] Although the margin-center dyad has been contested by a multiplicity of "centers," the question of "from" and "for" is urgent.

LEAVING AND RETURNS

It is Monday, November 22, 2010, and I have returned from a brief trip to Hong Kong, where I participated in a group art exhibition, to Phnom Penh, where I have been living for the past year and a half. I came back for the jubilant holiday throngs and riotous lights of the last evening of the annual Water Festival, a national three-day celebration in which millions of people from the provinces and countryside come to Phnom Penh to cheer their boat race teams along the riverside, stroll the capital's wide boulevards, eat street snacks, and partake in festivities such as free celebrity concerts, product booths, rides, and massive discount sales at most of the city's stores. In the twilight crowds gather near the sprawling lawns and promenades near the golden National Palace to see and be seen, to gaze at glittering barges resembling giant lit movie marquees. The inky river dimples with shimmering orbs as the sky sizzles with fireworks—all around, constellations of light and laughter. We could not know it would end in hundreds of deaths.

I am late, searching for my friend among the masses along the riverside. There is no cell phone reception. The crowds are thick; one can barely squeeze through. An ocean of revelers. Coming toward our designated spot in front of a restaurant/bar/disco popular with sexpats. I spot Chris's blond mane and lanky, six-foot-one frame towering above a sea of black hair. We go to our friend Sreymom's guesthouse down a quieter alley nearby and have a quick bite with her in the Riverside area. Exhausted, we go home afterward, although it is early, anticipating a studio visit with Leang Seckon the next day. In the morphing metropolis, mine is one among millions of recollections. Memory and modernity are not linear. Memory does not unravel as a single chronological narrative; it starts and stops unevenly. Similarly, development is uneven and discrepant, as Phnom Penh's diverse neighborhoods, including the Boeung Kak ghetto, the touristy Riverside area, and the swanky expat haven Boeung Keng Kang 1 reflect.[1] These neighborhoods have very different histories, stories, and hauntings.

It is Tuesday November 23, 2010, and the last day Seckon has in his Boeung Kak studio, where he has worked and lived with his family for the past twenty years. He has been kicked out, forcibly evacuated. Developers continue to fill the lake with sand, despite mounting protests. His studio flat, once teeming, full of paintings and furniture and people (his mother and cousins were always there), is now barren, a shell. Several months earlier he had moved many of his large paintings out, anticipating this day. A forgotten, tattered paintbrush lies on the floor. Instead of his usual towel, Seckon has wrapped himself in white fabric to meet friends who have come and lend him support. White is the color of mourning. When Chris and I visit him in the morning, he is alone, enveloped by white. On the studio's wide, empty white walls he has painted a mural as a memorial of sorts—a nāga, a dragon, that scales the four walls. Soon it, too, will be gone—debris on the street.

On the main road next to Seckon's studio lies Calmette Hospital. On the way back out, Chris and I drive past frantic families and bandaged bodies on gurneys. In front of the hospital there are two large signs—two giant grids of hundreds of faces that evoke the photographic grids at Tuol Sleng. Chris stops his motorcycle, wanting to take a closer look, despite my protests that we should just return home. Reluctantly, I join the small, solemn crowd in front of the signs. They are trying to find familiar faces among the color photos. As I was going to sleep the previous night, I received texts that hundreds had died in a human stampede around 10 p.m., triggered by panic that the Diamond Island (a.k.a. Koh Pich) bridge—a small bridge leading to the site of a large outdoor concert and fair during the festivities—would collapse. We had crossed the bridge on our way from Diamond Island back to the Riverside. The final count said that four hundred were injured and as many as three hundred and fifty had died. Seckon had said, "It was not earthquake or storm. It was nothing. Only fear. I am sad so many die because of nothing."

The photographed faces in rows in front of the hospital all have their eyes shut. Women are on the left sign; men, on the right. A small crowd huddles in front. A man recognizes a family member in one of the photographs at the hospital and cries hysterically, cradling his motorcycle helmet. I want to hold him. *I am so sorry, my brother.* I remember the stark midmorning light illuminating the grid of faces, many young and a few old, their eyes shut. On their faces, necks and closed eyes bloom with inky bruises. A constellation of bruises.

Cambodia's Prime Minister Hun Sen makes a televised public statement after the bridge stampede, calling it the "biggest tragedy we have experienced in the last thirty-one years, since the collapse of the Khmer Rouge regime."[2] For a brief moment, Cambodia is international news, this odd proclamation often accompanying headlines in the *Washington Post, New York Times.* Again, mainstream mass media represents Cambodians as traumatized, hysterical. Khmer bloggers and other pundits note that tragedies of similar magnitude sparked by government corruption and uncurbed development have been less visible. Boeung Kak is only one example of construction projects undertaken in service to "growth" that have displaced millions.

Many have tried to come up with explanations for the bridge accident, ranging from inadequate crowd control to inappropriate or insufficient police response. To people from the countryside not familiar with such structures, the gentle sway of the narrow suspension bridge felt like a harbinger of collapse. My hypothesis is that the panic spread so quickly among the masses because it triggered bodily memories and generational memories of distress: bombs and evacuations, disaster and despair. My own panic attacks, debilitating in my teens and twenties, were often triggered by large crowds or just a feeling of being overwhelmed, as I was as a boat refugee. Damage is relative. Damage depends on a host of relations. How and why destabilizing fear spreads is a mystery. Terror's initial onset spreads through the body and through the social body invisibly yet indelibly. Panic is a form of immediate collective trauma, at first unmediated by culture. At times it may seem instantaneous, but there is still a lag. The body's response to the upset mind lags, just as individual suffering later registers as a societal issue. Collective hurt becomes cultural trauma over time. "Trauma never happens once," as Shoshana Felman notes.[3] The original distress gets replayed, reevaluated, and reinforced in our minds and our communities as tragic incidents. We are stunned over and over. We want to remember and forget. The stories we tell ourselves and each other in conversations, in mass media, wrestle with the unfathomable depths.

We revisit pain again and again. Seckon's evacuation and the bridge accident are indelibly linked in my mind. I still cannot comprehend it, but they are linked by more than just the memory of my experiences that Tuesday morning. Private grief and loss was separated by a few meters of road between the studio and the hospital, a few minutes. Seckon's former life vanishes quietly, unremarked by the press and an unremarkable disappearance. Diamond Island's victims died spectacular deaths. In the international news for a day or two, the pornography of trampled anonymous brown bodies, wet faces contorted in agony. One private loss is invisible, the other losses are hypervisible—but in the end, they are also politically invisible.

The incidents in Boeung Kak and at the bridge encapsulate the traumas of modernization. The battle over Boeung Kak continues. Boeung Kak residents began a peaceful demonstration at Freedom Park on January 10, 2011. After a week of protests—congregating, holding signs, speaking to reporters—they gathered at the Chinese Embassy to deliver a petition to the ambassador to decry Shukaku Inc.'s involvement in the project. Riot police met them and dispersed the crowd, preventing the delivery.[4] Two days earlier, police had confiscated the two cameras of the *Phnom Penh Post* photographer Sovan Philong, who was documenting the evacuation of twenty families and the demolition of their homes. A local longtime nongovernmental organization (NGO) worker at the scene noted that such intimidation tactics have been commonplace for the villagers since 2008. As he commented, the connection between the government and private industry was clear from the police's actions, both in blocking protesters and in blocking reportage.[5] While Sovan got his cameras back after intervention from fellow journalists, NGO workers, and villagers, the police made him delete the images of the forced evacuations. The divide between the public good and private interests gets increasingly blurred as rapid development continues in Cambodia. The same holds true in Việt Nam.

Diamond Island (Koh Pich), which the bridge on which the stampede took place connects to the mainland, was also once a slum community. Originally eggplant farmland, it was cleared in 2004 to make way for commercial enterprises, residences for the elite, and future high-rises.[6] The area, which now features strip malls of multipurpose beige buildings for conventions and weddings and a grassy park area, will be redeveloped again. The $200 million plan calls for skyscrapers. It is being developed by the Overseas Cambodian Investment Company (OCIC), a firm controlled by Canadia Bank, which has ties to Prime Minister Hun Sen's in-laws.[7] The OCIC worked with the Cambodian government to host the Water Festival's outdoor concert to call attention to the area's retail offerings and increase foot traffic. Hun Sen is rumored to have a major stake in Diamond Island and the bank. After

242

the tragedy, the government refused to hold any parties accountable and to claim any responsibility for the accident. It instead offered compensation: families of the deceased received 5 million riel ($1,250) for funeral expenses; each injured person received 1 million riel ($250).[8] A friend of mine who lost a loved one is angry. She says a life is worth more than a thousand dollars.

Another friend, Bich from Sài Gòn, visited me the weekend following the bridge accident. She had a desire that she herself called morbid to see the bridge for herself. Blocked off and strewn with thousands of flowers, still colorfully lit, the bridge seemed incredibly small—almost a twinkling miniature bridge—compared with the larger-than-life scenes of duress in print and on television and computer screens. It was eerily quiet. Others were there, too: on vigil, they became new melancholics. This moment of mourning, inextricably tied in to dreams of the future and haunted by the past, marked a different horizon—discrepant limits. Within hauntology, as Derrida calls it, the past, present, and future are linked by the spectral.

Throughout this book I have argued for an ethics and poetics of return. Those of us who are haunted—beyond the horizon of mourning and waiting—also conjure visions of possibility within the impossible. Utopic horizons have been questioned by queer theorists such as Jack Halberstam, Lee Edelman, and others, for their assumptions of heteronormative futurity. Nonetheless, José Esteban Muñoz argues that queerness can be future-facing, a "not yet here" unguarded against possibilities of the present. To this aporia we must be "open, waiting for the event *as* justice."[9] The "messianic, including its revolutionary forms (and the messianic is always revolutionary; it has to be), would be urgency, imminence but, irreducible paradox, a waiting without *horizon* of expectation."[10] A future-oriented, forward-thinking ethics ("the messianic") is predicated on a turning back, a re-volution. As I traced in the introduction, revolt, *volver*, "to return, to become," and revolution are linked by notions of cyclical turning. Hence, the (ghostly) revenant is also (messianic) arrivant, as Derrida and Avery Gordon note. (In French, *revenir* means to come back.) By definition, the ghost "begins by coming back" to urgently address an injustice.[11] Ghosts are outside the contraints of time, yet bound to structures. The trauma studies scholar Jenny Edkins notes, "The memory of past traumas, [then] returns to haunt the structures of power that instigated the violence in the first place."[12] Through these continued hauntings, structures of violence—including cultural and academic institutions—shift. "One often finds oneself 'disrupting power' by returning (*re-venir*) to the scene of the crime (like a ghost)," writes the philosopher

Epilogue

Trevor Hoag.[13] Let us return, then, to the mise-en-scène of the crime, without expectations.

In this book, I have gone back and forth in time and space to highlight discrepant temporal embodiments and disembodiments. The rhetoric scholar Thomas Rickert observes, "Any haunting requires embodiment and emplacement, or a residence and an abode. In other words, haunting, by conjoining the spectral and the material, still requires sites of actualization as incarnation, embodiment, and placement."[14] These "sites of actualization" are embodied through art, by artists as well as places—real, imagined, and memorialized. This is the process of actualization, as envisaged by Jung, engaging the shades and the shadow self.

After the initial Diamond Island bridge incident, people kept coming, intentionally and by chance, myself included. Locals and tourists came to pay their respects or were drawn by television reports—revenants and arrivants. In the next few weeks, the next few years, and for a lifetime and more, these melancholics and their families will revisit the scene of disaster. Diamond Island—and, indeed, Phnom Penh—will change beyond recognition, the spectral and the material conjoined.

But that day we had not yet witnessed how the public, artists, and politicians would respond to, remember, and represent Diamond Island and Boeung Kak. A flirtatious evening turned into tragedy. Golden miles, the promising mirage of high-rises, obscure the desperation of those living on the edges. Desire and despair. Yet beyond the newly rebuilt Diamond Island bridge, on the horizon, is justice, an impossible, returning specter.

Preface

1. Rushdie keenly observes, "The past is a country from which we have all emigrated, [and therefore] its loss is part of our common humanity" (Rushdie, "Imaginary Homelands").

2. Several diasporic Vietnamese artists call Việt Nam home, including Hà Thúc Phu Nam, Đỉnh Q. Lê, Tuấn Andrew Nguyễn, Phi Phi Oanh Nguyễn (phiphiblackbox.com), and Rich Streitmetter-Trần (diacritic.org). Tiffany Chung lived in Sài Gòn for more than ten years and recently moved to Texas. All of the listed artists reside in Sài Gòn, with the exception of Phi Phi Oanh Nguyễn.

3. For more on the structures of art worlds and the relationships that sustain them, see Bourdieu, "The Historical Genesis of a Pure Aesthetic," 260–63. Summarizing Bourdieu on the primacy of avant-garde cultural practice, the sociologist David Gartman writes, "These cultural producers [artists] have more cultural capital (taste, knowledge, education) than economic capital (money); consequently, their works match the dispositions of consumers in the social field who similarly have more culture than money. Bourdieu calls these consumers of high art the dominated fraction of the dominant class, or the intellectual bourgeoisie, which includes all professions that rely on knowledge and education for a living. Lacking the money of the dominant fraction or economic bourgeoisie, these people prefer culture that is more cerebral than expensive, more ascetic than self-indulgent; just the kind of art that innovative, avant-garde artists struggling for symbolic profits in the restricted subfield are motivated to produce" (Gartman, "Bourdieu's Theory of Cultural Change," 258). For further reading, see Bourdieu, *The Field of Cultural Production*, 29–73; Bourdieu, *The Rules of Art*.

4. The description of the work reads, "Adrian Piper creates a poetic and philosophical duration performance in which the text 'Everything will be taken away' will be written, in henna, on an unspecified number of participants' foreheads that respond to an open call. The henna will be applied to respondents on May 1 and May 2. Written in reverse, the message becomes readable when seen through

the reflection of a mirror, and the dye is anticipated to endure on the skin for 1–2 weeks. The participants will be asked keep journals of their experiences and audience reactions during the project, then re-read the journals a year after the performance. Written directly on the forehead the text suggests the layered, shifting organization and loss of memory. It is both a promise and a threat. What will be taken away and what do we consider to be 'our' everything?" (Creative Time, "Six Actions for New York City," May 2007, accessed August 2020, https://creativetime .org/programs/archive/2007/performance/piper.html).

5. Mech Dara, "No Leaders Left to Stand Trial," *Phnom Penh Post*, November 19, 2018, accessed November 20, 2018, https://www.phnompenhpost.com /national-kr-tribunal/no-more-khmer-rouge-leaders-left-stand-trial.

6. Mech, "No Leaders Left to Stand Trial."

7. The Extraordinary Chambers in the Courts of Cambodia (ECCC) is available online at https://www.eccc.gov.kh/sites/default/files/documents/courtdoc /%5Bdate-in-tz%5D/E463_EN.pdf.

8. Mech, "No Leaders Left to Stand Trial."

9. Eli Meixler, "Why a Genocide Verdict in Cambodia Could Be the Last of Its Kind," *Time*, November 30, 2018, accessed December 1, 2018, http://time.com /5467567/cambodia-genocide-verdict-court-last-verdict/, https://www.ushmm .org/confront-genocide/cases/cambodia/violence/s-21.

10. Meixler, "Why a Genocide Verdict in Cambodia Could Be the Last of Its Kind."

11. Meixler, "Why a Genocide Verdict in Cambodia Could Be the Last of Its Kind."

12. Dara, "No Leaders Left to Stand Trial."

13. "Case 001," ECCC website, accessed October 24, 2017, https://www.eccc.gov .kh/en/case/topic/1.

Acknowledgments

1. bell hooks, *Bone Black: Memories of Girlhood*.

2. bell hooks, *All about Love*, 235.

Introduction. Risky Returns

1. "Performed, presented, or taking place again: a return engagement of the ballet; a return tennis match": *The Free Dictionary*, s.v. "return (*adj.*)," accessed February 3, 2014, https://www.thefreedictionary.com/returning#:~:text =Performed%2C%20presented%2C%20or%20taking%20place,plumbing%20 pipe%3B%20a%20return%20valve.

2. Williams, *Keywords*, 273.

3. Williams, *Keywords*, 271.

4. Williams, *Keywords*, 113.

5. Williams, *Keywords*, 274.

6. Williams writes about the term *revolution*, "In all its early uses it indicated a revolving movement in space or time: 'in whiche the other Planetes, as well as the Sonne, do finyshe their revolution and course according to their true tyme' (1559); 'from the day of the date heereof, to the full terme and revolution of seven yeeres next ensuing' (1589); 'they recoyl again, and return in a Vortical motion, and so continue their revolution for ever' (1664). This primary use, of a recurrent physical movement, survives mainly in a technical sense of engines: revolutions per minute" (Williams, *Keywords*, 270).

7. The term *invert* is used intentionally to evoke its historical usage as derogatory term for homosexuals.

8. Ahmed, *The Promise of Happiness*, 170.

9. Frantz Fanon, *The Wretched of the Earth*.

10. Frantz Fanon, *Conscience*.

11. Ahmed, *The Promise of Happiness*, 197.

12. Ahmed, *The Promise of Happiness*, 169.

13. Marcuse, *Counterrevolution and Revolt*, 107.

14. Art has an a priori political dimension. "By virtue of its own subversive quality, art is associated with revolutionary consciousness, but to the degree to which the prevailing consciousness of a class is affirmative, integrated, blunted, revolutionary art will be opposed to it" (Marcuse, *Counterrevolution and Revolt*, 125).

15. Marcuse, *Counterrevolution and Revolt*, 116.

16. Marcuse, *Counterrevolution and Revolt*, 128.

17. Ahmed, *The Promise of Happiness*, 54.

18. Williams, *The Long Revolution*, 44.

19. Scarry, *The Body in Pain*, 4.

20. Williams, *The Long Revolution*, 31.

21. Marcuse, *Eros and Civilization*, xx.

22. See Chapelle, *Nietzsche and Psychoanalysis*.

23. Nietzsche, *The Gay Science*, 273.

24. Thurman, *Inner Revolution*, 32.

25. Kōtō Uchiyama, *Opening the Hand of Thought: Foundations of Zen Buddhist Practice*, 288.

26. Williams, *The Long Revolution*, 31.

27. Dalai Lama, quoted in Goleman, *A Force for Good*, 119.

28. Dalai Lama XIV, *The Universe in a Single Atom*, 64.

29. Dalai Lama XIV, *The Universe in a Single Atom*, 524.

30. Dalai Lama XIV, *The Universe in a Single Atom*, 69.

31. Williams, *The Long Revolution*, 27, emphasis added.

32. Evolution and revolution appear to be temporal opposites, yet are aligned. Evolution connotes the slow biological Darwinian processes whereas revolution implies rapid leaps. Evolution, like revolution, is a cyclical process. Evolution's Latin root (*evolver*) means a rolling out (or unrolling a book). Shifting from the literal (literary book) to the metaphorical, evolution referred "both to the divine

247

creation and to the working-out, the developing formation, of Ideas or Ideal Principles. It is clear from the root sense . . . what is implied is the 'unrolling' of something that already exists" (Williams, *Keywords*, 120). Again, the creative act is a reiterative act—not spontaneously arising but eternal.

33. Appadurai, *Modernity at Large*, 31.

34. Benedict Anderson, *Imagined Communities: Reflections on the Origin and Spread of Nationalism*, 2016.

35. Rankine, *Citizen*, 134–35.

36. The *Washington Post*'s "National Police Shootings Database" is a Pulitzer Prize–winning project with links to individual cases. 999 people had been killed in 2019, https://www.washingtonpost.com/graphics/2019/national /police-shootings-2019/. Despite increasing public awareness, the number of shooting deaths have remained relatively steady since 2015 (see https://www .washingtonpost.com/investigations/four-years-in-a-row-police-nationwide -fatally-shoot-nearly-1000-people/2019/02/07/0cb3b098-020f-11e9-9122 -82e98f91ee6f_story.html).

37. For works on President Barack Obama's deportations and Khmer American exiles, see the art collaborative Studio Revolt's experimental videos *My Asian Americana* (Anida Yoeu Ali, Masahiro Sugano, codirectors, 2011) and *Return to Sender* (Anida Yoeu Ali, Masahiro Sugano, codirectors, 2012). Descriptions of the videos are available at Studio Revolt's website, http://loveinthetimeofwar.com /index.php/onlineonly/studio-revolt. See also Cesar Vegas and Margo Schlanger, "Advocate: Trump's Deportations Are Possible Because Obama and Congress Failed to Protect Immigrants," *Democracy Now!*, February 22, 2017, accessed December 1, 2017, https://www.democracynow.org/2017/2/22/advocate_trumps _deportations_are_possible_because.

38. Julie Hirschfield and Miriam Jordan, "Trump Plans 45,000 Limit on Refugees Admitted to US," *New York Times*, September 26, 2017, accessed December 8, 2017, https://www.nytimes.com/2017/09/26/us/politics/trump-plans-45000 -limit-on-refugees-admitted-to-us.html; Dara Lind, "The Trump Administration Doesn't Believe in the Global Refugee Crisis," Vox News, December 4, 2017, accessed December 10, 2017, https://www.vox.com/policy-and-politics/2017/10/3 /16379016/trump-refugees.

39. Williams, *Keywords*, 120.

40. "At the time I was deep into working on a history of the Vietnamese revolution and the origins of its exemplary tenacity and the reasons for its supporters' capacity to withstand unimaginable suffering"; Anthony Barnett, "Foreword to *The Long Revolution* by Raymond Williams," Open Democracy, December 16, 2011, accessed June 10, 2018, https://www.opendemocracy.net/anthony-barnett /we-live-in-revolutionary-times-but-what-does-this-mean.

41. Williams, *The Long Revolution*, 1–2, 6.

42. Long Bui, *Returns of War: South Vietnam and the Price of Refugee Memory*, 2018.

43. Williams, *The Long Revolution*, 37.

44. North Carolina is home to a significant number of Vietnamese refugees. The exhibition lasted from November 7, 2010, to January 30, 2011. According to the museum's website, "To create his unique 'chlorophyll prints,' Danh starts by selecting a suitable leaf, then places the leaf on a felt-covered board and rests a photographic negative directly on the leaf. The negative is chosen from Danh's collection of archival images that he has saved from magazines and other sources. Danh then places a sheet of glass over the leaf and exposes the leaf and negative to sunlight for a variable period of time—sometimes a week, sometimes several days—and lets the photosynthesis process of the sun and the leaf create the images. His most recent work uses the Daguerreotype process, the early 19th-century photographic process that also produces a single print that cannot be duplicated" (North Carolina Museum of Art, accessed December 8, 2017, http://ncartmuseum.org/exhibitions/binh_danh).

45. Gleeson, *Who Cares?*

46. Schlund-Vials, *War, Genocide, and Justice*, 17.

47. Lê's exhibition at the Museum of Modern Art took place from June 30, 2010, to January 24, 2011. The website describes the installation: "For *Projects 93*, Lê presents *The Farmers and The Helicopter* (2006), an installation comprised of [*sic*] a three-channel video and a helicopter hand-built from scrap parts by Le Van Danh, a farmer, and Tran Quoc Hai, a self-taught mechanic. Lê's video interlaces the personal recollections of the war by Vietnamese locals with clips from Western films. While many of the interviewees relay childhood memories of the horrors associated with helicopters during the war, the helicopter-makers share their vision of this machine as a means to make a better life for the Vietnamese people and bring strength to their community. Installed in adjacent galleries, the helicopter and the video projection offer a multilayered insight into the complex relationships between the Vietnamese individuals and the charged object of the helicopter" (exhibition description, Museum of Modern Art website, accessed January 16, 2011, https://www.moma.org/calendar/exhibitions/1058).

48. Landry and MacLean, *The Spivak Reader*, 214.

49. This segment on strategic cartographies is expanded and updated from the framework first presented in "Myriad Modernities: Southeast Asian Visual Cultures," a special issue of *Visual Anthropology* I coedited with Lan Duong. The double issue includes articles by Michelle Dizon, Janet Hoskins, Patrick Flores, Panivong Norindr, Nguyễn Tân Hoàng, Dredge Kang, Louisa Schein and Bee Vang. An artists' portfolio features work by Anida Yoeu Ali, Lang Ea, Sokuntevy Oeur, and Đinh Q. Lê, among others (*Visual Anthropology* 31, nos. 1–2 [2018]).

50. José Esteban Muñoz writes, "Disidentification is about recycling and rethinking encoded meaning. The process of disidentification scrambles and reconstructs the encoded message of a cultural text in a fashion that both exposes the encoded message's universalizing and exclusionary machinations and recircuits its workings to account for, include, and empower minority identities and identifications. Thus, disidentification is a step further than cracking open the code of the majority; it proceeds to use this code as raw material for representing

249

a disempowered politics or positionality that has been rendered unthinkable by the dominant culture" (Muñoz, *Disidentifications*, 31).

51. See Kim's critical cartography projects housed at the University of Southern California (http://slab.today/2014/09/maps) and an older Massachusetts Institute of Technology site (http://slab.scripts.mit.edu/wp/links/critical-cartography).

52. Petersen, *Migration into Art*, 7.

53. Leys, *Trauma*, 298.

54. It is telling, as a metaphor, that Damien was banished from god's kingdom, never to return. This eternal banishment of living in the underworld (the subconscious) gets reinterpreted as the return of the repressed, as hysteria, psychosis, and outbreaks.

55. Williams, *The Long Revolution*, 29.

56. LaCapra, *Writing History, Writing Trauma*, 142.

57. Judith Butler, *Frames of War: When Is Life Grievable?*, 9–12.

58. Becker, "Dealing with the Consequences of Organized Violence in Trauma Work."

59. Becker, "Dealing with the Consequences of Organized Violence in Trauma Work."

60. Bennett and Kennedy, *World Memory*, 4.

61. Bennett and Kennedy, *World Memory*, 7.

62. Bennett and Kennedy, *World Memory*, 5. Increasingly, postcolonial scholarship—which is cross-disciplinary by nature—has dealt with visual culture, including work by Gwendolyn Wright, Hamid Naficy, Panivong Norindr, Annie Coombes, Kobena Mercer, Janet Hoskins, Saloni Mathur, Macarena Gómez-Barris, Alloula Malek, Trinh T. Minh-ha, Coco Fusco, and Paul Gilroy.

63. Kaplan, *Trauma Culture*, 24.

64. Foster, *The Return of the Real*, 168.

65. Foster, *The Return of the Real*, 168.

66. Foster writes, "This strange rebirth of the author, this paradoxical condition of absentee authority, is a significant turn in contemporary art, criticism, and cultural politics" (Foster, *The Return of the Real*, 168).

67. Foster, *The Return of the Real*, x.

68. Crimp, "Getting the Warhol We Deserve."

69. Eng, *Racial Castration*, 81.

70. See, e.g., Carlos Castaneda, *The Art of Dreaming*; Michael Harner (Foundation for Shamanic Studies); Sandra Ingerman, *Soul Retrieval: Mending the Fragmented Self*; among others.

71. Nietzsche, *Thus Spoke Zarathustra: A Book for All and None*, 154.

72. Akira Mizuta Lippit, *Atomic Light (Shadow Optics)*, 3–16.

73. Halberstam, *The Queer Art of Failure*, 124.

74. Halberstam, *The Queer Art of Failure*, 124.

75. Judith Butler, *Precarious Life*, 28–30.

76. Jung, *Two Essays on Analytical Psychology*, 227.

77. Jung, *Collected Works of C. G. Jung*, 11:238–39.

78. Marcuse, *Counterrevolution and Revolt*, 93.

79. Marcuse, *Counterrevolution and Revolt*, 93.

80. Taylor, "Why Have There Been No Great Vietnamese Artists?," 160.

81. For more on the structures of art worlds and the relationships that sustain them, see Bourdieu, "The Historical Genesis of a Pure Aesthetic," 260–63.

82. Richard C. Paddock, "Vietnamese Art Has Never Been More Popular," *New York Times*, August 11, 2018, accessed August 9, 2018, https://www.nytimes.com/2017/08/11/arts/design/vietnamese-art-has-never-been-more-popular-but-the-market-is-full-of-fakes.html.

83. Jennifer Conlin, "The Awakening of Hanoi," *New York Times*, February 18, 2007, accessed August 9, 2018, https://www.nytimes.com/2007/02/18/travel/18hanoi.html.

84. See Ingrid Muan's articles, "Haunted Scenes: Painting and History in Phnom Penh," and "Musings on Museums from Phnom Penh."

85. Muan, "Citing Angkor."

86. Thompson, "Mnemotechnical Politics," 56, 225–40.

87. Alice Yang, Jonathan Hay, and Mimi Young, eds., *Why Asia?*

88. For a more comprehensive listing of art historians working on Southeast Asian contemporary and modern art history, from national foci to more regional emphases, see Antoinette, *Reworlding Art History*. Special journal issues on visual cultures in Southeast Asian contemporary art history include "Contemporaneity and Art in Southeast Asia," ed. Joan Kee and Patrick Flores, *Third Text* 25, no. 4 (2011), and "Myriad Modernities."

89. Pamela Corey, "Three Propositions for a Regional Profile: The History of Contemporary Art in Ho Chi Minh City," 135–44.

90. See Moira Roth, "Obdurate History: Dinh Q. Lê, the Vietnam War, Photography and Memoir," *Art Journal* 60, no. 1 (summer 2001): 38–53; and "Traveling Companions/Fractured Worlds," *Art Journal* 58 (1999): 82–93; her website has an archive of writing: http://www.moiraroth.net.

91. See T. J. Clark's *Farewell to an Idea: Episodes from a History of Modernism* and Thomas Crow's *The Rise of the Sixties: American and European Art in the Era of Dissent*.

92. Trouillot, *Silencing the Past*, 6.

93. Trouillot, "The Otherwise Modern: Caribbean Lessons from the Savage Slot," 220–37.

94. Chakrabarty, *Provincializing Europe*, 44; Nguyễn, *The Gift of Freedom*, 17.

95. Derrida, *On Cosmopolitanism and Forgiveness*.

96. Derrida, *Given Time*, 41.

97. Muñoz, *Cruising Utopia*, 182.

98. Muñoz, *Cruising Utopia*, 174.

99. The Derrida scholar Gerasimos Kakoliris notes that Derrida wrote about hospitality from the 1990s until 2004 (the year of his death) in *Autour de Jacques Derrida* (1999), *Adieu to Emmanuel Levinas* (1999), "Hospitality, Justice and Responsibility" (1999), "Hospitality" (2000), *Of Hospitality* (2000), "Hospitality"

(2002), and "The Principle of Hospitality" (2005) (Kakoliris, "Jacques Derrida on the Ethics of Hospitality," 145n5).

100. Derrida, "Hospitality" (2000), 176.

101. Raffoul, "The Subject of the Welcome," 214.

102. Derrida, *Adieu to Emmanuel Levinas*, 192.

103. Raffoul, "The Subject of the Welcome," 216, emphasis added.

104. Derrida, *Adieu to Emmanuel Levinas*, 79, emphasis added.

105. Derrida, *Adieu to Emmanuel Levinas*, 72.

106. Lim, *Translating Time*, 31.

107. Walter Benjamin, *Theses on the Philosophy of History*, 50.

108. Brunschwig et al., "The Global Financial Crisis."

109. Park et al., "Why Did Asian Countries Fare Better during the Global Financial Crisis than during the Asian Financial Crisis?," 135. Martin Khor of the *Sunday Observer* writes, "The Asian crisis began [in July 1997] when speculators brought down the Thai baht. Within months, the currencies of Indonesia, South Korea, and Malaysia were also affected. The East Asian Miracle turned into an Asian Financial Nightmare. Despite the affected countries receiving only praise before the crisis, weaknesses had built up, including current account deficits, low foreign reserves and high external debt. In particular, the countries had recently liberalised their financial system in line with international advice. This enabled local private companies to freely borrow from abroad, mainly in US dollars. Companies and banks in Korea, Indonesia, and Thailand had in each country rapidly accumulated over a hundred billion dollars of external loans. This was the Achilles heel that led their countries to crisis" (Martin Khor, "Bigger Global Crisis Started in 2008: Asian Financial Crisis Twenty Years Later," *Sunday Observer*, July 16, 2017, accessed October 27, 2018, http://www.sundayobserver.lk/2017/07/16/business/bigger-global-crisis-started-2008-asian-financial-crisis-20-years-later).

110. Park et al., "Why Did Asian Countries Fare Better during the Global Financial Crisis than during the Asian Financial Crisis?," 138.

111. Park et al., "Why Did Asian Countries Fare Better during the Global Financial Crisis than during the Asian Financial Crisis?," 107–9.

112. Schüller and Wogart, "The Emergence of Post-crisis Regional Financial Institutions in Asia."

113. In 2012–13, a number of significant international exhibitions featuring Cambodian contemporary art put Cambodia on the global art market's radar. This was part of a longer trajectory of Khmer artistic production that Pamela Corey marks as having emerged in 2003–10 from the post–Khmer Rouge era's cultural reconstruction and development. Corey writes, "In 2012 and 2013 Cambodian artists were showcased in some of the most prominent cities for contemporary art in the world. Works by sculptor Pich Sopheap, photographer Vandy Rattana, and the late painter Vann Nath were exhibited at Documenta (13) in Kassel, Germany. Pich enjoyed solo exhibitions at The Metropolitan Museum of Art and at his representative gallery, Tyler Rollins Fine Arts, in New York City, and in the group show Phnom Penh: Rescue Archaeology/Contemporary Art

and Urban Change, hosted by the Institut für Auslandsbeziehungen (Institute of Foreign Relations) in Berlin and Stuttgart. The Season of Cambodia Living Arts Festival occupied numerous center stages in New York City during the months of April and May 2013, organizing performances of dance, music, and theater, and through its Visual Arts Program, residencies, and exhibitions for ten visual artists and one curator." For an expanded discussion of timelines of Khmer contemporary art, see Corey, "The 'First' Cambodian Contemporary Artist," 61.

114. Muan, "Citing Angkor."

115. Corey, "The 'First' Cambodian Contemporary Artist," 64.

116. Lim, *Translating Time*, 32.

117. Cassidy, "The Real Cost of the 2008 Financial Crisis." The White House calls the 3.7 percent unemployment rate in August 2019 a "near-historic" low; it is comparable to White House press release, September 6, 2019, accessed September 13, 2019, https://www.whitehouse.gov/articles/u-s-unemployment-rate -remains-at-near-historic-low-of-3–7-percent-african-american-unemployment -rate-hits-new-series-low.

118. "The Origins of the Financial Crisis," *The Economist*, September 7, 2013, accessed October 29, 2018, https://www.economist.com/schools-brief/2013/09/07 /crash-course.

119. Tooze, *Crashed*, 20.

120. Brunschwig et al., "The Global Financial Crisis," 1–3.

121. In addition to these two models of viewing the 2008 fiscal crisis, there have been other stances: "More recently, there has been a more nuanced view of the global imbalances that emphasizes the unique role of the US financial markets to effectively intermediate world savings." Perhaps a major lesson that comes out of this analysis—and that has not yet been fully appreciated—is the importance of accelerating financial market development in Asia and, in particular, developing sound and liquid financial instruments as a means to contain the pressure for safe assets in the United States and the risk of global financial instability. For an in-depth analysis of Asia's responses to the 1997 and 2008 fiscal crises, see Brunschwig et al., "The Global Financial Crisis."

122. For more on Australia's trade shift away from Europe and toward Asia, see "Global Interaction Australia: New Links to Asia," episode 15 of *The Power of Place: Geography in the 21st Century*, video series, Annenberg Learner, 2003, accessed March 12, 2018, https://www.learner.org/resources/series180.html. See also "Australia and the World: Trade," Australian Department of Foreign Affairs and Trade website, accessed August 11, 2018, https://dfat.gov.au/about-australia /australia-world/Pages/trade.aspx.

123. Divya Skene, "ASEAN: Here Comes the Neighborhood," Australia Trade and Investment Commission, May 12, 2017, accessed December 6, 2018, https://www .austrade.gov.au/News/Economic-analysis/asean-here-comes-the-neighbourhood.

124. "The Economics of Australia Security in Asia," East Asia Forum, November 14, 2016, accessed August 1, 2020, https://www.eastasiaforum.org/2016/11/14 /the-economics-of-australias-security-in-asia/.

125. "Countries and Regions: Australia," European Commission, Council of the European Union, Brussels, May 22, 2018, accessed August 8, 2018, http://ec .europa.eu/trade/policy/countries-and-regions/countries/australia.

126. "Commission Welcomes Green Light to Start Trade Negotiations with Australia and New Zealand," European Commission, Council of the European Union, Brussels, May 22, 2018, accessed August 8, 2018, http://trade.ec.europa.eu /doclib/press/index.cfm?id=1843.

127. Schüller and Wogart, "The Emergence of Post-crisis Regional Financial Institutions in Asia," 488.

128. In 2017, European Union investment in Australia was $106 billion, with two-way trade valued at $98 billion: "Australia-EU Trade Statistics," Australian Department of Foreign Affairs and Trade, December 21, 2018, accessed August 8, 2018, https://dfat.gov.au/about-us/publications/trade-investment/business-envoy /Pages/january-2018/australia-eu-trade-statistics.aspx.

129. Chakrabarty, *Provincializing Europe*, 16.

130. Sylvia Tsai, "Salvage Operation: Patrick D. Flores," *Art Asia Pacific*, May–June 2015, 49, accessed June 5, 2018, http://artasiapacific.com/Magazine/93 /PatrickDFlores.

131. Kwon, *One Place after Another*, 166.

132. See Jay, "Scopic Regimes of Modernity."

133. Kwon, *One Place after Another*, 166.

134. See Bishop, *Artificial Hells*.

135. Susan Gunelius, "Understanding the New ROI of Marketing," *Forbes*, May 14, 2012, accessed July 24, 2016, http://www.forbes.com/sites/work-in -progress/2012/05/14/understanding-the-new-roi-of-marketing/#e0a908222fe9.

136. Williams, *Keywords*, 271.

137. Halberstam, *The Queer Art of Failure*, 129.

138. "Rules of engagement must be consistent while also accounting for a variety of potential scenarios and the political and military aspects of a given situation. They might describe appropriate action regarding unarmed mobs, the property of local civilians, the use of force in self-defense, the returning of hostile fire, the taking of prisoners, the level of hostility (that is, whether the country is at war), as well as a number of other issues" ("Rules of Engagement: Military Directives," *Encyclopaedia Brittannica*, accessed June 13, 2018, https://www.britannica .com/topic/rules-of-engagement-military-directives).

139. "Rules of Engagement."

140. United Nations, *Handbook on United Nations Multidimensional Peacekeeping Operations*, 140.

141. United Nations, *Handbook on United Nations Multidimensional Peacekeeping Operations*, 113–17.

142. Joint Doctrine for Military Operations Other than War, accessed June 12, 2018, https://www.globalsecurity.org/military/library/policy/army/fm/27–100 /chap8.htm#8.1.

143. "Rules of Engagement."

144. "Rules of Engagement."

145. See, e.g., Mirzoeff, "Invisible Empire," 21–44; Puar, *Terrorist Assemblages*.

146. Mirzoeff, "Invisible Empire," 27–40.

147. Cheang Sokha, "asean to Consider Border Talks," *Phnom Penh Post*, August 19, 2010.

148. Prashanth Parameswaran, "What's Next for Cambodia-Vietnam Military Ties in 2018?," *The Diplomat*, February 7, 2018, accessed February 10, 2018, https://thediplomat.com/2018/02/whats-next-for-vietnam-cambodia-military-ties-in-2018.

149. "Forum Promotes Vietnamese Cambodia Trade and Investment," *Nhân Dân*, July 10, 2019, accessed September 11, 2019, https://en.nhandan.org.vn/business/economy/item/7676002-forum-promotes-vietnam-%E2%80%93-cambodia-trade-and-investment-cooperation.html.

150. "Among Top Investors in Cambodia," *Việt Nam Investment Review*, July 4, 2017, accessed March 10, 2018, http://www.vir.com.vn/vn-among-top-investors-in-cambodia-48479.html.

151. "Central Bank Buys $6.38 Billion to Build up Reserves," *Việt Nam News*, May 4, 2019, accessed September 1, 2019, https://vietnamnews.vn/economy/519439/central-bank-buys-835-billion-to-build-foreign-reserves.html#jmQLDZImvORtbh7Y.97. "Vietnam's Record High Forex Reserves Help Ensure Economic Stability," *Hanoi Times*, April 11, 2020, accessed August 1, 2020, http://hanoitimes.vn/vietnam-record-high-forex-reserves-help-ensure-economic-stability-cbank-governor-311708.html.

152. Williams, *The Long Revolution*, 64.

153. For more, see Clifford Geertz, "Description: Toward and Interpretive Theory of Culture," in Geertz, *The Interpretation of Culture*, chap. 1. The author muses that we must continually "uncover the degree to which [an action's] meaning varies according to the pattern of life by which it is informed. Understanding a people's culture exposes their normalness without reducing their particularity" (Geertz, *The Interpretation of Culture*, 14).

154. Geertz, *The Interpretation of Culture*, i.

155. Schwenkel, *The American War in Contemporary Vietnam*, 14.

156. Rafael, "The Cultures of Area Studies in the United States," 91.

157. Foster, *The Return of the Real*, 198.

158. Machida, *Unsettled Visions*, 8.

159. Pratt, *Contact Zones*, 6–15.

160. Hall, "Cultural Identity and Diaspora," 21.

161. Demos notes that in general, attention to diasporas in the academic and art worlds emerged in the 1980s; to nomadism, in the 1990s; and to refugees and forced displacement, in the 2000s (Demos, *The Migrant Image*, 103).

162. Mathur, *The Migrant's Time*, ix.

163. Mathur, *The Migrant's Time*, ix.

164. Petersen, *Migration into Art*.

165. In *Migration into Art*, Anne Ring Petersen "concentrates on artists as professional labour migrants and considers the impact of migration and globalisation on

artists' career patterns and the conditions of being an artist" (Petersen, *Migration into Art*, 36).

166. Petersen, *Migration into Art*, 10.
167. Braziel and Mannur, *Theorizing Diaspora*, 4.
168. Palumbo-Liu, *Asian/American*, 344.
169. Braziel and Mannur, *Theorizing Diaspora*, 4.
170. Lowe, *Immigrant Acts*, 60–97.
171. Aguilar-San Juan, "Going Home," 25.
172. Palumbo-Liu, *Asian/American*, 345.
173. Carruthers, "Saigon from the Diaspora."
174. Um, "Exiled Memory," 833.
175. Um, *From the Land of Shadows*.
176. Deleuze and Guattari, *A Thousand Plateaus*, 422–23.
177. Deleuze and Guattari, *A Thousand Plateaus*, xvii.
178. Sara Ahmed, "Institutional as Usual," Feminist Killjoys (blog), October 24, 2017, accessed August 9, 2018, https://feministkilljoys.com/2017/10/24/institutional-as-usual.
179. Palumbo-Liu, *Asian/American*, 345.
180. Braziel and Mannur, *Theorizing Diaspora*, 8.
181. Szanton, *The Politics of Knowledge*.
182. The postcolonial theorist Gayatri Spivak wrote about the ways in which multivalent identitarian groups (nationalities, minorities, ethnicities) deliberately present themselves outwardly as a unified entity toward common goals or interests, despite differences. This is a "a strategic use of positivist essentialism in a scrupulously visible political interest" (Landry and MacLean, *The Spivak Reader*, 214).
183. For a discussion of the limitations and potential of area studies and a Southeast Asian American study, see Nguyen, "Refugee Memories and Asian American Critique."
184. Yến Lê Espiritu, *Body Counts: The Vietnam War and Militarized Refuge(es)*.
185. Espiritu, "Vietnam, the Philippines, Guam and California," 10–20.
186. Việt Thanh Nguyễn, "The Authenticity of the Anonymous," 58–67.
187. Lê and Min, "'Curatorial Conversations/Correspondences."
188. Việt Lê and Yong Soon Min, eds., "Việt Nam and Us," special issue of *BOL* (winter 2007).
189. M. T. Nguyễn, *The Gift of Freedom*, 32.
190. Derrida, *Given Time*, 44.
191. Ferguson, "The Gift of Freedom," 41.
192. Ferguson, "The Gift of Freedom," 49.
193. Ferguson, "The Gift of Freedom," 42.
194. Bataille, *The Accursed Share*, 70–72.
195. Gramsci, *Prison Notebooks*, 168.
196. Gramsci, *Prison Notebooks*, 41.

197. For more readings on self-reflexivity and positionality, see Foley, *Critical Ethnography*; hooks, *From Margin to Center*; Maher and Tetreault, *The Feminist Classroom*; Marcus, *Ethnography through Thick and Thin*.

198. Gramsci, *Prison Notebooks*, 169.

199. Ferguson observes, "When the economics of the objects are transcended, only the economics of relationship and affect endure. At the heart of the gift, then, stands the act of giving, not the need or pleasure of receipt. In the annihilation of the thing, the subjugation of the other is all that remains" (Ferguson, "The Gift of Freedom," 43).

200. Mimi Thi Nguyễn, *The Gift of Freedom*, 8.

201. Mimi Thi Nguyễn, *The Gift of Freedom*, 8.

202. Ferguson, "The Gift of Freedom," 44.

203. Việt Thanh Nguyễn, "Just Memory," 148.

204. Mimi Thi Nguyễn, *The Gift of Freedom*, 8.

205. Derrida, *Memoirs of the Blind*, 30.

Chapter One. What Remains

1. An earlier, shorter version of this chapter was published as Lê, "What Remains."

2. It is uncanny how Mike's story of departure mirrors mine. I fled at around the same age, also with my mother. My earliest childhood memory is also of an airplane and landing in America: I received a yellow nylon jacket to keep me warm. But unlike Siv, I reunited with my father rather than leaving him in going to the United States, and unlike Siv, I am the son of a man who did not live into my adulthood. Mike's return to Cambodia in 2002 reunited him with the father he could not remember; my first return to Việt Nam, in 2006, came after my father's death but reunited me with other father figures, such as my uncles.

3. Chandler notes that Indochina (both the region and the wars that took place there) is represented centripetally, as "places and events that happen to Americans; the war becomes 'America's longest'; it is inconceivable that the Vietnamese—or the Cambodians—should be allowed into the center of their own national stages, competent to make their own decisions and their own . . . history, and the perception is that Americans are something that are happening to *them*, rather than the inverse": Chandler, "'The Killing Fields' and Perceptions of Cambodian History."

4. Boyle, "Shattering Silence," 96.

5. For more on the concept of haunting, memory, and the effects of violence, see Gordon, *Ghostly Matters*.

6. "Neoliberal audiences" here refers to viewers situated in the global North. According to the *American Heritage Dictionary*, neoliberalism is a "political movement beginning in the 1960s that blends traditional liberal concerns for social justice with an emphasis on economic growth." The political philosopher Paul Treanor notes, "Neoliberalism is a philosophy in which the existence and operation of a market are valued in themselves, separately from any previous rela-

tionship with the production of goods and services . . . and where the operation of a market or market-like structure is seen as an ethic in itself, capable of acting as a guide for all human action, and substituting for all previously existing ethical beliefs": Paul Treanor, "Neoliberalism: Origins, Theory, Definition," accessed August 1, 2013, http://web.inter.nl.net/users/Paul.Treanor/neoliberalism.html.

7. In the *Loss* anthology, Eng and Kazanjian write, "The politics of mourning might be descriptive that create a process meeting between loss and history. . . . [They advocate for examining how] our losses have been animated for hopeful and hopeless politics": Eng and Kazanjian, *Loss*, 2.

8. Chandler, *A History of Cambodia*, 12–39.

9. For more on Cambodia's past and present, including current country statistics such as gross domestic product, see "Background Note: Cambodia," US Department of State, accessed September 26, 2010, http://www.state.gov/r/pa/ei/bgn/2732.htm.

10. Trouillot, *Silencing the Past*, 6. Trouillot examines the Haitian Revolution, the Alamo, the politics of Columbus Day, a proposed Disney theme park display on slavery, and other sites of social memory and erasure. By examining how memory is constructed within historical narratives, he reveals incompatible tendencies within historical discourse.

11. Chandler, "Revisiting the Past in Democratic Kampuchea," 288–300.

12. Etcheson, *After the Killing Fields*, 3–5.

13. Etcheson, *After the Killing Fields*, 4.

14. Duffy, "Toward a Culture of Human Rights in Cambodia," 91.

15. James Gibson, *The Perfect War*.

16. Young, *The Vietnam Wars*.

17. Robert Sheer, "Cambodia's Anguish: Made in the USA," *Los Angeles Times,* July 8, 1997.

18. Young, *The Vietnam Wars*, 235.

19. Moss, "*S-21: The Khmer Rouge Killing Machine* Review."

20. Duffy, "Toward a Culture of Human Rights in Cambodia," 85.

21. Duffy, "Toward a Culture of Human Rights in Cambodia," 84.

22. Hinton, *Why Did They Kill?*, 1.

23. Sheer, "Cambodia's Anguish."

24. Hinton, *Why Did They Kill?*, 2.

25. St. John, *Revolution, Reform and Regionalism in Southeast Asia*, 179–81.

26. "The Humbling of Hun Sen: Cambodia's Strongman Gets a Shock at the Polls," *The Economist,* Asia ed., August 3, 2013.

27. Ben Sokhean, "Hun Sen Thanks Voters amid CPP Claim of Assembly Sweep," *Phnom Penh Post*, accessed December 15, 2018, https://www.phnompenhpost.com/national/hun-sen-thanks-voters-amid-cpp-claim-assembly-sweep.

28. "Hen Sen: Cambodia's Strongman Prime Minister," *BBC News: Asia,* July 25, 2018, accessed December 15, 2018, https://www.bbc.com/news/world-asia-23257699.

29. Barensten, "Freud, Jung, and the Dangerous Supplement to Psychoanalysis."

30. Eng and Kazanjian, *Loss*, 3–7.

31. Schlund-Vials, *War, Genocide, and Justice*, 189.

32. Eng and Kazanjian, *Loss*, 5.

33. Parr, *The Deleuze Dictionary*.

34. Against Western notions of retributive action, Thompson reads the painter Vann Nath's silent, passive agency and "standing" as he engages his former S-21 prison guards in the film *S-21* as the embodiment of Buddhist ideals of nonattachment to *samsara*; Thompson, "Mnemotechnical Politics."

35. For futher reading, see Derrida and Spivak, *Of Grammatology*; Derrida, *Margins of Philosophy*; Derrida, *Limited Inc.*

36. Saussure's theories on structural linguistics paved the way for subsequent discussions on the gaps between representation, language, and culture in anthropology, psychoanalysis, media studies, and so on; Saussure, *Course in General Linguistics*.

37. Derrida, *Limited Inc.*, 236.

38. Derrida, *Limited Inc.*, 236, emphasis added.

39. Bernasconi, "Supplement," 19.

40. Derrida and Spivak, *Of Grammatology*, 144.

41. Panh's *Missing Picture* (2014), also about the Khmer Rouge genocide, was nominated for the Oscar for Best Foreign Language Film. In the *Japan Times* article, Panh also connects himself with his country, writing, "I don't have the impression of going to Los Angeles all alone. . . . I feel like I'm going with my whole country": "Cambodia Vies for First Oscar with 'Missing Picture,'" *Japan Times*, Asia Pacific ed., February 28, 2014, accessed September 16, 2018, https://www .japantimes.co.jp/news/2014/02/28/asia-pacific/cambodia-vies-for-first-oscar -with-missing-picture.

42. Derrida, *Margins of Philosophy*, 195.

43. Schlund-Vials frames the ongoing Khmer Rouge tribunal tribulations as a "(non)pursuit of justice": Schlund-Vials, *War, Genocide, and Justice*, 4–8.

44. Schlund-Vials, *War, Genocide, and Justice*, 17.

45. Freud, "Project for a Scientific Psychology," 398.

46. Bistoen et al., "Nachträglichkeit," 687.

47. Derrida, *Dissemination*, 125.

48. Derrida, *Dissemination*, 127.

49. Boyle, "Shattering Silence," 99.

50. Thompson, "Mnemotechnical Politics," 239.

51. Thompson, "Mnemotechnical Politics," 240.

52. Thompson, "Forgetting to Remember, Again: On Curatorial Practice and 'Cambodian Art' in the Wake of Genocide." See also Thompson's "Memoires du Cambodge."

53. Sturken, *Tangled Memories*, 8.

54. Alexander et al., *Cultural Trauma and Collective Identity*, 44.

55. Alexander et al., *Cultural Trauma and Collective Identity*, 78.

56. This phrase is from Jeffrey Alexander, "Social Construction of Moral Universals," in Alexander et al., *Cultural Trauma and Collective Identity*, 227–29.

57. Scarry, *The Body in Pain*, xiv.

58. Leshu Torchin, *Creating the Witness: Documenting Genocide on Film, Video, and the Internet*.

59. Lisa Moore, "Recovering the Past, Remembering Trauma," 47–63.

60. For more on the early East German documentary-filming process in post-genocide Cambodia, see Maquire, *Facing Death in Cambodia*, 94–96.

61. Sturken, *Tangled Memories*, 8.

62. Marshall McLuhan, *The Medium Is the Message*.

63. Sturken, *Tangled Memories*, 259.

64. Panh, "Bophana."

65. Rithy Panh, "Cambodia: A Wound That Will not Heal," UNESCO *Courier*, December 1999, accessed December 12, 2011, http://www.unesco.org/courier/1999 _12/uk/dossier/txt07.htm.

66. Panh, "Cambodia."

67. Panh, "Cambodia."

68. For more critical writing on Panh's work, see Hamilton, "Cambodian Genocide," 175; Boyle, "Trauma, Memory, Documentary"; Thompson, "Mnemotechnical Politics."

69. Keo, "Fact Sheet on 'S-21' Tuol Sleng Prison," 1.

70. Rithy Panh, dir., *S-21: The Khmer Rouge Killing Machine*, DVD, First Run Features, 2003.

71. Keo, "Fact Sheet on 'S-21' Tuol Sleng Prison," 2.

72. In the Documentation Center of Cambodia's fact sheet on S-21, Dacil Keo writes, "The release status of the 179 prisoners (of which 100 were soldiers) is based on numerous Khmer Rouge documents and interviews compiled primarily by Tuol Sleng Genocide Museum senior archivist Mr. Nean Yin. Most of the 179 who were released have disappeared and only a few are known to have survived after 1979. Of the 23 who survived after 1979, more than half have disappeared or have died since. Several of the survivors who are alive today have recently made the news: Norng Chanphal for being a witness for Case 001 of the Khmer Rouge Tribunal, Vann Nath and Chum Mei for being featured in documentary films, and Bou Meng for having a book published about him." For a detailed list of released prisoners and survivors, see Documentation Center of Cambodia (DC-Cam), accessed March 15, 2020, http://www.dccam.org/Archives/Documents /Confessions/pdf/Fact_Sheet_on_S-21_Tuol_Sleng_Prison.pdf.

73. Chandler, *Voices from S-21*, 4.

74. Duffy, "Toward a Culture of Human Rights in Cambodia," 91.

75. Chandler, *Voices from S-21*, 4.

76. Chandler, *Voices from S-21*.

77. Chandler, *Voices from S-21*, 5.

78. Chandler, *Voices from S-21*, 8.

79. Chandler, *Voices from S-21*.

80. Hinton, *Why Did They Kill?*, 4.

81. First Run Features, press release, December 30, 2003, New York.

82. Hinton, *Why Did They Kill?*, 5.

83. Christopher Shay, "The Khmer Rouge Tribunal: Cambodia's Healing Process," *Time,* November 30, 2009, accessed May 27, 2011, http://www.time.com/time/world/article/0,8599,1943373,00.html.

84. Thompson, "Mnemotechnical Politics," 225.

85. Thompson writes, "The association, explicitly made in these demands, between the remembrance of genocide and democratic political rehabilitation is firmly grounded in the twentieth-century experience of the Shoah in Europe and its Euro-American commemorative aftermath"; Thompson, "Mnemotechnical Politics," 225.

86. Rofel, "Discrepant Modernities and Their Discontents," 640–41.

87. Rofel, "Discrepant Modernities and Their Discontents," 641.

88. See Deleuze and Guattari, *A Thousand Plateaus*, chap. 12.

89. Rofel, "Discrepant Modernities and their Discontents," 640–43.

90. Rithy Panh, dir., *S-21: The Khmer Rouge Killing Machine*, documentary, 2003, at 37:50.

91. Adorno, *Minima Moralia*, 168.

92. Adorno states, "Indignation over cruelty diminishes in proportion as the victims are less like normal readers, the more they are swarthy, 'dirty', dago-like. The constantly encountered assertion that slaves, blacks, Japanese are like animals, monkeys, for example, is the key to the pogrom. . . . This throws as much light on the crimes as the spectators. Perhaps the social schematization of perception in anti-Semites is such that they do not see Jews as human beings at all"; Adorno, *Minima Moralia*, 105.

93. Panh, *S-21*, 1:27:25–1:30:24.

94. Vann, *A Cambodian Prison Portrait*.

95. Freud, "Mourning and Melancholia."

96. Freud, "Mourning and Melancholia," 244.

97. Freud, "Mourning and Melancholia," 240.

98. Freud, "Mourning and Melancholia," 240.

99. Freud, "Mourning and Melancholia," 248–50.

100. Freud, *Beyond the Pleasure Principle*, 14.

101. Panh, "Cambodia."

102. Eng and Kazanjian, *Loss*, 3.

103. Eng and Kazanjian, *Loss*, 4.

104. Eng and Kazanjian, *Loss*, 4.

105. Eng and Kazanjian, *Loss*, 4.

106. Tracing Vann Nath's artistic career before and after the Khmer Rouge, Corey writes, "Prior to 1975, [Vann] Nath had learned to paint from observation during his monkhood from the ages of seventeen to twenty-one, followed by enrollment in private painting courses and a subsequent apprenticeship, after which

he began to paint professionally, receiving commissions for portraits, landscapes, movie posters, and large-scale panel paintings. After 1975, the act of painting during his imprisonment was a form of coerced artistic labor, as he was directed by the regime to paint portraits of Pol Pot and other leaders, and subsequently the Vietnamese-backed regime of the PRK tasked him with illustrating nightmarish episodes of his imprisonment for the Tuol Sleng Museum of Genocide": Corey, "The 'First' Cambodian Contemporary Artist."

107. Corey, "The 'First' Cambodian Contemporary Artist," 85–86.

108. Thompson, "Forgetting to Remember Again," 83.

109. Freud, "Mourning and Melancholia," 243–44.

110. Thompson, "Mnemotechnical Politics," 240.

111. Felman and Laub, *Testimony*, 69.

112. Rithy Panh, interview with the author, July 26, 2010, Bophana Center, Phnom Penh.

113. Derek Elley writes in *Variety* that *S-21* "dissipates its impact through repetition and over-leisurely pacing"; Derek Elley, "Review of *S-21: The Khmer Rouge Killing Machine*," May 13, 2003, accessed May 13, 2003, https://variety.com/2003/film/markets-festivals/s21-the-khmer-rouge-killing-machine-1200541644.

114. Leslie Camhi, "The Banal Faces of Khmer Rouge Evil," *New York Times*, May 16, 2004, 24.

115. Hamilton, "Witness and Recuperation," 9.

116. Ann Hornaday, "'S-21': Cambodia's Bloody Hands," *Washington Post*, June 11, 2004, accessed September 27, 2018, http://www.washingtonpost.com/wp-dyn/articles/A33190-2004Jun10.html.

117. Thompson, "A Witness to Genocide," 26.

118. Cathy Caruth, *Unclaimed Experience: Trauma, Narrative, and History*.

119. Felman and Laub, *Testimony*, 70.

120. Ly and Muan, *The Legacy of Absence*.

121. Among the artists in the exhibition *The Legacy of Absence* were Tum Saren, Svay Ken, Vann Nath, Phy Chan Than, Ly Daravuth, Ngeth Sim, and Soueng Vannara. More information about the artists can be found in the print catalogue and online at https://asianart.com/exhibitions/legacy/index.html.

122. Thompson, "Mnemotechnical Politics," 232.

123. Thompson, "Mnemotechnical Politics," 233.

124. Thompson, "Mnemotechnical Politics," 233, emphasis added.

125. Thompson, "A Witness to Genocide," 27.

126. Thompson, "A Witness to Genocide," 27.

127. Felman and Laub, *Testimony*, 116.

128. See Human Rights Watch, "Cambodia Country Report 2010," accessed September 3, 2010, http://www.hrw.org/en/node/87393.

129. Rankings for 2016 by the organization Transparency International place Cambodia in the top twenty of most corrupt countries (156/176), with a score of 21/100 (with 0 indicating highly corrupt and 100 indicating clean). Transparency

International, accessed January 10, 2018, https://www.transparency.org/country/KHM#.

130. In addition to justice, corruption limits economic development, as it limits investment in the country: World Bank, *World Economic Forum,* December 3, 2012, accessed August 2, 2020, https://www.weforum.org/agenda/2012/12/does-foreign-aid-fuel-corruption/.

131. *Khmer Machas Srok Daily*, December 9, 2009 interview, accessed August 1, 2020, http://kmsdaily.blogspot.com.

132. *Khmer Machas Srok* 3, no.546, December 4, 2009, accessed December 4, 2009, https://khmernz.blogspot.com/2009/12/prime-minister-said-that-to-summon-more.html.

133. "The four top former Khmer Rouge leaders, who are at present already being detained, are the former head of state, Mr. Khieu Samphan; the former president of the National Assembly, Mr. Nuon Chea; the former Deputy Prime Minister and Minister of Foreign Affairs, Mr. Ieng Sary; and the former Minister of Social Affairs, Ms. Ieng Thirith; in addition, there is also the former S-21 (Tuol Sleng) prison chief Duch, who was a middle level leader, who was brought first to the hearings": *Khmer Machas Srok* 3, no. 546, December 4, 2009, 5.

134. Robbie Corey Poulet, "S-21 Chief Downplays Role in Final Statements," *Phnom Penh Post*, November 26, 2009, accessed November 27, 2009, https://www.phnompenhpost.com/national/s-21-chief-downplays-role-final-statements.

135. Shay, "The Khmer Rouge Tribunal," 3.

136. Poulet, "S-21 Chief Downplays Role in Final Statements."

137. Seth Mydans, "Cambodia Arrests Former Khmer Rouge Head of State," *New York Times*, November 20, 2007, accessed July 29, 2011, www.nytimes.com/2007/11/20/world/asia/20cambo.html.

138. Samphan, *L'histoire récente du Cambodge et mes prises de position.*

139. "Using smuggled footage, this documentary [*Burma VJ: Reporting from a Closed Country*] tells the story of the 2007 protests in Burma by thousands of monks": *Burma VJ*, directed by Anders Østergaard, starring Ko Muang and Aung San Suu Kyi," Internet Movie Database, http://www.imdb.com/video/imdb/vi1823277593/.

140. Duch, quoted in Shay, "The Khmer Rouge Tribunal," 4.

141. Panh interview.

142. Panh interview.

143. Mark Vlasic, "Life for Comrade Duch, a Milestone for International Justice," *The Guardian*, March 13, 2012, accessed March 14, 2012, https://www.theguardian.com/commentisfree/cifamerica/2012/mar/13/cambodia-khmer-rouge.

144. Seth Mydans, "Duch, Prison Chief Who Slaughtered for the Khmer Rouge, Is Dead at 77," *The New York Times*, September 1, 2020, accessed September 2, 2020, https://www.nytimes.com/2020/09/01/world/asia/duch-kaing-guek-eav-dead.html.

145. Zoe Murphy, "Chum Mey: Tuol Sleng Survivor," BBC *News*, July 26, 2010, accessed July 27, 2010, http://www.bbc.co.uk/news/world-asia-pacific-10602689 ?print=true.

146. Panh, "Cambodia," 30.

147. Việt Thanh Nguyễn, *Nothing Ever Dies*, 40, 267.

148. Eng and Kazanjian, *Loss*, 5.

149. Derrida, *Memoirs of the Blind*, 30.

150. Việt Thanh Nguyễn, *Nothing Ever Dies*, 12.

151. Việt Thanh Nguyễn, *Nothing Ever Dies*, 9.

152. Espiritu, *Militarized Refuge(es)*, 7.

153. Schlund-Vials, *War, Genocide and Justice*, 194.

154. Việt Thanh Nguyễn, *Nothing Ever Dies*, 76.

155. Việt Thanh Nguyễn, *Nothing Ever Dies*, 12.

156. Schlund-Vials, *War, Genocide, and Justice*, 18.

157. Eng and Kazanjian, *Loss*, 5.

158. Espiritu argues that Southeast Asian war refugees of the 1970s were seen as "returning" to Western countries that had a direct role in their displacement. This "return" was facilitated with greater ease as these powers had preexisting militarized routes and infrastructure in place. Espiritu, *Militarized Refuge(es)*, 7–20.

159. "Spencer Nakasako has over three decades of experience as an independent filmmaker. He won a National Emmy Award for *A.K.A. Don Bonus*, the video diary of a Cambodian refugee teenager that aired on the PBS series *P.O.V.* and screened at the Berlin International Film Festival. *Kelly Loves Tony*, a video diary about a Iu Mien refugee teenage couple growing up too fast in Oakland, California, also aired on *P.O.V.* His third film in his trilogy about Southeast Asian youth, *Refugee*, aired on the PBS series *Independent Lens*, and garnered major awards at the Hawaii International Film Festival and Hamptons Film Festival. He also wrote the screenplay and co-directed a feature film in Hong Kong, *Life Is Cheap . . . but Toilet Paper Is Expensive*, with Wayne Wang. . . . Besides consultancies and residencies at Stanford, Harvard, the Walker Art Center in Minneapolis, USC, UCLA, the Virginia Foundation for the Humanities, and the University of Toronto, to name a few, he has lectured in the Social Documentation graduate program at the University of California at Santa Cruz, and is currently a lecturer at the Graduate School of Journalism at the University of California at Berkeley. Nakasako is a member of the Writers Guild of America, and the Academy of Motion Picture Arts and Sciences": Faculty website for Spencer Nakasako, University of California, Berkeley, accessed September 27, 2018, https://journalism.berkeley .edu/person/spencer_nakasako.

160. Spencer Nakasako, "Director's Commentary," in Nakasako, *Refugee*.

161. Porthira Chhim, "Cambodian Americans," *Asian-Nation: The Landscape of Asian America*, accessed August 13, 2013, http://www.asian-nation.org /cambodian.shtml.

162. The Pew Research Center notes that 2000–2015 data are based on US Census information. The "2015 population estimates are from the 2015 American

Community Survey one-year estimates (American FactFinder)"; "Cambodians: Data on Asian Americans," Pew Research Center, December 8, 2007, accessed January 10, 2018, http://www.pewsocialtrends.org/fact-sheet/asian-americans -cambodians-in-the-u-s. The US Census population estimate for 2016 is 323,127, 513 Cambodians; American FactFinder, US Census, accessed January 11, 2018, https://factfinder.census.gov/faces/nav/jsf/pages/community_facts.xhtml. In 2010, 231,616 (84 percent) are identified as Cambodian and 45,051 are identified as part-Cambodian; American FactFinder, US Census, accessed August 13, 2013, http://www.Factfinder2.census.gov.

163. My-Thuan Tran, "Building a New Destination," *Los Angeles Times*, November 1, 2009, A43, A47.

164. Ong, *Buddha Is Hiding*.

165. Cheng, *The Melancholy of Race*, 9.

166. Um, "Exiled Memory," 836.

167. *Logos* is described as "discourse," speech, father; *logos* also represents the father—chief, capital, goods, "for only the 'living' discourse, only a spoken word (and not a speech's theme, object or subject) can have a father"; Derrida, *Dissemination*, 78–81.

168. Hughes, "Memory and Sovereignty in Post-1979 Cambodia: Choeung Ek and Local Genocide Memorials," 257–79.

169. Yaeger, "Consuming Trauma; or, The Pleasures of Merely Circulating," 25–51.

170. Yaeger, "Consuming Trauma," 26.

171. Alexander et al., *Cultural Trauma and Collective Identity*.

172. Oliver, *Women as Weapons of War*, 106.

173. Miller and Tougaw, *Extremities: Trauma, Testimony and Community*.

174. Derrida, *The Work of Mourning*, 41–42.

175. Derrida, *The Work of Mourning*, 159.

176. Derrida, *The Work of Mourning*, 160.

177. Vann, *A Cambodian Prison Portrait*, 117.

Chapter Two. The Art Part

1. Gilroy, *The Black Atlantic: Modernity and Double Consciousness*.

2. Foucault, *Discipline and Punish*.

3. Hinton, *Why Did They Kill?*, 5.

4. Chandler, *The Tragedy of Cambodian History*, 1.

5. An earlier, shorter excerpt from this chapter was published in Lê, "Many Returns."

6. Small, "Embodies Economies," 238.

7. Small, "Embodies Economies," 238.

8. Việt Nam Studies Group discussion thread on the term *Việt Kiều*, March 3–12, 2009, accessed August 8, 2018, https://sites.google.com/a/uw.edu /vietnamstudiesgroup/discussion-networking/vsg-discussion-list-archives/vsg -discussion-2009/viet-kieu.

9. Taylor, "Running the Earth," 206.

10. Sue Hajdu critiques the politics of representation as it pertains to returnees within the international art market, writing, "In Vietnam and Cambodia, artists that have come to represent these countries in recent years are often returnees. . . . The presence of such artists sometimes inspires local artists or meets with resentment, particularly due to strategic global positioning or when shows claiming to represent these countries gloss over bio-data or the existence of 'buddy-curating' or cliques. With this region so fresh on the international arena, the opportunities are small and the outcome-risks are high. Thorough curatorial research into the dynamics and activity at ground level is rare and the situation is aggravated by 'instant noodle curators' who drop in for twenty-four hours, meet a few familiar names, then just add water. Curatorial principles fluctuate, with locals sometimes overshadowed by more articulate returnees, or the standards of complexity, conceptualism, criticality and originality de rigueur for overseas-educated artists being more leniently applied to locals, or trumped by market forces. A lingering exoticism means that international artists or photojournalists with long-standing practices in Thailand, Cambodia and Vietnam are frequently ignored" (Hajdu, "Missing the Mekong," 267–69).

11. Spivak, *The Spivak Reader*, 269.

12. Lowe, *Immigrant Acts*, 206–7.

13. Mimi Thi Nguyễn, *The Gift of Freedom*, 666.

14. Sharon Mizota, "Review: Vietnam's Art Shows Off Its Depth and Diversity in This L.A. Show," *Los Angeles Times*, August 6, 2019, accessed September 5, 2019, https://www.latimes.com/entertainment-arts/story/2019-08-07/mistake-room -vietnam-art-show.

15. *Where the Sea Remembers*, curator's statement, The Mistake Room, Los Angeles, July 13, 2019, accessed August 1, 2019, http://www.tmr.la /ewherethesearemembers.

16. Catherine Woman, "Vietnamese Artists Born after the War Offer a Fresh Perspective on the Asian Nation," *Los Angeles Magazine*, July 15, 2019, accessed September 15, 2019, https://www.lamag.com/culturefiles/where-the-sea -remembers.

17. Mizota, "Review: Vietnam's Art Shows Off Its Depth."

18. Spivak, *The Spivak Reader*, 269.

19. Grosz, "Criticism, Feminism and the Institution," 1.

20. Fried, *Art and Objecthood*.

21. Heidegger, "The Origin of the Work of Art," 170.

22. Heidegger, "The Origin of the Work of Art," 199.

23. Peter van der Krogt writes, "The term *chorographia* was defined by Ptolemy as a representation of 'localities such as harbors, farms, villages, river courses and such'; the function of chorography was 'to paint a true likeness and not merely to give exact positions and size.' Chorography therefore is a visual representation that can be understood as a portrait of place. Occasionally the term *chorographer* was used in the Renaissance for maps and map-making of sub-national or county areas. . . . Most

modern European languages derive their word for map from the Greek word *chartès* (χάρτης)" (van der Krogt, "The Origin of the Word 'Cartography,'" 125).

24. Biehl and Locke, "Deleuze and the Anthropology of Becoming," 317.

25. Antoinette, *Reworlding Art History*, li.

26. Vint, "Becoming Other," 287.

27. Vint, "Becoming Other," 287.

28. Rofel, "Discrepant Modernities and Their Discontents."

29. Deleuze and Guattari, *A Thousand Plateaus*, 238.

30. For more on cultural capital, see Bourdieu, "The Forms of Capital."

31. Taylor, "Why Have There Been No Great Vietnamese Artists?," 49–50.

32. For more on the development of the Vietnamese economy over the twelve years, see Keith Bradsher, "Vietnam's Roaring Economy Is Set for World Stage," *New York Times*, October 25, 2006; Clay Chandler and Sheridan Prasso, "Vietnam VROOM: Asia's Second-Fastest Economy Takes the Global Stage," *Fortune*, November 21, 2006; Michael C. Moynihan, "The Ho Chi Minh City Statement," *Reason*, February 26, 2008; Martha Ann Overland, "Vietnam's Troubled Economy," *Time*, June 9, 2008; "Vietnam's Economic Prospects Improve Further, with GDP Projected to Expand by 6.8 Percent in 2018," *World Bank*, June 14, 2018; "Vietnam's Foreign Reserves Reach at an All-Time High of $63 billion," *Hanoi Times*, May 7, 2018, http://www.hanoitimes.vn/economy/2018/05/81e0c633/vietnam-s-foreign-reserves-at-all-time-high-of-us-63-billion.

33. "Economic Recession Goes Down" (interview with Lê Xuân Nghiã), *VietNamNet*, March 16, 2009.

34. World Trade Organization, "General Council Approves Việt Nam 's Membership," press release, January 11, 2007, access January 12, 2007, http://www.wto.org/english/news_e/pres06_e/pr455_e.htm; "Việt Nam Joins WTO," World Trade Organization, January 11, 2007, www.wto.org/english/news_e/news07_e/acc_vietnam_11jan07_e.htm.

35. For more on globalization and its impact on contemporary art, see Bydler, *The Global Art World Inc.*

36. Taylor has written extensively on contemporary art in Việt Nam; see Taylor, *Painters in Hanoi*; Taylor, "Whose Art Are We Studying?"

37. The biannual Festival Huế showcases artists and performances (visual art, music, theater, performance art, traditional arts, and so on) from twenty-seven countries. The festival's theme—"Cultural Heritage with Integration and Development"—is telling in terms of the impact of economic development.

38. Central Intelligence Agency, *The World Factbook 2019*.

39. L'Espace (http://www.ambafrance-vn.org/rubrique.php3?id_rubrique=265), the Goethe Institute (http://www.goethe.de/ins/vn/han/enindex.htm), and the British Council (http://www.britishcouncil.org/vietnam) all provide language instruction and have archival holdings. The British Council (http://www.hanoigrapevine.com) also supports Hanoi Grapevine, a website and group email list that features ongoing updates on cultural events in Hà Nội and Sài Gòn.

40. Describing the avant-garde art scene, the critic and painter Joe Fyfe notes, "The Vietnamese government has not been friendly to this work and the artists have felt more comfortable with the extra ring of protection that an international organization provides"; Joe Fyfe, "Report from Hanoi: Rienke Enghardt and Tran Trung Tin at Art Vietnam, Hanoi," Artcritical.com, November 2006, accessed December 2006, http://www.artcritical.com/fyfe/JFHanoi.htm.

41. *Mission civilisatrice*, French for "civilizing mission," was one of the main phrases for French colonial expansion into West Africa, Indochina, and Algeria in the nineteenth and early twentieth centuries; see Koro-Ljungberg et al., "Mission Civilisatrice."

42. For more on the development of contemporary art in Việt Nam, see Kraevskaia, *Từ Hoài Cổ Hướng Sang Miền Đất Mới*; Nguyễn Nhu Huy, "Asian Art Report," *Arthub*, December 3, 2006, accessed December 30, 2008, http://www.nhuhuy.com/htmls/weblogs_detail_en.php?logid=228&f=1&mon=11&ye=2006.

43. For Đào Anh Khánh's website, see http://www.daoanhkhanh.com. Ryllega Gallery was also an active alternative art space; see the gallery's website, at http://www.ryllegahanoi.com.

44. See the Nhà Sàn Collective website at http://nhasan.org.

45. Art Vietnam (www.artvietnamgallery.com) is one of the most prominent commercial spaces in Hà Nội. Suzanne Lecht, a Texan who has lived in Việt Nam since the early 1990s, runs it (Suzanne Lecht, interview with the author, May 3, 2006, Hà Nội). Other galleries have had varying life spans, including Bui Gallery (http://www.thebuigallery.com), Suffusive Gallery (http://www.suffusiveart.com), Studio Thơ (http://www.studiotho.com), and Maison des Arts (http://maisondesartshanoi.com), among others.

46. Quỳnh Phạm also regularly hosts artists' talks in conjunction with her exhibitions at the Galerie Quynh. Salon Saigon has regular rotating commercial exhibitions, which feature a roster of their artists. Llouquet also curates the founder's permanent collection, which, according to the website, "focuses on how artists put in perspective Vietnamese tradition and heritage with current issues" and includes artworks by Bùi Công Khánh, Tiffany Chung, Hà Mạnh Thắng, Hoàng Dương Cầm, Chinh Lê, Dinh Q. Lê, Lê Hoàng Bích Phượng, Lê Thừa Tiến, Lê Thúy, Nguyễn BanGa, Nguyễn Hữu Trâm Kha, Nguyễn Mạnh Hùng, Nguyễn Phương Linh, Oanh Phi Phi, The Propeller Group, Trần Trọng Vũ, Truc Anh, Trương Tiến Trà, Trương Tân, and Võ Trân Châu, as well as emerging Vietnamese artists.

47. For more on Streitmatter-Tran and his practice, see his website at http://www.diacritic.org.

48. Founded in 1982, IDECAF has an exhibition space, library, and screening room. According to its website, at http://www.idecaf.gov.vn, IDECAF "is an agency under the Department of Foreign Affairs of Hồ Chí Minh City. Institute [offers language] training in French and [aims to create] favorable conditions for

strengthening and developing bilateral [Vietnamese—French] partnerships in the field of culture." Before 1982, the organization was known as the French Culture Institute and was under the auspices of the French Embassy.

In the past, the "artist-run initiative" *albb* (which stands for *a little blah blah*) organized artist talks, residencies, and exhibitions. It was cofounded in 2003 by the Sài Gòn–based artists Sue Hajdu, Nguyễn Như Huy, and Motoko Uda. Starting in 2010, it concentrated on a single large project per year with related programming. It is no longer active.

49. Ungar, "Re-gendering Vietnam," 312–13.

50. Thu-hương, *The Ironies of Freedom*, xv, 144.

51. Hồ Tài, *The Country of Memory*.

52. Mana Magat, "Sex and Drugs Sell," *Eastern Horizons*, no. 14, June 2003, November 24, 2006, http://www.unaids.org.vn/event/sexndrugs.htm.

53. Trinh, *Women, Native, Other*.

54. Trinh, *When the Moon Waxes Red*.

55. Kraevskaia, *Từ Hoài Cổ Hướng Sang Miền Đất Mới*.

56. Three female artists out of approximately one hundred total students attended the EBAI (Taylor, *Painters in Hanoi*).

57. For more on Vietnamese female artists, including historical and contemporary developments, see Taylor, *Changing Identities*, 19–22.

58. Taylor, "Why Have There Been No Great Vietnamese Artists?," 149–65.

59. See Taylor, "Invisible Painters."

60. For more on the exhibition *0395A.ĐC*, see the website at http://factoryartscentre.com/en/event/a-solo-exhibition-by-ly-hoang-ly.

61. "An Artist and Her Work: Dinh Y Nhi: Nguyen Qui Duc visits with Hanoi artist Dinh Y Nhi," *Things Asian*, June 1, 1995, accessed July 5, 2005, http://thingsasian.com/story/artist-and-her-work-dinh-y-nhi.

62. Charles Keyes, "Presidential Address: 'The Peoples of Asia'—Science and Politics in the Classification of Ethnic Groups in Thailand, China, and Vietnam," 1163–203.

63. "Vietnamese Artist Exhibits in Canada," *VietNamBridge*, June 12, 2013, https://english.vietnamnet.vn/fms/artentertainment/77001/vietnamese-artist-exhibits-paintings-in-canada.html.

64. *Asia Art Archive* notes that Tham Poong "shows the uneasy 'emigration' of one's mental and emotional self from a rural structure of life to a more urbanized and dynamic society" ("Artist Profile," *Asia Art Archive*, accessed August 22, 2018, https://aaa.org.hk/en/collection/search/archive/salon-natasha-archive-emigration/object/curriculum-vitae-of-dinh-thi-tham-poong).

65. Fizen Yuen, "Vietnamese Artist Phan Thao Nguyen Won the Signature Art Prize," *Video Art Asia*, July 10, 2018, https://www.cobosocial.com/dossiers/phan-thao-nguyen-won-the-signature-art-prize.

66. See Foster, *The Return of the Real*.

67. An-My Lê was born in Sài Gòn in 1960 and is now based in New York. She received her master of fine arts in photography from Yale University in 1993. For

images of An-My Lê's work, see the Murray Guy Gallery website at http://www
.murrayguy.com/an_my/main.html.

68. In her catalogue essay for Lê's solo exhibition *Small Wars* at the Museum of Contemporary Photography, Chicago, October 27, 2006–January 6, 2007, the curator Karen Irvine wrote, "Lê was often asked to participate in the reenactments, her ethnicity presumably adding an element of authenticity to the make-believe. Over the course of the project she acted various roles ranging from that of a translator to, disconcertingly, a member of the Viet Cong. On occasion she included herself in her photographs, as she performed for the male audience that became, in actuality, her real subject. Sensitive to the fact that what motivates such men is often a complex web of psychological need, fantasy, and a passion for history, Lê did not make a mockery of their actions. In fact, some of her most heavily theatrical images she produced were the ones that she considered the least successful and ultimately edited out of the series. This strategy of avoiding parody allows viewers to form their own opinions of the events and, hopefully, to remember the gravity at their root" (Karen Irvine, "Under the Clouds of War," Museum of Contemporary Photography, Columbia College, Chicago, accessed March 19, 2009, http://www.mocp.org/exhibitions/2000/6/an-my-le-small-wars .php).

69. Liza Nguyễn was born in 1979 in France. She received her master of arts at La Sorbonne in Paris in 1994.

70. Liza Nguyễn, *Souvenirs from Vietnam*, exhibition brochure, Gallery 44, Toronto, 2007. See also the artist's website at http://www.liza-nguyen.com.

71. Young, *The Vietnam Wars*.

72. I think of Walter Benjamin's angel of history, face turned toward the past, with wreckage and detritus piling up at his feet.

73. Uncanny experiences can arise when one "doubts whether an apparently animate being is really alive; or conversely, whether a lifeless object might not be in fact inanimate" (Freud, "The Uncanny," 139).

74. Love is a secondhand emotion, to paraphrase Tina Turner (Terry Britten and Graham Lyle, "What's Love Got to Do with It?," Capitol Records, 1984).

75. Taylor, *Painters in Hanoi*, 103.

76. Interview with Llouquet and Chung, Hô Chì Minh City, May 2008.

77. For more on Le Mois de l'Image, see the website at https://hanoigrapevine .com/2008/09/hcmc-le-mois-de-limage, September 30, 2008, accessed August 1, 2020.

78. Chung's *Vietnam, Past Is Prologue* ran from March 15 to August 25, 2019, and was curated by Sarah Newman. The publicity text on the exhibition's website highlights the Vietnam War: "The project stems from the facts of her own life. Chung's father was a pilot in the South Vietnamese army who fought alongside American forces, and the family immigrated to the United States as part of the post-1975 exodus from that country. Chung examines the narratives that have been used to understand the war and its aftermath, and probes how the America we know today was shaped by Vietnam. . . . Based in painstaking primary

research, *Vietnam, Past Is Prologue* is broad and richly textured, illuminating both the war's scale and the personal stakes of people affected by it. The exhibition features a new series of video interviews with former Vietnamese refugees in Houston, Texas; Southern California; and Northern Virginia that has been commissioned by the Smithsonian American Art Museum for this exhibition" ("Tiffany Chung: Vietnam, Past Is Prologue," Smithsonian American Art Museum, accessed August 28, 2018, https://americanart.si.edu/exhibitions/chung).

79. "Tiffany Chung."

80. Đinh Q. Lê, interview with the author, Hô Chì Minh City, August 30, 2006.

81. By "originality" I mean both original concepts and original works of art. Benjamin's famous essay discusses the role of mass media and mass reproduction in shattering an original artwork's "aura" (reverence and awe experienced in the presence of an original work of art). Now the artwork is endlessly reproduced, allowing for revolutionary potential. "Instead of being based on ritual," Benjamin writes, art "begins to be based on another practice—politics" (Benjamin, "The Work of Art in the Age of Mechanical Reproduction," 1935).

82. Bourdieu, *Distinction*.

83. *Milk* artist statement, Galerie Quynh, 2008.

84. Sandrine Llouquet, interview with the author, August 8, 2008, Hô Chì Minh City.

85. Llouquet interview.

86. Ong, *Flexible Citizenship*. Ong defines "flexible citizenship" as "flexible practices, strategies, and disciplines associated with transnational capitalism" that create new "modes of subject making and new kinds of valorized subjectivity" (Ong, *Flexible Citizenship*, 17–19).

87. Phạm Gia Kiêm, "Message of H.E. Mr. Pham Gia Khiem, Deputy Prime Minister and Minister of Foreign Affairs, to the Overseas Vietnamese Community," Visa Exemption for Vietnamese Residents Overseas, Bộ Ngoại Giao Việt Nam (Ministry of Foreign Affairs), August 29, 2007, accessed March 27, 2009, http://mienthithucvk.mofa.gov.vn/Default.aspx?alias=mienthithucvk.mofa.gov.vn/en.

88. Nguyễn, "A New Narrative"; David Fullbrook, "Vietnamese I[nformation] T[echnology] Follows Taiwan's Example," *Asia Times*, January 27, 2007.

89. Nguyễn, "A New Narrative."

90. MacLean, *The Government of Distrust*, xiii.

91. Book description, University of Wisconsin Press, accessed August 8, 2018, https://uwpress.wisc.edu/books/5055.htm.

92. Nguyễn-võ, "The Red Seedlings of the Central Highlands."

93. Quỳnh Phạm, *Trời ơi!* catalog essay, May 18, 2009, accessed August 1, 2010, http://www.sandrinellouquet.net/article-31640369.html.

94. Ann Friedberg, "The Mobilized and Virtual Gaze in Modernity," 20–28.

95. Jay, "Scopic Regimes of Modernity."

96. Deleuze and Guattari, *A Thousand Plateaus*, 238.

97. Freud, "The Uncanny," 247.

98. Freud, "The Uncanny," 230, emphasis added. In the essay, Freud attempts to delineate the evasive boundaries and qualities of uncanniness. As the sociologist Avery Gordon suggests, "Uncanny experiences are haunting experiences" (Gordon, *Ghostly Matters*, 50). Uncanniness can be said to be related to fear, as well as to the familiar and the unfamiliar. Tracing the genealogy of the uncanny, Freud notes that "the quality of uncanniness can only come from the fact of the 'double' being a creation to a very early mental stage, long since surmounted— a stage, incidentally, at which it wore a more friendly aspect. The 'double' has become a thing of terror, just as, after the collapse of their religion, the gods turned into demons" (Freud, "The Uncanny," 236).

99. Althusser, "Ideology and Ideological State Apparatuses."

100. Thayer and Amer, *Vietnamese Foreign Policy in Transition*.

101. Ong, *Flexible Citizenship*, 17.

102. Deleuze and Guattari, *A Thousand Plateaus*, 237–38.

103. MacLean, *The Government of Distrust*, 100.

104. Cherniavsky, *Neocitizenship*, 47.

105. Adam Jezar, *World Economic Forum*, April 23, 2018, accessed August 8, 2018, https://www.weforum.org/agenda/2018/04/what-is-civil-society.

106. Writing from a US perspective, Cherniavsky notes that citizen-centered political change may be a paradox, yet we continue "to assign to the agency of 'citizens' political actions no longer directed toward government institutions grown unresponsive and indifferent to popular political mandates and demands" (Cherniavsky, *Neocitizenship*). Civil society is the crux of such a paradox. "Such popular mobilizations are increasingly structured on the model of self-organizing groups and coalitions addressing corporations and other private entities, so that the very form of the action indexes the retreat of governmental agencies (legislative, executive, or juridical) once meant to mediate the relation of elements within the polity, and thus signals the erosion of the terrain on which we have historically understood the 'citizen' to operate" (Cherniavsky, *Neocitizenship*, 3).

107. Deleuze and Guattari, *A Thousand Plateaus*, 238.

108. Cherniavsky, *Neocitizenship*, 5.

109. Cherniavsky, *Neocitizenship*, 12.

110. The approval was granted in November 2008. "Under the amended law, foreigners eligible to take out Vietnamese citizenship and retain their origin nationalities would include those who: a) marry Vietnamese citizens or have Vietnamese parents or children; b) receive certificates or medals of merit from the State or the Government for their contribution to the country; and/or c) those whose citizenship would benefit Vietnam's socio-economic development, science, national security or defense. These categories of foreigners would be exempted from some Vietnamese citizenship criteria, such as being able to speak Vietnamese and residing in the country for at least five years" ("Vietnam House Approves Dual Citizenship for Expats, Diaspora," *Thanh Nhien News*, November 15, 2008, http://www.thanhniennews.com/politics/?catid=1&newsid=43761).

111. "Vietnam House Approves Dual Citizenship for Expats, Diaspora."

112. "Vietnam to Allow Dual Citizenship," *Agence France-Presse*, November 14, 2008, http://blog.vietnam-aujourdhui.info/post/2008/11/15/Vietnam-to-allow-dual-nationality.

113. Associated Press, "Vietnam to Allow Dual Citizenship," *International Herald Tribune*, November 17, 2008, accessed November 21, 2008, http://www.iht.com/articles/ap/2008/11/17/asia/AS-Vietnam-Dual-Citizenship.php.

114. A general overview of the Housing Law enacted on July 1, 2006, is available online in English translation at http://www.freshfields.com/publications/pdfs/2006/15848.pdf.

115. "Property Ownership Restrictions Loosened for Vietnamese," *Pacific Bridge*, vol. 8, no. 3, March 4, 2008, accessed March 27, 2009, http://www.pacificbridge.com/asianews.asp?id=353.

116. This follows a revision to the Housing Law (Art. 126) in July 2006. Previously, Vietnamese expatriates were not allowed to own any property. Overseas Vietnamese who retain Vietnamese citizenship may be able to own several homes, as well; the National Assembly continues to debate this point. Under this proposal, only 750,000 out of the two million overseas Vietnamese who have retained Vietnamese citizenship would be eligible to own multiple homes in Việt Nam.

117. "Nguyen Quang Thong, the newspaper's Editor-in-Chief, nailed the problem down: 'A lack of subsequent legal documents clarifying relevant procedures means the law is yet to be implemented practically'" (Minh Hung, "It's Still Hard for Foreigners, Viet Kieu to Buy Houses in Vietnam," *Thanh Nien News*, September 15, 2017, accessed October 29, 2017, http://www.thanhniennews.com/business/its-still-hard-for-foreigners-viet-kieu-to-buy-houses-in-vietnam-51323.html).

118. Dan Stapleton, "Vietnam's Rapid Growth Fuels Housing Boom," *Financial Times*, March 30, 2018, https://www.ft.com/content/e5170f58-2d07-11e8-97ec-4bd3494d5f14.

119. "In 2015, Vietnam hit $12.25 billion in remittances. To put this in perspective, Vietnam's GDP in 2015 was $193.6 billion. That's 6%. That's a significant sum. Remember that foreign direct investment into Vietnam was just $23 billion in the same year. In other words, the Vietnamese diaspora remitted almost half of what foreign investors put into Vietnam" (Anh Minh Do, "Are Viet Kieus Givers or Takers in Vietnam's Rise?," *Vietcetera*, December 7, 2016, accessed October 31, 2017, http://vietcetera.com/are-viet-kieus-really-vietnams-secret-weapon).

120. According to the World Bank, Việt Nam is among "the world's top 10 recipients of remittances in 2017" ("Vietnam's Foreign Reserves Reach an All-Time High").

121. Hung Le, "Vietnam Is Ninth Highest Receiver of Remittances," *VnExpress International*, January 30, 2019, https://e.vnexpress.net/news/business/economy/vietnam-is-ninth-highest-receiver-of-remittances-3876047.html.

122. Ivan V. Small, "How Vietnamese-Americans and other 'Viet Kieu' Fuel Capitalist Dreams with Remittances," *This Week in Asia*, July 27, 2019, accessed

September 5, 2019, https://www.scmp.com/week-asia/opinion/article/3020310
/how-vietnamese-americans-and-other-viet-kieu-fuel-capitalist.

123. The *International Herald Tribune* article states, "There are an estimated 3.5 million ethnic Vietnamese living overseas, many of whom fled the country by boat after the end of the Vietnam War in 1975 and sought citizenship in their new home countries. Many maintain close ties with Vietnam, opening businesses and sending more than $6 billion to the country last year" ("Vietnam to Allow Dual Citizenship").

124. "Property Ownership Restrictions Loosened for Vietnamese."

125. In response to a question about dual citizenship and children born outside of Việt Nam, the Ministry of Justice told a reporter, "The Law on Citizenship confers citizenship based on consanguinity. In other words, if the parents are Vietnamese citizens, their children will naturally be Vietnamese citizens no matter where they were born. If one of the parents is not of Vietnamese citizenship, the parents can choose Vietnamese citizenship for their children. Because the granting of citizenship is based on consanguinity, children born in Vietnam to foreign couples will not have Vietnamese citizenship. But, in cases of children whose parents can't be determined or who were abandoned in Vietnam, the children will be granted Vietnamese citizenship. In terms of international adoption, the law of Vietnam provides that Vietnamese children who are adopted by foreign couples will retain their Vietnamese citizenship until [they are] 18 years old and then have a right to choose their citizenship" ("Lawmakers May Recognize Dual Citizenship for Overseas Vietnamese" [interview with Trần Thật], *Tuổi Trẻ (Youth)*, January 28, 2008, accessed March 27, 2009, http://english.vietnamnet .vn/social/2008/02/770835).

126. "Lawmakers May Recognize Dual Citizenship for Overseas Vietnamese."

127. Deleuze and Guattari, *A Thousand Plateaus*, 238.

128. The đổi mới economic reforms involved successive stages of opening up and closing off Việt Nam to market forces.

129. Huggan, *Maps and Mapping Strategies in Contemporary Canadian and Australian Fiction*, 11.

130. Deleuze and Guattari, *A Thousand Plateaus*, 238.

131. For Cherniavsky, US electoral politics "operates on a plane of hyperreality." She writes, "The public called forth from the data streams—including the 'electorate' emerged from the endless political polls—is, of course, perfectly unreal, a model of no actual or original thing . . . the corporate person, like contemporary iterations of an American public, is a simulacrum" (Cherniavsky, "Refugees from this Native Dreamland," 295).

132. Huggan, *Maps and Mapping Strategies in Contemporary Canadian and Australian Fiction*.

133. Kim, *Sidewalk City*, 63.

134. Tiffany Chung artist statement, 2007, Galerie Quynh, Hồ Chí Minh City.

135. Klaus Rohland and Christine Delvoie, "Infrastructure Strategy: Cross-sectoral issues," World Bank report, June 2006, accessed June 12, 2007,

http://siteresources.worldbank.org/INTEAPINFRASTRUCT/Resources
/CrossSectoralIssues.pdf.

136. See Palen, *The Urban World*.

137. K. Bardhan Pranab and Dilip Mookherjee, "Capture and Governance at
Local and National Levels," 135–39.

138. Howard, *Garden Cities of To-morrow*.

139. Chuh and Shimakawa, *Orientations*.

140. Rofel, *Other Modernities*.

141. Kim, *Sidewalk City*, 85.

142. "[Hồ Chì Minh City] Metro: Is The End in Sight?" *City Pass Guide*,
August 13, 2018, https://www.citypassguide.com/en/living/ho-chi-minh-city
/transportation/blog/hcmc-metro-is-the-end-in-sight.

143. Tali Trigg, "First Metro Projects in Vietnam Risk Bigger Problems than
Delays," Scientific American, March 6, 2008, https://blogs.scientificamerican.com
/plugged-in/first-metro-projects-in-vietnam-risk-bigger-problems-than-delays.

144. Michael Takatarski, "Vietnam's Tale of Two Metros: One Built by the
Japanese, the Other by the Chinese," *This Week in Asia*, July 30, 2017, https://www
.scmp.com/week-asia/business/article/2104149/vietnams-tale-two-metros-one
-built-japanese-and-other-chinese.

145. Trigg, "First Metro Projects in Vietnam Risk Bigger Problems than
Delays."

146. Kim, *Sidewalk City*, 85.

147. Takatarski, "Vietnam's Tale of Two Metros."

148. "In Bangkok, there was a 1 kilometer (0.62 mile) gap (and a missing
station) between the Purple and Blue Lines, causing commuters to opt to drive
or take a bus than pay two different fares. The Thai government was finally able
to find an operator to build the missing link in 2017, connecting the Blue and
Purple lines": Sisithorn Ongdee, "Bangkok Commuters Left Out of the Loop,"
The Nation, December 30, 2017, http://www.nationmultimedia.com/detail/politics
/30303147.

149. Takatarksi details several other safety issues of the Hà Nội line, writing,
"On November 6, 2014, several reels of steel fell from the construction site of a
flyover on the line, killing a motorbike driver and injuring two more passers-by.
The following month, a 10-metre-high section of scaffolding fell from the same
flyover, trapping three people in a taxi that was travelling beneath it. In 2015, the
line drew criticism when people noticed that the track, which runs above major
thoroughfares and intersections, looked wavy, raising concerns over its safety.
That August a steel bar fell from another construction site onto a car, nearly
killing the driver. . . . This May [2017], a government inspection team detected
rust on sections of the train track that hadn't been covered in protective paint. A
number of loose joints were found as well. Vietnam's Ministry of Transport has
responded swiftly to these incidents by calling for improved safety measures, and
while there hasn't been an accident in roughly two years, the project's reputation
is poor": Takatarski, "Vietnam's Tale of Two Metros."

150. Takatarski, "Vietnam's Tale of Two Metros."

151. Kim, *Sidewalk City*, 68.

152. Turcotte, "Prologomena to Uncovering Alter/Native Scripts," 144.

153. Rofel, "Discrepant Modernities and Their Discontents," 637–49.

154. Carruthers, "Cute Logics of the Multicultural and the Consumption of the Vietnamese Exotic in Japan," 401–29.

155. The historic avant-garde shift from Paris to New York reflects in part diasporic movement during World War II, when top European modernists sought refuge in America. The confluence of European émigrés seeking survival and artistic freedom and America's postwar economic might and rash of collectors, critics, and institutions responsive to avant-garde practices rezoned the cultural landscape to its current coordinates.

156. Yúdice, *The Expediency of Culture*.

157. Cieslikowski, *World Development Indicators 2008*.

158. "Collectors' appetites for Chinese contemporary art has abated slightly in recent auctions, while prices for Indonesian artists have jumped in the past year. That suggests rising young Vietnamese artists may soon come into their own as the auction houses and collectors keep trying to chase the next 'big thing'" (Matt Miller, "The Vogue for Vietnam," *Deal Newsweekly*, September 26, 2008).

159. See Bourdieu, *Distinction*, 233. He writes, "The endless changes in fashion result from the objective orchestration between, on the one hand, the logic of the struggles internal to the field of production, which are organized in terms of the opposition old/new . . . and, on the other hand, the logic of struggles internal to the field of the dominant class, which, as we have seen, oppose the dominant and the dominated fractions, or, more precisely, the established and the challengers." See also Bourdieu, "The Field of Cultural Production."

160. Miller, "The Vogue for Vietnam."

161. Yue is number eight on *Artnet*'s January 2017 list of top-selling living Chinese artists: Henri Neuendorf, "Who Are the Most Popular Living Chinese Artists?" *Artnet News*, January 12, 2017, accessed August 19, 2018, https://news.artnet.com/market/most-popular-living-chinese-artists-813356.

162. For more about Yue Minjun, see the website at http://www.yueminjun.com.

163. "Chinese Contemporary Artist Yue Minjung," *State of the Arts*, March 21, 2018, accessed April 21, 2018, https://stateoftheartsnyc.wordpress.com/2018/03/21/chinese-contemporary-artist-yue-minjun.

164. Tingting Dai, "The Painted Messages: Trauma in Contemporary Chinese Art," unpublished master's thesis, California College of the Arts, San Francisco, 2018.

165. The writer and editor Alec Ash, based in Beijing, notes that the "more conceptual" artists of the "post-90s" include "Zhao, who cuts cubes out of antique Buddhist statues; Cao Fei, a video and digital-media artist concerned with urban decay; and Guo Hongwei, who arranges tiny piles of concrete ash, decorates empty rooms in colorful streaks, and paints intricate collections of

birds, rocks, and leaves" (Alec Ash, "Why Young Chinese Artists Are Avoiding Political Art," *The Atlantic*, July 26, 2018, accessed August 20, 2018, https://www.theatlantic.com/entertainment/archive/2018/07/young-chinese-artists/565040.

166. Scot Reyburn, "The Biggest-Selling Artist at Auction Is a Name You May Not Know," *New York Times*, June 2, 2017, https://www.nytimes.com/2017/06/02/arts/china-art-auction-zhang-daqian.html.

167. Articles on the "rise" of Vietnamese contemporary art have appeared since the mid-1990s and continue through today. They include Sonia Kolesnikov-Jessop, "Vietnam's Rising Generation Awaits Recognition in the Sale Room," *International Herald Tribune*, March 26, 2008, and Jennifer Conlin, "The Awakening of Hanoi," *New York Times*, February 18, 2007. Vietnamese art has been proclaimed to be "in vogue" for more than a decade (see Philip Shenon, "Success Overnight, in a Sense: Vietnam's Artists Are in Vogue," *New York Times*, November 29, 1994).

168. Patrick Rhine, "Southeast Asian Gallerist Willie Valentine Retires from Commercial Art World," *Art Radar Asia*, September 10, 2012, accessed June 19, 2014, http://artradarjournal.com/2012/10/09/southeast-asian-gallerist-valentine-willie-retires-from-commercial-world.

169. Tyler Rollins Fine Art archived gallery statement, September 10, 2012, accessed October 12, 2014, https://www.mutualart.com/Gallery/Tyler-Rollins-Fine-Art/961F077708B5FF38#more.

170. Bourdieu et al., *The Love of Art*.

171. I later discuss an international "ranking system" for artists. Bourdieu also uses the term *distinction* as a mark of difference—art used as a filter of class divides through connoisseurship: Bourdieu et al., *The Love of Art*, 111.

172. As mentioned earlier, the title of Taylor's "Why Have There Been No Great Vietnamese Artists?" references Linda Nochlin's seminal essay "Why Have There Been No Great Women Artists?"

173. I chose not to write in depth about Nguyễn-Hatsushiba and Lê for this chapter because so much critical work has already been written about both of them. I wrote about Đinh Q. Lê's work in Lê, "The Art of War."

Chapter Three. Personal and Public Archives

1. Ketelaar, "Tacit Narratives," 132.

2. Ketelaar, *The Archival Image*.

3. Brothman, "Jacques Derrida, Archive Fever," 191.

4. Manoff, "Theories of the Archive from Across the Disciplines," 13.

5. Derrida, *Archive Fever*, 10 (translation of Jacques Derrida, *Mal d'archive* [Paris: Galilée, 1995]).

6. Derrida, *Archive Fever*, 11.

7. Derrida, *Archive Fever*, 15.

8. Weaver, *Ideologies of Forgetting: Rape in the Vietnam War*.

9. Weaver, *Ideologies of Forgetting: Rape in the Vietnam War*. "The falseness of a judgment is to us not necessarily an objection to a judgment. . . . The question is to what extent it is life-advancing, life-preserving, species-preserving, perhaps even species-breeding" (Nietzsche, *Beyond Good and Evil*, 4).

10. Derrida, *Archive Fever*, 14.

11. Shetty and Bellamy, "Postcolonialism's Archive Fever," 36.

12. Ly, "Of Scent and Sensibility."

13. Ly, "Of Scent and Sensibility," 68.

14. Jean Armour Polly coined this term in 1992; see "Brief Timeline of the Internet," Webopedia, May 24, 2007, http://www.webopedia.com/quick_ref/timeline.asp.

15. Brothman, "Jacques Derrida, Archive Fever," 190–91.

16. Derrida, *Archive Fever*, 17.

17. The HBO documentary *The Conscience of Nhem En* (2009), directed by Steven Okazaki, was nominated for an Oscar.

18. Truong and Slavick, "War, Memory, the Artist and the Politics of Language."

19. Moore, "Flowers Come from My Mouth."

20. Moore, "Flowers Come from My Mouth," 12.

21. Leang Seckon, interview by the author, Mutrak Gallery, Phnom Penh, October 3, 2010.

22. See Brown, "The Emergence of Black Women Artists."

23. The strikes occurred outside the Garment Processing Factory in the Meanchey district of Phnom Penh. Dene Heren-Chen with Aun Pheap, "Three Month Strike in Cambodia Factory," *Womens Wear Daily*, December 5, 2013, https://wwd.com/business-news/government-trade/three-month-strike-in-cambodia-factory-7300970.

24. "Cambodia Textile Workers Killed during Pay Protest," *BBC News*, January 3, 2014, https://www.bbc.com/news/av/world-asia-25593553/cambodian-textile-workers-killed-during-pay-protest.

25. "Cambodia Hikes Minimum Wage for Textiles Workers by 11 Percent from 2018," Reuters, October 5, 2017, https://www.reuters.com/article/cambodia-economy-garmentworkers-wages/cambodia-hikes-minimum-wage-for-textiles-workers-by-11-pct-from-2018-idUSL4N1MG1Q6.

26. Business and Human Rights Resource Centre, "Cambodia: NGO Fact Finding Mission Documents Exploitative Working Conditions at Garment Factories Supplying International Brands," Human Rights Now, April 16, 2015, accessed February 12, 2018, https://business-humanrights.org/en/cambodia-ngo-fact-finding-mission-documents-exploitative-working-conditions-at-garment-factories-supplying-intl-brands#c123889. In 2010, the average monthly wage for garment workers was US$56 a month; Prak Chan Tul, "Cambodian Workers Strike, Seek Higher Wages," Reuters, September 13, 2010, http://www.reuters.com/article/idUSSGE67U09320100913.

27. "Hundreds Faint in a Factory," Radio Free Asia, August 24, 2011, accessed February 12, 2018, https://www.rfa.org/english/news/cambodia/faintings-08252011182914.html.

28. Mom Kunthear, "Mass Collapse at Garment Factory," *Phnom Penh Post*, August 24, 2011.

29. Tep Nimol and Vincent MacIsaac, "H&M in Second Mass Faint," *Phnom Penh Post*, August 26, 2011.

30. Business and Human Rights Resource Centre, "Cambodia."

31. "Cambodian Textile Workers Killed During Pay Protest," BBC *News*, January 3, 2014, accessed January 4, 2014, https://www.bbc.com/news/av/world-asia -25593553/cambodian-textile-workers-killed-during-pay-protest.

32. The Por Sanchey district is about 6.25 miles (10 kilometers) from Phnom Penh's city center. It is the largest of the twelve districts and, due to high prices in the city center, is an emerging hub for residential developments. This protest for missing wages was resolved within a few hours of the road blockade, but Chey Sopha, a former Ghim Li Factory employee, noted that protests often do not result in any solution (Sen David, "Protesting Workers Block National Road 4," *Khmer Times*, September 18, 2018, accessed November 18, 2018, https://www .khmertimeskh.com/50534057/protesting-workers-block-national-road-4).

33. Yon Sineat and Daphne Chen, "Workers Protest Factory Shutdowns," *Phnom Penh Post*, February 9, 2018, accessed November 18, 2018, https://www .phnompenhpost.com/national/workers-protest-factory-shutdowns.

34. Sineat and Chen, "Workers Protest Factory Shutdowns."

35. Sineat and Chen, "Workers Protest Factory Shutdowns."

36. "Cambodia Hikes Minimum Wage for Textiles Workers by 11 Percent from 2018."

37. Prak Chan Thul, "Cambodia Hikes Textile Workers' Minimum Wage, Falls Short of Union Demands," Reuters, October 5, 2018, accessed October 17, 2008, https://www.reuters.com/article/us-cambodia-garment/cambodia-hikes-textile -workers-minimum-wage-falls-short-of-union-demands-idUSKCN1MF18B.

38. "Cambodia Hikes Minimum Wage for Textiles Workers by 11 Percent from 2018."

39. "Garment Workers in Cambodia Fear EU Trade Threat, Makers Optimistic," *Asahi Shimbun*, October 17, 2018, accessed November 18, 2018, http://www .asahi.com/ajw/articles/AJ201810170041.html.

40. "Garment Workers in Cambodia Fear EU Trade."

41. The compliance matrix used by BFC contains twenty-one "critical issues," including work conditions, wages, and access to unions. The critical issues are "categorized mainly from the Compliance Assessment Tool's Fundamental Rights cluster of compliance points, along with Occupational Safety and Health; Compensation; and Contracts and Human Resources clusters," according to BFC, which has been reporting on these issues, along with low-compliance factories and strikes, and releasing the information publicly since 2014. With the release of cycle 11, the Transparency Database has accumulated information gathered from 1,580 assessment reports covering 579 garment factories that possess an export license in Cambodia since 2014 (Better Factories Cambodia, *Better Factories Cambodia Transparency Database Report, 11th Cycle, September 2018*, accessed

November 19, 2018, http://betterfactories.org/transparency/uploads/eeaf8-bfc
-transparency-database-report-cycle-11th.pdf).

42. "Unpaid Garment Workers Protest in Cambodia," *Apparel Resources*,
April 20, 2018, accessed November 17, 2018, https://apparelresources.com
/business-news/sustainability/unpaid-garment-workers-protest-cambodia.

43. "Garment Workers in Cambodia Fear EU Trade Threat."

44. "Garment Workers in Cambodia Fear EU Trade Threat."

45. Leang Seckon, interview with the author, Boeung Kak, Phnom Penh,
November 25, 2009.

46. Moore, "Flowers Come from My Mouth."

47. Trungpa, *The Myth of Freedom and the Way of Meditation*.

48. Thompson, *Engendering the Buddhist State*.

49. Seckon interview (2010).

50. Quoted in Shaw-Jackson, *Heavy Skirt*, 6–7.

51. Shaw-Jackson, *Heavy Skirt*.

52. Quoted in Shaw-Jackson, *Heavy Skirt*, 5.

53. The report also states: "Hun Sen has been linked to a wide range of serious
human rights violations: extrajudicial killings, torture, arbitrary arrests, summary
trials, censorship, bans on assembly and association, and a national network of
spies and informers intended to frighten and intimidate the public into submission. Hun Sen's main tactic has been the threat and use of force. During his time
in power, hundreds of opposition figures, journalists, trade union leaders, and
others have been killed in politically motivated attacks. Although in many cases
the killers are known, in not one case has there been a credible investigation and
prosecution, let alone conviction. Worse, many have been promoted: the Ministry
of Defense and Ministry of Interior websites listing senior military and police
officials are a veritable Who's Who of human rights abusers. This report describes
the human rights record of Hun Sen since his time as a Khmer Rouge commander during the 1970s. It is based on materials in Khmer, English, Vietnamese,
and Chinese. These include official and other Cambodian documents; interviews
with Cambodian officials and other Cambodians by Human Rights Watch, other
non-governmental organizations, journalists, and academics, and United Nations records, foreign government reports, and Cambodian court proceedings"
("Thirty Years of Hun Sen: Violence, Repression, and Corruption in Cambodia,"
Human Rights Watch, January 12, 2015, accessed February 14, 2018, https://www
.hrw.org/report/2015/01/12/30-years-hun-sen/violence-repression-and-corruption
-cambodia).

54. "Continue to Investigate Kem Ley Killing: Significant Questions Remain
after Guilty Verdict," Human Rights Watch, March 23, 2017, accessed February 14,
2018, https://www.hrw.org/news/2017/03/23/cambodia-continue-investigate-kem
-ley-killing.

55. Human Rights Watch's country profile for Cambodia outlines government
censorship this way: "Media defamation cases are no longer covered by the penal
code but by Cambodia's 1995 press law, which does not carry criminal liability

or imprisonment as a penalty. During 2009 at least 10 government critics were prosecuted for criminal defamation and disinformation based on complaints by government and military officials. Among those convicted were four journalists, two of whom were jailed on disinformation charges: opposition editor Hang Chakra, sentenced to one year's imprisonment in June, and journalist Ros Sokhet, sentenced to two years' imprisonment in November. In July editor Dam Sith closed *Moneaksekar Khmer*, one of Cambodia's oldest opposition papers, as the only way to prevent government lawsuits that could have landed him in prison. Criminal defamation, disinformation, and incitement lawsuits were also filed against opposition Sam Rainsy Party (SRP) members, including party leader Sam Rainsy, SRP parliamentarians Mu Sochua and Ho Vann, and SRP youth activist Soung Sophorn. Prime Minister Hun Sen pressed defamation charges against the lawyer defending SRP cases, spurring the lawyer's withdrawal from the cases in July. As a result, Mu Sochua lacked legal counsel during her July 24 trial, in which she was found guilty of defaming the prime minister and ordered to pay US$4,100 in fines and compensation" ("Cambodia: Events of 2009," Human Rights Watch, accessed September 11, 2010, http://www.hrw.org /en/node/87393).

56. Seckon interview (2009).

57. Corey, "The 'First' Cambodian Contemporary Artist," 67.

58. Seckon interview (2009).

59. Figures can be misleading. The World Bank's "Doing Business" report ranks Cambodia 145 out of 158 countries. The World Economic Forum has a different ranking: Cambodia is ranked #109 out of 138 countries for business climate, barring Myanmar (Burma), countries not included on the survey. The rankings are based on the following factors: "The forum's annual competitiveness study scores 110 factors across 12 areas affecting an economy's business climate: institutions, infrastructure, macroeconomic environment, health, education, goods and labour market efficiency, financial market development, technological readiness, market size, business sophistication, and innovation."

60. Quoted in Moore, "Flowers Come from My Mouth," 13.

61. Seckon interview (2009).

62. Corey, "The 'First' Cambodian Contemporary Artist," 67.

63. Corey, "The 'First' Cambodian Contemporary Artist," 67.

64. For more information on the Tonlé Sap, see the website at https://www .eater.com/2017/12/29/16823664/tonle-sap-drought-cambodia.

65. According to the World Bank, foreign direct investment to Cambodia in 2019 was $3.706 billion; see real-time updates at https://data.worldbank.org /indicator/BX.KLT.DINV.CD.WD?locations=KH.

66. Two-wheeled carriages attached to a motorcycle commonly used as taxis.

67. "Cambodia's Economy in 2010: After Unusual Year, Is Recovery on Its Way for Workers and Entrepreneurs?," World Bank blog, accessed June 19, 2009, http://blogs.worldbank.org/eastasiapacific/node/2858.

68. Since the IMF started monitoring Cambodia in 1988, this is the first negative growth indicator. The economic downturn is due to social distancing lockdown protocols. ("Cambodia's GDP to See Negative Growth in 2020: IMF," *The Cambodia Daily*, April 18, 2020, accessed August 5, 2020, https://english .cambodiadaily.com/business/cambodias-gdp-to-see-negative-growth-in-2020 -imf-162970/).

69. The National Bank of Cambodia report is titled, "Macroeconomic Prospects and Financial Sector in 2017 and Outlook for 2018." See also May Kunmakara, "Economy to Grow at 6.9 Percent in 2018, NBC," *Khmer Times*, January 11, 2018, accessed February 15, 2018, http://www.khmertimeskh.com/50101290 /economy-grow-6-9-percent-2018-nbc.

70. The Business and Human Rights Resource Centre invited eight international garment companies to respond to human rights labor abuses; five (Celio, H&M, Inditex, M&S, and Uniqlo [part of Fast Retailing]) responded, and three (Adler Modemaerkte, Calzedonia, and Nygard) did not (Business and Human Rights Resource Centre, "Cambodia").

71. Galasso and Ravallion, "Decentralized Targeting of an Antipoverty Program," 705–27.

72. United Nations Development Program, "The International Day for the Eradication of Poverty: Middle Income Cambodia's Three Poverty Challenges," October 17, 2017, accessed February 15, 2018, http://www.kh.undp.org/content /cambodia/en/home/ourperspective/middle-income-cambodia-three-poverty -challenges.html.

73. World Bank in Cambodia Country Overview, accessed September 20, 2019, http://www.worldbank.org/en/country/cambodia/overview.

74. World Bank in Cambodia Country Overview.

75. United Nations Development Program, "The International Day for the Eradication of Poverty."

76. Asian Development Bank, "Cambodia and ADB," accessed February 15, 2018, https://www.adb.org/countries/cambodia/main.

77. For more on Trương's work, see her website, at http://hongantruong.com.

78. Pelaud et al., *Troubling Borders*, 89.

79. Pelaud et al., *Troubling Borders*, 112.

80. The John Simon Guggenheim Award is a prestigious competition held annually for permanent citizens of the United States and Canada; there are approximately three thousand applicants, and 175 fellowships are awarded. The average award is $43,000. There is a separate category of competition for permanent residents of Latin America and the Caribbean. For information about Hồng-Ân Trương's 2019 fellowship, see the John Simon Guggenheim Memorial Foundation website, at https://www.gf.org/fellows/all-fellows/hong-an-truong.

81. Daniel Quiles, "Interview with Hương Ngô and Hồng-Ân Trương," *ArtForum*, March 16, 2018, accessed September 9, 2019, https://www.artforum .com/interviews/huong-ngo-and-hong-an-truong-on-their-work-in-being-new -photography-2018-74649.

82. Mimi Thi Nguyễn, *The Gift of Freedom*, 183.

83. LÊ THI DIEM THÚY explores family, memory, and colonial representation in her performance piece *Carte Postale* (2010) (LÊ THI DIEM THÚY, discussion with the author, Phnom Penh, April 18, 2010).

84. For more on diasporic identity and experimental videos including the practice of Ming Yuen S. Ma, Trinh T. Minh-ha, and Nguyễn Tân Hoàng, see Mimura, *Ghostlife of Third Cinema*.

85. Võ, interview with Trương, *diaCritics*, 2009.

86. Zie Zong and Jeanne Batalova, "Vietnamese Immigrants in the United States," Migration Policy Institute, June 8, 2016, accessed February 15, 2018, https://www.migrationpolicy.org/article/vietnamese-immigrants-united-states.

87. The largest Vietnamese communities living abroad are in California (418,249) and Texas (107,027). The third-largest group consists of Vietnamese studying and working in the Soviet bloc who remained after the end of the Soviet Union. The fourth-largest group lives in other Asian countries, most of whom live in South Korea or Taiwan as economic migrant workers or mail-order brides; see Grieco, "The Foreign Born from Vietnam" (2004); and Alperin and Batalova, "The Foreign Born from Vietnam" (2018).

88. The website for the PBS documentary *Art21: Art in the Twenty-first Century* (http://www.pbs.org/art21) features images of An-My Lê's work. A discussion of Đình Q. Lê and An-My Lê's work appears in Lê and Min, *transPOP*, 12–37. Jun Nguyễn-Hatsushiba is represented by the Lehman Maupin Gallery (www .lehmannmaupin.com/#/artists/jun-nguyen-hatsushiba) in New York.

89. Jay, "Scopic Regimes of Modernity."

90. Theresa Hak Kyung Cha, *Dictee*.

91. Jay, "Scopic Regimes of Modernity."

92. This line is from William Butler Yeats's poem "The Second Coming": "Turning and turning in the widening gyre / the falcon cannot hear the falconer; / Things fall apart; the centre cannot hold."

93. Nguyễn, "Seeing Double."

94. Jay, "Scopic Regimes of Modernity."

95. This is an inexact translation of the French woman's narrative: "He's stripped me naked, this is what I wanted. I desired him more than anything else. I couldn't help but look for him. I couldn't help but do otherwise . . . I wanted to disappear in his gaze until I disappeared myself . . . The sheets were soaked with blood . . . We were lying in bed smoking cigarettes" (translated from French with help from David Picard).

96. I borrow this term from W. E. B. Du Bois, who coined it in *The Souls of Black Folk*. He wrote, "After the Egyptian and Indian, the Greek and Roman, the Teuton and Mongolian, the Negro is a sort of seventh son, born with a veil, and gifted with second-sight in this American world—a world which yields him no true self-consciousness, *but only lets him see himself through the revelation of the other world. It is a peculiar sensation, this double-consciousness, this sense of always looking at one's self through the eyes of others, of measuring one's soul by*

the tape of a world that looks on in amused contempt and pity. One ever feels his twoness—an American, a Negro; two warring souls, two thoughts, two unreconciled strivings; two warring ideals in one dark body, whose dogged strength alone keeps it from being torn asunder. The history of the American Negro is the history of this strife—this longing to attain self-conscious manhood, to merge his double self into a better and truer self" (Du Bois, *The Souls of Black Folk*, 3–5).

97. Lacan, Jacques, *The Four Fundamental Concepts of Psychoanalysis*.

98. Foucault states that among utopias, "unreal spaces," and heterotopias— "real sites" in which he includes cemeteries, prisons, museums, theaters, libraries, brothels, ships (changeable in their forms, but more or less cohesive in their respective functions)—lies the *mirror*, a space of absence and presence, both utopic and heterotopic (Foucault, "Of Other Spaces," 3–4).

99. See Norindr, *Phantasmic Indochina*.

100. For more on American filmic representations of the Việt Nam War, see Sturken, *Tangled Memories*.

101. Kingston, *Simon and Garfunkel*, 69.

102. Interview with Trương (2010).

103. Steyerl and Berardi, *The Wretched of the Screen*.

104. Mimi Thi Nguyễn, *The Gift of Freedom*, 186.

105. Fall, *Hell in a Very Small Place*, 469.

106. Mimi Thi Nguyễn, *The Gift of Freedom*, 188.

107. Việt Thanh Nguyễn, *Nothing Ever Dies*, 9.

108. Mimi Thi Nguyễn, *The Gift of Freedom*, 189.

109. Different institutional demands on the postmodern subject may create discrepant—and occasionally conflicting—affiliations. The editors of *Translocal Geographies* apply Appadurai's concept of "disjunct affiliations" to the contradictory impulses of deterritorialized cultural production with the desire for situatedness. Appadurai writes, "For many national citizens, the practicalities of residence and the ideologies of home, soil and roots are often disjunct, so that the territorial referents of civic loyalty are increasingly divided for many persons among different spatial horizons: work loyalties, residential loyalties, and religious loyalties may create disjunct registers of affiliation. This is true whether migration of populations is across small or large distances and whether or not these movements link traverse to international boundaries" (Appadurai, *Modernity at Large*, 47). See also Brickell and Datta, "Introduction," 3–6. Appadurai is quoted on 13.

110. Mitchell, *Questions of Modernity*, 13.

111. Mitchell, *Questions of Modernity*, 24.

112. Anderson, *Imagined Communities*.

113. Walter Benjamin, *Reflections: Essays, Aphorisms, Autobiographical Writings*; Henri Bergson, *Time and Free Will*.

114. Mimi Thi Nguyễn, *The Gift of Freedom*, 185.

115. Mimi Thi Nguyễn, *The Gift of Freedom*, 189.

116. Mitchell, *Questions of Modernity*, 23.

117. Mitchell, *Questions of Modernity*, 29.

118. Derrida, *Archive Fever*, 12, emphasis added.

119. Derrida, *The Gift of Death*.

Chapter 4. Town and Country

1. Zwolinski and Wertheimer, "Exploitation."

2. Zwolinski and Wertheimer, "Exploitation," 25.

3. Bachelard, *The Poetics of Space*, 231.

4. Harms, *Saigon's Edge*, 122.

5. Harms, *Saigon's Edge*, 123.

6. "Word Origin and History," Dictionary.com, s.v. *exploit, exploitation* (n.): "1803, 'productive working' of something, a positive word among those who used it first, though regarded as Gallicism, from French *exploitation*, noun of action from *exploiter* (see exploit [v.]). Bad sense developed 1830s–50s, in part from influence of French socialist writings (especially Saint-Simon), also perhaps influenced by U.S. antislavery writing; and the insulting word was hurled at activities it once had crowned as praise. It follows from this science [conceived by Saint-Simon] that the tendency of the human race is from a state of antagonism to that of an universal peaceful association—from the dominating influence of the military spirit to that of the *industriel* one; from what they call *l'exploitation de l'homme par l'homme* to the *exploitation* of the globe by industry. ['Quarterly Review,' April & July 1831]. . . . v. c. 1400 *espleiten, esploiten* 'to accomplish, achieve, fulfill,' from Old French *esploitier, espleiter*, from *esploit* (see exploit [n.]). . . . The sense of 'use selfishly' first recorded 1838, from French, perhaps extended from use of the word with reference to mines, etc. (cf. exploitation). Related: *Exploited; exploiting*. As an adjective form, *exploitative* (1882) is from French; *exploitive* (by 1859) appears to be a native formation."

7. Olga Viso, "*Documenta (13)*: The Uncommodifiable Quinquennial," *Walker Art Center Magazine*, August 9, 2012, accessed December 9, 2018, https://walkerart.org/magazine/olga-viso-reviews-documenta-13.

8. Roberta Smith, "Art Show as Unruly Organism: *Documenta 13* in Kassel, Germany," *New York Times*, June 14, 2018, accessed December 9, 2018, https://www.nytimes.com/2012/06/15/arts/design/documenta-13-in-kassel-germany.html.

9. Smith, "Art Show as Unruly Organism."

10. Corey, "The 'First' Cambodian Contemporary Artist."

11. Cambodia Living Arts was founded under the guidance of the nonprofit incubator Marion Institute, in southeastern Massachussetts. According to the website Visitsemass.com, the institute was founded in 1993 as a "nonprofit that acts as an incubator for a diverse array of programs and projects that delve into the root cause of an issue and seeks to create deep and positive change. We work with individuals, schools and communities to inspire change in the areas of

health and healing, sustainability, green economics, environmental education, spirituality and much more."

12. *Season of Cambodia* is organized by Cambodia Living Arts. For information, see the website, at http://www.seasonofcambodia.org.

13. For images of the *Rang Phnom Flower* installation, see the Tyler Rollins Fine Art website, at http://www.trfineart.com/exhibition/sopheap-pich-rang -phnom-flower/#info.

14. The Tyler Rollins Fine Arts website (www.trfineart.com/artist/sopheap -pich) notes that "Sopheap Pich is widely considered to be Cambodia's most internationally prominent contemporary artist; . . . [his works] have been acquired by numerous major museums, including: the Centre Pompidou, Paris; the Metropolitan Museum of Art, New York; and M+, Hong Kong."

15. "Artist Sopheap Pich, Survivor of Cambodian Genocide, is Alumni Artist-in-Residence at UMass Amherst," March 30, 2012, accessed August 5, 2020, https://www.umass.edu/newsoffice/article/artist-sopheap-pich-survivor -cambodian-genocide-alumni-artist-residence-umass-amherst.

16. Pich, "Artist Statement," *Silence and Cycles*, Tyler Rollins Fine Art New York, emphasis added.

17. Brian Curtin, "Sopheap Pich, H Gallery Thailand" (exhibition review), September 1, 2007, accessed October 2, 2008, http://www.trfineart.com/wp -content/uploads/2016/10/Frieze.pdf.

18. Jonathan Goodman, "Sopheap Pich: Return to Cambodia," *Sculpture Magazine*, September 1, 2011, accessed August 5, 2020, http://www.trfineart.com/wp -content/uploads/2016/10/Sculpture_magazine_2011-09_return_to_cambodia .pdf.

19. Ron Gluckman, "Battle for Boeung Kak Lake," *Far Eastern Economic Times*, October 6, 2008, 30–33.

20. Ananth Baliga and Khouth Sophak Chakrya, "Boeung Kak: A Disastrous Decade," *Phnom Penh Post*, February 3, 2017, accessed November 23, 2018, https:// www.phnompenhpost.com/national-post-depth-politics/boeung-kak-disastrous -decade.

21. "Cambodia Land Management and Administration Project," Bank Information Center, October 10, 2008, accessed November 2, 2009, https:// bankinformationcenter.org/en-us/project/cambodia-land-management-and -administration-project/.

22. Describing the formal complaint filed against the World Bank, the Bank Information Center notes, "It alleges that the Bank breached its operational policies by failing to adequately supervise the Land Management and Administration Project . . . , which has denied urban poor and other vulnerable households due process rights and protection against increasing land-grabbing and forced evictions in Cambodia" (Bank Information Center, "World Bank Agrees to Full Investigation into Land Activities in Cambodia," press release, April 28, 2010, accessed April 3, 2010, http://ki-media.blogspot.com/2010/04/world-bank-agrees-to-full -investigation.html).

23. Bank Information Center, "World Bank Agrees to Full Investigation into Land Activities in Cambodia." According to its website (www.bicusa.org), the Bank Information Center "partners with civil society in developing and transition countries to influence the World Bank and other international financial institutions to promote social and economic justice and ecological sustainability."

24. "About Us," World Bank website (www.worldbank.org).

25. Bank Information Center, "World Bank Agrees to Full Investigation into Land Activities in Cambodia."

26. Guy de Launey, "Cambodia Lake Battle: How Boeung Kak Became a Puddle," BBC News, Phnom Penh, August 14, 2011, accessed November 23, 2018, https://www.bbc.com/news/business-14488100.

27. Personal conversation, October 2, 2010.

28. Artist interview with the author, Phnom Penh, October 2, 2010.

29. "Two Foreign Companies Investing in Boeung Kak Lake Area Withdraw," Khmer Machas Srok, vol. 4, no. 629, March 18, 2010.

30. Cambodia Development Watch states in its June 2010 report: "Later the [Municipality of Phnom Penh] announced that a private construction company named 7NG has proposed a plan to the [municipality] for providing alternative housing for thousands of residents due to be evicted from Phnom Penh's Boeung Kak area. According to the proposed plan the families will be allowed to stay at current location for 4 years and will pay US$0.64/day/family for four years to the company as a deposit amount. After four years, the families will move to new houses and will pay an additional US$0.42/day/family for six years and subsequently get the ownership of the house. The total costs of the new house will therefore amount to US$1,854 measured in 2007 prices. The alternate housing are [sic] said to be composed of 20 [meter] × 5 [meter] lots but there is no detail available about the location of the housing lots. The new housing will be provided with a road, electricity, water, sewage system, a school, a hospital and a pagoda according to the proposal. A representative of 7NG said his company is currently working with [the Municipality of Phnom Penh] on a project involving more than 1000 h[ectares] of land which will be used to provide affordable housing for the poor" ("Boeung Kak Lake Lease Agreement Some Questions for Discussion," Cambodia Development Watch, June 7, 2010, accessed June 11, 2010, http://www.cambodia.org/downloads/pdf/DPP_CambodiaDevelopmentWatchJune07Final_English.pdf).

31. The terms are taken from the publicity material for MacLean's book at the University of Wisconsin Press website, accessed September 7, 2018, https://uwpress.wisc.edu/books/5055.htm.

32. MacLean, The Government of Mistrust, xii.

33. De Launey, "Cambodia Lake Battle."

34. The World Bank's self-critical report and withdrawal from future Khmer lending has not left a fiscal vacuum, as there are plenty of investors. This admission of partial responsibility may explain why the bank decided to take the unusual step of suspending its lending to Cambodia. The country's international

donors are usually reluctant to attach conditions to their aid. The bank's country director, Annette Dixon, issued a statement saying, "Until an agreement is reached with the residents of Boeung Kak Lake we do not expect to provide any new lending to Cambodia." The Cambodian authorities reacted with little more than a shrug, perhaps mindful that billions of dollars of Chinese money is now pouring into the country, on top of hundreds of millions in aid from long-standing donors. An official spokesman said that Cambodia "no longer appreciate[d]" World Bank loans" (de Launey, "Cambodia Lake Battle").

35. US Senate, *The International Financial Institutions*.

36. De Launey, "Cambodia Lake Battle."

37. Philip Heijman, "Chinese Money Is Driving One of Asia's Fastest Property Booms," Bloomberg News, September 10, 2018, https://www.bloomberg.com/news/features/2018-09-10/chinese-money-is-driving-a-property-boom-in-cambodia.

38. Heijman, "Chinese Money Is Driving One of Asia's Fastest Property Booms."

39. Baliga and Chakrya, "Boeung Kak."

40. Luc Forsyth and Gareth Bright, "The Vanishing Lakes of Phnom Penh," *The Diplomat*, February 17, 2016, https://thediplomat.com/2016/02/the-vanishing-lakes-of-phnom-penh.

41. Forsyth and Bright, "The Vanishing Lakes of Phnom Penh."

42. An article posted by the LICADHO details the activist's detention. "Tep Vanny was arrested on 15 August 2016 and charged during a peaceful protest supporting five jailed human rights defenders. She was subsequently found guilty of 'insulting a public official' and sentenced to six days in prison. While she was detained, three long dormant cases related to other peaceful protests were reactivated. The single mother of two is currently serving a 30 month sentence": "Religious Ceremony at Boeung Kak to Call for Tep Vanny Release," LICADHO, Phnom Penh, August 15, 2018, accessed November 24, 2018, http://www.licadho-cambodia.org/flashnews.php?perm=252.

43. "Supreme Court Upholds Tep Vanny Conviction," LICADHO, Phnom Penh, February 7, 2018, accessed November 24, 2018, http://www.licadho-cambodia.org/flashnews.php?perm=231.

44. LICADHO reported on Vanny's release on August 20, 2018. "Tep Vanny was released from prison on Monday after receiving two pardons—one for a 30 month sentence she was serving in Correctional Center 2 and for another six-month conviction. Her release coincided with the release of political analyst Kim Sok who had finished his sentence last Friday and former Radio Free Asia journalists Uon Chhin and Yeang Sothearin who were released on bail on Tuesday" (LICADHO, "Flash Info: Boeung Kak Lake Activists Get Suspended Sentences," August 15, 2018, Phnom Penh, http://www.licadho-cambodia.org/flashnews.php?perm=253).

45. LICADHO, "Flash Info."

46. LICADHO, "Flash Info."

47. BTI is an independent foundation with an international database dedicated to monitoring market and democratic reforms worldwide. According to its website (www.bfna.org), its research, publishing, and advocacy materials are geared toward promoting "reform processes" and "the principles of entrepreneurial activity." According to the BTI 2018 Cambodia Country Report, intermittent legislative threats—as well as physical violence—have a been a way for the Hun Sen regime to retain political control. "In the political arena, Prime Minister Hun Sen does not depend on the permanent show of force to maintain his power after sidelining all rivals inside and outside of his ruling [Cambodian People's Party]. Instead, threats and intimidation legal persecution—based on fabricated allegations and show trials—have become the main tool against the opposition and independent civil society organizations for years. However, as the murder of independent political commentator and activist Kem Ley proves, violence still remains a means of last resort in the regime's efforts to defend its political power. So far, this threat has been regarded as sufficiently credible by the people, causing a high degree of reluctance for outright confrontation with the regime" (Bertelsmann Stiftung, BTI 2018 Cambodia Country Report, 28–29).

48. Bertelsmann Stiftung, BTI 2018 Cambodia Country Report, 11.

49. Bank Information Center, "World Bank Agrees to Full Investigation into Land Activities in Cambodia."

50. Heijman, "Chinese Money Is Driving One of Asia's Fastest Property Booms."

51. Heijman, "Chinese Money Is Driving One of Asia's Fastest Property Booms."

52. David Hutt, "To Be Down, Out and in Debt in Cambodia," *Asia Times*, September 14, 2018, accessed November 24, 2018, http://www.atimes.com/article/to-be-down-out-and-in-debt-in-cambodia.

53. Hutt, "To Be Down, Out and in Debt in Cambodia."

54. Hutt, "To Be Down, Out and in Debt in Cambodia."

55. Hutt, "To Be Down, Out and in Debt in Cambodia."

56. Hutt, "To Be Down, Out and in Debt in Cambodia."

57. According to Hutt, instead of standard methods of looking at income level to determine poverty, "multidensional poverty" indicators examine a wide range of contributing factors. The MPI data looked beyond income to understand how people experience poverty in multiple and simultaneous ways. It identifies how people are being left behind across three key dimensions—health, education, and living standards, with those lacking such things as clean water, sanitation, adequate nutrition, or primary education. Traditional poverty measures—often calculated by the number of people who earn less than $1.90 a day—shed light on how little people earn but not on how they experience poverty in their daily lives (Hutt, "To Be Down, Out and in Debt in Cambodia").

58. Bertelsmann Stiftung, BTI 2018 Cambodia Country Report, 29.

59. Pich, "Artist Statement," *The Pulse Within* catalog, Tyler Rollins Fine Art.

60. Pich, "Artist Statement," *The Pulse Within* catalog.

61. Pich, "Artist Statement," *The Pulse Within* catalog.

62. Đinh Q. Lê, personal conversation, Hồ Chí Minh City, December 2007.

63. Curtin, "Sopheap Pich, H Gallery Thailand" review, October 2016, accessed November 2017, http://www.trfineart.com/wp-content/uploads/2016/10/Frieze.pdf.

64. Curtin, "Sopheap Pich, H Gallery Thailand," emphasis added.

65. Curtin, "Sopheap Pich, H Gallery Thailand."

66. Curtin, "Sopheap Pich, H Gallery Thailand."

67. Curtin, "Sopheap Pich, H Gallery Thailand."

68. The Cambodia Cultural Profile site is no longer active.

69. Ly, "Of Texture and Tactile Memory," 8.

70. Gluckman, "Battle for Boeung Kak Lake."

71. Gluckman, "Battle for Boeung Kak Lake."

72. Sopheap Pich, "Artist Statement," Headlands Center for the Arts, 2016, http://www.headlands.org/artist/sopheap-pich.

73. Pich, "Artist Statement" (2016).

74. *Expanses* press release, November 1, 2018, accessed November 2, 2018, http://www.trfineart.com/wp-content/uploads/2018/11/Pich-Press-Release-2018 -web-1.pdf.

75. Nowak et al., "Identification and Determination of Ergot Alkaloids in Morning Glory Cultivars."

76. For more information on symptoms and permutations, see the database entries for articles on ergot alkoloids at Science Direct, at https://www .sciencedirect.com/topics/neuroscience/ergot-alkaloids.

77. In 2008, an article in the *Chicago Tribune* noted that ingesting morning glory seeds as a drug was on the rise among teenagers. "The use of morning glory seeds as a recreational drug is just beginning to register nationally. After hearing in March . . . the Ohio Early Warning Network issued an alert to school, health and law-enforcement officials" (Theresa Vargas, "Wake Up Call on the Danger of Seeds," *Chicago Tribune*, May 4, 2008, accessed November 23, 2018, https://www .chicagotribune.com/news/ct-xpm-2006-05-04-0605040163-story.html).

78. Pich, quoted on the Tyler Rollins Fine Art website, http://www.trfineart .com/exhibition/sopheap-pich-morning-glory/#info.

79. The World Bank figures are based on the UNDP's World Urbanization Prospect, last revised in 2018, accessed September 20, 2019, https://data.worldbank .org/indicator/SP.RUR.TOTL.ZS?locations=VN.

80. The census conducted on April 1, 2009, puts the Vietnamese population at 85.8 million people. Đỗ Thức, deputy director general of the General Statistics Office of Việt Nam and standing member of the Central Steering Committee, reported, "By 00:00 April 1, 2009, Vietnam had 85,789,573 million people, of which 25,374,262 persons were residing in urban areas, accounting for 29.6 percent of the total; and 43,307,024 were women, with a sex-ratio of 98.1 men per 100 women. Vietnam's population increased by 9.47 million, at an annual population growth rate of 1.2 percent in mid period of two censuses of 1999 and 2009, decreasing fast as compared to period 1989–1999. This rate was different among provinces, especially for regions with high economic growth" (General Statistics

Office of Việt Nam, "Conference of Releasing the 2009 Population and Housing Census Preliminary Results," August 14, 2009, http://www.gso.gov.vn/default_en .aspx?tabid=462&idmid=2&ItemID=9198). In comparison, the 1999 Việt Nam census states that the population is about 76,323,173 ("Monthly Statistical Information," General Statistics Office of Việt Nam, http://www.gso.gov.vn/default_en .aspx?tabid=476&idmid=4&ItemID=1841).

81. The Australian National University hosts an annual conference on Việt Nam that focuses on political economy and socioeconomic change. The 2009 session, held in Canberra, was called Vietnam Update: Migration Nation.

82. Matthew Pike, "Made in Vietnam: The Country's Top Ten Exports," *Culture Trip: Vietnam*, May 18, 2018, accessed September 20, 2019, https://theculturetrip .com/asia/vietnam/articles/made-in-vietnam-the-countrys-top-10-exports.

83. Global manufacturing hubs maybe shifting. Kyssha Mah writes, "China's Pearl River Delta, long known as one of the key factory centers for the world's manufacturers (particularly those from Hong Kong) has now become too costly for many companies to stay in the region" (Kyssha Mah, "An Introduction to Vietnam's Import and Export Industries," *Vietnam Briefing*, November 19, 2018, accessed December 1, 2018, https://www.vietnam-briefing.com/news /introduction-vietnams-export-import-industries.html).

84. Mah, "An Introduction to Vietnam's Import and Export Industries."

85. Dezan Shira and Associates produces the *Vietnam Briefing* website, on which Mah's "An Introduction to Vietnam's Import and Export Industries" article is featured.

86. Mah, "An Introduction to Vietnam's Import and Export Industries."

87. Founded in 1991 at a meeting in The Hague, UNPO is "an international, nonviolent and democratic membership organisation." There were originally fifteen member nations; they numbered forty in 1998. The organization's members, according to the UNPO website (https://unpo.org), "are indigenous peoples, minorities, unrecognised States and occupied territories that have joined together to defend their political, social and cultural rights, to preserve their environments and to promote their right to self-determination." "About UNPO," November 19, 2018, accessed December 1, 2018, https://unpo.org/section/2.

88. "UNPO Concerned about Impacts of EU-Vietnam F[ree] T[rade] A[greement] on Human Rights," UNPO, September 21, 2018, accessed December 9, 2018, https://unpo.org/article/21108.

89. Kennedy and Williams, "The Past without the Pain."

90. Author interview with Phan Quang, Hồ Chí Minh City, September 15, 2010.

91. Author interview with Phan Quang, Hồ Chí Minh City, September 15, 2010.

92. Prabhu L. Pingali and Võ-Tong Xuan, "Vietnam: Decollectivization and Rice Productivity Growth," 697–718.

93. Roger Nelson, "Swiming in Sand: Growing Rice under an Umbrella," catalog essay, November 25, 2014, accessed December 25, 2014, http://www

.pegasos5.com/wp-content/uploads/pdf/Catalogue%20-%20Swimming%20in%20
Sand%3B%20Growing%20Rice%20under%20an%20Umbrella.pdf.

94. Tucker, *Monet in the '90s*.

95. For more on Byron Kim's recent practice, see the Hosfelt Gallery website,
at http://hosfeltgallery.com/index.php?p=artists&a=Byron%20Kim.

96. Author interview with Phan Quang, Hồ Chí Minh City, September 15,
2010.

97. Ravallion and Van der Walle, *Breaking Up the Collective Farm*.

98. Here I compare US State Department statistics on Việt Nam's economy a
decade apart. Việt Nam's performance in 2009 (overall) and 2019 (bilateral US
relations) breaks down this way:

[2009] Agriculture, forestry, and fisheries (20.7 percent of GDP, 2009): *Principal products*—rice, coffee, cashews, maize, pepper (spice), sweet potato,
pork, peanut, cotton, plus extensive aquaculture of both fish and shellfish
species. *Cultivated land*—12.2 million hectares. *Land use*—21 percent arable;
28 percent forest and woodland; 51 percent other. Industry and construction
(40.3 percent of GDP, 2009): *Principal types*—mining and quarrying, manufacturing, electricity, gas, water supply, cement, phosphate, and steel. Services
(39.1 percent of GDP, 2009): *Principal types*—tourism, wholesale and retail,
repair of vehicles and personal goods, hotel and restaurant, transport storage,
telecommunications. Trade (2009): *Exports*—$56.6 billion (first quarter 2010:
$14.0 billion). *Principal exports*—crude oil, garments/textiles, footwear, fishery
and seafood products, rice (world's second-largest exporter), pepper (spice;
world's largest exporter), wood products, coffee, rubber, handicrafts. *Major
export partners*—US, EU, Japan, China, Australia, Singapore, Germany, and
the United Kingdom.

[2019] Bilateral Economic Relations
Since entry into force of the US-Vietnam bilateral trade agreement in 2001,
trade between the two countries and US investment in Vietnam have grown
dramatically. The United States and Vietnam have concluded a trade and
investment framework agreement; they also have signed textile, air transport,
and maritime agreements. US exports to Vietnam include agricultural products, machinery, yarn/fabric, and vehicles. US imports from Vietnam include
apparel, footwear, furniture and bedding, agricultural products, seafood, and
electrical machinery. US-Vietnam bilateral trade has grown from $451 million
in 1995 to nearly $52 billion in 2016. In 2016, Vietnam was America's fastest
growing export market. US exports to Vietnam grew by 77 percent between
2014–16. US exports to Vietnam were worth over $10 billion in 2016, and US
imports in 2016 were worth $42 billion. US investment in Vietnam has grown
significantly over the past eight years to nearly $10 billion. The United States
and Vietnam intend to establish the US-Vietnam Joint Commission on Civil
Nuclear Cooperation to facilitate the implementation of the 123 Agreement on
the peaceful uses of nuclear activity, which came into force in October 2014.

An expanding civil nuclear partnership will help reduce emissions from the global power sector and establish the highest standards of nuclear safety, security, and nonproliferation. (US Department of State, "US Relations with Vietnam," December 11, 2017, accessed September 20, 2019, http://www.state .gov/r/pa/ei/bgn/4130.htm)

99. "According to figures from the National Bureau of Statistics, urban per capita income was US$2,525 against rural per capita net income of US$754. . . . Government researchers have warned that effective measures must be taken in the coming years to narrow the difference between the rich and the poor in order to maintain social cohesion. This is in contrast to the latest report from the Organization for Economic Cooperation and Development . . . , which concluded that the gap between the rich and the poor in China was decreasing thanks to increased welfare spending and major adjustments to the labor market for reducing disparities" ("China Urban Rural Income Gap Widest in 32 Years," *China Economic Review*, March 3, 2010, accessed August 18, 2010, http:// www.chinaeconomicreview.com/dailybriefing/2010_03_03/China_urban-rural _income_gap_widest_in_32_years.html).

100. "The Rural-Urban Divide: Ending Apartheid," *The Economist*, April 19, 2014, accessed September 20, 2019, https://www.economist.com/news/special -report/21600798-chinas-reforms-work-its-citizens-have-be-made-more-equal -ending-apartheid.

101. China's ranking as the world's second-largest economy can be misleading. "In news conferences, on talk shows and in editorial pages, commentators have hastened to pooh-pooh the statistics, saying they are wrong, misleading or meaningless. They compare China not to Japan or the United States, but to Albania— both have annual per capita income of about $3,600" (*Los Angeles Times*, August 20, 2010). China's rapid socioeconomic growth is "incomplete," proclaims the World Bank. "Although China has made impressive economic and social development gains, its market reforms are incomplete, and its per capita income remains that of a developing country and only about a quarter of the average for high-income countries. The country is on track to eliminate absolute poverty by 2020 according to China's current poverty standard (per capita rural net income of [renminbi] 2,300 per year in 2010 constant prices). However, there are still an estimated 372.8 million people below the 'upper middle income' international poverty line of $5.50 a day" ("The World Bank in China," World Bank, October 1, 2019, accessed October 16, 2019, https://www.worldbank.org/en/country/china /overview).

102. Central Intelligence Agency, *The World Factbook 2009*.

103. Xinhua News Agency, "Over 7 Million Chinese Return to Rural Areas to Start Businesses," *China Daily*, January 21, 2018, http://www.chinadaily.com.cn/a /201801/21/WS5a645c6ea3106e7dcc135914.html.

104. UNDP, Human Development Report, 62.

105. "China Urban Rural Income Gap Widest in 32 Years," *China Economic Review*.

106. Dominque Patton, "China Seeks to Rejuvenate Countryside with 2018 Rural Policy," Reuters, February 4, 2018, accessed February 22, 2018, https://www.reuters.com/article/china-policy-agriculture/china-seeks-to-rejuvenate-countryside-with-2018-rural-policy-idINKBN1FO06M.

107. *Blue Book of Cities in China*.

108. Phan Quang, "Artist Statement," *A Farmer's Diary*, Galerie Quynh, Hồ Chí Minh City, October 2010.

109. In a founding myth, Âu Cơ, a mountain fairy, marries a sea dragon, Lạc Long Quân, and gives birth to Việt Nam's ancestors.

110. Harms, *Saigon's Edge*, 121.

111. "Phan Quang Synopsis," Galerie Quynh, http://galeriequynh.com/exhibition/a-farmers-diary.

112. Harms, *Saigon's Edge*, 125.

113. Phan Quang interview.

114. Simon Lewis, "Same-Sex Marriage Ban Lifted in Vietnam but a Year Later Discrimination Remains," *Time*, January 19, 2016, http://time.com/4184240/same-sex-gay-lgbt-marriage-ban-lifted-vietnam.

115. "How to Buy a House or Land in Vietnam," *City Pass Guide*, December 11, 2018, https://www.citypassguide.com/en/living/ho-chi-minh-city/real-estate/blog/how-to-buy-a-house-or-land-in-vietnam.

116. Phạm, "How Do the Vietnamese Lose Face?," 229.

117. Harms, *Saigon's Edge*, 123.

118. Philip Taylor, *Fragments of the Present: Searching for Modernity in Vietnam's South*.

119. Zoe Butt, *Poetic Politic* exhibition catalog, December 12, 2012, accessed December 10, 2018, https://kadist.org/wp-content/uploads/2016/04/sanartcatalog_final_0_0.pdf.

120. "Rooster in Vietnamese Folklore," *Sài Gòn: Việt Nam Bridge*, January 29, 2017, accessed December 10, 2018, https://english.vietnamnet.vn/fms/art-entertainment/171873/rooster-in-vietnam-folklore.html.

121. The Alice in Chains song "Rooster" is about the lead singer's father, who served during the Việt Nam War and suffered post-traumatic stress disorder (see Eric Milzarski, "Why 'Rooster' Was the Greatest Song to Honor a Father's Service," March 13, 2018, https://www.wearethemighty.com/music/why-rooster-was-the-greatest-song-to-honor-a-fathers-service; "Vietnam," History of the 101st Airborne Division: Screaming Eagles, n.d., http://screamingeagles__10.tripod.com/101st_played_an_important_part_i.htm).

122. Butt, *Poetic Politic*.

123. Roger Nelson, "And That Which Is Known," exhibition catalog essay, Yavuz Gallery, accessed December 10, 2018, https://rogerincambodia.files.wordpress.com/2015/05/roger-catalogue-final.pdf.

124. Ben Valentine, "Photographing the Forgotten Vietnamese Widows of Japanese W[orld] W[ar] II Soldiers," July 19, 2016, accessed September 20, 2019,

https://hyperallergic.com/306502/photographing-the-forgotten-vietnamese
-widows-of-japanese-wwii-soldiers.

125. Benjamin, *Reflections: Essays, Aphorisms, Autobiographical Writings.*

126. Griffiths, *Agent Orange: "Collateral Damage."*

127. "Vietnam, US Complete Cleanup of Toxic Chemical from Airport," Associated Press, November 7, 2018, accessed December 2, 2018, https://www.apnews
.com/3a686cd385184f6789b4aa672a0939cf.

128. Phil Stewart, "US Prepares for Biggest-Ever Agent Orange Cleanup in
Vietnam," Reuters, October 17, 2018, https://www.reuters.com/article/us-vietnam
-usa-mattis/u-s-prepares-for-biggest-ever-agent-orange-cleanup-in-vietnam
-idUSKCN1MR1U4.

129. Daniel Malloy, "US Helps Defuse Vietnam's Dioxin Hotspots Blamed on
Agent Orange," *Washington Post*, April 8, 2016.

130. Martha Graybow, "U.S. Court Upholds Dismissal of Agent Orange Suit."
Reuters, February 22, 2008, accessed July 17, 2009, http://www.reuters.com/article
/latestCrisis/idUSN22581489.

131. See Gammeltoft, "Figures of Transversality."

132. Gammeltoft, *Women's Bodies, Women's Worries.*

133. Fox, "One Significant Ghost."

134. "Vietnam, US Complete Cleanup of Toxic Chemical from Airport."

135. Stewart, "US Prepares for Biggest-Ever Agent Orange Cleanup in Vietnam."

136. "Vietnam, US Complete Cleanup of Toxic Chemical from Airport."

137. Stewart, "US Prepares for Biggest-Ever Agent Orange Cleanup in
Vietnam."

138. Stewart, "US Prepares for Biggest-Ever Agent Orange Cleanup in
Vietnam."

139. Fox, "One Significant Ghost."

140. "Vietnam, US Complete Cleanup of Toxic Chemical from Airport."

141. Graybow, "U.S. Court Upholds Dismissal of Agent Orange Suit." The
April 2019 census states there are 96.2 million people living in Việt Nam: "Vietnam's Population Reaches over 96.2 Million, Ranking Fifteenth in the World:
2019 Census," *Nhân Dân*, July 11, 2019, https://en.nhandan.org.vn/society/item
/7680202-vietnam%E2%80%99s-population-reaches-over-96-2-million-ranking
-15th-in-the-world-2019-census.html. In 2008, the population estimate was 86
million: Central Intelligence Agency, *The World Factbook 2009.* As noted earlier,
the 1999 Việt Nam census gives the population as 76,323,173.

142. Graybow, "U.S. Court Upholds Dismissal of Agent Orange Suit."

143. "Vietnam, US Complete Cleanup of Toxic Chemical from Airport."

144. "US Prepares for Cleanup of Agent Orange in Vietnam," *Gulf Times,*
October 17, 2018, accessed October 18, 2018, https://www.gulf-times.com/story
/609795/US-prepares-for-cleanup-of-Agent-Orange-in-Vietnam.

145. Stewart, "US Prepares for Biggest-Ever Agent Orange Cleanup in
Vietnam."

146. "Vietnam, US Complete Cleanup of Toxic Chemical from Airport."

147. Fox, "Speaking with Vietnamese Women on the Consequences of War," 107–20.

148. Fox, "One Significant Ghost," 242–43.

149. "Agricultural Exports Reach $15 B[illion] in 2016," *Việt Nam News*, June 29, 2016, accessed June 30, 2016, http://vietnamnews.vn/economy/298718 /agriculture-exports-reach-15b-in-2016.html.

150. "Agricultural Export Value up 2 percent First Seven Months of 2019," *Việt Nam News*, August 7, 2019, https://vietnamnews.vn/economy/523672/agricultural -export-value-up-2-in-first-seven-months-of-2019.html#BsqO7Fl4Eo0QroSJ.97.

151. Netherlands Enterprise Agency, "Factsheet: Agriculture in Vietnam," Netherlands Enterprise Agency, The Hague, 2018, accessed September 21, 2019, https://www.rvo.nl/sites/default/files/2017/11/factsheet-agriculture-in-vietnam .pdf. The Netherlands Enterprise Agency is under the Dutch Ministry of Economic Affairs and Climate Policy, with its work commissioned by the European Union.

152. The World Bank, "Taking Stock: An Update on Vietnam's Recent Economic Developments," June 2018, accessed July 3, 2019, http:// documents1.worldbank.org/curated/en/536421528929689515/pdf/127168-WP -TakingStockENG-PUBLIC.pdf.

153. "'A U.S. District Court judge in Brooklyn, New York ruled in March 2005 that the plaintiffs failed to show that use of agent orange, a plant killer supplied to the U.S. military in Vietnam, violated a ban on the use of poisonous weapons in war and that the lawsuit did not prove the plaintiffs' health problems were linked to the chemical. Although the herbicide campaign may have been controversial, the record before us supports the conclusion that agent orange was used as a defoliant and not as a poison designed for or targeting human populations,' Judge Roger Miner wrote for the three-judge appeals court panel. The court also upheld two other Agent Orange rulings, including one in a case that was brought by veterans and their families who said their health problems did not become apparent until after a 1984 class-action settlement was reached with a group of veterans. In that case, the Second Circuit found that, as government contractors, the chemical companies could be shielded from liability. . . . The plaintiffs had sought class-action status for millions of Vietnamese people in a case that, if successful, could have resulted in billions of dollars in damages and the costs of environmental cleanup in Vietnam": Graybow, "Court Upholds Dismissal of Agent Orange Suit."

154. Graybow, "Court Upholds Dismissal of Agent Orange Suit."

155. "HDNET World Report Investigates the Devastating Effects of Agent Orange 30 Years after the Vietnam War," press release, February 24, 2009, posted to the Việt Nam Studies Group discussion thread, February 26, 2009, https:// sites.google.com/a/uw.edu/vietnamstudiesgroup/discussion-networking/vsg -discussion-list-archives/vsg-discussion-2009/hdnet.

156. "In 2010, the U.S. Department of Veterans Affairs provided $16.2 billion in compensation to 1,095,473 Vietnam-era veterans. . . . The agency does not

relate these service-connected benefit figures directly to Agent Orange/dioxin exposure. . . . The U.S. Department of Veterans Affairs now allows compensation to anyone who had 'boots on the ground' in Vietnam or served on particular U.S. Navy ships offshore from 1962 to 1975 (about 2.8 million people) and suffers from any of these diseases: soft-tissue sarcoma, non-Hodgkins lymphoma, Hodgkin's disease, chloracne, chronic lymphocytic leukemia, respiratory cancer, prostate cancer, multiple myeloma, amyloidosis, peripheral neuropathy, porphyria cutanea tarda, type II diabetes, and spina bifida in offspring . . . ; Parkinson's Disease, hairy cell leukemia and ischemic heart disease were added to this list in 2009. The V[eterans] A[dministration] also allows compensation for children of female veterans who served in Vietnam who have achondroplasia, cleft lip or cleft palate, congenital heart disease, clubfoot, esophageal and intestinal atresia, Hallerman-Streiff syndrome, hip dysplasia, Hirschsprung Disease, hydrocephalus, hypospadias, imperforate anus, neural tube defects (including spina bifida, encephalocele, and anencephaly), Poland syndrome, pyloric stenosis, fused digits, tracheal or esophageal fistula, undescended testicle and Williams syndrome. All U.S. compensation is for service in Vietnam and is not specifically linked to exposure to any of the herbicides or to dioxin" ("Agent Orange and US Veterans," Aspen Institute, August 2011, accessed June 9, 2019, https://www.aspeninstitute.org/programs/agent-orange-in-vietnam-program/agent-orange-and-u-s-veterans).

157. "Even if the National Academy of Medicine's forthcoming [2019] report does find definitive evidence of a link between Agent Orange and esophageal cancer, that's no guarantee the disease will be added to the list of approved service-related illnesses. Though the academy's past reports have recognized 50 diseases that fall under the 'limited or suggestive' evidentiary category, the V[eterans] A[dministration] has only approved 14. Hypertension and bladder cancer are two examples of diseases the academy listed in its 2016 report as having some research suggesting a link with service exposure, but which the V[eterans] A[dministration] has thus far not added" (Eoin Higgins, "Agent Orange May Be Responsible for More Veteran Deaths than the Government Is Willing to Recognize," *Huffington Post*, July 17, 2018, https://www.huffingtonpost.com/entry/agent-orange-may-be-responsible-for-more-veteran-deaths-than-the-government-is-willing-to-recognize_us_5b05b4f1e4b07c4ea1046787).

158. Svetvilas, "The Art of War," 27–28.

159. Select exhibitions featuring *Damaged Gene* include *Slew Release* (Bishopsgate Goodsyard, London, 1999), *humor us* (Los Angeles Municipal Art Gallery, 2008), and *Agent Orange: Landscape, Body, Image* (California Museum of Photography, University of California, Riverside, 2009).

160. Kennedy and Williams, "The Past without the Pain," 135–63.

161. Kennedy and Williams, "The Past without the Pain," 145.

162. Hồ Tài, *The Country of Memory*, 1–20.

163. Taylor, "Playing with National Politics," 4.

164. "China Provides Aid for Infrastructure," *Kampuchea Thmey*, col. 8, no. 2075, October 18–19, 2009.

165. The artist Harrell Fletcher has rephotographed the images from the War Remnants Museum for a traveling photographic series commenting on historical representation and appropriation.

166. Alexander et al., *Cultural Trauma and Collective Identity*.

167. Benjamin, *The Arcades Project*.

168. Trouillot, *Silencing the Past*, 27.

169. Huyssen, "Geographies of Modernism in a Globalizing World," 192.

170. Gaonkar, *Alternative Modernities*.

171. Rofel, "Discrepant Modernities and Their Discontents," 638.

172. Rofel, "Discrepant Modernities and Their Discontents," 638.

173. Chakrabarty, *Provincializing Europe*, 16.

Epilogue. Leaving and Returns

1. Rofel, *Desiring China*.

2. "Cambodia Mourns Worst Tragedy after Murderous Pol Pot Regime," *NBC News*, November 23, 2010, accessed November 23, 2010.

3. Felman and Laub, *Testimony*, 69.

4. Save Boeung Kak website, accessed February 12, 2011, http://www.saveboeungkak.com. The site is no longer active. WordPress archive, accessed September 21, 2019, https://saveboeungkak.wordpress.com.

5. Khouth Sophakchakrya, "Lakeside Families Homeless," *Phnom Penh Post*, January 16, 2011, accessed February 7, 2011, http://www.phnompenhpost.com/index.php/2011011646107/National-news/lakeside-families-homeless.html.

6. Strangio, *Hun Sen's Cambodia*.

7. Strangio, *Hun Sen's Cambodia*, 147.

8. Sopheng Cheang, "Cambodia: Festival Stampede Kills at Least 345," Associated Press, November 23, 2010, accessed September 21, 2019, https://www.cbc.ca/news/world/cambodia-festival-stampede-kills-345-1.872870.

9. Derrida, *Spectres of Marx*, 168.

10. Derrida, *Spectres of Marx*, 168, emphasis added.

11. Derrida, *Spectres of Marx*, 11.

12. Edkins, *Trauma and the Memory of Politics*, 59.

13. Hoag, "Ghosts of Memory," 7.

14. Rickert, *Ambient Rhetoric*, 101.

Adorno, Theodor. *Minima Moralia: Reflections from Damaged Life*. Translated by E. F. N. Jephcott. London: Verso, 1978.

Aguilar-San Juan, Karin. "Going Home: Enacting Justice in Queer Asian America." In *Feminist Theory Reader: Local and Global Perspectives*, edited by Carole R. McCann and Seung-kyung Kim, 267–76. New York: Routledge, 2003.

Ahmed, Sara. *The Promise of Happiness*. Durham, NC: Duke University Press, 2010.

Alexander, Jeffrey C., Ron Eyerman, Bernard Giesen, et al., eds. *Cultural Trauma and Collective Identity*. Berkeley: University of California Press, 2004.

Alperin, Elijah, and Jeanne Batalova. "The Foreign Born from Vietnam in the United States." Migration Policy Institute, Spotlight, September 13, 2018. Accessed April 9, 2019. https://www.migrationpolicy.org/article/vietnamese -immigrants-united-states-5.

Althusser, Louis. "Ideology and Ideological State Apparatuses." In *Lenin and Philosophy and Other Essays*. London: Monthly Review Press, 1972.

Antoinette, Michelle. *Reworlding Art History: Encounters with Contemporary Southeast Asian Art after 1990*. Cross/Cultures, vol. 178. Leiden: Brill Rodopi, 2014.

Appadurai, Arjun. *Modernity at Large: Cultural Dimensions of Globalization*. Minneapolis: University of Minnesota Press, 1996.

Bachelard, Gaston. *The Poetics of Space*. London: Penguin, 2014.

Bank Information Center. "World Bank Agrees to Full Investigation into Land Activities in Cambodia." Press release, April 28, 2010.

Barensten, Gord. "Freud, Jung, and the Dangerous Supplement to Psychoanalysis." *Mosaic* 44, no. 4 (2011): 195–211.

Bataille, Georges. *The Accursed Share: An Essay on General Economy*. Translated by Robert Hurley. New York: Zone Books, 1988.

Becker, David. "Dealing with the Consequences of Organized Violence in Trauma Work." In *Berghof Handbook for Conflict Transformation*, edited by Alexandra Austin, 1–21. Berlin: Berghof Research Center for Constructive Conflict Management, 2001.

Benjamin, Walter. *The Arcades Project.* Translated by Howard Eiland and Kevin McLaughlin. Cambridge, MA: Harvard University Press, 2002.

Benjamin, Walter. *Reflections: Essays, Aphorisms, Autobiographical Writings.* New York: Harcourt Brace Jovanovich, 1978.

Benjamin, Walter. "The Work of Art in the Age of Mechanical Reproduction." In *Illuminations*, edited by Hannah Arendt, translated by Harry Zohn, 217–51. New York: Schocken, 1977.

Bennett, Jill, and Rosanne Kennedy, eds. *World Memory: Personal Trajectories in Global Time.* Hampshire, UK: Macmillan, 2003.

Bergson, Henri. *Time and Free Will: An Essay on the Immediate Data of Consciousness.* Translated by F. L. Pogson. Whitefish, MT: Kessinger Publishing Company, 1910.

Bernasconi, Robert. "Supplement." In *Jacques Derrida: Key Concepts*, edited by Claire Colebrook. Abingdon, UK: Routledge, 2015.

Bhabha, Homi. "Of Mimicry and Man." In *The Location of Culture*, by Homi Bhabha, 121–31. New York: Routledge, 1994.

Biehl, João, and Peter Locke. "Deleuze and the Anthropology of Becoming." *Current Anthropology* 51, no. 3 (June 2010): 317–51.

Bishop, Claire. *Artificial Hells: Participatory Art and the Politics of Spectatorship.* London: Verso, 2012.

Bistoen, Gregory, Stijn Vanheule, and Stef Craps. "Nachträglichkeit: A Freudian Perspective on Delayed Traumatic Reactions." *Theory and Psychology* 24, no. 5 (2014): 668–87.

Blue Book of Cities in China: Annual Report on Urban Development of China No. 3. Beijing: Chinese Academy of Social Sciences, 2010.

Bourdieu, Pierre. *Distinction: A Social Critique of the Judgment of Taste.* Cambridge, MA: Harvard University Press, 1984.

Bourdieu, Pierre. "The Field of Cultural Production." In *The Field of Cultural Production*, edited by Randal Johnson, 29–73. New York: Columbia University Press, 1993.

Bourdieu, Pierre. "The Forms of Capital." In *Handbook for Theory and Research for the Sociology of Education*, edited by J. G. Richardson, 241–58. Westport, CT: Greenwood, 1986.

Bourdieu, Pierre. "The Historical Genesis of a Pure Aesthetic." In *The Field of Cultural Production*, edited by Randal Johnson, 29–73. New York: Columbia University Press, 1993.

Bourdieu, Pierre. *The Rules of Art.* Stanford, CA: Stanford University Press, 1996.

Bourdieu, Pierre, and Alain Darbel, with Dominique Schnapper. *The Love of Art: European Art Museums and Their Public.* Translated by Caroline Beattie and Nick Merriman. Stanford, CA: Stanford University Press, 1990.

Boyle, Deirdre. "Shattering Silence: Traumatic Memory and Reenactment in Rithy Panh's *S-21: The Khmer Rouge Killing Machine*." *Framework* 50, nos. 1–2 (spring–fall 2009): 95–106.

Boyle, Deidre. "Trauma, Memory, Documentary: Re-enactment in Two Films by Rithy Panh (Cambodia) and Garin Nugroho (Indonesia)." In *Documentary Testimonies: Archives of Suffering*, edited by Janet Walker and Bhaskar Sarkar, 155–72. New York: Routledge, 2010.

Braziel, Jana E., and Anita Mannur. *Theorizing Diaspora: A Reader*. Malden, MA: Blackwell, 2010.

Brothman, Brien. "Jacques Derrida, Archive Fever" (review). *Archivaria* 43 (1996): 191–92.

Brown, Kay. "The Emergence of Black Women Artists: The 1970s, New York." *International Review of African American Art* 15, no. 1 (1998): 45–52.

Brunschwig, Sonia, Bruno Carrasco, Tadateru Hayashi, et al. "The Global Financial Crisis: Impact on Asia and Emerging Consensus." ADB Publication, no. 3. Asia Development Bank, Manila, 2011.

BTI 2018 Cambodia Country Report. Gütersloh, Germany: Bertelsmann Stiftung, 2018.

Bui, Long. *Returns of War: South Vietnam and the Price of Refugee Memory*. New York: New York University Press, 2018.

Butler, Judith. *Frames of War: When Is Life Grievable?* London: Verso, 2016.

Butler, Judith. *Gender Trouble: Feminism and the Subversion of Identity*. New York: Routledge, 1999.

Butler, Judith. *Precarious Life: The Powers of Mourning and Violence*. London: Verso, 2020.

Butt, Zoe, ed. *Poetic Politic*. Exhibition catalog. San Francisco: Kadist Foundation, 2012. Accessed December 10, 2018. https://kadist.org/wp-content/uploads/2016/04/sanartcatalog_final_0_0.pdf.

Bydler, Charlotte. *The Global Art World Inc.: On the Globalization of Contemporary Art*. Uppsala, Sweden: Uppsala University, 2004.

Carroll, Lewis. *Alice's Adventures in Wonderland*. New York: Doubleday, Page, 1907.

Carruthers, Ashley. "Cute Logics of the Multicultural and the Consumption of the Vietnamese Exotic in Japan." *Positions* 12, no. 2 (2006): 401–29.

Carruthers, Ashley. "Saigon from the Diaspora." *Singapore Journal of Tropical Geography* 29 (2008): 68–86.

Caruth, Cathy. *Unclaimed Experience: Trauma, Narrative, and History*. Baltimore: Johns Hopkins University Press, 1996.

Cassidy, John. "The Real Cost of the 2008 Financial Crisis." *New Yorker*, September 17, 2018. Accessed October 11, 2019. https://www.newyorker.com/magazine/2018/09/17/the-real-cost-of-the-2008-financial-crisis.

Castaneda, Carlos. *The Art of Dreaming*. Shaftesbury, UK: Element, 2004.

Central Intelligence Agency. *The World Factbook 2009*. Washington, DC: Central Intelligence Agency, 2009.

Chakrabarty, Dipesh. *Provincializing Europe: Postcolonial Thought and Historical Difference*. Princeton, NJ: Princeton University Press, 2000.

Chandler, David P. *A History of Cambodia*. Boulder, CO: Westview, 2008.

Chandler, David P. "'The Killing Fields' and Perceptions of Cambodian History." *Pacific Affairs* 59, no. 1 (spring 1986): 92–97.

Chandler, David P. "Revisiting the Past in Democratic Kampuchea: When Was the Birthday of the Party?" *Pacific Affairs* 56, no. 2 (summer 1983): 288–300.

Chandler, David P. *The Tragedy of Cambodian History: Politics, War, and Revolution since 1945.* New Haven, CT: Yale University Press, 1991.

Chandler, David P. *Voices from S-21: Terror and History in Pol Pot's Secret Prison.* Berkeley: University of California Press, 1994.

Chapelle, Daniel. *Nietzsche and Psychoanalysis.* Albany: State University of New York Press, 1993.

Cheng, Anne Anlin. *The Melancholy of Race.* Oxford: Oxford University Press, 2000.

Cherniavsky, Eva. *Neocitizenship: Political Culture after Democracy.* New York: New York University Press, 2017.

Cherniavsky, Eva. "'Refugees from This Native Dreamland': Life Narratives of Occupy Wall Street." *Life and Writing Corporate Personhood* 37, no. 1 (winter 2014): 279–99.

Chuh, Kandice, and Karen Shimakawa, eds. *Orientations: Mapping Studies in the Asian Diaspora.* Durham, NC: Duke University Press, 2001.

Cieslikowski, David. *World Development Indicators 2008.* Washington, DC: World Bank, 2009.

Corey, Pamela. "The 'First' Cambodian Contemporary Artist." *Udaya* 12 (2014): 61–94.

Corey, Pamela. "Three Propositions for a Regional Profile: The History of Contemporary Art in Ho Chi Minh City." In *Arts du Vietnam: Nouvelles approches*, ed. Caroline Herbelin, Béatrice Wisniewski, and Françoise Dalex, 135–44. Rennes, France: Presses Universitaires de Rennes, 2015.

Crimp, Douglas. "Getting the Warhol We Deserve." *Social Text*, no. 59 (summer 1999): 40–66.

Curtin, Brian. "Sopheap Pich, H Gallery Thailand" (exhibition review). *Frieze*, September 1, 2007, http://www.trfineart.com/wp-content/uploads/2016/10/Frieze.pdf.

Dalai Lama XIV Bstan-'dzin-rgya-mtsho. *The Universe in a Single Atom: How Science and Spirituality Can Serve Our World.* London: Abacus, 2009.

Deleuze, Gilles, and Félix Guattari. *A Thousand Plateaus: Capitalism and Schizophrenia.* Translated by Brian Massumi. London: Athlone, 1988.

Demos, T. J. *The Migrant Image: The Art and Politics of Documentary during Global Crisis.* Durham, NC: Duke University Press, 2013.

Derrida, Jacques. *Adieu to Emmanuel Levinas.* Translated by Pascale-Anne Brault and Michael Naas. Stanford, CA: Stanford University Press, 1999.

Derrida, Jacques. *Archive Fever: A Freudian Impression.* Translated by Eric Prenowitz. Chicago: University of Chicago Press, 1996.

Derrida, Jacques. *Autour de Jacques Derrida. Manifeste pour l'hospitalité.* Edited by Mohammed Seffahi. Paris: Paroles l'Aube, 1999.

Derrida, Jacques. *Dissemination*. Translated by Barbara Johnson. Chicago: University of Chicago Press, 1981.

Derrida, Jacques. *The Gift of Death*. Translated by David Wills. Chicago: University of Chicago Press, [1991] 1995.

Derrida, Jacques. *Given Time: Counterfeit Money*. Translated by Peggy Kamuf. Chicago: University of Chicago Press, 1992.

Derrida, Jacques. "Hospitality." *Angelaki* 5, no. 3 (December 2000): 3–18.

Derrida, Jacques. "Hospitality." In *Acts of Religion*, edited by Gil Anidjar, 358–420. New York: Routledge, 2002.

Derrida, Jacques. "Hospitality, Justice and Responsibility: A Dialogue with Jacques Derrida." In *Questioning Ethics: Contemporary Debates in Philosophy*, edited by Richard Kearney and Mark Dooley, 65–83. London: Routledge, 1999.

Derrida, Jacques. *Limited Inc*. Evanston, IL: Northwestern University Press, 1988.

Derrida, Jacques. *Margins of Philosophy*. Chicago: University of Chicago Press, 1982.

Derrida, Jacques. *Memoirs of the Blind: The Self-Portrait and Other Ruins*. Chicago: University of Chicago Press, 1993.

Derrida, Jacques. *Of Hospitality*. Translated by Rachel Bowlby. Stanford, CA: Stanford University Press, 2000.

Derrida, Jacques. *On Cosmopolitanism and Forgiveness*. London: Routledge, 2001.

Derrida, Jacques. "The Principle of Hospitality." In *Paper Machine*, translated by Rachel Bowlby, 6–9. Stanford, CA: Stanford University Press, 2005.

Derrida, Jacques. *Specters of Marx: The State of the Debt, the Work of Mourning, and the New International*. New York: Routledge, 1994.

Derrida, Jacques. *The Work of Mourning*. Chicago: University of Chicago Press, 2001.

Derrida, Jacques, and Gayatri Chakravorty Spivak. *Of Grammatology*. Baltimore: Johns Hopkins University Press, 1976.

Duffy, Terence. "Toward a Culture of Human Rights in Cambodia." *Human Rights Quarterly* 16, no. 1 (February 1994): 82–104.

Duiker, William J. *Ho Chi Minh: A Life*. New York: Hyperion, 2000.

Duras, Marguerite. *L'amante anglaise*. Paris: Gallimard, 1967.

Edkins, Jenny. *Trauma and the Memory of Politics*. Cambridge: Cambridge University Press, 2003.

Eng, David L. *Racial Castration: Managing Masculinity in Asian America*. Durham, NC: Duke University Press, 2007.

Eng, David L., and David Kazanjian, eds. *Loss: The Politics of Mourning*. Berkeley: University of California Press, 2003.

Espiritu, Yến Lê. *Body Counts: The Vietnam War and Militarized Refuge(es)*. Berkeley: University of California Press, 2014.

Espiritu, Yến Lê. "Vietnam, the Philippines, Guam and California: Connecting the Dots of U.S. Military Empire." York Asia Colloquia Papers, vol. 6, no. 2. York University, Ontario, June 14, 2016. Accessed July 16, 2016. http://ycar

.apps01.yorku.ca/wp-content/uploads/2013/09/Espiritu-Vietnam-the
-Philippines-Guam-and-California-1.pdf.

Etcheson, Craig. *After the Killing Fields: Lessons from the Cambodian Genocide.* Westport, CT: Praeger, 2005.

Fanon, Frantz. *Black Skin, White Masks.* London: Penguin Books, [1952] 2020.

Fanon, Frantz. *The Wretched of the Earth.* New York: Grove, [1961] 2004.

Felman, Shoshana, and Dori Laub. *Testimony: Crises of Witnessing in Literature, Psychoanalysis, and History.* New York: Routledge, 1992.

Ferguson, Kennan R. "The Gift of Freedom." *Social Text* 25, no. 2 (2007): 39–52.

Foley, Douglas E. *Critical Ethnography: The Reflexive Turn.* Thousand Oaks, CA: SAGE, 2001.

Foster, Hal. *The Return of the Real: The Avant-Garde at the End of the Century.* Cambridge, MA: MIT Press, 1996.

Foucault, Michel. *Discipline and Punish: The Birth of the Prison.* Translated by Alan Sheridan. New York: Pantheon, 1977.

Foucault, Michel. "Of Other Spaces." Translated by Jay Miskowiec. *Diacritics* 16, no. 1 (spring 1986): 22–27.

Fox, Diane. "One Significant Ghost: Agent Orange Narratives of Trauma, Survival, and Responsibility." PhD diss., University of Washington, Seattle, 2007.

Fox, Diane. "Speaking with Vietnamese Women on the Consequences of War: Writing against Silence and Forgetting," In *Le Việt Nam au feminin/Vietnam: Women's Realities*, ed. Gisele Bousquet and Nora A. Taylor, 107–20. Paris: Les Indes Savantes, 2005.

Freud, Sigmund. *Beyond the Pleasure Principle.* New York: W. W. Norton, 1959.

Freud, Sigmund. "Mourning and Melancholia" (1917). In *The Standard Edition of the Complete Psychological Works of Sigmund Freud*, edited and translated by James Strachey, vol. 17, 239–60. London: Hogarth, 1955.

Freud, Sigmund. "Project for a Scientific Psychology" (1895). In *The Standard Edition of the Complete Psychological Works of Sigmund Freud*, vol. I, edited and translated by James Strachey, 283–397. London: Hogarth, 1975.

Freud, Sigmund. "The Uncanny" (1917). In *The Standard Edition of the Complete Psychological Works of Sigmund Freud*, vol. 17, edited and translated by James Strachey, 217–56. London: Hogarth, 1955.

Fried, Michael. *Art and Objecthood: Essays and Reviews.* Chicago: University of Chicago Press, 1998.

Friedberg, Ann. "The Mobilized and Virtual Gaze in Modernity." In *Window Shopping: Cinema and the Postmodern*, by Ann Friedberg, 20–28. Berkeley: University of California Press, 2007.

Galasso, Emanuela, and Martin Ravallion. "Decentralized Targeting of an Antipoverty Program." *Journal of Public Economics* 89, no. 4 (2005): 705–27.

Gammeltoft, Tine M. "Figures of Transversality: State Power and Prenatal Screening in Contemporary Vietnam." *American Ethnologist* 35, no. 4 (2008): 570–87.

Gammeltoft, Tine M. *Women's Bodies, Women's Worries: Health and Family Planning in a Vietnamese Rural Community.* Oxford: Routledge, 1999.

Gaonkar, Dilip. *Alternative Modernities*. Public Culture no. 11. Durham, NC: Duke University Press, 1999.

Gartman, David. "Bourdieu's Theory of Cultural Change: Explication, Application, Critique." *Sociological Theory* 20, no. 2 (July 2002): 255–77.

Geertz, Clifford. *The Interpretation of Cultures*. New York: Basic, 1973.

Gibson, James William. *The Perfect War: Technowar in Vietnam*. New York: Random House, 1986.

Gilroy, Paul. *The Black Atlantic: Modernity and Double Consciousness*. Cambridge, MA: Harvard University Press, 1993.

Gleeson, Erin. *Who Cares? Sixteen Essays on Curating in Asia*. Hong Kong: Para/Site Art Space, 2010.

Goleman, Daniel. *A Force for Good: The Dalai Lama's Vision for Our World*. London: Bloomsbury, 2016.

Gordon, Avery. *Ghostly Matters: Haunting and the Sociological Imagination*. Minneapolis: University of Minnesota Press, 1997.

Gramsci, Antonio. *Prison Notebooks, Volume 3*. Translated by Joseph A. Buttigieg. New York: Columbia University Press, 2007.

Gramsci, Antonio. *Selections from the Prison Notebooks of Antonio Gramsci*. Edited by Quintin Hoare and Geoffrey Nowell-Smith. New York: International Publishers, 1971.

Grieco, Elizabeth. "The Foreign Born from Vietnam in the United States in 2000." Migration Policy Institute, Spotlight, February 1, 2004. Accessed January 2, 2002. https://www.migrationpolicy.org/article/foreign-born-vietnam-united -states-2000.

Griffiths, Philip Jones. *Agent Orange: "Collateral Damage" in Việt Nam*. London: Trolley, 2003.

Grosz, Elizabeth. "Criticism, Feminism and the Institution: An Interview with Gayatri Chakravorty Spivak." In *Post-colonial Critic: Interviews, Strategies, Dialogues*, by Gayatry Chakravorty Spivak, edited by Sarah Harasym, 1–17. New York: Routledge, 1990.

Hajdu, Sue. "Missing the Mekong." *Contemporary Art and Visual Culture Broadsheet* 38, no. 4 (2009): 186–89.

Halberstam, Jack [Judith]. *The Queer Art of Failure*. Durham, NC: Duke University Press, 2013.

Hall, Stuart. "Cultural Identity and Diaspora." In *Diaspora and Visual Culture*, edited by Nicholas Mirzoeff, 235. London: Routledge, 2000.

Hamilton, Annette. "Cambodian Genocide: Ethics and Aesthetics in the Cinema of Rithy Panh." In *Holocaust Intersections: Genocide and Visual Culture at the New Millennium*, edited by Axel Bangert, Robert S. C. Gordon, and Libby Saxton, 170–90. Leeds, UK: Maney, 2013.

Hamilton, Annette. "Witness and Recuperation: Cambodia's New Documentary Cinema." *Concentric: Literary and Cultural Studies* 39, no. 1 (March 2013): 7–30.

Harms, Erik. *Saigon's Edge: On the Margins of Ho Chi Minh City*. Minneapolis: University of Minnesota Press, 2011.

Heidegger, Martin. "The Origin of the Work of Art." In *Basic Writings: From Being and Time (1927) to the Task of Thinking (1964)*, edited by David Farrell Krell, 143–212. New York: HarperCollins, 1993.

Hinton, Alexander Laban. *Why Did They Kill? Cambodia in the Shadow of Genocide*. Berkeley: University of California Press, 2005.

Hoag, Trevor L. "Ghosts of Memory: Mournful Performance and the Rhetorical Event of Haunting (Or: Specters of Occupy)." *Liminalities* 10, nos. 3–4 (2014): 2–22.

hooks, bell. *All About Love: New Visions*. New York: William Morrow, 2000.

hooks, bell. *Bone Black: Memories of Girlhood*. New York: Henry Holt, 1996.

hooks, bell. *From Margin to Center*. Boston: South End, 1984.

Hồ Tài, Huệ-Tâm, ed. *The Country of Memory: Remaking the Past in Late Socialist Vietnam*. Berkeley: University of California Press, 2001.

Howard, Ebenezer. *Garden Cities of To-morrow*. Eastbourne, UK: Attic, 1985.

Huggan, Graham. *Maps and Mapping Strategies in Contemporary Canadian and Australian Fiction*. Toronto: University of Toronto Press, 1994.

Hughes, Rachel. "Memory and Sovereignty in Post-1979 Cambodia: Choeung Ek and Local Genocide Memorials." In *Genocide in Cambodia and Rwanda: New Perspectives*, edited by Susan E. Cook, 257–79. New Brunswick, NJ: Transaction, 2006.

Human Rights Watch. *On the Margins: Human Rights Abuses of Ethnic Khmer in Vietnam's Mekong Delta*. New York: Human Rights Watch, 2009.

Huyssen, Andreas. "Geographies of Modernism in a Globalizing World." *New German Critique 100* 34, no. 1 (winter 2007).

Jay, Martin. "Scopic Regimes of Modernity." In *Vision and Visuality*, edited by Hal Foster, 5–20. Seattle: Bay, 1988.

Jung, C. G. *Collected Works of C. G. Jung, Volume 11: Psychology and Religion: West and East*. New Haven, CT: Princeton University Press, 2014.

Jung, C. G. *Two Essays on Analytical Psychology*. Translated by R. F. C. Hul. New York: Pantheon, 1953.

Kakoliris, Gerasimos. "Jacques Derrida on the Ethics of Hospitality." In *The Ethics of Subjectivity: Perspectives since the Dawn of Modernity*, edited by Elvis Imafidon, 144–56. London: Palgrave Macmillan, 2015.

Kaplan, E. Ann. *Trauma Culture: The Politics of Terror and Loss in Media and Literature*. New Brunswick, NJ: Rutgers University Press, 2005.

Kennedy, Laurel B., and Mary Rose Williams. "The Past without the Pain: The Manufacture of Nostalgia in Vietnam's Tourist Industry." In *The Country of Memory*, edited by Tài Hồ Huệ-Tâm, 135–63. Berkeley: University of California Press, 2001.

Keo, Dacil. "Fact Sheet on 'S-21' Tuol Sleng Prison." *Searching for the Truth* magazine. December 6. Phnom Penh: Documentation Center of Cambodia, 2010.

Ketelaar, Eric. *The Archival Image: Collected Essays*. Hilversum, Netherlands: Verloren, 1997.

Ketelaar, Eric. "Tacit Narratives: The Meanings of Archives." *Archival Science* 1 (2001): 131–41.

Keyes, Charles. "Presidential Address: 'The Peoples of Asia'—Science and Politics in the Classification of Ethnic Groups in Thailand, China, and Vietnam." *Journal of Asian Studies* 61, no. 4 (November 2002): 1163–203.

Kim, Annette Miae. *Sidewalk City: Remapping Public Space in Ho Chi Minh City.* Chicago: University of Chicago Press, 2015.

Kingston, Victoria. *Simon and Garfunkel: The Biography.* New York: Fromm International, 1999.

Koro-Ljungberg, Mirka, Marco Gemignani, Shane Chaplin, Sharon Hayes, and Ivy Haoyin Hsieh. "'Mission Civilisatrice': Fixing Scientific Evidence and Other Practices of Neo-colonialism in Social Sciences." *International Review of Qualitative Research* 1, no. 4 (2009): 491–513.

Kraevskaia, Natalia. *Từ Hoài Cổ Hướng Sang Miền Đất Mới* [From nostalgia toward exploration]. Hanoi: Kim Đồng, 2005.

Kwon, Miwon. *One Place after Another: Site-Specific Art and Locational Identity.* Cambridge, MA: MIT Press, 2002.

Kyung Cha, Theresa Hak. *Dictee.* Berkeley: University of California Press, 2009.

Lacan, Jacques. *The Four Fundamental Concepts of Psychoanalysis.* Seminars of Jacques Lacan, Book 11. New York: W. W. Norton, 1988.

LaCapra, Dominick. *Writing History, Writing Trauma.* Baltimore: Johns Hopkins University Press, 2014.

Landry, Donna, and Gerald MacLean, eds. *The Spivak Reader.* New York: Routledge, 1996.

Lê, Việt. "The Art of War: Vietnamese American Visual Artists Đinh Q. Lê, Ann Phông and Nguyễn Tân Hoàng." *Amerasia Journal* 31, no. 2 (2005): 23–35.

Lê, Việt. "Many Returns: Contemporary Vietnamese Diasporic Artists-Organizers in Hồ Chí Minh City." In *Modern and Southeast Asian Art: An Anthology*, edited by Nora Taylor and Boreth Ly, 85–116. Ithaca, NY: Cornell University Press, 2011.

Lê, Việt. "What Remains: Returns Representation, and Traumatic Memory in *S-21: The Khmer Rouge Killing Machine* and *Refugee.*" *American Quarterly* 66, no. 2 (June 2014): 301–32.

Lê, Việt, and Yong Soon Min. "Curatorial Conversations/Correspondences." In *transPOP: Korea Vietnam Remix.* Exhibition catalog, edited by Việt Lê and Yong Soon Min, 12–37. Seoul: Arko Art Center, 2008.

Ledgerwood, Judy. "The Cambodian Tuol Sleng Museum of Genocidal Crimes: National Narrative." *Museum Anthropology* 21, no. 1 (1997): 82–98.

Leys, Ruth. *Trauma: A Genealogy.* Chicago: University of Chicago Press, 2007.

Lim, Bliss Cua. *Translating Time: Cinema, the Fantastic, and Temporal Critique.* Durham, NC: Duke University Press, 2009.

Lippit, Akira Mizuta. *Atomic Light (Shadow Optics).* Minneapolis: University of Minnesota Press, 2005.

Lippit, Akira Mizuta. *Electric Animal: Toward a Rhetoric of Wildlife*. Minneapolis: University of Minnesota Press, 2000.

Lowe, Lisa. *Immigrant Acts: On Asian American Cultural Politics*. Durham, NC: Duke University Press, 1996.

Ly, Boreth. "Of Scent and Sensibility: Embodied Ways of Seeing in Southeast Asian Cultures." *Suvannabhumi Multidisciplinary Journal of Southeast Asian Studies* 10, no. 1 (June 2018): 63–91.

Ly, Boreth. "Of Texture and Tactile Memory: Situating Sopheap Pich's Work in a Global and Local Perspective." In *The Pulse Within: Sopheap Pich*. Exhibition catalog, 6–10. New York: Tyler Rollins Fine Art, 2010.

Ly, Daravuth, and Ingrid Muan. *The Legacy of Absence: A Cambodian Story*. Phnom Penh: Reyum Gallery, 2000.

Machida, Margo. *Unsettled Visions: Contemporary Asian American Artists and the Social Imaginary*. Durham, NC: Duke University Press, 2008.

MacLean, Ken. *The Government of Mistrust: Illegibility and Bureaucratic Power in Socialist Vietnam*. Madison: University of Wisconsin Press, 2013.

Maguire, Peter. *Facing Death in Cambodia*. New York: Columbia University Press, 2012.

Maher, Francis A., and Mary Kay Tetreault. *The Feminist Classroom*. New York: Basic, 1994.

Manoff, Marlene. "Theories of the Archive from across the Disciplines." *Portal: Libraries and the Academy* 4 no. 1 (2004): 9–25.

Marcus, George. *Ethnography through Thick and Thin*. Princeton, NJ: Princeton University Press, 1998.

Marcuse, Herbert. *Counterrevolution and Revolt*. Boston: Beacon, 1972.

Mathur, Saloni, ed. *The Migrant's Time: Rethinking Art History and Diaspora*. New Haven, CT: Yale University Press, 2011.

McLuhan, Marshall. *The Medium Is the Message: An Inventory of Effects*. New York: Bantam, 1967.

Miller, Nancy K., and Jason Tougaw, eds. *Extremities: Trauma, Testimony, and Community*. Urbana: University of Illinois Press, 2002.

Mimura, Glen. *Ghostlife of Third Cinema: Asian American Film and Video*. Minneapolis: University of Minnesota Press, 2009.

Mirzoeff, Nicholas. "Invisible Empire: Visual Culture, Embodied Spectacle, and Abu Ghraib." *Radical History Review*, no. 95 (2006): 21–44.

Mitchell, Timothy, ed. *Questions of Modernity*. Minneapolis: University of Minnesota Press, 2000.

Moore, Lisa. "Recovering the Past, Remembering Trauma: The Politics of Commemoration at Sites of Atrocity." *Journal of Public and International Affairs* 20 (spring 2009): 47–63.

Moss, Laurence S. "*S-21: The Khmer Rouge Killing Machine* Review." *American Journal of Economics and Sociology* 64, no. 4 (October 2005): 1096–101.

Muan, Ingrid. "Citing Angkor: The 'Cambodian Arts' in the Age of Restoration, 1918–2000." PhD diss., Columbia University, New York, 2001.

Muan, Ingrid. "Haunted Scenes: Painting and History in Phnom Penh." *Udaya Journal of Khmer Studies* 6 (2005): 15–37.

Muan, Ingrid. "Musings on Museums from Phnom Penh." In *Museum Frictions: Public Cultures/Global Transformations*, edited by Ivan Karp, Corinne Ann Kratz, Lynn Szwaja, Tomás Ybarra-Frausto, 257–85. Durham, NC: Duke University Press, 2006.

Muan, Ingrid, Daravuth Ly, and Ashley Thompson. *Visions of the Future: An Exhibition of Contemporary Cambodian Art*. Phnom Penh: Reyum Institute of Arts and Culture, 2002.

Muñoz, José Esteban. *Cruising Utopia: The Then and There of Queer Futurity*. New York: New York University Press, 2019.

Muñoz, José Esteban. *Disidentifications: Queers of Color and the Performance of Politics*. Minneapolis: University of Minnesota Press, 1999.

Nath, Vann. *A Cambodian Prison Portrait: One Year in the Khmer Rouge's S-21*. Bangkok: White Lotus, 1998.

Nguyễn, Mimi Thi. *The Gift of Freedom: War, Debt, and Other Refugee Passages*. Durham, NC: Duke University Press, 2012.

Nguyễn, Thao. "A New Narrative: Perspectives from the Post–Việt Nam War Generation." Paper presented at the Echoes of a War Conference, Casual Arts Centre, Sydney, April 17–18, 2009.

Nguyễn, Việt Thanh. "The Authenticity of the Anonymous." *TransPOP: Korea Vietnam Remix*. Exhibition catalog, edited by Việt Lê and Yong Soon Min, 58–67. Seoul: Arko Art Center, 2007.

Nguyễn, Việt Thanh. "Just Memory: War and the Ethics of Remembrance." *American Literary History* 25, no. 1 (spring 2013): 144–63.

Nguyễn, Việt Thanh. *Nothing Ever Dies: Vietnam and the Memory of War*. Cambridge, MA: Harvard University Press, 2017.

Nguyễn, Việt Thanh. "Seeing Double: The Films of R. Hong-an Truong." *Postmodern Culture* 17, no. 1 (September 2006): 17–24.

Nguyễn-võ, Thu-hương. *The Ironies of Freedom: Sex, Culture, and Neoliberal Governance in Vietnam*. Seattle: University of Washington Press, 2007.

Nguyễn-võ Thu-hương. "'The Red Seedlings of the Central Highlands': Social Relatedness and Political Integration of Select Ethnic Minority Groups in Post-War Vietnam." In *Connected and Disconnected in Viet Nam: Remaking Social Relations in a Post-socialist Nation*, edited by Philip Taylor, 173–202. Canberra: Australian National University Press, 2016.

Nietzsche, Friedrich Wilhelm. *The Gay Science*. Translated by Walter Kaufmann. New York: Vintage, 1974.

Nietzsche, Friedrich Wilhelm. *The Gay Science*. Translated by J. Nauckhoff. Cambridge: Cambridge University Press, 2001.

Nietzsche, Friedrich Wilhelm. *The Gay Science*. Translated by Thomas Common. Boston: Dover, 2006.

Nietzsche, Friedrich W., and Walter A. Kaufmann. *Thus Spoke Zarathustra: A Book for All and None*. New York: Viking Penguin, 1978.

Bibliography

Norindr, Panivong. *Phantasmatic Indochina: French Colonial Ideology in Architecture, Film and Literature*. Durham, NC: Duke University Press, 1996.

Nowak, Julia, Michał Woźniakiewicz, Piotr Klepacki, Anna Sowa, and Paweł Kościelniak. "Identification and Determination of Ergot Alkaloids in Morning Glory Cultivars." *Analytical and Bioanalytical Chemistry* 408, no. 12 (2016): 3093–102.

Oliver, Kelly. *Women as Weapons of War*. New York: Columbia University Press, 2007.

Ong, Aihwa. *Buddha Is Hiding: Refugees, Citizenship, and the New America*. Berkeley: University of California Press, 2003.

Ong, Aihwa. *Flexible Citizenship: The Cultural Logics of Transnationality*. Durham, NC: Duke University Press, 1999.

Owen, Taylor, and Ben Kiernan. "Bombs over Cambodia." *The Walrus* (October 2006): 62–69.

Palen, J. John. *The Urban World*. New York: McGraw-Hill, 1992.

Palumbo-Liu, David. *Asian/American: Historical Crossings of a Racial Frontier*. Stanford, CA: Stanford University Press, 1999.

Panh, Rithy. "Bophana: A Cambodian Tragedy." *Mānoa: In the Shadow of Ângkor* 16, no. 1 (2004): 108–26.

Park, Donghuyn, Arief Ramayandi, and Kwanho Shin. "Why Did Asian Countries Fare Better during the Global Financial Crisis than during the Asian Financial Crisis?" In *Responding to Financial Crisis: Lessons from Asia Then, the United States and Europe Now*, edited by Changyong Rhee and Adam S. Posen, 103–39. Manila: Asian Development Bank, 2013.

Parr, Adrian. *The Deleuze Dictionary*. Edinburgh: Edinburgh University Press, 2010.

Puar, Jasbir K. *Terrorist Assemblages: Homonationalism in Queer Times*. Durham, NC: Duke University Press, 2017.

Pelaud, Isabelle T., Lan P. Duong, Mariam B. Lam, and Kathy L. Nguyễn. *Troubling Borders: An Anthology of Art and Literature by Southeast Asian Women in the Diaspora*. Seattle: University of Washington Press, 2014.

Petersen, Anne Ring. *Migration into Art: Transcultural Identities and Art-Making in a Globalised World*. Manchester, UK: Manchester University Press, 2018.

Phạm, Thị Hồng Nhung. "How Do the Vietnamese Lose Face? Understanding the Concept of Face through Self-Reported, Face Loss Incidents." *International Journal of Language and Linguistics* 2, no. 3 (2014): 223–31.

Pich, Sopheap. "Artist Statement." In *The Pulse Within: Sopheap Pich*. Exhibition catalog, 2–4. New York: Tyler Rollins Fine Arts, 2010.

Pingali, Prabhu L., and Võ-Tong Xuan. "Vietnam: Decollectivization and Rice Productivity Growth." *Economic Development and Cultural Change* 40, no. 4 (1992): 697–718.

Pranab, K. Bardhan, and Dilip Mookherjee. "Capture and Governance at Local and National Levels." *American Economic Review* 90, no. 2 (2000): 135–39.

Rafael, Vicente L. "The Cultures of Area Studies in the United States." *Social Text*, no. 41 (winter 1994): 91–111.

Raffoul, François. "The Subject of the Welcome." *Symposium* 2, no. 2 (fall 1998): 211–22.

Rankine, Claudia. *Citizen: An American Lyric.* London: Penguin, 2015.

Ravallion, Martin, and Dominique van der Walle. *Breaking Up the Collective Farm: Welfare Outcomes of Vietnam's Massive Land Privatization.* Policy Research Working Paper Series 2710. Washington, DC: World Bank, 2001.

Rickert, Thomas. *Ambient Rhetoric: The Attunements of Rhetorical Being.* Pittsburgh: University of Pittsburgh Press, 2013.

Rofel, Lisa. *Desiring China: Experiments in Neoliberalism, Sexuality, and Public Culture.* Durham, NC: Duke University Press, 2007.

Rofel, Lisa. "Discrepant Modernities and Their Discontents." *Positions: East Asia Cultures Critique* 9, no. 3: 637–49.

Rofel, Lisa. *Other Modernities: Gendered Yearnings in China after Socialism.* Berkeley: University of California Press, 1999.

Rōshi, Uchiyama Kōshō, Thomas Wright, Jishō C. Warner, and Shohaku Okumura. *Opening the Hand of Thought: Foundations of Zen Buddhist Practice.* Boston: Wisdom Publications, 2005.

Roth, Moira. "Obdurate History: Dinh Q. Lê, the Vietnam War, Photography and Memory." *Art Journal* 60, no. 1 (summer 2001): 38–53.

Roth, Moira. "Traveling Companions/Fractured Worlds." *Art Journal* 58 (1999): 82–93.

Rushdie, Salman. "Imaginary Homelands." In *Imaginary Homelands*, by Salman Rushdie, 9–12. London: Granta, 1991.

Samphan, Khieu. *L'histoire récente du Cambodge et mes prises de position* [Reflection on Cambodian history to the era of Democratic Kampuchea]. Paris: L'Harmattan, 2004.

Saussure, Ferdinand de. *Course in General Linguistics.* Edited by Charles Bally and Albert Sechehaye. Translated by Wade Baskin. New York: McGraw-Hill, 1966.

Scarry, Elaine. *The Body in Pain: The Making and Unmaking of the World.* Oxford: Oxford University Press, 1987.

Schlund-Vials, Cathy J. *War, Genocide, and Justice: Cambodian American Memory Work.* Minneapolis: University of Minnesota Press, 2012.

Schüller, Margot, and Jan Peter Wogart. "The Emergence of Post-crisis Regional Financial Institutions in Asia—with a Little Help from Europe." *Asia Europe Journal* 15, no. 4 (December 2017): 483–501.

Schwenkel, Christina. *The American War in Contemporary Vietnam: Transnational Remembrance and Representation.* Bloomington: Indiana University Press, 2009.

Shetty, Sandhya, and Elizabeth J. Bellamy. "Postcolonialism's Archive Fever." *Diacritics* 30, no. 1 (2000): 25–48.

Small, Ivan. "Embodies Economies: Vietnamese Transnational Migration and Return Regimes." *Sojourn* 27, no. 2 (October 2012): 234–59.

Steyerl, Hito, and Franco Berardi. *The Wretched of the Screen*. Berlin: Sternberg, 2012.

St. John, Ronald Bruce. *Revolution, Reform and Regionalism in Southeast Asia: Cambodia, Laos and Vietnam*. London: Routledge, 2006.

Strangio, Sebastian. *Hun Sen's Cambodia*. New Haven, CT: Yale University Press, 2014.

Sturken, Marita. *Tangled Memories: The Vietnam War, the AIDS Epidemic, and the Politics of Remembering*. Berkeley: University of California Press, 1997.

Svetvilas, Chanika. "The Art of War." *Dialogue* (spring–summer 1999): 27–28.

Szanton, David L. *The Politics of Knowledge: Area Studies and the Disciplines*. Berkeley: University of California Press, 2004.

Taylor, Nora A. *Changing Identities: Recent Works by Women Artists from Vietnam*. Exhibition catalog, edited by Barbara Tran and Penny Kiser. Washington, DC: International Art and Artists, 2007.

Taylor, Nora A. "Invisible Painters: From the Cultural Revolution to *Doi Moi*." In *Asian Women Artists*, edited by Dynah Dysart and Hannah Fink. Sydney: Art Asia Pacific, 1996.

Taylor, Nora A. *Painters in Hanoi*. Honolulu: University of Hawai'i Press, 2004.

Taylor, Nora A. "Playing with National Politics: Vietnamese Artists' Visions of War." *Obieg*, no. 2 (2016). Accessed August 9, 2020. https://obieg.u -jazdowski.pl/en/numery/azja/playing-with-national-politics--vietnamese -artists----visions-of-war.

Taylor, Nora A. "Running the Earth: Jun Nguyen-Hatsushiba's Breathing Is Free: 12,756.3." In *The Migrant's Time: Rethinking Art History and Diaspora*, edited by Saloni Mathur, 206–26. New Haven, CT: Yale University Press, 2011.

Taylor, Nora A. "Whose Art Are We Studying? Writing Vietnamese Art History from Colonialism to the Present." In *Studies in Southeast Asian Art: Essays in Honor of Stanley J. O' Connor*, edited by Nora A. Taylor, 143–57. Ithaca, NY: Cornell University Press, 2000.

Taylor, Nora A. "Why Have There Been No Great Vietnamese Artists?" *Michigan Quarterly Review* 44, no. 1 (2006): 149–65.

Taylor, Philip. *Fragments of the Present: Searching for Modernity in Vietnam's South*. Honolulu: University of Hawai'i Press, 2001.

Thayer, Carl A., and Ramses Amer, eds. *Vietnamese Foreign Policy in Transition*. Singapore: Institute of Southeast Asian Studies, 1999.

Thompson, Ashley. *Engendering the Buddhist State: Territory, Sovereignty and Sexual Difference in the Inventions of Angkor*. New York: Routledge, 2016.

Thompson, Ashley. "Forgetting to Remember, Again: On Curatorial Practice and 'Cambodian Art' in the Wake of Genocide." *Diacritics* 41, no. 2 (2013): 82–109.

Thompson, Ashley. "Mémoires du Cambodge." PhD diss., Université de Paris 8, 1999.

Thompson, Ashley. "Mnemotechnical Politics: Rithy Panh's Cinematic Archive and the Return of Cambodia's Past." In *Modern and Contemporary Southeast Asian Art: An Anthology*, Southeast Asia Program Publications, no. 56, edited by Nora A. Taylor and Boreth Ly, 225–40. Ithaca, NY: Cornell University Press, 2012.

Thompson, Ashley. "A Witness to Genocide: Vann Nath." In *Contemporary Buddhists*, edited by Justin McDaniel, Jeffrey Samuels, and Mark Rowe, 25–27. Honolulu: University of Hawai'i Press, 2016.

Thurman, Robert A. F. *Inner Revolution: Life, Liberty, and the Pursuit of Real Happiness*. New York: Riverhead, 1999.

Tooze, Adam J. *Crashed: How a Decade of Financial Crises Changed the World*. New York: Penguin, 2019.

Torchin, Leshu. *Creating the Witness: Documenting Genocide on Film, Video, and the Internet*. Minneapolis: University of Minnesota Press, 2012.

Torchin, Leshu. "Mediation and Remediation: La Praole Filmée in Rithy Panh's *The Missing Picture (L'Image Manquante)*." *Film Quarterly* 68, no. 1 (2014): 32–41.

Trinh T. Minh-ha. *When the Moon Waxes Red: Representation, Gender, and Cultural Politics*, 81–105. New York and London: Routledge, 1991.

Trinh T. Minh-ha. *Women, Native, Other: Writing Postcoloniality and Feminism*. Bloomington: Indiana University Press, 1969.

Trouillot, Michel-Rolph. "The Otherwise Modern: Caribbean Lessons from the Savage Slot." In *Critically Modern*, edited by B. M. Knauft, 220–37. Bloomington: Indiana University Press, 2002.

Trouillot, Michel-Rolph. *Silencing the Past: Power and the Production of History*. Boston: Beacon, 1995.

Trungpa, Chogyam. *The Myth of Freedom and the Way of Meditation*. Boston: Shambhala, 1976.

Trương, Hồng-Ân, and elin o'Hara slavick. "War, Memory, the Artist and the Politics of Language." *Asia-Pacific Journal* 8, no. 31 (August 2, 2010). http://japanfocus.org/-Hong_An-Truong/3393.

Tucker, Paul Hayes. *Monet in the '90s: The Series Paintings*. New Haven, CT: Yale University Press, 1989.

Turcotte, Gerry. "Prologomena to Uncovering Alter/Native Scripts." In *A Talent(ed) Digger: Creations, Cameos and Essays in Honor of Anna Rutherford*, edited by Hena Maes-Jelinek, Gordon Collier, and Geoffrey V. Davis, 145–50. Amsterdam: Editions Rodopi, 1996.

Um, Khatharya. "Exiled Memory: History, Identity, and Remembering in Southeast Asia and Southeast Asian Diaspora." *Positions* 20, no. 3 (June 20, 2012): 831–50.

Um, Khatharya. *From the Land of Shadows: War, Revolution, and the Making of the Cambodian Diaspora*. New York: New York University Press, 2015.

United Nations. *Handbook on United Nations Multidimensional Peacekeeping Operations*, 2018. Accessed June 18, 2018. http://www.un.org/en/peacekeeping/documents/Peacekeeping-Handbook_UN_Dec2003.pdf.

313

United Nations Development Program. *Human Development Report 2009*. New York: Palgrave Macmillan, 2009.

US Senate, Committee on Foreign Relations, 111th Cong. *The International Financial Institutions: A Call for Change*. Washington, DC: US Government Printing Office, 2010.

van der Krogt, Peter. "The Origin of the Word 'Cartography.'" *E-Perimetron* 10, no. 3 (2015): 124–42.

Vint, Sherryl. "Becoming Other: Animals, Kinship, and Butler's 'Clay's Ark.'" *Science Fiction Studies* 32, no. 2 (July 2005): 281–300.

Weaver, Gina Marie. *Ideologies of Forgetting: Rape in the Vietnam War*. New York: State University of New York Press, 2010.

Williams, Raymond. *Keywords: A Vocabulary of Culture and Society*, rev. ed. Oxford: Oxford University Press, 1985.

Williams, Raymond. *The Long Revolution*. London: Chatto and Windus, 1961.

Yaeger, Patricia. "Consuming Trauma; or, The Pleasures of Merely Circulating," 25–51.

Yang, Alice, Jonathan Hay, and Mimi Young, eds. *Why Asia? Contemporary Asian and Asian American Art*. New York: New York University Press, 1998.

Young, Marilyn. *The Vietnam Wars, 1945–1990*. New York: HarperCollins, 1991.

Yúdice, George. *The Expediency of Culture: Uses of Culture in the Global Era*. Durham, NC: Duke University Press, 2003.

Zwolinski, Matt, and Alan Wertheimer. "Exploitation." In *The Stanford Encyclopedia of Philosophy*, edited by Edward N. Zalta, summer 2017 ed. https://plato.stanford.edu/archives/sum2017/entries/exploitation.

index

Page numbers with an *f* indicate figures; *plate* refers to the color plates.

Ong, Aihwa, 49, 95; on "flexible citizenship," 129, 135; outsourced workers of, 127–28; on "worlding," 108
Open Society Justice, 76–77
Orientalism, 39, 176
Orozco-Valdivia, Nicolas, 109
outsourced artists' assistants, 126–28, 148, 195, 208
Overseas Cambodian Investment Company (OCIC), 242
overseas Vietnamese. See Việt Kiều
Oxfam (NGO), 203–4
Oxford Poverty and Human Development Initiative (OPHI), 204

Palen, J. John, 141
Palumbo-Liu, David, 44–46
Panh, Rithy, 26, 72–73; Bophana Audiovisual Center and, 89; Hamilton on, 85; on immigration experience, 73, 259n41
—works of: "Cambodia: A Wound That Will Not Heal," 90–91; Irradiated, 73; The Missing Picture, 73, 259n41; S-21: The Khmer Rouge Killing Machine, 49, 66–91, 100–104
Park, Donghyun, 31
Pen Sovann, 87–88
Peret, Bertrand, 132
Persian Gulf War, 78
Petersen, Anne Ring, 14, 42, 256n165
Phạm, Quỳnh, 269n46
Phạm Gia Kiêm, 129, 139, 272n87
Phạm Thị Hồng Nhung, 222
Phạm Văn Đồng, 177
Phan Quang, 50, 189–93, 212–25, 233–37; exhibitions of, 193, 214–15; urban/rural tropes of, 191
—works of: Dream, plate 23, 220–21; "Life of a Farmer," plate 21, plate 22, 217–18; Re/Cover No. 5, plate 25, 223–25; Space/Limit, plate 24, 223; The Umbrella, plates 19–20, 216–18
Phan Thảo Nguyên, 120, 121
Philippines, 213
Picasso, Pablo, 147

Pich, Sopheap, 50, 189–212, 233–37; exhibitions of, 193, 194, 195, 207, 211, 253n113; materials of, 206–12; on Nath, 82; outsourced workers of, 195, 208; Rollins on, 195, 196, 212, 277n169, 286n14; Seckon and, 199–200; urban/rural tropes of, 191
—works of: Caged Heart, plate 17, 209; Cycle, plate 14, 196–97, 223; Expanses, plate 18, 195, 211; Junk Nutrients, plate 16, 205–6, 209; Morning Glory, 195, 211–12, 290n77; The Pulse Within, plate 14, 195, 198, 204; Raft, plate 15, 204–5; Rang Phenom Flower, 195–96
Piper, Adrian, 245n4
Plato, 7, 15–16, 64, 65
Podolsky, Boris, 7
Pollack, Jackson, 21, 24
psychoanalysis, 15, 16, 52, 69, 179–80. See also Freud, Sigmund

quê ("country"), 215–16, 219, 222–23
queer theory, 67, 112, 243
quilting, 158

Rafael, Vincente L., 39
Raffoul, François, 29
Rāmāyana, 169
Ramayandi, Arief, 31
Ranariddh, Norodom, 62
Rankine, Claudia, 8
ready-made objects, 20, 52
Reagan, Ronald, 94
Refugee (2003 film), plate 3, 49, 57–59, 66–72, 94–104
refugees, 43–44, 95, 126; boat people as, 58, 120, 174, 179, 241, 274n123; critical studies of, 47–49; Espiritu on, 93, 94, 264n158; Syrian, 58, 126
remains, 57–59
return engagements, 45, 191; definitions of, 1–2, 4, 82; gift exchange and, 51; individual/institutional, 190; Nietzsche and, 94
return investments, 137–39

323

www.ingramcontent.com/pod-product-compliance
Lightning Source LLC
Chambersburg PA
CBHW051209170526
45166CB00005B/1816